RECOVERING INFORMAL LEARNIN

Lifelong Learning Book Series

VOLUME 7

Aims & Scope
"Lifelong Learning" has become a central theme in education and community development. Both international and national agencies, governments and educational institutions have adopted the idea of lifelong learning as their major theme for address and attention over the next ten years. They realize that it is only by getting people committed to the idea of education both life-wide and lifelong that the goals of economic advancement, social emancipation and personal growth will be attained.

The *Lifelong Learning Book Series* aims to keep scholars and professionals informed about and abreast of current developments and to advance research and scholarship in the domain of Lifelong Learning. It further aims to provide learning and teaching materials, serve as a forum for scholarly and professional debate and offer a rich fund of resources for researchers, policy-makers, scholars, professionals and practitioners in the field.

The volumes in this international Series are multi-disciplinary in orientation, polymathic in origin, range and reach, and variegated in range and complexity. They are written by researchers, professionals and practitioners working widely across the international arena in lifelong learning and are orientated towards policy improvement and educational betterment throughout the life cycle.

For other titles published in this series, go to
www.springer.com/series/6227

Recovering Informal Learning
Wisdom, Judgement
and Community

by

PAUL HAGER
University of Technology, Sydney, Australia

and

JOHN HALLIDAY
University of Strathclyde, Glasgow, UK

 Springer

A C.I.P. Catalogue record for this book is available from the Library of Congress.

ISBN 978-1-4020-9295-4 (PB)
ISBN 978-1-4020-5345-0 (HB)
ISBN 978-1-4020-5346-7 (e-book)

Published by Springer,
P.O. Box 17, 3300 AA Dordrecht, The Netherlands.

www.springer.com

Printed on acid-free paper

As societies become more complex in structure and resources, the need of formal or intentional teaching and learning increases. As formal teaching and training grow in extent, there is the danger of creating an undesirable split between the experience gained in more direct associations and what is acquired in school. This danger was never greater than at the present time, on account of the rapid growth in the last few centuries of knowledge and technical modes of skill.

(Dewey 1966: 9)

Table of Contents

PREFACE

We wish to thank the following for help with the production of this book:
The Carnegie Trust for the Universities of Scotland for financial help with travel which enabled us to meet to complete the book.
The Universities of Strathclyde and of Technology, Sydney
The OVAL Research Group at UTS for hosting John Halliday during late 2005.

Special thanks are due to the many interviewees who gave their time freely and generously to enable our compilation of exemplars and case studies. Most wished to remain anonymous. Our intention has been to alter the details of their accounts sufficiently so that others cannot recognise them. In all cases they seem to us to be good informal learners. They may well have become involved because they shared with us the suspicion that informal learning is far more significant than is often acknowledged.

The various exemplars and case studies discussed in this book resulted from the research work undertaken with others. Here we take the opportunity to list the projects and project teams, and to acknowledge the work of our research colleagues.

In Scotland:
Dorothy Russell for compiling some of the case exemplars.

In Australia:
Charles' story
'*Changing Nature of Work*', Board of Vocational Education and Training project – researchers: Paul Hager and Bernice Melville.

Anne's story, Alison's story, Jack's story and Maria's story
'*Judgement at Work*' project – researchers: Paul Hager, David Beckett, Carole Hooper and Bernice Melville.

Martin's story and Financial literacy case study
'*Context, Judgement and Informal Learning at Work*', Australian Research Council Discovery Grant No. DP0453091 – researchers: Paul Hager, Jim Athanasou, John Halliday and Mary Johnsson. (The Financial literacy exemplar (Chapter ten, section 2.3.2) is an edited version with permission of a more extensive case study written by Mary Johnsson.)

Permission to include extracts from the following previously published material is also gratefully acknowledged:

HALLIDAY, J.S. (2001) 'Lifelong Learning, changing economies and the world of work', in D. Aspin, J. Chapman, M. Hatton & Y. Sawano (eds.) *The International Handbook on Lifelong Learning*. Dordrecht/Boston/London: Kluwer Academic Publishers, 93–108.

HALLIDAY, J.S. (1996) 'Empiricism in Vocational Education and Training', *Educational Philosophy and Theory*, 28:1, 40–57.

HALLIDAY, J.S. (1999) 'Political Liberalism and Citizenship Education: towards curriculum reform', *British Journal of Educational Studies*, 47:1, 43–56.

HALLIDAY, J.S. (2001) 'Reason, education and liberalism: family resemblance within an overlapping consensus, *Studies in Philosophy and Education*, 20, 225–234.

HALLIDAY, J.S. & HAGER, P. (2002) 'Context, Judgement and Learning at Work', *Educational Theory*, 52:4, 429–445.

HALLIDAY, J.S. (2004) 'Distributive Justice and Vocational Education', *British Journal of Educational Studies*, 22:4, 151–165.

HAGER, P. (2001) 'Lifelong Learning and the Contribution of Informal Learning', in D. Aspin, J. Chapman, M. Hatton & Y. Sawano (eds.) *The International Handbook of Lifelong Learning*. Dordrecht/Boston/London: Kluwer Academic Publishers, 79–92.

HAGER, P. (2005) 'Philosophical Accounts of Learning', *Educational Philosophy and Theory*, 37: 5, 649-66.

HAGER, P. (2005) 'Current Theories of Workplace Learning: A Critical Assessment', in Bascia N., Cumming A., Datnow A., Leithwood K. & Livingstone D. (eds.) *International Handbook of Educational Policy*. Part Two. Dordrecht: Springer, 829–846.

EDITORIAL BY SERIES EDITORS

This volume is a further flowering from the *International Handbook of Lifelong Learning*, which was jointly edited by David Aspin, Judith Chapman, Yukiko Sawano and Michael Hatton, published by Springer (formerly known as Kluwer Academic Publishers) in 2001. In the *International Handbook* we laid down a set of agenda for future research and development, analysis and expansion, strategies and guidelines in the field of lifelong learning. It had become clear that the domain of lifelong learning was a rich and fertile ground for setting out and summarising, comparing and criticising the heterogeneous scope and remit of policies, proposals, and practices in its different constitutive parts across the international arena. Certainly the scholars, researchers, policy makers and educators with whom we discussed these matters seemed to agree with us that each of the themes that were taken up in individual chapters of the original *International Handbook* would merit separate volumes of their own – to say nothing of the other possibilities that a more extended mapping, analysis and exploration of the field might generate.

This volume is an outcome of one of the important issues that were raised in the *International Handbook*. It is the work of Paul Hager and John Halliday. They argue that for too long theories and practices of learning have been dominated by the requirements of formal learning. They seek in this book to persuade readers, through philosophical argument and empirically grounded examples, that the balance should be shifted back towards the informal. Their arguments and examples are taken from informal learning in very diverse circumstances, such as in leisure activities, as a preparation for and as a part of work, and as a means of surviving undesirable circumstances like "dead end" jobs and incarceration. Informal learning can be fruitfully thought of as developing the capacity to make context sensitive judgments during ongoing practical involvements of a variety of kinds. Such involvements are necessarily indeterminate and opportunistic. Hence there is a major challenge to policy makers in shifting the balance towards informal learning without destroying the very things that are desirable about informal learning and indeed learning in general. The book has implications therefore for formal learning too and the ways in which teaching might proceed within formally constituted educational institutions such as schools and colleges.

There are some key points to be found in the case this book presents:

1. Many current theories of learning, particularly those that concern workplace learning, rely upon the metaphor of participation in communities of practice. These so-called theories of situated cognition are, however, not without some problems, to which people such as Biesta have drawn attention: "The magic spell cast by Jean Lave and Etienne Enger's situated learning has led many to believe that education is a process of participation in 'communities of practice'.... If there has ever been a time in which we need a critical re-examination of the idea of 'practice' in order to counter

its conservative and conserving connotations, it may well be now". The
book aims to provide just such a critical re-examination. It challenges many
common taken-for-granted assumptions about learning in a way that connects with much of the Deweyan literature and work from the philosophy
of Alisdair MacIntyre.

2. The authors argue that 'community' is nothing like so stable as is commonly supposed. Nor is the associated concept of 'consensus'. They therefore draw upon work from both the communitarian and liberal traditions to
move towards a new position that highlights the roles that contingency and
opportunity play in learning. Such roles point towards the importance of informal learning. Yet the authors also trace the way that educational polices
in general, and lifelong learning policies in particular, have led to an increasing emphasis on formal learning. The authors argue that a main problem with this emphasis – quite apart from the fact that it is likely to be of
little use to many people – is that it leads, to borrow Wain's phrase, to a
"panopticon" society. In such a society people are compelled or coerced to
attend institutions of formal education, not so much out of an interest on
what is on offer there, but as unwilling participants in forms of their own
social control and surveillance.

3. The authors clearly wish to avoid the slide into such a "panopticon" society
and urge, through argument and exemplars, that learning is best conceived
of as developing an ability to make contextually sensitive judgments. This
emphasis on judgment and the variability of contexts resonates with their
political analyses of variability and contingency, to provide a promising
new theory of learning with, as their exemplars show, widespread applicability. Theirs is thus no conservative or conserving theory: it calls for radical changes in the way learning is conceived and in the way policies for
learning are framed.

4. The book is thus in many ways a challenge to policy-makers, theorists and
practitioners to think anew and to question existing conceptions of learning. For the authors the concept of learning has become so distorted by an
increased emphasis on the formal, that it almost prevents the kind of
imaginative leaps in policy-making that could envisage learning and doing
as co-existing. No longer would learning be seen as a preliminary to getting
a job or doing a job better. Rather it should be seen as part of life, supplemented but not removed by, formal learning opportunities.

5. The work includes many interesting empirically-grounded exemplars of
informal learning, including learning through leisure (hobbies, crafts and so
on); learning while preparing for work; learning for continuing vocational
development; and learning for surviving (e.g. unemployment, dead-end
jobs etc..)

6. There is one excellent extensive chapter which explains carefully why human beings cannot think about learning in metaphor-free ways. There are
several distinctive metaphors employed in relation to learning, each one involving its own epistemological and ontological assumptions, as well as a
series of subsidiary metaphors. Each of these distinctive metaphors and

their attendant assumptions and subsidiary metaphors is outlined in detail. It seems that one metaphor cluster, the propositional learning one, has been elevated to the position of 'single, preferred account of learning'. Crucial problems for common understandings of learning have been created by the ascendancy of this single preferred account of learning. For policies concerned with lifelong learning such a single account is not only of little use, but is positively damaging: it militates against the whole notion of the availability and utility of different learning styles, modes and signatures that individual learners may bring to their activities. So the book invites us to undertake a reappraisal of what lifelong learning might mean.

This awareness is supported, in the first chapter of the book, by a quotation from Chris Duke: "This transposition of language denies legitimacy to the kinds of learning that are not recognised in educational theory and policy-making. The scope of learning, lifelong and life-wide, mysterious, little understood and invisible, is reduced to that which the 'empire of education' can reach". It is to the authors' credit that they carry the implications of this assertion into an elaboration of an account of learning that might go some way towards making lifelong learning a little less mysterious, much better understood and far more visible, and in this way be of benefit to all learners generally.

We are pleased that this important and radical work helps carry forward the agenda of the Springer Series on Lifelong Learning. We thank the anonymous international reviewers and assessors who have considered and reviewed this proposal and who have played such a significant part in the progress of this work to completion. We trust that its readers will find it as stimulating, thought-provoking and controversial as we who have overseen this project and its development have found it: we commend it with confidence to all those working in this field. We are sure that this further volume in the Springer Series will provide the wide range of constituencies working in the domain of lifelong learning with a rich range of new material for their consideration and further investigation. We hope that it will encourage their continuing critical thinking, research and development, academic and scholarly production, and individual, institutional and professional progress.

June 2006   David Aspin and Judith Chapman

INTRODUCTION

This book presents a theory of informal learning, which is illustrated throughout with exemplars of cases involving individuals and organisations. Our central thesis is that currently the balance within both policies and practices of lifelong learning has shifted too far towards formal learning. That imbalance should be corrected. We indicate some practical and policy oriented implications of what such corrections would involve and we attempt to illustrate some societal benefits that would result from making them. In summary we argue that too much is spent on the provision of formal learning opportunities and not enough on the provision of opportunities for informal learning. It is not as though informal learning is unpopular or unsuccessful. Indeed we provide evidence to support the view both that it is very popular and that it can be very successful. It is limited not by human interest. Rather it is limited at the practical level by a lack of opportunities. More importantly perhaps at the theoretical level it is limited by a lack of awareness of the richness and variety of practice at all levels. We include in our argument not only considerations of income, status and class but also considerations of the richness of apparently mundane practices which so easily can be missed by those obsessed with the former type of consideration.

1. WHAT IS INFORMAL LEARNING?

Distinctions are problematic. Boundaries may be blurred. Some categories can be made to fit either side of a distinction and the very act of making a distinction opens up some possibilities and closes down others (Edwards *et al.* 2004). Moreover to name something is to position it somewhere in a nexus of power relations that are sustained by the rhetorical force of the naming term. Naming something also positions the nominators somewhere on a spectrum of values. In a research-based book such as this, it is tempting then to try to avoid such positioning. It is tempting to problematise, to draw attention to complexity, sometimes to change the nouns that comprise a distinction into adjectives that describe qualities that may be located along a spectrum. In that way, it is possible to sit on the fence and allow an undefined notion of context to do the evaluative work. This latter appears to be the approach adopted by Colley, Hodkinson & Malcolm (2003) in their report to the English Learning and Skills Council on formal and informal learning. They find

> It is not possible to separate out informal/non formal learning from formal learning in ways that have broad applicability or agreement .... Attributes of in/formality are interrelated differently in different situations. *(Extracted from the Executive Summary)*

We disagree with these findings. It seems to us that the distinction between formal and informal learning is both useful and, in most contexts, easily made. We met nobody in the course of compiling our case exemplars, who had any difficulty understanding this distinction. For us, formal learning is that which takes place as intended within formally constituted educational institutions such as schools, colleges, universities, training centres and so on. Typically it follows a prescribed framework whether or not actual attendance at the institution is necessary. Sometimes there are quite specific outcomes. On other occasions there is more of a kind of broad direction or aim. In all cases however those partaking of courses of formal learning have an idea of what they are likely to learn and they accept that that learning will to some extent be under the control of the institution. Informal learning covers all other situations in which people learn including those occasions when in the course of living they learn without sometimes intending to learn. It also includes those situations within formal educational institutions when some things are learnt which are not directly intended by those employed by the institution.

It is true of course that there are borderline cases but as Wittgenstein (1953) points out, that does not make a distinction useless. Rather he refers to a rule governing the ways such things as distinction are made as standing "there like a signpost" (1953: PI 85) and he asks

> Does the sign-post leave no doubt open about the way I have to go? Does it show which direction I am to take when I have passed it; whether along the road or the foot path or cross-country? But where is it said which way I am to follow it; whether in the direction of its finger or (e.g.) in the opposite one? *(1953: PI 85)*

The rule directs a way to go but it cannot compel anyone to go that way. For most purposes the rule serves its purpose. Where a mistake is made, again according to Wittgenstein, is to imagine that a distinction can only be useful if rules can be formulated to govern their application in all cases. Such imagining leads to the mistaken views that it must be possible to define a term before it can be used on all contexts and that all uses of that term must share something fundamental in common. Once this view is accepted then it is easy to see the attractions of an opposing, but equally mistaken view that informality and formality are attributes applicable to all learning contexts. In the first chapter we show how some commentators on the literature surrounding learning have made such mistakes.

We might imagine a person seeking work forced to attend a course of formal learning in order to secure their social security benefit where the course content is of little interest and where most of what is learnt will be learnt informally. Our definitions above will be useful in such a situation. Again our definitions are useful in the situation where someone learns informally while at the same time being enrolled on a chosen course of study. Moreover our definitions allow us to make sense in policy and practical terms of the idea that there is necessarily a balance to be struck between formal and informal learning and that one is not inherently superior to another.

In this we follow John Dewey who argued that all learning is worthwhile. As he puts it 'the very process of living together educates' (1966: 6). While education enables the young to come to take part in the social practices of the community into which they are born such enabling is 'not automatic'. Therefore for Dewey while formal learning at school and elsewhere is important, he (1966: 4-7) cautions that:

Schools are indeed, one important method of the transmission which forms the dispositions of the young but it is only one means and, compared with other agencies, a relatively superficial means. .... [yet] As civilisation advances, ... an ability to share effectively in adult activities depends upon a prior training given with this end in view. .... The task of teaching certain things is delegated to a special group of persons.

In other words while it would be and was possible to learn without attendance at schools and other institutions, current society is sufficiently complicated that without formal learning far too many people would miss out on what might be regarded as key societal practices for harmonious and productive living. Dewey is aware that there is always a danger with such teaching that it becomes remote from the day to day practicalities of everyday life – it becomes 'relatively technical and artificial'.

Hence one of the weightiest problems with which the philosophy of education has to cope is the method of keeping a proper balance between the informal and the formal, the incidental and the intentional modes of education *(Dewey 1966: 9)*.

The problem of determining what forms of learning are worthwhile is shifted by Dewey to one of maintaining an appropriate balance between the formal and the informal. There is a need for formal learning because without it, the initiation of the young into the practices of a society would be too much a matter of happenstance. There are some things that are so fundamental to the educational well being of everyone that formal educational institutions exist to promote them. Crucially though for policy and practice, it is important to maintain a balance with informal learning.

2. THE CENTRAL ARGUMENT

Our central argument then is that currently the balance is shifted too far towards the formal. Quite simply we seek to persuade readers through philosophical argument and empirically grounded examples, that the balance should be shifted more towards the informal. The assumption implicit in many policies, theories and practices concerned with lifelong learning, that such learning must be predominantly formal, is wrong in our view and potentially dangerous for harmonious societal development.

On our view the richness of the educative possibilities of informal learning within a liberal society depends upon the particular circumstances into which children are born. That means that for us as for Dewey the content of the formal curriculum must necessarily vary depending upon the particular backgrounds of children. For example children who are brought up in certain kinds of community such as farming or fishing communities will necessarily be initiated informally into certain practices and not others.

Curriculum is not entirely a philosophical concern though. Rather it involves political concerns, which are informed by empirical investigation of the informal learning undertaken by each child. Worthwhile learning is education, which may be conceived as cultural transmission between generations. For Dewey and for us the type of transmission that should be favoured is that which encourages the

greatest 'variety of mutually shared interests' (1966: 322) and that is a democratic
society.

We have not got very far however and what in our view is currently lacking is
an adequate theory of informal learning. Writing at the end of the United King-
dom's multi-million pound programme of research into The Learning Society, the
Director notes 'that informal learning was much more significant than many of
[the researchers] had previously recognised.' (Coffield 2000: 1). We go further in
arguing that a continuing over-emphasis on formal learning is actually harmful for
any reasonable conception of a learning society guided by principles of lifelong
learning. For some time we have recognised that it is mistaken to hold a rationalist
conception of learning through which theory is supposed to guide practice. By implication it is also mistaken to hold on to the idea that the best way to improve
practice in the workplace or elsewhere is through formal theoretical learning,
which then is somehow practically applied.

We also recognise however that it is mistaken to put too much faith in the idea
of communities of practice (Lave & Wenger 1991) as bases for informal learning
of a non-rationalistic sort. It is mistaken to hold on to the idea that informal learning is best conceived as a series of apprenticeships within communities of practice. Such an idea is often based on an unexamined notion of practice which at
worst suggests that all practices are equally worthwhile. The idea also fails to account for the widely held educational principle that it is good to be a generalist
with a broad grasp of what are held to be main features of societal practices while
at the same time being a specialist in just a few.

Rather we have come to see that what is required is a different conception of rationalism which is much less determinate than commonly supposed. In this book
we develop a theory of learning which puts the notion of judgement in context to
the fore. We theorise learning as the growing capacity to make appropriate context
sensitive judgements. This notion offers a less deterministic account of learning
because contexts are nested and layered in a way that problematises the identification of relevant context. Such nesting and layering also problematises the notion
of a community of practice and suggests that learning is often sufficiently opportunistic for it to be difficult to sustain the idea of community. We therefore re-
examine the notions of community and consensus to set out a less cosy but more
realistic account of community than is often suggested in the literature. This re-
examination involves a revised relationship between opportunity and wisdom. It
might be imagined that our view of learning is most relevant to those concerned
with informal learning in the workplace and elsewhere. We point out that this
view also has strong implications for those concerned with formal education in
general and the school curriculum in particular.

The developing account of learning is illustrated throughout the book by a
number of excerpts from empirically based exemplars dealing with such topics as
hobbies, crafts, professions, learning to survive, and keeping vocationally relevant
in a rapidly changing field. These exemplars are developed in an attempt to illustrate the overall range of the theory presented. However, we hope that they also
serve to show some of the richness of learning from practice, a richness that is not
fully captured in theoretical discussions of learning. The book concludes by setting

out the implications of this account for policy makers concerned not only with lifelong learning but school education too. Part of our advice to them is that the term 'learning' now comes so loaded with undesirable connotations that it may be time to try to find some new term to describe a developing ability to make contextually sensitive judgments. Such a new term would aim to capture the sense of lifelong development and achievement. That is to avoid the connotation of 'learner' as powerless and, as yet, incapable. A new term would aim to get away from the view of learning as preparing towards one of learning as becoming. It is hoped that policy makers, theorists, practitioners and those simply wanting to live more fulfilling lives may find some things of interest in the book.

3. OUTLINE OF THE BOOK

We begin with a wide-ranging review of the literature concerned with informal, workplace and lifelong learning. We argue that these three distinctive concepts of learning converge much more than has hitherto been supposed. We claim that recognition of this convergence provides new insights into the nature of learning itself. Throughout the book we attempt to tease out such insights. We argue that hitherto there has been an undue emphasis on the cognitive aspects of human life as if through cognitive endeavour alone all practical problems are best solved. Such an emphasis is related to an over reliance on a type of rationalism which puts means-ends rationality to the fore. The emphasis leads both to a concentration on knowledge as a fundamental explanatory category and on a type of instrumentalism, which suggests that knowledge is the best guide to appropriate action. Since it is hard to see how knowledge of a theoretical kind could possibly be 'acquired' other than through attendance at institutions specifically set up to 'transmit' it to learners, then it is not difficult to see how an undue emphasis on formal learning arises.

We also argue that policies concerned with lifelong learning often conflate learning with education with societal development in general. Again there is an implicit instrumentalism in much policy discourse, which suggests that societal development depends fundamentally on sound economic performance, which in turn depends upon appropriate formal learning. Our account is more complex than this. It is not entirely clear just what vision of societal development is favoured by the various versions of lifelong learning that can be found in the literature. To be sure there is an uneasy tension between humanistic and neo-liberal versions, yet it is hard to see anyone now supposing that a humanistic vision of society can be achieved without at least some concern for the implications of global capitalism.

It is widely regarded that lifelong learning conceived as formal learning is an obviously good thing. The question can be asked however 'Who wants to learn forever?' at least in this way. Moreover the strand of lifelong learning that has emerged in the workplace as continuing professional development raises a similar question. The review therefore includes current literature on workplace learning. This shows that there is a tendency in the literature to base practical recommendations on a single theory of learning. For example, much of this literature is based on concepts surrounding situated cognition (Lave & Wenger 1991, Lave 1996,

Wenger 1998). There are at least two problems with this particular literature. The first is that much of it is based on the idea that a single account of learning is what is required. The second is that it misses out on a normative account of practice. Interesting though it might be to theorise about how people learn, for us that is less interesting than theorising about what they should learn. Empirical investigation might enable the former type of theorising, but it is unlikely to enable the latter.

Chapter two is a genealogical account of development of policies towards lifelong learning which attempts to show how a deep-seated empiricist epistemology lay largely unexamined within the democracies of Britain and Australia so that instrumentalism in this area grew into a fairly restrictive sense of vocationalism. It is argued that this deep seated empiricism made it hardly surprising that researchers in the area tended to concentrate on formal learning. The idea that the outcomes of learning could be something measurable and describable gave rise to the idea that learning is a product describable and measurable in behavioural terms. The so-called competence revolution (Hyland 1997) developed that idea so that it became common place to describe the desirable learning outcomes of formal learning in behavioural terms and to group these into occupational families.

It could be argued that this was all part of a wider move to end the public sector's monopoly of formal learning. In an increasingly tight jobs market, vocational qualifications became the keys to securing well paid employment. The certificates of competence became promissory notes of a job. In a very real sense a certificate became a product for which people would pay. The performance criteria that had to be satisfied in order that a certificate to be awarded could also be regarded as products of formal learning. It was then easy for governments to legitimate the idea of a market in formal learning through which products would be sold through different providers both public and private to deliver these products in the most efficient ways. Policies for lifelong learning simply continued the same trend. Once formal learning at school might have been regarded as sufficient to act as a passport for lifelong employment. But now, in a globalised economy in which change is stressed above all else, formal learning is seen to be needed throughout life to keep up to date with rapidly changing employment fields and consumer demands. Hardly surprising therefore that researchers tried to work out what forms of formal learning could best match this policy agenda.

Once it became accepted that learning is a kind of product, then it was not unreasonable to want to be able to specify that product. Once the product was specified then formal learning and formal institutions for learning became all the more prevalent. After all within such institutions and as a preliminary to joining such institutions, learners are supposed to know just what it is they are to learn. Indeed in recent decades under the influence of behavioural learning theory, it has become commonplace to specify the products of learning in behavioural terms as if a quite specific learning outcome could be guaranteed without risk to the learner (see Blake et al. 1998). Not only that but those of a neo-liberal persuasion then saw these specifications of products of learning as the means of introducing much needed market reforms to what previously had been public sector provision of learning opportunities. It became increasingly attractive to governments concerned to reduce the size of public sector expenditure to privatise the opportunities for learning. The dominant metaphors and assumptions that supported the product view seemed to enable them to do this.

As has been said, however, there was something wrong with the metaphysics and epistemology that underpinned these developments. It should hardly surprise us that the logical contradictions of these developments are becoming increasingly apparent. For example it is becoming increasingly difficult to find evidence to support the view that many of the jobs currently on offer do require increased formal learning. Moreover the phenomenon known as credentialism, to which attention was drawn by Collins (1979), has grown apace. A problem arises however because there is a limit to the exchange value of different qualifications. As it becomes increasingly expensive to acquire credentials with high exchange value, some learners simply 'drop out' of the formal learning society.

In chapter three we attempt to show an impending sense of crisis in formal education and in all forms of 'front loaded' formal educational provision which take the form of promissory notes for successful future practice. While it might be imagined that informal learning is essentially a private concern and formal learning a public concern, we attempt to show how such imagining arises and how it gets us off on entirely the wrong foot in considering lifelong learning in postmodernity. In chapter four we go on to argue that learning is necessarily opportunistic at both the individual and communal level. We outline a crisis within liberal democratic societies that arises because of misplaced attraction to a non-perfectionist liberalism such as that of Rawls (1971, 1993). According to this argument both the neo-liberals got it wrong by focusing on the private and the communitarians got it wrong by supposing that community was more stable than it actually can be at the present time. We argue against the idea that there exists a kind of overlapping consensus that can be used to guide educational policy. The development of personal autonomy as a guide to learning may no longer be of much use. What we need is a kind of liberalism that can hold good against postmodernism. Our guide here is Manuel Castells (1996, 1997, 1998) and his idea of a network society. Our keywords are contingency and opportunity, as outlined in chapter 4. We suggest that it is precisely because so many people currently slip through the net of formal learning, and are likely to slip through any further nets in the form of formal schemes of lifelong learning, that provides us with the most hope that the significance of informal learning can be recognised.

While we seek to redress a balance in favour of informal learning, we are aware of the risks involved in such an attempt. Just as it is argued that formal learning has become a central part of a panopticon society (Wain 2004), it can also be argued that any systems designed to encourage informal learning could easily function as part of such a society too. Moreover systems which promote informal learning may serve as a rather cheap type of panopticon at that. In short an adequate theory of informal learning may be precisely what is not needed at the present time. We are sensitive to this possibility and our theory brings risk and uncertainty in learning to the fore. Risk and uncertainty are resistant to systematisation. Attempts to make lifelong learning risk free and its outcomes determined in advance are what have led to a present state of crisis. A different way of thinking about the State's interest in encouraging learning is required. We argue that a renewed focus on informal learning opens up the possibility of recognising practices that have gone largely unnoticed as educative practices and that such recognition is overdue.

In chapter five we begin to rethink learning. We argue that a single account of learning is always unlikely to be sufficient and describe how metaphor seems essential to enable us to talk and think about learning. Yet metaphor not only enables but restricts our thinking. For learning is an 'essentially contested' term (Gallie 1956) and the metaphors that we use to describe learning reflect the different meanings that are ascribed to the term. Metaphor both reveals and conceals however. With close scrutiny it becomes apparent that some of the ontological assumptions that are hidden through the use of metaphor are seriously deficient. Unsurprisingly the view that learning is essentially the acquisition of a product comes in for most criticism.

The chapter concludes with some desiderata for a better understanding of learning as a dialectical interplay of product and process and a greater awareness of the ways that metaphors shapes our understanding of and practices in learning. In summary we think that learning is concerned primarily with the development of the capacity to judge well whether that judging is concerned with the appropriateness of actions or speech. On this view learning is holistic. It involves not only individual bodies but the organisations and communities of which they are a part. It makes sense to talk of organisations as well as individuals learning. The outcomes of learning cannot always or even often be written down. Since the learner is part of the world then learning alters both learner and the world of which she is a part. There is a view of learning as the ability to rehearse certain behavioural repertoire in a formal context, which may or may not share a resemblance with the practical context in which the learning has real point. In contrast to this view we advance an alternative that all learning is primarily contextual and that an understanding of context is crucial to any theory of learning. We also consider the idea that learning itself is metaphorical and that the metaphor of learning now carries considerable unhelpful baggage in the form of associations with such qualities as helplessness, powerlessness and incompetence.

In chapter six we begin to outline our preferred informal learning theory as the developing ability to make judgments with ever increasing contextual sensitivity. Plainly there are two key terms in need of expansion and explanation here – context and judgment. We start with the term 'context'. We argue that the learning of propositions within formal learning has distorted commonly held views of learning to such an extent that it is hard now to conceive of propositions as things to be learnt practically as and when required. In contrast to the widely accepted view that definitions of terms are essential prerequisites for successful uses of those terms in a variety of contexts, we argue that definitions are but one type of use appropriate in some contexts but not in others. Indeed in most practical contexts definitions are of no use at all.

We also argue that learning is holistic in that learner, learning and context cannot be sharply distinguished once and for all. For us learning is a transactional relationship in which both learners and their environment change together. That is so because learners are part of the environment. Likewise, rather than being something that is located within learners, learning encompasses both learner and their environment. Such a relationship is coherent with our post empiricist epistemology in which the distinction between a knowing subject and an object to be known is rejected.

It might appear then as if context is an infinitely expandable concept, one that can be used to interpret in an apparently infinite number of ways the judgments that are made. That appearance is deceptive for two main reasons. First the infinite regress is blocked by the actual experience of a learner and not by any possible experience. Moreover, it is her particular interest at any one time that limits interpretation, not any possible interest that she might have. Second the fact that contextuality is considerably more complex than might be imagined does not mean that nothing of significant generality can be said about it and in this and the next chapter we attempt to do just this. We attempt to explain the sense in which contexts are nested and layered, the distinction between implicit and explicit context and crucially the ways in which one interpretation or one set of contextual factors might be preferred in a general sense over another.

In chapter seven we attempt to elucidate the other key term in our theory – practice. We argue that the most obvious way of making sense of 'judgment' is through the notion of a practice. For example to make the judgment that wine is blood would simply be wrong within the practice of chemistry. To make the same judgment within certain religious practices would not only be true but central to what it means to be practically engaged in a religious sense. Coming to make the right judgment therefore depends upon there being a means of discriminating between practices and, for us, the goods that are involved in the practice. The work of Alasdair MacIntyre is widely acknowledged (e.g. Kemmis 2005, Smeyers & Burbules 2005) to be central to a proper understanding of practice and we examine his work in detail, particularly his distinction between internal and external goods. In terms of influence however, it seems uncontroversial to claim that the situated cognition theorists Jean Lave and Etienne Wenger are prominent in the field of workplace learning. In this chapter we compare MacIntyre's use of the term practice with that of Lave and Wenger and argue that Macintyre gives us a better possibility for a normative account of practice than the situated cognitivists. The work of MacIntyre is not without its difficulties however and, in the course of this chapter, we examine some of these difficulties associated with his notions of internal and external goods, practices and institutions, narrative unity and traditions. Indeed, we take care to try to avoid turning what potentially are helpful distinctions into the kind of uncritically accepted dualisms that Dewey so railed against and which restrict out thinking in unhelpful ways. We try to hold on to the idea that it is through an appreciation and valuing of internal goods that we have the best chance of resisting the systematisation that is built into an over formalised view of learning.

The idea of contextualising judgments with reference to the practices that give those judgments meaning appears promising. Certainly this idea can be used to account for the idea of learning as enculturation. A problem arises however once it is realised that the same activity can be contextualised within a range of practices and that to differing extents everyone comes to be involved in such a range. The ways in which they describe their practical judgments is part of their identity and it is generally agreed that learning should enable them not only to become enculturated but also individuated, so that they come in a sense to be able to choose the range of their practical involvements. It is agreed that such choice should be based on some expanding notion of personal characteristics rather than on the basis of the power that others have over them.

For example the context for the activity of cutting wood might be through the practice of carpentry. But there are other ways of contextualising that activity or the judgments that guide that activity. Cutting wood may be contextualised through the practice of boatbuilding or it could be contextualised through the life plan of someone to sail around the world or in a myriad of other possible ways. It is the possibility that there are these other ways that enables us to avoid what would otherwise become an infinite regress of chasing an ultimate context for a judgment. For us there is no ultimate context. Rather there is a series of recursive possibilities for contextualising judgments across practices and within what we go on to argue are nests of contexts moving from the specific to the more general. There is no certainty that such recursion will be productive but there are guides that can help us. One such guide may be produced by a theoretical discussion of the type that is found in this book.

In chapter eight we compare the idea that there can be no context-free judgment with the idea taken from post empiricist philosophy of science that there can be no theory free observation statement. As Dewey points out, implicit context provides the background against which we make sense of explicit context. Sometimes however that implicit context is brought to the surface, challenged and modified again in a similar way to Kuhn's (1962) description of the case of the overthrow of a paradigmatic theory in natural science. This comparison forms the background to our argument that judgments are often framed against implicit context. In those cases it makes little sense to write of judgment as if it were an action or prompt for an action distinct from the ordinary flow of activity that is exhibited by a competent practitioner. In other cases it is clear that judgments are framed against explicit features of context such as the type of practice within which the judgment is located.

Practices are not all of a piece, however, and we refer again to the work of Alasdair MacIntyre to show how those that are rich in what he calls internal goods might be preferred over those that are mere instruments in the pursuit of external goods such as money, status or power. We may say that judgments form part of activities which form part of practices. We adapt MacIntyre's (1981: 187) distinction so that for us a practice is

> ..... any coherent and complex form of socially established collection of human activities that is identifiable by a single word or phrase. Through this form goods are realised in the course of trying to achieve those standards of excellence which are appropriate to and partly definitive of the form with the result that human powers to achieve excellence, and human conceptions of the goods involved, are systematically extended.

...ich in turn is guided by the recognition of human capacities, which enable good practice. It is such recognition that in the end forms a goal for a lifelong learner, for without it no sense of learning can be made. Learning becomes vacuous and there are no clear criteria to guide one sort of practical development from another.

In chapter ten we draw together and summarise main features of our account of informal learning theory that has been presented throughout the book. We then discuss the practical implications of this account for a range of learning situations, including some examples of societal practices that have not, till that stage, figured prominently in the book. Finally, we present a series of conclusions and implications that centre around the need to shift the balance from over-reliance on formal learning more towards informal learning, together with a pressing need to rethink our common assumptions about learning.

Our account of reason is based within the Enlightenment tradition of liberal humanism. We recognise that that tradition is currently under some strain and we understand why some commentators describe it now as being in a state of terminal crisis. We hold, however, that it is the best available. In any case we have no option other than to work within it for that is where we belong. Our book is quite simply an attempt within that tradition to analyse a problem, to describe it, to propose solutions and to outline the practical implications of those solutions. In this way we seek to convince. Liberal humanism may be in crisis, but that crisis need not be terminal and we prefer a politics of hope. We are not attracted by a seemingly endless series of initiatives made by those with power to attempt to control the learning of those with less power. Nor are we attracted, however, by the work of those whose intellectual efforts seem to stop at unmasking such control. It may be unfair for Rorty to characterise the latter as 'the Foucauldian academic left' and we do not agree with his nationalism, but there is surely something in his claim that this group:

> Is exactly the sort of left that the oligarchy dreams of: A left whose members are so busy unmasking the present that they have no time to discuss what laws need to be passed in order to create a better future. *(Rorty 1998: 139)*

Post or late modernity (Giddens 1992) presents challenges for liberal humanism. Practical change in some areas seems so rapid that it is hard to conceptualise in terms of progress or otherwise. It just happens. It is episodic. It is not readily conceptualised within any one practice and it may not be helpful to conceptualise it at all. Life is too short to try. There is a radical contingency about some of our practical associations. Discerning any sense of continuity or cohesion between them seems hopeless. If we were to generalise from this observation we might wonder why anyone would bother about learning at all.

There is a growing sense of crisis in values within which political liberalism struggles to cope. Different cultural forms of life seem to share less and less that would enable rational decision making on a democratic basis. There is a growing sense that the effects of power are so ubiquitous and unpredictable that even if a shared sense of values could be discovered, the best intentions of those who tried to act upon such a shared sense would be distorted and compromised. From this comes a loss of confidence in any notion of objectivity or of disinterest. Everything and everyone appears interested. It appears as if their interests should be deciphered in a way that does not appear naive but while this is done a pernicious relativism gains hold. Notions of right-wrong, better-worse, knowledge-belief become blurred. It is easier to go along with the flow. In the meantime there are those who have to try to deal with the consequences of this sense of crisis at an immediate level that theorists such as the writers generally avoid. We are thinking in particular here of those teachers who are supposed formally to teach others who actually do not want to learn in that way.

CHAPTER ONE

LIFELONG, INFORMAL AND WORKPLACE LEARNING

This chapter sets the scene for much of the rest of the book by outlining and reviewing main themes from the literature on three notionally distinct areas of learning. The three areas, lifelong learning, informal learning, and workplace learning, are notionally distinct in that each has an identifiable literature in its own right. Part of the argument of this book is that these three distinctive concepts of learning converge much more than has hitherto been supposed. We claim that recognition of this convergence provides new insights into the nature of learning itself. These insights are at the heart of a main theme of this book, which is the claim that there needs to be a rethink of the balance between formal and informal learning in the lives of citizens. Currently, the balance is too far towards the formal.

The first main section of this chapter outlines the origins and main understandings of lifelong learning, including the main assumptions that these understandings make about the nature of learning. Then some common criticisms of lifelong learning are discussed. These criticisms are shown to make assumptions about the nature of learning that heavily favour formal learning, whilst marginalizing informal learning. Because informal learning is central to our argument, we then review relevant literature on this topic, including debates about its definition and its connections or otherwise with formal learning. We then turn to an overview of the literature on workplace learning, the third notionally different type of learning that is vital to our argument.

1. ORIGINS AND MAIN UNDERSTANDINGS OF LIFELONG LEARNING

The concept of lifelong education came to major prominence in the cultural and intellectual ferment of the late 1960's. It was proposed by both UNESCO and the Council of Europe as the "master concept" for ensuring that educational opportunities were spread over the whole of a person's lifetime. The UNESCO position, which was centred on the concept of "lifelong learning", saw

> ..... lifelong education as involving a fundamental transformation of society, so that the whole of society becomes a learning resource for each individual. *(Cropley 1979: 105).*

The philosophical basis of the UNESCO position was one that saw the society of the future as a scientific humanist learning society. The vision, articulated at length in the famous Faure report, *Learning To Be* (UNESCO 1972), was that well organised lifelong education would enable all citizens to participate fully in this scientific humanism.

The Council of Europe's position was focused on the concept of *"education permanente"*. As such it was targeted more on the role of cultural policy in changing society. The Council saw *education permanente* as a means of "preserving and renewing" the European cultural heritage and, at the same time, "as a strategy for promoting European cultural integration" (Kallen 1979: 51). As well, the concept of lifelong education was also significantly connected to the different, but related OECD concept of recurrent education (see, e.g., Kallen 1979). Unlike the concept of *lifelong education*, recurrent education was specifically focussed on *lifelong learning*. In short, there were seemingly small, but ultimately vital, differences amongst the main proponents of lifelong education in the 1960's and 1970's. Thus, as various commentators (e.g. Duke 2001) have noted, the seeds of inevitable conceptual conflict were present from the start.

Duke (2001: 501) traces much of the subsequent conceptual conflict to, firstly, confusion between lifelong *education* and lifelong *learning* by many writers, and, secondly, to misunderstanding of the concept of *education permanente*. For Duke, slipping between lifelong *education* and lifelong *learning* has various unfortunate results as will be discussed below. Likewise, rendering *education permanente* into English, inaccurately and misleadingly, as 'permanent education' only served to reinforce and inflame hostility from sceptics about lifelong education. (In this book, we will use lifelong learning as the preferred term, except when we specifically want to emphasise lifelong education).

Another interesting perspective on the conflicts inherent in the various proposals for lifelong education/lifelong learning is provided by Bagnall (2001). He argues that three different "progressive sentiments" suffuse much of this literature. One is the "democratic progressive" sentiment that he locates in the work of Faure (UNESCO 1972), Gelpi (1985), Freire (1972) and others. Its focus is on "cultural reform through education" (Bagnall 2001: 37). For the democratic progressive sentiment:

> The purpose of education is to inform social action for the development of a more humane, tolerant, just and egalitarian society of liberated, empowered individuals, acting collegially in the public good. Education is seen as informing both social action itself and the reflective and discursive evaluation of that action: an ongoing process of action and reflection, together commonly labelled 'praxis'.
> *(Bagnall 2001: 37)*

Bagnall argues that, on this view, lifelong education ".... is seen as being, first and foremost, a public good. It is from the public good that the private, individual benefit flows" (Bagnall 2001: 38).

Another "progressive sentiment" identified by Bagnall is the so-called "individual progressive" sentiment, which he traces to much traditional adult education writing (such as Houle (1980), Knowles (1980), Lawson (1979), and Paterson

(1979)), as well as to the Dewey tradition. Its purpose of eduction is individual growth and development of various kinds reflecting slightly different kinds of liberatory commitments:

> ...... liberation from ignorance (through individual enlightenment), from dependence (through individual empowerment), from constraint (through the individual transformation of perspectives), or from inadequacy (through individual development). *(Bagnall 2001: 36)*

These four different liberatory commitments respectively imply somewhat different central purposes for education:

- intellectual development, usually through academic disciplines;
- practical social and political organisational skills;
- transformation and transcendence of individual frameworks and assumptions, in particular those developed by passive acculturation;
- individual growth and development of a Deweyan kind.

These purposes in turn imply slightly different bases for lifelong learning:

- the sheer breadth, depth and ever-expanding nature of human knowledge;
- the changing developmental needs of people to remain in control of their lives at different stages;
- the ongoing need for educational transformation of individuals to counter conformism;
- the endless process of human growth in an evolving social world.

Whereas the first sentiment focused on education as a public social good, with benefits flowing also to individuals, the individual progressive sentiment views education as primarily concerned with the development of individuals, with the public good following automatically from successfully taking care of individual needs.

Finally, according to Bagnall, there is the "adaptive progressive" sentiment which focuses centrally on lifelong learning as a response to ongoing cultural change. Adaptive learning in the face of cultural change is seen as the means of avoiding deprivation, poverty and dependence. For this sentiment, the purposes for education centre on the learner gaining the "freedom ... to enjoy the good life, to contribute constructively to society, and to pursue one's interests" (Bagnall 2001: 39). Major sources for this sentiment cited by Bagnall include Cropley (1977), Knapper & Cropley (1985), Jessup (1969) and Kozlowski (1995). On this view, the basis for adopting lifelong learning is the impact of accelerating cultural change on the learning needs of individuals of all ages, as well as on the learning needs of groups, such as organizations and even nations.

Thus, the adaptive progressive sentiment views education "as being directed to a process of lifelong adaptation to the changing cultural context .... to allow learners to manage their own actions *as* lifelong learners" (Bagnall 2001: 39). Here education can be seen as both a public and a private good, though beyond the compulsory sector the focus tends to be on the private, as individuals and organizations enhance their capacity to profit from the changing cultural context.

Despite its strong humanistic origins, the concept of lifelong education received wide criticism and rejection from many educational writers in the 1970's. This led to the concepts of lifelong education and lifelong learning falling somewhat from favour in the 1980's. As the preceding discussion has demonstrated, there were more than enough differences of view amongst proponents of both to confirm Duke's contention that "the seeds of inevitable conceptual conflict were present from the start". Certainly these differences and ambiguities were highlighted by critics.

However, lifelong education and lifelong learning were never entirely off the educational agenda. For instance, Long (in Long, Apps and Hiemstra 1985: 66ff.) noted, there were various ongoing interacting forces that together served to build up continuing increasing pressure for lifelong learning provision. Long classified and discussed these in terms of "three critical foundations of lifelong learning" as follows:

-   Lifelong learning – a basic human need
-   Social and technological factors (including the increasing failure of the 'front end' model of vocational education)
-   Institutional pressures (these include both "philosophical pressures" – education as a good in itself – and "practical pressures" – public demands placed on educational institutions).

It is notable that these pressures could conceivably produce a range of outcomes. At one extreme, a minimalist view of lifelong education could be achieved, i.e. a society in which there is reasonably adequate provision of adult education. Perhaps many present industrialised countries have approached this situation. Arguably, there is already consensus about a minimalist view of lifelong education. However, many proponents of lifelong education and lifelong learning are seeking much more than this. Duke (2001: 502) argues that a minimalist view trivialises lifelong learning. Formal education providers, seeking to expand their student load, have latched onto the notion of lifelong learning as a marketing ploy for their courses, particularly ones involving new forms of delivery, such as web-based offerings and ones available on off-peak radio and television. For Duke, this trivialises the powerful concept of lifelong learning by reducing it to adult and continuing education.

At the other extreme, a maximalist view of lifelong education, favoured by Duke, seeks nothing less than a learning society. While learning societies can take various forms, proponents of lifelong education typically favour one that is democratic, where the learning society is "a shared, pluralistic and participatory 'form of life' in Dewey's sense .... rather than a simple set of institutions and constitutional guarantees" (Wain 1987: 202; Wain 1993: 68). What are the prospects for consensus emerging in respect of this maximalist view of lifelong education?

According to Duke:

..... in its fullest meaning, creating a learning society is truly ambitious. It implies developing in a society the capability to learn from and change as a result of
experience and reflection. ... lifelong and societal learning becomes a call for active citizenship .... *(Duke 2001: 507)*

This richer meaning of the learning society is outside of the ken of most policy
makers. Not only does it imply a redirecting of formal education provision, but it
also points to the importance of the kinds of informal learning that are the focus of
this book. But, as Duke points out, the "powerful metaphor of a learning society is
almost always reduced to providing more opportunities for individuals " (Duke
2001: 507). In the process, the role and potential of informal learning in the learning society is overlooked. Thus, coming from a somewhat different perspective,
Duke concurs with our view, developed at length in this book, that informal learning has been neglected vis-a-vis formal learning in lifelong learning policy.

A clear instance of the kind of policy reductionism identified by Duke occurred
in the 1998 Australian West report *Learning for Life*:

..... in a learning society primary responsibility for learning and choosing when
to learn rests with the individual. The individual should be prepared to explore
learning options and to invest time, money and effort. *(quoted by Duke 2001:
506-7)*

Following its period of relative dormancy in the 1980s, the concept of lifelong
education has returned to favour from the 1990's onwards, particularly under the
guise of lifelong learning. Amongst other things, the notion of lifelong learning
sits well with OECD neo-liberal economic agendas. As Boshier (1998: 13) put it:

There has been a shift from a neo-Marxist or anarchistic-utopian template for reform (the Faure report) to a neo-liberal, functionalist rendition (OECD) orches-
trated as a corollary of globalisation and hyper capitalism.

Inevitably, the current OECD take on lifelong learning will be condemned by many
for not being humanistic enough. Yet the OECD will not be left in sole charge of the
agenda. Undoubtedly, their understanding of what lifelong learning might be will be
challenged and renovated by others. For instance, Edwards (1997: Ch. 6) identifies
three distinct discourses that construct differing versions of the learning society.
Coffield (2000) discusses ten models of a learning society all of which were in-
stanced to some extent in his empirical research project. Thus plurality of interpretations remains despite OECD intentions. Our worry is that too often, the crucial role
of informal learning in any sort of learning society is missed. To show this, we turn
to five common criticisms of the lifelong learning concept. In each case the argument is distorted by informal learning being overlooked.

2. SOME COMMON CRITICISMS OF THE CONCEPT OF LIFELONG LEARNING

As already noted in this chapter, the concept of lifelong learning has attracted a variety of criticisms from its very beginnings. In this section we will consider five prime examples of these criticisms as follows:

– Who wants to learn forever?
– The concept of lifelong learning seen to be too promiscuous since it treats all learning as being of the same status, i.e. the problem of undesirable learning.
– Education as a major social control mechanism and, hence, lifelong education as a threat of more and permanent control.
– Lifelong learning as supporting a highly inequitable status quo.
– Lifelong learning as encouraging abdication of responsibility by governments.

In discussing each of these criticisms, we will be considering the main assumptions that each of them makes about the nature of learning. It will emerge that a central common assumption is the marginal significance of informal learning. Other common associated assumptions, which reflect common sense understandings of learning, include:

– Learning as accumulation of objects in a container.
– To be any good learning should be of a particular favoured kind.

Who Wants to Learn forever?

For many people, formal education courses are something to be endured for various extrinsic purposes, e.g. to gain the qualification needed for a job, to satisfy the expectations of parents, to improve one's standard of living, etc. For such people, reaching the end of the course is all that matters. After that, you can 'throw away the books'. Of course, this is a very anti-educational view of learning. However, for those who harbour this view of learning, the notion of lifelong learning, taken literally, is somewhat threatening, if not sinister. It conjures up suggestions of lifelong attendance at classes with a never ending stream of assignments and examinations to be completed. Some of this perceived threat is suggested by the title of the Illich and Verne 1976 book, *Imprisoned in the Global Classroom*. (Similar images have been suggested by titles employed by other authors, e.g. Falk 1998, Ohliger 1974, Halliday 2003). Another strand of this thinking is represented by the negative connotations of 'credential creep' (as discussed briefly earlier in this book).

However this response takes a very narrow view of lifelong learning. It equates learning with formal learning in classrooms, thereby leaving informal learning completely out of the picture. Note that worries about credential creep are centred on pressures to accumulate formal educational qualifications. Thus this response smuggles in the assumption that for learning to be any good, it should be of a particular kind favoured in formal courses, the learning of propositional knowledge. If one adds to this the common sense assumption that learning involves the accumulation of objects (products) in a container (the mind), it further conjures up the spectre of the mind bursting at the seams. If too many files are crammed into the filing cabinet, it will disintegrate.

Overall, this criticism of the concept of lifelong learning is flawed by a failure to appreciate the rich scope of the term learning. There is a lot more to learning, and lifelong learning, than participation in formal courses.

2.2 The Concept of Lifelong Learning Seen to be too Promiscuous since it Treats All Learning as being of the Same Status

Probably the main conceptual argument advanced by its critics against the notion of lifelong education hinges on the charge that it uses the terms 'lifelong education' and 'lifelong learning' interchangeably, thereby confusing education and learning. These critics argue that education involves stringent criteria of quality of learning, criteria which everyday instances of learning simply fail to meet. Hence, education is viewed as being much more exclusive than mere learning. Lawson (1982) presented the argument very succinctly as follows: The lifelong education movement confuses learning with education. But education is much narrower than learning. Hence 'lifelong learning' debases education.

Related arguments are common in the literature. For instance, Boshier, a supporter of lifelong education as against lifelong learning, argues that:

> Education is the optimal (and usually systematic) arrangement of external conditions that foster learning. Education is a provided service. Lifelong education requires that someone – often government or other agencies – develops policy and devotes resources to education that will preferably occur in a broad array of informal, non-formal and formal settings. *(Boshier 1998: 8-9)*

So Boshier sees lifelong education as eliciting resource commitments from government and other organizations. However in contrast, he thinks that lifelong learning, with its "notion of the autonomous free-floating individual learner as consumer" (1998: 9), will only encourage a push towards further privatisation of education. He puts it this way:

> Lifelong learning is a way of abdicating responsibility, of avoiding hard choices by putting learning on the open market. If the learner as consumer doesn't decide to take advantage of available opportunities, then it is his or her fault. It is easier to blame the victim than overcome structural or psycho-cultural barriers to participation. *(Boshier 1998: 9)*

Thus, according to Boshier, 'lifelong learning' debases education in a sense somewhat different from Lawson's view, in that it shifts responsibility for education from government to individual learners.

Likewise, Collins (1998: 46) worries that the discourse of lifelong learning tends to valorise learning, thereby forgetting that some learning is undesirable. For instance, some informal learning might be a blockage to any more learning happening. So it becomes necessary to 'unlearn' this learning, before any further learning can occur. However, it is well known that similar undesirable learning can occur within formal learning situations. For instance, people can learn, falsely, that they are poor learners. So, while accepting that this is a significant issue, we doubt that it is one that is especially relevant to the shift from lifelong education to lifelong learning. As this book proceeds, it will be made clear that not all informal learning is equally valuable. As we will demonstrate, there are criteria for distinguishing the sound from the less sound.

However, Duke offers a somewhat more subtle and convincing interpretation of the matters raised by Lawson and Boshier. He does indeed agree that "... hopeless confusion arises from indiscriminately swapping around the words 'education' and 'learning'." (Duke 2001: 508). But, according to Duke, there are several strands to this confusion. Firstly, there is a tendency, arising from liberal individualist assumptions combined with supposedly egalitarian trends, to substitute the terms 'learner' and 'learning' for 'education'. In these times of customer focus and business practices applied to education, the individual learner becomes properly the focus of attention rather than the provider or the system. This supposedly 'democratic' emphasis on learners, and their choices amongst the many forms and modes of learning available, shifts the focus away from education itself. It also deflects attention from important issues such as publicly funded education and inequitable access. Thus, in a somewhat different sense, Duke agrees that there is ".... poverty of comprehension revealed by the shift from education to learning." (2001: 508).

However, Duke points to a second, and more important, outcome of confusing education with learning. Far from education being debased by the shift to lifelong learning discourse, Duke thinks the influence is the other way around. He argues that slipping between lifelong *education* and lifelong *learning* results in learning becomes subsumed into educational provision. For him, learning becomes limited or debased by being confused with education in this way.

> The problem from a policy perspective, in terms of educational or other intervention to foster learning, is that the language of 'learning' constantly flips over into the imperialism of educational provision. *(Duke 2001: 508)*

In this move of 'learning' being absorbed into educational provision, a very unfortunate consequence follows:

> ..... it unintentionally leaves out any kind of learning not recognised by the individual concerned as learning and, normally, which is not manifest in some course or other purposeful educational support activity. *This equates education, training and other activities intended to support learning with learning itself.* Learning is seen only in terms of provision. *(Duke 2001: 508) (our emphasis)*

Duke sums this up in a passage that might well serve as an epigraph for this book:

> This transposition of language denies legitimacy to the kinds of learning that are not recognised in educational theory and policy-making. The scope of learning, lifelong and life-wide, mysterious, little understood and invisible, is reduced to that which the 'empire of education' can reach. *(Duke 2001: 509)*

In arguing that lifelong education policy has encouraged the colonisation of informal learning by the formal education sector, Duke has pointed out one strand of our key argument in this book that lifelong education policy has moved too far in favour of the formal. Other strands of this key argument will be highlighted as the book unfolds.

Once again in this section we find the prevalence of the assumption that only the kinds of systematic learning that are the province of formal education systems are educationally valid. The different kinds of informal learning, that occur in everyday contexts, are, with no attempt at serious examination, viewed as, at best, dubious. With the exception of Duke, this assumption is characteristic of all of the writers discussed. Lawson assumes an 'only the best will do' principle. For Lawson, it is self-evident that formal education involves stringent criteria of quality about what is learnt. But by definition, informal learning of all kinds simply fails to meet these criteria. So it is judged inferior. In Boshier's case, the claim is that publicly funded educational provision ensures quality standards for learning, because it is offered as a service. Boshier seems to fear that marketising education will dilute criteria of quality, thereby allowing whatever instances of learning that people drift into, to count as worthwhile learning.

But there are flaws in this kind of reasoning. Firstly, as Duke pointed out, it assumes that informal learning will be brought under the criteria of formal learning and thereby be found wanting. It dismisses out of hand all learning that is not specifiable according to formal criteria, much of it "mysterious, little understood and invisible" as Duke so eloquently put it. It is not the claim of this book that informal learning should displace its formal counterparts. Rather a rich understanding of learning needs to recognise that both formal and informal are indispensable, and neither is reducible to the other. The key issue then is 'how to achieve a judicious balance of the two'? In this book we want to argue strongly, with Duke, that there are many kinds of informal learning that are valuable, indeed indispensable, that do not fit formal criteria, yet which have been largely overlooked because of the prevalence of the 'only the best will do' formal assumption. We further maintain in this book that understandings of lifelong learning and of the learning society that fail to recognise this hitherto marginalised learning, are fatally defective. Thus, our conclusion is that critics who maintain that the shift from lifelong education to lifelong learning debases education, are closing off in advance possibilities for developing viable understandings of the learning society.

Since learning is clearly a wider notion than education, it was only to be expected that, unlike the case of lifelong education, understandings of lifelong learning would tend towards a maximalist view. That is, that the favoured notion of lifelong learning would embrace learning in any type of setting ranging from formal educational systems of all kinds, through diverse sorts of non-formal educational provision, to the limitless situations and contexts in which informal learning can occur. Certainly, a maximalist view of this sort is implied in much of the policy literature on lifelong learning. However, as Duke cautioned, the hegemony exerted by the formal education system in deciding what learning is to be valued and how it is to be assessed and accredited, ensured that 'learning' was read by most as 'formal learning'. This poses a major problem for proponents of lifelong learning in most of its forms.

The hegemonic influence of the formal education system on the relative valuation of different forms of learning is illustrated by the usual way in which the nonformal and informal educational sectors are defined. They are defined by what they are perceived to lack in relation to the formal sector, i.e. formal assessment of learning and/or the awarding of formal credentials. Informal learning of most kinds is especially lacking in these kinds of characteristics that are valued in the formal education system.

However, we should not accept at face value the oft-repeated claims by critics that proponents of lifelong education have conflated education with learning. Wain (1987, 1993) has strongly denied that this is so. Firstly, Wain argues that we need to distinguish the normative definition of education from its technical definition. Then applying the work of Lakatos (1978) on research programmes, Wain maintains that the normative definition of education belongs in the ideological core of an educational research programme; while its technical definition belongs in the operational belt. (See Wain 1987: 47; Wain 1993: 65). Following Lakatos, the normative definition of education is adhered to rigidly, while the technical definition can be revised and expanded as the operational belt evolves so as to advance the ideological core of the research program. Wain argues that Lawson, wedded to his exclusive understanding of 'education', reads 'education' normatively whenever he encounters it in writing on lifelong education. This leads him to the mistaken conclusion that proponents of lifelong education conflate all learning with education.

Wain makes the further, interesting, claim that we should view lifelong education's relation to lifelong learning as one of process to product. In viewing lifelong education as process (Wain 1987: 50; Wain 1993: 66), Wain intends that the focus be on all the kinds of learning that can contribute to the process of individual growth, i.e. formal, non-formal and informal learning. He does not, of course, mean that all instances of any of these are always educational – only that all three are relevant to education. Wain's concern is how to enhance the education of learners. The kinds of informal learning that are the main focus of this book are seen by Wain as being very relevant here.

Wain's viewing of lifelong learning as product, on the other hand, highlights the wide scope of learnt products. Wain argues that if education rather than learning is viewed as a product the focus shifts to matters such as what content should be taught?; by whom?; and by what teaching methods?. Once these questions come to the fore, informal learning becomes invisible. Thus, Wain rebuts the typical assumption by critics of lifelong education that for learning to be educational, it must be intentional. By distinguishing between process and product in the way he does, Wain evades the charge that he conflates learning with education. The Lawson argument therefore fails as a critique of the concept of lifelong education because its first premise ('The lifelong education movement confuses learning with education') is false. How convincing is Wain's defence of lifelong education as a process? While it does accord with the views of many other proponents of lifelong education, we question later in the book the ultimacy of the process/product distinction. We prefer to view the processes and products of learning as being in dialectical interaction.

2.3 Education as a Major Social Control Mechanism and, Hence, Lifelong Education as a Threat of More and Permanent Control

As is well known, various writers have viewed education as a form of social control. Hence the notion of *lifelong* education raises the spectre of *permanent* control (e.g. Falk 1998, Collins 1998, Ohliger 1974). Duke refers to

> .... scepticism .... about the colonisation of life and learning by the professions and agents of the State. *(2002: 503)*

Thus sceptics have charged that lifelong education is an ideology primarily designed to manipulate workers into being more productive. The argument goes that having expelled the adversarial workplace at the front door, what has intruded through the back door is a subtle form of surveillance, inducing in the new 'flatter', more ostensibly democratic workplace, strategies of compliance, such as 'discourses of competence and management' (Usher and Edwards 1994: Ch. 5, drawing on Foucault). Thus, some fear that lifelong learning might constitute a new version of the panopticon, the perfect instrument for surveillance and control.

We are sympathetic to these arguments, particularly as they apply to formal education provision. In chapters two and three, we develop these ideas further, drawing particularly on the work of Foucault. However, we there argue that the surveillance and control argument holds up particularly if lifelong education and lifelong learning are interpreted as provision of *formal* education. But, we argue, if the kinds of informal learning that are the focus of this book are brought into the picture, then surveillance and control are mitigated. Thus, this particular criticism of lifelong learning is blunted by the account of informal learning and lifelong learning, centred on practices in context, that is developed later in this book. While this criticism rightly points to potential dangers of the notion of lifelong learning, attention to the wider possibilities of informal learning will be shown to render this issue more complex.

2.4 Lifelong Learning as Supporting a Highly Inequitable Status Quo

Contemporary lifelong learning is charged with abandoning the "democratic progressive" sentiment (that was discussed earlier in this chapter). Its aim of "social action for the development of a more humane, tolerant, just and egalitarian society" is simply not on the radar of current favoured versions of lifelong learning.

The latter is seen to focus on matters such as the vocationalization of education, the development of basic life and core skills, and the marketing of credentials. All of this is seen to consolidate existing powerful interests, whilst jettisoning former egalitarian initiatives (Baptiste 1999, Collins 1998, Bagnall 2001: 44-46).

According to Boshier, the shift from lifelong education to lifelong learning is symptomatic of the decline of the democratic progressive sentiment:

> .... lifelong learning denotes a less emancipatory and more oppressive set of relationships than does lifelong education. Lifelong learning discourses render social conditions (and inequality) invisible. Predatory capitalism is unproblematized. Lifelong learning tends to be nested in an ideology of vocationalism. Learning is for acquiring skills that will enable the learner to work harder, faster and smarter and, as such, enable their employer to better compete in the global economy. These days, lifelong learning often denotes the unproblematized notion of the savvy individual consumer surfing the Internet. *(Boshier 1998: 8)*

Once again, these criticisms focus on lifelong education and lifelong learning viewed as formal education provision. Later in the book (e.g. chapter three), we critique various instances of this formal education response to lifelong education and lifelong learning. This is part of our overall claim that policy responses to lifelong learning have been too heavily weighted towards formal education arrangements. Shifting the balance towards informal learning, in the ways that we recommend later in the book, will serve to alleviate this criticism of lifelong learning.

2.5 Lifelong Learning as Encouraging Abdication of Responsibility by Governments

Bagnall (1990) presented the following conceptual argument against the notion of lifelong education: If all learning is to count as education, then governments will be tempted to close down, or at least severely reduce, formal and non-formal education provision. They will argue that people can learn informally for free. In Foucauldian terms, if lifelong formal learning might possibly offer a new version of the panopticon, it is still very resource intensive. If the same can be achieved from lifelong informal learning, then a much cheaper panopticon looks to be an attractive alternative possibility for governments.

So Bagnall thinks that lifelong education, and presumably lifelong learning, by bringing informal learning to public attention, will encourage governments to abandon financial commitments to formal educational provision. As already noted in section 2.2, Boshier presented an argument that is closely related to the Bagnall one. Boshier saw lifelong learning as encouraging a push towards further privatisation of education, thereby shifting responsibility for education from government to individual learners.

According to Wain, his earlier criticism of Lawson (section 2.2 above) also applies to Bagnall's argument. He charges that Bagnall has interpreted 'education' normatively whenever it occurs in the lifelong education literature, whereas Wain contends that it is often being used in the technical sense. He claims that this leads

Bagnall to the erroneous conclusion that proponents of lifelong education conflate all learning with education. So the first premise of Bagnall's argument is false.

In any case, Bagnall's argument seems to assume that public resources available for lifelong learning should be directed to formal educational agencies. As Duke argues, the concept of the learning society requires a fundamental rethink of current educational systems. He laments the

> .... failure to engage the concept of lifelong learning within the institutional imperatives of school and schooling. *(Duke 2001: 501)*

Later in this book we recommend that policy makers should shift the lifelong learning policy balance more towards arrangements that would encourage informal learning. Thus we consider that basic assumptions behind this criticism of lifelong learning are dubious or debatable. Certainly, we argue that lifelong learning should encourage governments to rethink their commitments. But this does not entail an abdication of responsibility.

3. THE LITERATURE OF INFORMAL LEARNING

A main theme of this book is that a rich understanding of lifelong learning is contingent on according a proper balance to the roles of both formal and informal learning. As already suggested, understanding of lifelong learning has been hindered by either too much focus on formal learning or, where informal learning has been given due consideration, an impoverished account of what informal learning is has usually been invoked. Thus, this book aims to both rejuvenate understandings of informal learning and, using this, to develop the promised richer understanding of lifelong learning.

In recent decades there has been a growing discussion of the differences and similarities between formal and informal learning. A third category, non-formal learning, is also commonly invoked in these discussions. In some cases non-formal learning is viewed as being halfway between formal and informal learning; in other cases it is used interchangeably with the term informal learning. A detailed and illuminating critical overview of this literature is provided by Colley, Hodkinson & Malcolm (2003).

In this section, we will firstly outline and discuss some main themes from the literature on the differences and similarities between formal and informal learning. This discussion will draw heavily on the work of Colley, Hodkinson & Malcolm (2003). Secondly we will present our own understanding of the notion of informal learning, an understanding that will be exemplified and expanded on by the many and various case studies that will be referred to throughout the book. Finally in this section, given that we disagree with some of the conclusions of Colley, Hodkinson & Malcolm about informal learning, we will offer a critique of their position, one that will serve to present more sharply our own views on these issues.

3.1 Distinguishing Formal Learning and Informal Learning

Colley, Hodkinson & Malcolm (2003) provides a very useful survey of approaches to characterising informal learning. They classify these approaches into two main clusters:

- Predominantly theoretical approaches, and
- Predominantly political approaches

(There is also a small third cluster that combines these two).

The predominantly theoretical approaches focus mainly on learning in the workplace while taking a broad view of what such learning is. Authors discussed include Eraut (2000), Billett (2002), Beckett & Hager (2002), and Hodkinson & Hodkinson (2004a). Together these present somewhat different attempts to characterise informal learning. Eraut (2000) offers five features that distinguish formal learning, with informal learning being said to lack these. But Colley, Hodkinson & Malcolm (2003: 18) query what happens to the learning situations that exhibit some but not all of Eraut's five features. By locating all learning in participatory social practices, Billett (2002) questions whether supposed differences between formal and informal learning are very significant. He thinks that when we focus on the actual learning, there are plenty of relevant similarities between formal and informal learning. The Beckett & Hager (2002) work discussed by Colley, Hodkinson & Malcolm presents six key features of informal learning at work. These are considered in the next section (3.2) of this chapter. However, it should be noted that they are not features claimed to characterise all informal learning. Rather they are features of one kind of informal learning, viz. the informal learning that flows from practice. This is precisely the kind of learning that is the particular focus of this book.

Hodkinson & Hodkinson (2004a) argue that there are different types of workplace learning and present a suggestive six-fold classification of it (Figure 1).

	Intentional/planned	**Unintentional/unplanned**
Learning that which is already known to others	Planned learning of that which others know	Socialisation into an existing community of practice
Development of existing capability	Planned/intended learning to refine existing capability	Unplanned improvement of ongoing practice
Learning that which is new in the workplace (or treated as such)	Planned/intended learning to do that which has not been done before	Unplanned learning of something not previously done

Figure 1. Types of Workplace Learning (Hodkinson & Hodkinson 2004a)

It is worth noting that the informal learning which is the focus of this book is captured in the unintentional/unplanned column of Figure 1. The second main cluster of approaches to characterising formal and informal learning that Colley, Hodkinson & Malcolm identify are "predominantly political approaches". These approaches encompass two types:

- A utilitarian approach common in policy documents, which focuses mostly on workplace learning but with a narrower, more instrumentalist view of learning than was evident in the theoretical approaches outlined above.
- An emancipatory political approach exhibited, for example, by radical traditions of adult and community education.

Colley, Hodkinson & Malcolm consider five examples of this second approach. Some seek to sharply distinguish formal and non-formal for various blunt purposes, e.g. economic development agencies seeking to classify current educational provision in developing countries. However, most of the writers that they consider suggest that there is no hard and fast boundary between formal and informal. Some posit a continuum, e.g. Stern & Sommerlad (1999) propose a ten-step continuum from the formal to the informal.

Finally, Colley, Hodkinson & Malcolm discuss a detailed approach by Livingstone (2001) that subtly combines elements of the theoretical and political approaches to distinguish between four categories: formal education, non-formal education, informal education/training, and informal learning. (Livingstone's fourth category is closely descriptive of the informal learning that is the main focus of this book).

We accept the overall Colley, Hodkinson & Malcolm conclusion that there is no prospect of distinguishing formal from informal learning in such a way that all instances fall on one side or other of the boundary. However, our position, as already explained, is that the existence of intractable borderline instances needs in no way invalidate or reduce the usefulness of a given distinction. Accordingly, we think that their strategy of celebrating the attributes of both the formal and informal, that they allege are present in all instances of learning, to be an over-reaction to the existence of intractable borderline instances. In effect, they are claiming that *all* cases are borderline. We regard this conclusion as implausible. Our case for this view is presented in section 3.3 below.

3.2 Our Understanding of Informal Learning

In this section we present our own understanding of the notion of informal learning. As the term 'informal' suggests, informal learning is usually characterised by what it lacks in relation to formal learning. Formal learning typically applies to a situation that includes these three items: a specified curriculum, taught by a designated teacher, with the extent of the learning attained by individual learners being assessed and certified. Thus, (as was stated in the Introduction to this book), for us formal learning:

..... is that which takes place as intended within formally constituted educational institutions such as schools, colleges universities, training centres and so on. Typically it follows a prescribed framework whether or not actual attendance at the institution is necessary. Sometimes there are quite specific outcomes. On other occasions there is more of a kind of broad direction or aim. In all cases however those partaking of courses of formal learning have an idea of what they are likely to learn and they accept that that learning will to some extent be under the control of the institution.

All other situations in which people learn are for us informal learning situations. Paradigmatic informal learning, such as the learning attained by a proficient practitioner during the course of their engagement in practice, lacks each of the features identified above for formal learning. Our attempt to characterise such informal learning in positive rather negative terms is as follows:

╱ *The informal learning from the practice of work can be thought of as the development of an evolving capacity to make context-sensitive judgments in changing contexts.* ╭

This is our working definition of informal learning for the purposes of this book. We argue that this is a distinctive kind of learning that cannot be gained elsewhere. As Beckett & Hager comment:

> People can learn from their experience of practice to further improve their subsequent practice. This does not mean that all learning is equally useful (people can learn bad habits for example). Nor does it mean that earlier learning from formal courses is irrelevant for daily workplace practice (such learning often plays a significant part in workplace practice). Rather the claim is that informal workplace learning of the right kind appears to be an essential component of proficient practice in most, if not all, occupations. *(Beckett & Hager 2002: 114)*

Beckett and Hager go on to discuss six key features of informal learning at work that they claim are important for understanding it (Beckett & Hager 2002: 115). It is:

1. Organic/holistic
2. Contextual
3. Activity- and experience-based
4. Arises in situations where learning is not the main aim
5. Activated by individual learners rather than by teachers/trainers
6. Often collaborative/collegial

If this kind of informal learning is as important and necessary, as we suggest that it is in order that novices will develop into proficient practitioners, why has this largely escaped notice? The answer is that this kind of informal learning lacks almost all of the features that are usually thought of as characterising education. Faced with such 'chalk and cheese' differences, people simply assume that such informal learning cannot be part of education. In earlier work (Hager 2001: 80-81), these 'chalk and cheese' differences were set out as follows:

- Teachers/trainers are in control in both formal learning in educational institutions and in formal on-the-job training, whereas it is the learner who is in control (if anyone is) in informal learning at work. That is, formal learning is planned, but informal learning at work is often unplanned.
- The learning that takes place in educational institutions and in on-the-job training is largely predictable as it is prescribed by formal curricula, competency standards, learning outcomes, etc. Informal learning at work is much less predictable as there is no formal curriculum or prescribed outcomes.
- In both educational institutions and formal on-the-job training, learning is largely explicit (the learner is expected to be able to articulate what has been learnt, e.g. in a written examination, in oral answers to instructor questioning, or in being required to perform appropriate activities as a result of the training). In informal learning at work, the learning is often implicit or tacit (the learner is commonly unaware of the extent of their learning) even though the learner might be well aware of the outcomes of such learning, e.g. that they are able to perform their job much better.
- In both formal classrooms and on-the-job training the emphasis is on teaching/training and on the content and structure of what is taught/trained (largely as a consequence of the three previous points). Whereas in informal learning at work the emphasis is on learning and on the learner.
- In both formal classrooms and on-the-job training the focus is usually on learners as individuals and on individual learning. In informal learning at work, the learning is often collaborative and/or collegial.
- Learning in formal classrooms is uncontextualised, i.e. there is an emphasis on general principles rather than their specific applications. While formal on-the-job training is typically somewhat contextualised, even here there is some emphasis on the general e.g. the training might be aimed at general industry standards. However, informal learning at work is by its nature highly contextualised.
- The learning that takes place in educational institutions and in on-the-job training is conceptualised typically in terms of theory (or knowledge) and practice (application of theory and knowledge). The learning that comes from informal learning at work, on the other hand, seems to be most appropriately thought of as seamless know how.

We can see from the above that formal learning/education and on-the-job training have more in common with one another than either one has with informal learning at work. This is somewhat surprising because education and training are often viewed as antithetical to one another. This only serves to reinforce the point that for informal learning to be taken seriously as a vital part of a practitioner's overall education, a major change of mindset is needed. Our aim in this book is to achieve just this, and in the process, to establish the vital role of informal learning in any viable understanding of lifelong learning and the learning society.

At this point it is worth noting that none of the people we interviewed in developing the exemplars and case studies were confused about *informal* learning as such. It was a concept that was generally well understood. In a few cases, people thought of learning as something different from working, so they held that when you were working learning was not happening as well. ('You cannot be doing two things at once'). For this minority group, informal learning about work occurred when they organised various learning activities for themselves, such as later reflection on what had happened at work, or discussion of it with colleagues, or undertaking some research to make sense of it. Even here, though, they were clear on what it meant for the learning to be *informal*. So, although, as discussed in this book, various theorists and policymakers seem to have difficulty with the concept, *back at the rough ground* (Wittgenstein 1953: PI 107) there is no such problem.

3.3 A Critique of the Colley, Hodkinson & Malcolm Position on Informal Learning

Colley, Hodkinson & Malcolm (2003) provide the most comprehensive and well-grounded overview and analysis of the informal learning literature that has appeared in recent times. As well as synthesising and evaluating previous literature in an impressive and concise way, they offer an innovative and radical proposal for how the concept of informal learning should be treated in the future. This includes a radical questioning of the term 'informal learning' itself, a questioning that, at first glance, leaves one wondering whether it should have any uses other than certain very limited ones.

Although we have some sympathy for several features of the overall Colley, Hodkinson & Malcolm analysis, there are some key aspects of it that we will question in this section. We will maintain that not only are the kinds of cases that we describe in this book accurately characterised as 'informal learning', but that some of their arguments for thinking otherwise are far from convincing. We begin, then, with an overview of their position, followed by our own critique of that position.

The Colley, Hodkinson & Malcolm position rests on two main principles:

1. We should "see attributes of informality and formality as present in all learning situations" (2003, Executive Summary (non-numbered page)).
2. The attributes of informality and formality are *interrelated* in crucial ways in all learning situations.

Their argument for the first principle stems from two sources. Firstly, from their survey and summary of the main approaches by other authors to characterising informal learning. Foregrounding the differences and inconsistencies between the various authors that they identified in their survey, Colley, Hodkinson & Malcolm conclude that

> .... it is not possible to clearly define separate ideal types of formal and informal learning which bear any relation to actual learning experiences. *(2003: 64)*

The second source of argument for their first principle is their consideration of different actual learning experiences, in many and diverse contexts. Here they claim to be able to identify characteristics of formality and informality in virtually all of them. (Their preferred term is "attributes of in/formality" to represent the idea that elements of the supposed formal, non-formal and informal are to be found in any learning situation). Thus their first principle strongly denies that real learning situations are ever purely formal, informal or non-formal.

Their second principle emphasises the crucial idea of the *interrelatedness* of these attributes of in/formality. This interrelatedness includes the following ideas:

LIFELONG, INFORMAL AND WORKPLACE LEARNING

- Attributes of formality and informality are interrelated in different ways in different learning situations.
- Those attributes and their interrelationships influence the nature and effectiveness of learning in any situation.
- Those interrelationships and effects can only be properly understood if learning is examined in relation to the wider contexts in which it takes place. This is particularly important when considering issues of empowerment and oppression. *(Colley, Hodkinson & Malcolm 2003: 65)*

So, the attributes of formality and informality are claimed to interact with one another to shape the learning in any given situation. But, this claim is merely asserted rather than argued for in any detail. This means that the exact nature of this interaction is left less than clear. In their defence, Colley, Hodkinson & Malcolm do maintain that this interaction will be distinctive for every given case. However, this should not preclude something more specific being said about these allegedly crucial interactions. It is notable that even when they consider individual cases in some detail, the supposed interactions of the attributes of formality and informality are invariably described in very general terms such as the following: they are said to "interpenetrate in a wide range of contexts" (2003: 32); they are "complex interrelationships" (2003: 35); they exhibit a "particular balance" in a given case (2003: 64).

These, then, are the two principles that together are claimed to cast doubt on the viability of the notion of informal learning as a distinct category. However, we argue that there are a number of aspects of these two principles that make them somewhat problematic. As we have seen, the Colley, Hodkinson & Malcolm argument for the first principle, that attributes of informality and formality as present in all learning situations, relies on two sources. We argue that neither provides a convincing support for this first principle.

Their first source was the differences and inconsistencies that they identified between various authors in their survey of the main approaches to characterising informal learning. This lack of agreement on clear-cut criteria, for characterising a given learning situation as formal or informal, led Colley, Hodkinson & Malcolm to the conclusion that the two notions are inextricably connected. However, the point has been made earlier (in the Introduction), drawing on the work of Wittgenstein, that to establish that a distinction is faced with unclear borderline cases, in no way invalidates the usefulness or applicability of the distinction to typical cases. For instance, there are no clear criteria for establishing how much hair thinning is required before someone is correctly described as being bald. Baldness has no established boundaries, but it remains a useful concept. Its imprecision with respect to borderline cases, hardly seems reason enough for us to recommend that our future language usage be altered to a claim that everyone partakes in attributes of baldness and hirsuteness, and that we need to recognise that the interrelationships between these two attributes are very complex. Even in areas of human endeavour where precision is usually favoured, there are perfectly useful distinctions that include seemingly intractable borderline cases, e.g. living/non-living. Overall:

> For a concept to be useful, all that is required is that it is defined for some cases,
> so that some things would definitely fall under it, and others definitely would not.
> *(Glock 1996: 100)*

But the informal learning/formal learning distinction clearly meets this requirement. It is clear, then, that the first strand of the Colley, Hodkinson & Malcolm
argument for their first principle fails.

Colley, Hodkinson & Malcolm do, it is true, accept that we should not jettison
the formal learning/informal learning distinction entirely (2003: 65). Rather they
urge that we should be careful with how we use it:

> ..... any such uses should be carefully developed for particular purposes, and au-
> thors should make clear in what senses they are using the term(s) and why.
> *(Colley, Hodkinson & Malcolm 2003: 65)*

We can accept their caution that authors should make clear in what senses they are
using the term(s) and why. In our view, this is quite compatible with the formal
learning/informal learning distinction being a very useful one despite the existence
of borderline cases.

The second source of the arguments that Colley, Hodkinson & Malcolm mount,
in favour of their first principle, is their close consideration of actual learning
situations. They claim that careful analysis of learning situations shows that attributes of informality and formality are present in all cases. Here, we acknowledge
that, at first sight, their claim that all learning has attributes of formality and informality is a strong, and interesting, one. However, we believe that it is weakened
somewhat when it is realised that the terms formal and informal are being used
rather broadly, and even ambiguously, in the argument.

Let us begin with the notion of formal in its most general sense, since Colley,
Hodkinson & Malcolm do deploy the term in several different senses. In the most
general sense of the term, to say of something that it has attributes of formality is a
very weak claim indeed. For instance, all matter has a form, so it follows that all
material objects have an attribute of formality in common. Clearly, while true, this
statement does not say very much. A similar point can be made about the related
notion of structure. Once again, all material objects have a structure. Here we
might be getting just a bit closer to important differences and similarities, e.g.
whether the particular material object is a gas, a liquid or a solid, but these are still
properties at a fairly high level of abstraction. To say, as some do, that learning at
school has a formal structure, but so also does work activity, so therefore learning
at work is not significantly different from learning at school, is to fall for the fallacy that having high level of abstraction properties in common means that low
level differences are unimportant.

Clearly, if the notion of formal is used in its most general sense, then literally
everything will have attributes of formality. Colley, Hodkinson & Malcolm do not
quite deploy the term formal in this highly general sense, but they do get their
'joint attributes of informality and formality' thesis off the ground by employing
formal and informal in the distinct senses in which they are applied to manners,
dress, and interpersonal relations. But formal and informal in relation to manners,
dress, and interpersonal relations, is describing a different category from formal

and informal in relation to learning. As we defined 'formal' earlier, "those partaking of courses of formal learning have an idea of what they are likely to learn and they accept that that learning will to some extent be under the control of the institution". This control of the learning that characterises formal learning is manifest in a specified curriculum, a duly appointed teacher, assessment processes, etc. From this perspective, manners and dress of teacher and students, and interpersonal relations between them, are not significant factors in whether or not learning is formal. They are in a different category. To confuse the sense in which learning is formal with the sense in which manners, dress and interpersonal relations can be formal, is to commit a category mistake.

But Colley, Hodkinson & Malcolm want to include teachers' approaches to students (how they address them, what sorts of things they chat about to them (2003: 34); presumably even what clothing they wear) in the formal/informal learning mix. Likewise, according to them, if someone ostensibly learning informally from practice looks up some information in a book or asks someone who knows, they view this as a formal element in an otherwise largely informal mix (2003: 44). Thus, Colley, Hodkinson & Malcolm set it up so that unless a teacher's interaction with students is purely formal in an old-fashioned etiquette sense (using formal modes of address, formal protocols for asking questions, etc.), then their teaching must be significantly informal. Indeed, current recommended modes of interpersonal interaction would seem to guarantee in advance that their thesis is proven.

However, this is achieved only at the cost of implausibly attenuating the senses of formal and informal used in the discussion. In the sense of 'formal' that should be the focus of such discussions, the formal aspects of a teacher's interactions with students stem from the teacher's authority, both in relation to course content and as the person responsible for enhancing and monitoring the learning. Similarly, the implication, that someone looking up a dictionary at home is engaging in formal learning, again shows that the senses of formal and informal have been attenuated by Colley, Hodkinson & Malcolm well beyond the senses of these terms as deployed in the previous section in the outline of attempts to differentiate formal and informal learning.

Thus by seriously attenuating the senses of 'formal' and 'informal' that are brought into the discussion, in ways such as these, it is not surprising that they think they can make good their 'joint attributes of informality and formality' thesis. This capacity to identify all kinds of nuances that might be labelled formal or informal, as the case may be, is enhanced by their strategy of analysing the actual learning situations that they consider under each of the four distinct headings of *process, location and setting, purposes,* and *content.* When formal and informal are used in attenuated senses, these four headings simply multiply the possibilities.

So far, this discussion has cast doubt on the strength of the Colley, Hodkinson & Malcolm first principle that attributes of informality and formality are present in all learning situations. But if our charge that they achieve this by employing very attenuated senses of formal and informal is solidly grounded, then it also casts doubt on their second principle concerning the interrelatedness of the formal and informal attributes. As already suggested above, what they say about this interrelatedness is fairly vague (they "interpenetrate in a wide range of contexts"; they are "complex interrelationships"; they exhibit a "particular balance" in a given case). This is not surprising. What can we say of any substance about the interrelationship between a subject being very formal in traditional curriculum and assessment terms; but the teacher being very informal in his interpersonal dealings with the students? The likely answer is 'that all depends'. In the case of some students this particular combination might well be motivating; in other cases it might very well have the opposite effect. In any case, if as argued above, formal and informal are being deployed in a number of very different senses, important interrelationships might be fewer than Colley, Hodkinson & Malcolm suggest. In the senses in which the learning that is the focus of this book is informal, its significant involvements with the formal are somewhat less than Colley, Hodkinson & Malcolm have supposed.

At the most general level, there is an asymmetry in the two halves of their claim that the formal and informal are interconnected. The first strand of their argument, that all formal learning is accompanied by attributes of informality follows almost by definition (i.e. it is almost a truism). Once we realise that it is hard to imagine situations of human activity in which some informal learning might not occur, *a fortiori*, informal learning of some kind virtually always occurs in formal learning situations. But it is also noteworthy that in the actual case studies that they discuss, it is easy and useful (they do it), to distinguish the formal from the informal. The two certainly are not so entwined as to be inextricably blended. So, *prima facie*, this challenges their second principle. It also supports their claim that they are not trying to do away with formal/informal distinction altogether. This situation surely illustrates the ongoing usefulness of the distinction.

However the second strand of the Colley, Hodkinson & Malcolm argument, that all informal learning is accompanied by attributes of formality, far from being a truism, is only given plausibility by attenuating the meanings of the terms formal and informal, as already shown. As well, to claim that so-called informal learning is formal in the sense that the situation in which it occurs (e.g. a workplace) has a structure is an extraordinarily weak claim. All objects have a structure, but normally the differences between them as objects are much more relevant than the fact that they have this commonality at a high level of generality. So, overall, we conclude that the two principles, while interesting and suggestive, have less teeth than is claimed by Colley, Hodkinson & Malcolm.

It has been a main claim in the above discussion that Colley, Hodkinson & Malcolm make their case by illegitimately attenuating the meanings of the terms formal and informal. Our claim is that in these attenuated forms, the formal and informal attributes that they identify have little or nothing to do with the learning that might be occurring. Attributing them to the learning is to make a category mistake. In order to illustrate what we mean here, let us consider a couple of cases that intuition tells us are paradigmatic of informal learning.

Case A – Person X who has moved to a new suburb consults the railway timetable to learn what time train they need to catch to arrive at work in the city by 8.30am.

For most of us, this would count as an unproblematic case of informal learning. There is no teacher, no set learning outcomes (except what the learner sets for herself), and no assessment of whether learning has occurred (except perhaps arrival at work by 8.30am). To be sure the train timetable is formal in the sense that it is an official document that sets out arrival and departure times of trains, station by station, in an orderly and sequential manner. However, this has nothing to do with the senses in which learning is formal. To think otherwise is to make a category error. Hence this case is a paradigm of informal learning, since it exhibits no formal attributes.

But Colley, Hodkinson & Malcolm would not acquiesce so easily. For them the timetable is a formal document. As their own case studies show, consulting a formal document (any written document?) introduces attributes of formality into the learning situation. So according to them, this seemingly paradigm case of informal learning 'proves' their mixed attributes thesis. Or does it? Let us turn to Case B.

Case B – Person Y who has moved to a new suburb, not having a railway timetable to consult, goes to the Information Desk at the Central Railway Station to learn what time train they need to catch to arrive at work in the city by 8.30am.

For most of us, this would again count as an unproblematic case of informal learning, one that is not significantly different from Case A. It involves asking an official rather than reading the timetable. Surely this makes no difference to the learning being informal. As with Case A, there is no curriculum, teacher, assessment, etc. But contrary to our intuition that there is no significant difference and, hence, that again we have a paradigmatic case of informal learning, Colley, Hodkinson & Malcolm are committed, by the evidence of their own case analyses, to maintaining that this is an instance of learning in which the formal greatly outweighs the informal. Why so? Because unlike Case A, Case B is absolutely saturated with attributes of formality, including:

- Attendance at an official 'Information Desk'
- Consulting an 'expert'
- The expert wears an official uniform
- The expert wears a badge proclaiming their expertise
- Awaiting one's turn in a formal queue
- Consulting of formal documents by the expert
- Formal mode of addressing customers (the expert has completed a customer service course)
- Train times printed onto an information slip that is handed to the customer

(Virtually all of these (or their opposites) feature in the Colley, Hodkinson & Malcolm case studies as instances of formal (or informal) attributes).

In short, the sheer totality of these attributes of formality appears likely to outweigh the informal attributes in what we had thought was a paradigm case of informal learning. Common sense tells that *qua* learning, there is no significant difference between cases A and B – both are paradigms of informal learning. But Colley, Hodkinson & Malcolm seem to be committed to the view that case B has many more attributes of formality than does case A.

How are we to choose between these two understandings of the situation? Our view is that the common sense understanding is correct. Why? Because we believe that although the so-called attributes of formality may have all kinds of sociological, anthropological, phenomenological, socio-cultural, etc.... significance, they have little or nothing to do with understanding the learning involved and with why this learning is paradigmatically informal. That is, *qua learning*, these attributes of formality are largely irrelevant. Thinking otherwise arises from category mistakes. So the general claim that all learning situations feature attributes of formality and informality is questioned in that it is suggested that many of these attributes have little or no connection to the learning that is taking place.

Having set out their two principles about attributes of formality and informality, Colley, Hodkinson & Malcolm (2003) then outline and analyse a varied range of case studies of learning in order to illustrate the supposed applicability of their principles. However, when our critique of the principles is applied to the case studies, far from being saturated with joint attributes of formality and informality, most turn out to be straightforward cases of either formal or informal learning, with only a few being on the borderline. We will conclude this section by discussing a number of relevant issues that arise from our analysis and critique of the Colley, Hodkinson & Malcolm case studies.

They start with a series of case studies that in our view are clear examples of formal learning. We reject virtually all of the attributions of informal learning that they make for these case studies. Firstly, they categorise workplace placements, which typically occur as an integral part of a formal course, as informal on the grounds that "the prime purpose of the organization is not the learning of students" (Colley, Hodkinson & Malcolm 2003: 33). However, work placements in which students' performance is assessed against specified criteria are arguably a kind of formal workplace training. As we explained in the previous section, such formal workplace training arrangements have much more in common with formal course delivery than they do with the kind of informal learning from practice that is the main focus of this book.

Secondly, Colley, Hodkinson & Malcolm (2003: 34) classify as clearly informal the advice given to students on how they are expected to dress for work placements. We are puzzled as to why they regard this as a clear-cut case of informal learning. The issue here is that the dress code is being enforced by the lecturer/tutor who is running a formal occupational course. In terms of our discussion in the previous section, this is undoubtedly a case of formal learning. In fact, we would think that formal courses that prepare people for occupations would be deficient if they failed to alert students to the dress standards that prevail on work sites where they will be placed. It might not be always written down specifically in the curriculum, but such advice, in our view, is a taken-for-granted component of formal courses that prepare candidates for specific occupations, even more so when they involve work placements. Construction courses should ensure that students arrive on-site wearing sturdy boots; laboratory courses require a protective coat and protection of feet. In all such cases this advice about occupational norms is certainly learning that is firmly under the control of teachers/trainers. In our view it is clearly a type of formal learning.

Thirdly, they characterise as informal the 'hidden curriculum' kinds of learning that we accept occurs in any formal learning situation. This includes how students learn to relate to one another, how these interactions shape a student's growing sense of themselves as an adult person, etc. As already suggested, the fact is that this kind of informal learning can be readily separated from the formal aspects of the course. The two certainly are not so entwined as to be inextricably blended. So, *prima facie*, this challenges their second principle. The trouble is that it is never possible to predict how the two will interact. For instance they discuss a nursery nursing course that exemplifies fairly dated views about the roles of women. Some students will no doubt be happily and smoothly inducted into the nursery nursing culture. Others will not: 'With my marks I can obtain a better job than this'. Or 'I cannot stand these old-fashioned attitudes – I need a change'. It seems that there is no sense of tangled interrelationships of the formal and informal that will have any explanatory power. Are we to say that, for students who are smoothly inducted into the nursery nursing culture, the formal and informal are inextricably blended; yet for those who drop out, the two are not so blended? Any such explanation as this is after the event, and, hence, unconvincing.

Fourthly, they attempt to impute informal attributes to what are essentially mainstream formal courses by invoking their four distinct headings of process, location and setting, purposes, and content. An example of the informal aspects of *process* is the 'breezy' way a tutor interacts with students by phone and email. This is another example of 'proving' their thesis by seriously attenuating the senses of 'formal' and 'informal' employed in the analysis. An instance of supposed informal aspects of *location and setting* involves a course where the students learn at home at their own pace and in their own time. But students taking formal face-to-face courses also study at home, choose when to write their assignments, choose how many subjects to take, etc. Is their course thereby rendered informal? Once again, the senses of 'formal' and 'informal' are being attenuated to breaking point. The informal aspects of *purposes* are said to be the various motivations and purposes revealed by individual students that can be added to the official formal purpose of the course. If these really render the learning informal to any significant extent, then there are some bizarre consequences. For example, it would follow that someone who was studying law, in part because her parents expected it, was thereby rendering the formal law course as significantly informal. Once again, 'formal' and 'informal' are being stretched to the limits of credibility. Fortunately, when it comes to *content*, Colley, Hodkinson & Malcolm are usually prepared to accept that it is unequivocally formal.

A further series of case studies presented by Colley, Hodkinson & Malcolm are ones that are, in our view, uncontroversially centred on informal learning. Colley, Hodkinson & Malcolm, of course, claim to be able to show these cases also involve strong formal elements. Not surprisingly, virtually all of these supposed formal attributes are 'formal' in the kinds of attenuated senses discussed above. They appear to us to be not closely connected with the learning involved.

Next, Colley, Hodkinson & Malcolm also consider a few cases of non-formal learning, i.e. located at the borderline of formal and informal learning. In these we do find a mixture of formal and informal attributes in play that are closely connected with the learning. For example, traditionally many Workers' Educational Association (WEA) offerings have involved a set course of lectures and readings, but have had no formal assessment. But the WEA has been under increasing pressure from funding bodies to demonstrate that specific learning outcomes are being achieved. So WEA courses have hitherto featured an interesting mix of formal and informal attributes, but are under growing pressure to become much more unequivocally formal.

Colley, Hodkinson & Malcolm complete their case studies by considering various kinds of mentoring. Mentoring can vary from very formal to more informal ('natural') kinds. We classify mentoring as basically formal, with some of the more 'informal' cases being borderline between formal and informal. Finally, it is notable that none of the many cases that Colley, Hodkinson & Malcolm have considered in detail are typical of the informal learning situations that we are considering in this book. Probably the closest is a case of learning from social action, one which they agree is strongly informal. The only formal attributes that they attribute to it are ones that we have already claimed involve highly attenuated meanings of the term 'formal'.

4. THE LITERATURE OF WORKPLACE LEARNING

The purpose of this section is to provide an overview of main themes from the literature on workplace learning and to relate these themes to the central ideas of this book. Theorisations of workplace learning fall into two main categories – those that focus on learning as a product and those that focus on learning as a process. (For a more detailed account than can be provided here see Hager 2005b). The former theorisations tend to invoke the acquisition metaphor for thinking about learning; the latter rely more on the participation metaphor. As Sfard (1998) has argued, *acquisition* and *participation* have been the two most influential metaphors for understanding learning. At first glance, the learning as process approach, together with the participation metaphor, look more promising in relation to the themes of informal learning and its key role in lifelong learning that are the focus of this book. However, as will be discussed in chapter five, matters are more complex than this.

It is also tempting to line up the older theories of workplace learning, that emphasise learning as the acquisition of specified products, with human capital theory and its focus on the individual learner. This leaves the more recent theories, ones that emphasise learning as a participatory process, to be aligned with social capital theory, and its focus on learning communities. However, this binary is too simplistic since some significant learning theories reject the assumption that learning has to be exclusively either individual or social.

> These theories accept that, while all learning is in some sense social, this is compatible with some instances of learning being learning by individuals, and other instances of learning occurring at the communal level. So at least some of the social learning theories to be discussed later include a place for learning by individuals that is different from pure communal learning. Thus, it is a plausible initial claim that both individual and social learning are different but important dimensions of workplace learning. *(Hager 2005b: 830)*

Some of the best known early theorising of workplace learning comes from the 1970s. Springing from fields such as organisational psychology and management theory, classic texts are Argyris and Schön (1974, 1978), Schön (1983, 1987), and Marsick and Watkins (1990). This work gave rise to some very influential distinctions and concepts, such as:

- single loop learning (in which the learner exhibits reactive behaviour in order to adapt to changing circumstances) vs. double loop learning (in which the learner reflectively amends or adds to previous learning in selecting a suitable course of action to deal with a challenging situation);
- a practitioner's theory-in-use (inferred from what they actually do in given circumstances) vs. their espoused theory (the theory that they claim their actions exemplify);
- the reflective practitioner, knowing-in-action and reflecting-in-action;
- informal and incidental learning.

The theories that comprise this first main category of workplace learning theories have a range of common features (Hager 2005b: 832-3):

- They centre of individual learners.
- They focus mainly on the rational, cognitive aspects of work performance.
- Work performance tends to be conceived as thinking or reflection followed by application of the thinking or reflection – this is especially evident in Schön's work.
- Learning itself is taken for granted and not theorised or problematised. This means in practice that, as Elkjaer (2003) points out, they tend to assume that workplace learning is akin to formal learning, thereby favouring the acquisition metaphor.
- They downplay the importance of social, organisational and cultural factors in workplace learning and performance. (In stating that these factors are downplayed, it is accepted that some of the theorists mentioned above do take some account of them. For instance, Marsick and Watkins accept the importance of "organizational context" (1990: 210). But they do so in the limited sense that organizational context is the environment in which the individual, the unit of human capital theory, is learning informally and incidentally. As will be argued shortly, in the second main category of accounts of workplace learning, the roles of social, organisational and cultural factors in workplace learning and performance are much stronger than this).

The second main category of workplace learning theories is characterised by a recognition that workplace learning and performance are embodied phenomena, phenomena that are significantly shaped by social, organisational and cultural factors, that extend well beyond the individual (Hager 2005b: 834-5). These theories view workplace learning as seamlessly integrating a range of human qualities that extends well beyond just rationality. This means that these theories tend to problematise, or at least rethink the notion of learning. Earlier learning theorists such as Dewey and Vygotsky have been major influences on much of this work. Main examples of workplace learning theories in this second category include:

Situated learning theories
Lave and Wenger (1991) have popularised notions such as workplaces as 'communities of practice' and 'legitimate peripheral participation' as the social learning process that novices go through to become full members of the community of practice. Their work has popularised ideas such as the importance of apprenticeship in learning and learning as participation in a community of practice. Rather than viewing learning as the acquisition of discrete items, they regard the beginner as learning how to function appropriately in a given social, cultural and physical environment. On this view, the learning is something that is outside of the learner's head, or even body. Instead it takes place in the framework of participation, i.e. in a network of relations. As Hodkinson and Hodkinson (2004b, 2004c) show, Lave and Wenger (1991) left the key notion of community of practice rather vague, while assigning it wide applicability as an account of learning. Responding to this weakness, Wenger (1998) gives a more precise account of what constitutes a community of practice, but in the process he greatly reduces the incidence of such communities. But as Hodkinson and Hodkinson (2004b, 2004c) conclude, this move deflates the Lave and Wenger claim to have developed a general sociocultural account of learning. There is also a question mark over how well the participation metaphor favoured by Lave and Wenger accounts for change. It is quite possible to have successful participation while resisting all change. Some sects and religious orders achieve this. Perhaps Lave and Wenger rely too much on a single factor, participation, to carry the explanatory load of their theorising. (The work of Lave and Wenger will be discussed further in chapter seven).

Activity theory
Engeström (1999, 2001) regards workplaces as being activity systems comprised of various components including items such as workplace rules, the division of labour, and mediating artifacts. Engeström views learning as occurring during work processes within such activity systems. Learning happens according to Engeström because the activity systems continually exhibit contradictions and tensions that have to be resolved. Engeström's activity systems clearly incorporate social, organisational and cultural factors. It has been doubted by critics whether it is plausible to claim that all learning at work occurs from contradictions and tensions within the activity system. As well Engeström posits a dialectical interplay between the learner and the activity system. This raises the unresolved question: to what extent is the learner a locus of learning as against the system being the locus? Perhaps also, the key single notion of contradictions in activity systems carries too much explanatory load in Engeström's theorising. In his ongoing research centred on activity systems, Engeström notes a trend whereby collaborative expertise is

increasingly important in work, whilst expertise based on individuals is in sharp decline (Engeström 2004). According to Engeström, this collaborative expertise is enabled by practitioners being willing to cross established boundaries, and to negotiate with disparate other practitioners to improvise 'knots' of collaboration.

Situated learning theories and activity theory have both influenced a host of recent writing on learning at work. Though sometimes quite critical of earlier versions of these theories (e.g. Fuller *et al.* 2005), this recent writing generally seeks to amplify and elucidate the implications of the crucial idea that learning is socially and culturally situated. A brief outline of main work by some major contributors to this recent writing will be given here. Eraut, an early advocate of the idea that professional knowledge is of a distinctive kind (Eraut 1994), has been investigating the various kinds of knowledge employed in the practice of work and how these kinds of knowledge differ from the knowledge presented in vocational preparation courses (Eraut *et al.* 1998). Based on these differences, Eraut's writings point to the importance of learning opportunities at work. Thus, Eraut has been focusing on how to close the gap between the two kinds of knowledge. This has led him to propose a five-step model of transfer (Eraut 2004b). A main ongoing concern of Eraut's work is the learning by individual practitioners and ways to make the various kinds of learning explicit. Billett is another researcher to have focused on the opportunities (or 'affordances') for making learning at work more likely to happen. He has postulated a relational interdependency between individuals' intentional actions and practices in the workplace, that is, between individual agency and constraints/affordances of the work environment (Billett 2004a, 2004b). Billett has sought also to minimise apparent differences between formal and informal learning, arguing that workplace have their own pedagogical features (Billett 2002: 56).

Hodkinson and Hodkinson, although sympathetic to the idea that attributes of formality and informality coexist (see section 3.3 of this chapter), want to stress the striking variety of kinds of learning irrespective of the formal and informal categorisation. For instance, unlike some other theorists, they view both social and individual learning as important analytical categories in their work. According to them, neither Lave and Wenger nor Engeström have sufficiently recognised the diversity of kinds of learning, thereby reducing the explanatory value of their theorising (Hodkinson and Hodkinson 2004a: 261). Fuller and Unwin (2003, 2004) have drawn on and developed situated learning theory to investigate the learning of apprentices. Influenced by Engeström, they have proposed an expansive-restrictive continuum as a framework for understanding both the barriers to and opportunities for learning at work. Guile and Young (e.g. 1998, 1999, 2003) have also produced valuable work on vocational learning that shows the influence of Vygotsky and of social learning theory generally. Brown (e.g. Brown, Rhodes & Carter 2004), also influenced by both situated learning theory and activity theory, has investigated learning at work in a diverse range of settings.

Research by Rainbird, Munro & Holly (2004b) shows a further facet of the need to problematise the 'community of practice' concept. Communities of practice are often assumed to be consensual and participative. But such communities are frequently located within structures that exhibit differentiated power relations that constrain some individuals and groups more so than others. Evans, Kersh & Sakamoto (2004) have drawn attention to the significance of the tacit dimension of knowledge and skills, with particular emphasis on the gendered construction of such knowledge and skills. Their work shows that life experiences other than formal education or paid work are important sources of various attributes that are largely tacit, yet which can be important in work performance. This kind of knowledge and skills can become pivotal to learning in new and unfamiliar environments, particularly in circumstances where deployment of such tacit attributes is valued and encouraged.

There is, then, a rich and growing body of work that has sought to apply and extend both situated learning theory and activity theory as ways of understanding learning at work. Overall, this research encompasses both formal and informal aspects of learning at work. The kind of informal learning at work, which is our prime focus in this book, is but a small part of this broader spectrum of learning. Nor is it the main concern of most of the work reviewed above. Thus, we view our project in this book as being complementary to the above work, rather than as an attempt to displace it.

Major ongoing issues in the literature on workplace learning include:
How best to understand learning?
How to encompass both individual and communal learning?
How to encompass both tacit and explicit aspects of learning?
How to arrange work to maximise workplace learning?

As this book develops its account of workplace learning as context-sensitive judgment making situated in practices, it will be proposing answers to each of these questions.

5. LIFELONG LEARNING AS A STIMULUS TO RECONCEPTUALISE LEARNING

This chapter has argued that a rethink of the vital relationship between informal and lifelong learning should lead to a fresh approach to understanding the concept of lifelong learning. Indeed it serves as a stimulus to reconceptualising learning itself. We need to conceive of learning as something much wider than schooling and formal education. After all mass formal education is only a recent happening in historical terms. Much valuable learning occurred in communities before the advent of mass education. As education has become more tied in with the economy, the assumed tight connection between learning and formal provision has only been strengthened. After all, economists can work with the hard data associated with formal provision (number of enrolments, number of completions, number of course hours, etc.). Whereas quantitative data on informal learning remains something much more elusive. Chapter five will outline our attempt at this reconceptualisation of learning. Before then, over the course of several chapters, we examine and critique the various ways that lifelong learning, formal education provision and economic wellbeing have become entwined in educational policy and practice over several decades. We argue that this has resulted in a range of unforseen and unintended consequences that only serve to hinder steps towards a learning society. These undesirable consequences can be summarised as an imbalance between formal and informal learning, one in which there is too much focus on the former and unwarranted neglect of the latter.

CHAPTER TWO

A BRIEF GENEALOGY OF LIFELONG LEARNING

Lifelong learning looks like a good thing then. It resonates with the notions of renewal, of keeping up to date in a rapidly changing world. Yet as Field (2005) points out lifelong learning is difficult for policy makers to embrace. Procedurally lifelong learning cuts across government sectoral boundaries. It is for example not only concerned with supply to the labour market but demand – human resource development in drag as Boshier (1998) put it. It is also concerned with social justice because few now dispute the claims that those who have benefited most from learning tend to want more of it and that their continuing interest in formal learning has served them very nicely. Lifelong learning is not amenable to target setting and the audit culture (Apple 2005). It is not amenable to short term measurable objectives. Tying money in with soft objectives is not attractive to government concerned with value for money in the public sector. Yet there was a time, which Wain (2004: Ch 1) documents and which was reviewed in chapter one, when utopian visions of lifelong learning were popular and appeared to be attractive to international organisations. As this chapter explains, however, the attractions of a version of lifelong learning as vocational education soon came to the fore and it remains currently dominant. This version has considerable legitimacy through its espoused measurability of inputs and outputs. Much of it may be delivered though Vocational Education and Training (VET) Colleges which may be regarded as the most amenable education sector to bring about change. In Australia these are commonly known as Technical and Further Education (TAFE) Colleges and in the UK, simply as Further Education (FE). Moreover powerful institutions such as the World Bank are attracted to a deterministic human capital model of learning rather than what might appear to them as 'woolly' notions of social and cultural capital.

In the light of a reference to the World Bank it is appropriate to contextualise this genealogy at the outset within western liberal democracies. While the argument in this book is in support of greater attention towards informal learning within the developed world, it is worth noting that within the under developed world, informal learning appears to have been conspicuously ineffective. For example relatively few people have been successful in becoming literate through informal means. As Bown (1990: 346) notes in her survey of literacy world-wide:

..... while the *proportions* of non-literates are declining, the actual *numbers* are rising, owing to rapid population increases. Whereas there were 705 million adult non-literates in the world in 1950, there were an estimated 876 million in 2000 (of whom 563 million were women). ... the kind of literacy generally provided is meagre in amount and quality.

And in a telling conclusion, Bown goes on:

> There are therefore still very large numbers of people over the age of 15 who are
> excluded from even the very beginning of educational access.

It is not of course that these people have learnt nothing – far from it. Rather, it is that for Bown and others, significant learning necessarily involves literacy using such tools as books, pens and paper. It seems that unless there is an interest in using these tools and people around who are accomplished in their use, then informal learning of basic literacy will not occur. The requirements of interest to learn and sources of expertise may be taken to be appropriate to any account of informal learning. Or to put it another way in connection with the theory of informal learning presented here, unless traditions include practices involving literacy then those practices cannot be learnt. Formal attempts to teach literacy will necessarily conflict with certain traditional forms of life and it could be argued (and in the case of literacy probably would be argued) that such challenges should be encouraged.

In other cases things are not so obvious. For example in what cases should the religious practices of a society be challenged through formal learning imposed from a rival tradition? Or practices involving the subjugation of women or involving cruelty to animals? In what circumstances is it justifiable to force people to learn some things in school formally against what at the time appears like their better interests to learn other things informally? These are big questions that we are not able to answer in this chapter. What we can do is to try to illustrate some of the issues that are at stake in our attempt to restore a proper balance between formal and informal learning. We begin with a brief recollection of what life was like in western liberal democracies before formal learning became established. We conclude with an explanation of how an academic education turns out to be the best form of vocational education for many people and we give some exemplars of the effects of this.

1. LEARNING AND LIVING

It is important to remember amid current talk about lifelong learning that there is nothing new about such learning. It is not necessarily helpful to draw a distinction between learning and living. It has been normal to learn in the course of living long before there were even institutions concerned with formal learning such as schools. Moreover it has been normal to assess our learning and that of others in the course of living. It is worth remembering that people did all kinds of imaginative, useful and beautiful things long before there was talk of the sort referred to above. Great bridges, churches, houses, songs and so on came into existence long before it was fashionable to distinguish between work, living and learning in so sharp a way as is the case now. It is also worth remembering that such enduring creations were not products of the applications of courses of formal learning. Finally it is worth noting that people assessed each others' works informally too without the need for checklists, examinations and credentials of one bureaucratic sort or another. It was possible then to get along perfectly well without reliance on a type of precision which is supposed to be assured when practice follows theory. Yet despite these rather obvious observations, the idea that theory should guide practice and its associated idea of technical rationality has come to the fore and has remained to the fore even now within policies concerned to promote lifelong learning.

According to Altrichter, Posch and Somekh (1993), the three main assumptions of technical rationality are:

• There are general solutions to practical problems.
• These solutions can be developed outside practical situations (in research or administrative centres).
• The solutions can be translated into practitioners' actions by means of publications, training, administrative orders, etc.

So despite these obvious observations which indicate that there are alternative conceptions of rationality that enable productive development, we argue that the influence of technical rationality remains strong and that it distorts conceptions of what lifelong learning might be within postmodernity. One of the main reasons for its strong influence is that it coheres with an empiricist epistemology, a dualist metaphysics and a neutralist liberal democratic vision of societal development all of which are firmly embedded in what looks like common sense. Most importantly, though, technical rationality supports the idea that there is just one 'theoretical' context that can somehow govern applications in a multitude of other 'practical' contexts characterised famously as a 'swamp' (Schön, 1987: 3) Who, for example would want to try and navigate a swamp if there was the prospect of controlling it from a theoretical parapet above as it were?

Once however findings from research into notions of a learning society and lifelong learning began to emerge, anomalies appeared and one of the most important anomalies concerned the place of informal learning. Informal learning is of course precisely that type of learning that has always gone on and that is least explainable in terms of technical rationality. As one of our respondents put it:

> I mean you just do things and you learn, then you do other things and you learn some more. It's hard to say how but that's life!

Such a response is problematic for those using money collected from public taxation to develop policies to promote lifelong learning. That is because it is not at all clear that everyone has equal opportunities to do things that best enable or sustain learning. Indeed there is ample evidence that they do not. As we indicated in chapter one, the temptation for policy makers and theorists of lifelong learning was to try and formalise it. In that way there was at least the prospect of describing it, quantifying it and distributing it according to some principles of social justice.

Writing at the end of the UK's multimillion pound ESRC funded research programme into The Learning Society, the Director Coffield (2000: 1) observed:

> If all learning were to be represented by an iceberg ... the submerged two thirds of the structure would be needed to convey the much greater importance of informal learning. ... [Yet] none of the 14 projects [supported within the programme] was

funded to study informal learning as its central focus. However, as internal meetings
of the project directors got underway and debates began it became increasingly clear
… that informal learning was much more significant than many of us had previously
recognised.

Within the field of workplace learning too, the significance of informal learning is
also being increasingly recognised (Evans, Hodkinson & Unwin 2002). Rather
than indicating the need for planned interventions in work in the form of short
courses or training modules, current theories of workplace learning highlight the
importance of conditions that facilitate workers learning from each other and their
surroundings. In this regard the notions of social capital, cultural capital and habi-
tus have come to the fore in an attempt to theorise the sociocultural dimensions in
learning (Ecclestone & Prior 2003).

Eraut (1997) is one among many who notes that the discourse about lifetime
learning has been dominated by the providers of formal education and training.
We argue later that this dominance of formal learning has also led to an emphasis
on particular types of learning theory characterised as 'product' theories. Broadly
these theories assume that learning is primarily an individual activity which adopts
the 'mind as container' metaphor (Bereiter 2002). This implies that the products of
learning are relatively stable over time and that the learning of different learners is in
a sense the same. These assumptions enable formal systems of assessment within
educational institutions and indeed formal systems of whole class instruction.

Now while these assumptions seem reasonable in the case of children learning
such things as the names of the capital cities of the countries of the world, they are
not so reasonable in the case of learning such things as how to operate a machine.
That is particularly the case where the operational outcome is only desirable at a
particular time under the control of an individual or group who happen to be
charged or paid to achieve that outcome. Nor are these assumptions reasonable in
the case of learning to behave morally, learning to live in a general sense in reasonable harmony with others, and, indeed, many other kinds of learning where
neither the precise outcome nor the precise method of achieving that outcome are
specifiable in advance.

Nevertheless, there are many advantages from a policy-maker's point of view
in adopting the idea that learning might be the acquisition of products. First, this
idea appears to make learning transparent and easily understandable. Second, it
appears to enable the equitable distribution of learning, and, third, it appears to enable some measure of value-for money. It seems entirely plausible that learners
might know what it is they are to learn and that they might seek the most efficient
way of achieving that learning. Efficiency might best be seen to be achieved
through instituting a market in the providers of learning. No longer might public
sector educational institutions maintain expensive monopoly provision of learning.
The idea of learning as a product facilitates competition between different providers thus ensuring efficient delivery of products or services, or so the story goes.
While the story has come in for much criticism, it is easy to see the attractions to
governments, concerned to reduce the size of public sector expenditure, of the
learning as product idea. In summary learners choose the products of learning in

which they have an interest and the provider of that learning. Inefficient and unattractive providers simply go out of business. But what are the products that learners acquire and how might anyone know that they have achieved them?

2. LEARNING AND THE ECONOMY

To answer these questions it is necessary to refer to the so-called competence revolution (Hyland 1994). During the 1970's there was a resurgence of interest in behavioural learning theory and the products of learning came to be specified at least for some types of 'vocational' learning in behavioural terms. So-called competencies are broken down into performance criteria which specify the desired forms of behaviour that learners are supposed to demonstrate when they have acquired the product. It might be wondered however what would attract learners to pay for the acquisition of products that are specifiable and in many cases attainable in advance of their payment? On the face of it – not very much. However when competencies were arranged into occupational training families drawn up by experts to specify what is supposed to be required to perform well in particular jobs, then the attractions become clearer. The ultimate product learners want is a job which in turn is the key to money, social relations and much else besides. To achieve a job it is necessary to undertake some formal learning which includes some final 'official' recognition of competence which could then serve as a promissory note for the acquisition of a job. Thus learners, aided to some extent by government, pay to get a job which then enables both their own material rewards and increased economic productivity for the nation. According to this summary learning is indeed part of a virtuous circle.

Throughout the 80's till the present, this circle has been dominant. As the English Department for Education and Skills recently put it:

> It is crucial that education policies are viewed from an economic perspective *(DFES 2003: 4)*

Later:

> It is essential that the labour market and the wider economy are considered when making education policy, and increasingly so. *(DFES 2003: 6)*

It is not only economic productivity that appears to be ensured through adoption of the learning – jobs – improved economy circle, but social justice too. As the DFES put it:

> High quality learning is strongly linked with higher earnings, lower chances of becoming unemployed, better health and reduced crime. *(DFES 2003: 4)*

Later:

> By developing the skills of the current and future workforce, the Department's poli-
> cies are helping to create both a more prosperous society and a more equal one.
> *(DFES 2003: 8)*

Yet this chapter presents compelling evidence that in the UK high quality learning
and its associated benefits are best ensured through the acquisition of what might
be termed 'academic' skills and that it is only a minority who acquire them. The
acquisition of practical skills comes a poor second and, in some cases, shares third
place with those who appear to have benefited little from the many millions that
are put into the provision of formal educational opportunities of any kind. (DFES
2003: 13, 17, 19; Sianesi 2003: 1-2)

So while it therefore appears entirely reasonable for governments to want to
move as many people as possible from third and second positions to first, there are
at least two problems associated with such an attempt. First it seems highly
unlikely that national economic prosperity would result if everyone became aca-
demically engaged. Second social justice involves not only the principle of equality but also two other principles which may be summarised as truth and just desert.
These three principles are always in some degree of tension (see Halliday 2004,
for a fuller discussion of this tension). Those who put time money and effort into
formal learning on the basis of a promissory note of employment are entitled to
expect proportionate reward for their efforts time and money. They do not expect
that they will receive the same as someone who has not undertaken such learning.
Increasingly however, research into the rates of return of different types of formal
learning challenges this expectation (Applebaum, Bernhardt & Murnane 2005;
Ashton & Green 1996; Berg 1973; Brown & Hesketh 2004; Conlon 2002;
Dearden *et al.* 2002; Keep 2003; Lafer 2002; Robinson 1997b; Sianesi 2003; Wolf
2002).

In her summary of research in the British context, Sianesi notes that:

> The most robust findings to date are that ... academic qualifications generally earn
> higher rewards. ... Qualifications which on the other hand seem to fail to generate any
> wage premium for males or females are ... vocational qualifications, RSA, BTEC, ap-
> prenticeship and most notably NVQ level 2 and below. *(Sianesi 2003: 1-2)*

No one imagines that there could ever be equal rewards given for different types
of work. Indeed it would be hard to know the basis on which equality in reward
was to be decided. Yet a main problem with uncritical acceptance of the learning –
jobs – economy circle within social policy is that it encourages all learners to acquire academic qualifications which have the highest returns. At the same time,
learning for the acquisition of what are called 'intermediate level qualifications',
which lead to such worthwhile practices as plumbing, building and social care, is
avoided. All policy makers can do about this is complain.

> Economic performance has also been held back by a shortage of intermediate-level
> qualifications. *(DFES 2003: 14)*

It is hardly surprising that there is such a shortage because according to the logic of the learning – jobs – economy circle, students will seek learning with the highest rates of return which are not at intermediate level.

> The returns to holding a degree have generally remained high. *(DFES 2003: 30)*

And:

> The demand for higher level qualifications, especially at degree level, is set to increase further in the future. *(DFES 2003: 39)*

If everyone pursues learning that can lead to a degree then it is not possible for higher level qualifications to maintain their promissory exchange value. This will result in increased levels of disappointment and potentially greater levels of social injustice. That is because those who have invested in their education as government encourages them to do and who have acquired debts as a result, may find themselves even poorer than they would have been without such investment. In the UK, for example, an increasing proportion of 16-21 year olds are undertaking formal education programmes and paying to do so. An increasing proportion of these support themselves in part time work while so doing (DFES 2001). At the end of 2000, it is estimated that 58 per cent of 16 to 18 year olds in England and Wales were in employment. This illustrates that the type of learning they undertook pre-16 was a very good vocational education for them.

It might appear strange then that the main area of expansion has come in vocational education post-18. Both in further education colleges and in higher education institutions, 2 million students were enrolled at the end of 2000, typically obtaining degrees and Ordinary or Higher National Certificates/ Diplomas. In addition since their introduction in 1987, just under 3.2 million National Vocational Qualifications had been awarded up to the end of September 2000. The majority of these were at level 2 (59 per cent), with about 19 per cent at level 1 and 22 per cent at level 3 or above. 117 thousand General National Vocational Qualifications were awarded in 1999/00 compared with 113 thousand in 1998/99 and 103 thousand in 1997/98. The Autumn 2000 Labour force survey (LFS) estimates that a further 729 thousand people, who did not hold a full National Vocational Qualification, held a unit towards such a qualification. Not all of these qualifications are awarded while people are unemployed of course. Without going into the precise details of what and who is involved, it seems that something like perhaps 4 or 5 million people in the UK, one tenth of the population has been involved in some vocational education post 18.

Yet the bulk of these vocational qualifications were at the lowest levels and most people were able to secure work and perform their jobs satisfactorily without them. Moreover according to Wolf (2002: ch 6) the growth in the number of vocational qualifications awarded in further and higher education at the higher levels is the result not so much of increased demands for higher level skills. Rather 'the tyranny of numbers' simply racks up the stakes in attempting to secure for employers the best new employees and for prospective employees the best employment. That means that whatever government or individuals do, the requirement for social equality can never be achieved. It also means that a requirement for proportionate reward can also never be achieved because there is bound to be a polarisation that has nothing to do with effort between those who form the bottom part of the normal distribution and those at the top. Whereas once results at 'O' or 'A' levels were sufficient for employers to select new staff, now qualifications beyond those levels are also considered important. Prospective employees have no choice other than to try to achieve them if they want to have any chance of securing what appears to be good employment. The result is that many employees are over-qualified for the jobs they are expected to do (Wolf 2002).

Yet despite these impressive rates of participation, the British government persists with the view that many are still missing out on formal learning. For example, in her plea to widen participation in further education, Kennedy (1997) argues that the case for widening is irresistible on grounds of justice alone. Nowhere does she say how many are excluded even though she laments the student support system, which seems to lead to so many students failing to complete or begin courses of formal education.

> It forced people to cease courses leading to worthwhile qualifications and sustained employability to take up short-term unskilled jobs. *(Kennedy 1997: 70)*

Someone has to do these jobs and what is the evidence that these so called worthwhile qualifications are indeed worthwhile? What seems to receive little consideration anywhere in this uncritical call for inclusion through vocational education is that all economies need large numbers of people to perform work where satisfactory performance of such work is unrelated to a vocational education. Such performance is much more likely to be related to the degree to which those who do such work feel they are being rewarded and respected for it. A qualification is no substitute for such reward and respect.

Yet concerted efforts have been put into trying to persuade recalcitrant learners and workers to attend formal educational institutions. Government has even been prepared to go so far as to pay professionals to visit public houses trying to persuade drinkers to go and take part in such formal programmes of learning! (Chisholm 1997: 45) Quite apart from the moral issues that are involved in this example of what is called 'Inn-tuition', there is also the issue of whether it is wise to discount the informal learning that might take place during the course of a drink!

3. VOCATIONAL EDUCATION

It is worth noting that the term 'vocational education' is used to mean a number of quite different things among which are: a poor general education for workers, a practical education, a technical education, an industrial education, a scientific education, an engineering education, an education for basic skills. For the moment we accept the Scottish Further Education Funding Council (SFEFC 2002) definition:

> A vocational course is defined as a course primarily designed to prepare students for, or to increase their knowledge, skill or proficiency in, an employment or profession.

A vocational education is supposed to enable people to secure paid employment or to improve their ability to perform in employment. Given that different forms of work will be paid differentially, then plainly a vocational education is a means to secure positional advantage. This is certainly true for individuals. It is probably true for companies. It is also true for states which quite reasonably might expect and have expected that the educational system should be a means of securing greater national economic prosperity. Policy documentation concerned with lifelong learning is littered with references to vocational education being a prime means of securing national economic advantage (Commission of the European Communities 1994, 1997, OECD 1973, Delors 1996, Department for Education and Employment 1998, World Bank 1996, Scottish Office 1998).

There is a variety of forms of paid work through which people contribute to national economic prosperity and a flourishing civic culture. Social justice seems to require that governments should try to ensure that educational opportunities are distributed and arranged in such a way as to enable every citizen a reasonable chance of securing a job with a fair level of remuneration. Plainly no government, even one attempting to run a command economy, can guarantee everyone with the appropriate qualifications a job of their choice. It is equally unreasonable, however, for governments to invoke some concept of employability which makes it appear as if the only determinant (and problem) in the fitting of individuals to jobs was located on the supply side.

While we may imagine someone vocationally qualified unable to secure a job in the area of their vocational qualification, it would be implausible to claim that a qualification was vocational if no-one with such a qualification was able to secure a job in the area of that vocational qualification. If an individual invests a certain amount of time, effort and expenditure in pursuing a series of educational opportunities which lead to a qualification which purports to guarantee their ability to do a certain type of work, then they have a right to expect a reasonable chance of securing such a job and improving their ability once in it. Governments too might be seen to have a similar interest on behalf of taxpayers who wish to see that their investment does indeed have economic returns.

In summary then, an education may only reasonably be described as vocational if, at least some of those who partake of it, secure work for which the education purported to be a preparation and are more capable of carrying out that work than they would have been had they not partaken of it. Both the State and the individual may be seen to invest in such an education and social justice requires that, in the main, the investment should stand a reasonable chance of securing a proportionate reward. The requirement for social justice also suggests that no particular group is excluded from such investment or systematically channeled into certain types of vocational education that are known to offer poor investment returns.

4. ACADEMIC EDUCATION

We have already referred to the terms vocational and academic and indicated that academic qualifications have in general more exchange value than their vocational counterparts. It is important to clarify the distinction between these terms. As has been argued elsewhere (Halliday 1996), the basis of this distinction is not necessarily that one is narrowly seen as preparation for a particular job whereas the other floats free of instrumental considerations, for the benefit of only a leisured elite who need not worry about earning a living. Rather, the basis of the distinction is more plausibly that 'academic' practices typically exclude the use of the tools other than pens, books, paper and computers, whereas vocational practices often include the use of other sorts of tool, such as brushes, drills and vehicles. But there are many 'academic' forms of work too. Hence all educational activities may be seen as vocational in that they prepare people for different types of work to some degree. In many cases what traditionally has been termed an 'academic' education turns out to be the very best vocational education as we have seen.

Alison Wolf reminds us that when the vocational is emphasised, it becomes the type of education some enthusiastically advocate for other people's children. (Wolf 2002: Ch. 3) What Wolf hints at here is that those social practices known as academic practices serve as gateway practices to individual economic prosperity in a way that their 'vocational' equivalents do not. She provides abundant evidence that this is the case. Were students single-mindedly to base their judgements about what is worth learning and when on purely instrumental considerations relating to what they are likely to earn, then the evidence is clear that they should not pursue vocational qualifications at all. As Wolf concludes (2002: 37):

> ..... employers in the brave new knowledge economy are after just those traditional academic skills that schools have always tried to promote.

In summary as Ashton and Green (1996: 65) report, there does seem to be an impressive correlation between earnings and academic education. Better primary and secondary schooling seems to correlate with better economic returns, but more formal education after school does not, except for those going on to high status, well-paid employment.

It is hardly surprising, therefore, that when free to do so, people increasingly choose programmes that lead to qualifications of a general academic kind, precisely because they recognise that these qualifications have high exchange value, and because flexibility is the key to having most chance of securing a good job. It simply makes no sense to follow the VQ framework with its atomised competencies and performance criteria based on yesterday's practice (see Halliday 1996). The growth in vocational qualifications came at the lower end and for those already in work who, by and large, were not free to determine whether they should bother with these qualifications at all. They were generally required to attend formal educational institutions to achieve such qualifications because otherwise they would suffer financial loss through withdrawal of benefits or some other means.

Yet all economies require a number of what might appear to be lower-skilled jobs within social practices such as cleaning, carrying and food serving that nevertheless are vital for the proper functioning of a well-ordered society. Moreover it is important that those jobs are done well and properly recognised. Not only that, but it is perfectly conceivable for such supposedly low-skills workers to be highly educated in a general sense and for the major point for them of their work to be the external rewards that the work brings, which in turn provides them with the means to pursue an educated interest in some pastime. As we argue (Halliday & Hager 2002), the prime context for understanding the judgements that they make at work may well be their hobby of windsurfing, for example, which they undertake during their spare time. Of course the difficulty with this view is that unless rates of pay are sufficiently high for supposed 'low skills work' and such work intrinsically valuable to some degree, then there will be little point in doing it well.

The picture is complex and there is considerable evidence that people do not put monetary reward above all other considerations in their views of work. Nor indeed do they seem to be over-calculative in their approach to what is worth learning and with whom. There are good reasons for this. According to Clark and Oswald (1996), the degree of perceptions of happiness at work does not seem to depend much on the absolute level of remuneration workers receive. Rather it does depend upon individual earnings relative to others in the same work place. Moreover it seems that people value a sense of justice in the workplace, even if that means them forgoing some of their remuneration. The authors also find that holding income constant, satisfaction at work declines with increasing levels of education. So while requirements for social justice might appear to suggest that different groups in society ought to have some degree of equality of opportunity in securing well-paid work, their relative degrees of satisfaction and happiness may be more related to their perceptions of the relative earnings of those in the same group than across all groups. Difficulty with interpreting this empirical evidence is compounded by the conceptual difficulties there are in outlining and prioritising the different kinds of happiness and satisfaction that might be secured through work. Moreover it is impossible for students to have a proper informed basis on which to try to maximise their gains, as it were, quite apart from the fact that monetary gains are not the only kind from which they may benefit. That is because their potential gain depends upon how others interpret their chances of securing gains in the light of the laws of supply and demand. If everyone chooses a type of vocational education that in the past has led to the best rewards then it is clear that such a choice is unlikely to do so in the future. They are subject to a version of the prisoner's dilemma. Finally we cannot assume that higher wages reflect higher contribution to overall good.

As Wolf (2002: 27) puts it:

> In reality, earnings reflect a great deal more than individual productivity. The amount paid to different groups and different individuals also depends heavily on the way in which a society is organised overall.

Now as far as we are aware there is no entirely reliable measure of what might be called the quality of work or job satisfaction. Moreover it may be that systematic attempts to acquire such a measure are inevitably distorted by the very specific contexts within which people work. What might appear to be an awful job from an outsider's point of view might be very acceptable for those who enjoy each other's company. (See Keep & Mayhew 2002, Green & Gallie 2002 for further elaboration of this point).

The overall point that emerges from this discussion of a vocational education is that it is mistaken for educational policy to encourage too instrumental an orientation among learners. A clearer case of what amounts to a state endorsed promissory note than that provided by a vocational qualification is hard to find. Yet, as we have seen, in too many cases the promissory note is invalid. And it is invalid because it is not possible to contextualise in advance the kind of rewards people secure from their work or study, nor what those rewards will lead on to in the future. To be sure there are some social practices generally of the academic kind that seem to function as gatekeepers to certain high status occupations and perhaps that will always be the case. But high status occupations are not the only worthwhile forms of employment and no society would survive for long without other forms of employment being performed well. Moreover it might be preferable to decouple status from earnings. What we now need is a fresh account of curriculum and policy that pays attention to the notions of contingency and opportunity that our argument has highlighted. There will always be a hierarchy of earnings that different forms of employment enable. No doubt the present large differentials in such earnings are not easy to justify on the grounds of effort and time that the different forms of employment require. But it is not an educational task to try to justify or modify such differentials, nor to pretend that the efforts that are put into different forms of learning are likely to be proportionate to the rewards that are secured as a result of such learning.

In summary it is mistaken to imagine that in general the more formal education an individual undertakes, the more that individual earns. While this is true for some people with some qualifications, it is not generally true for all. So-called vocational forms of learning do not in many cases enable learners to secure work in a given area. Those who start out from certain kinds of family and societal backgrounds tend to benefit most from what is termed an academic education and the evidence that courses of vocational education compensate for some perceived disadvantage is not clear.

5. HIGH AND LOW SKILLS

Ashton and Green (1996), Winch (2002) and others distinguish between a high skills equilibrium (HSE) and a low skills equilibrium (LSE). They make the point that nations exhibit the characteristics of an HSE and an LSE in differing degrees. While there is no room here to outline all these characteristics, it is important to note that within an HSE, vocational qualifications may be seen as a kind of property because the state regulates employment through such qualifications. Germany would be an example here. In a real sense a vocational qualification and courses leading to the award of such qualifications enable participants and holders to reach a degree of financial security and prosperity. Thus they enable more people to have a stake in the society of which they are a part than might be possible if attempts were made to distribute land and real estate more equitably. They may thus serve as a form of goods to be distributed on the basis of their promissory exchange value. Plainly the justice of their distribution depends upon the extent to which their promise can be realised and that depends not only upon the supply of people with such qualifications and the quality of the education that led to those qualifications, but also upon demand. Moreover it probably depends on some regulation of all three, which is something that British and American Governments have tended to resist, and such lack of regulation is related to the characteristics of an LSE. Nevertheless it is easy to see why any government might wish to attempt to sustain the view that a vocational qualification is property worth having.

In contrast to countries in which the labour market is regulated, deregulated markets in the UK and the USA lead to a proliferation of changing structures all of which may be seen as attempts to sustain the idea that formal learning leading to vocational qualifications has promissory exchange value. Acronyms proliferate that are based on government departments, qualifications authorities and special funding bodies set up to support research and practice in the area of vocational education (Keep 2003; Lafer 2002; Wolf 2002). Often these are unashamedly short term in their aims and methods (Felstead 1993). This should not surprise us. Adoption of the circle suggests that education and economic success are like fresh air and fun – obvious good things to be maximised! It is hardly surprising then that an increasing proportion of 16 to 21 year olds are undertaking formal education programmes. Not everyone is convinced however, especially those older people who feel they have lived fulfilled lives without significant formal learning. We introduce a number of cases so as to illustrate this claim.

6. PERSONAL STORIES

6.1 Older People

6.1.1 Andrew Dalton's story
(Andrew Dalton's letter, as follows, appeared in the Sydney Morning Herald 20.12.05, page 12)

You can't pick up a book or article on social trends these days without reading about how grim life will be for people without formal skills and qualifications, how their chances of employment are virtually non-existent, and the devastating effects that being without a job has on one's self-esteem and ability to lead a normal life.

As a member of this group of people supposedly condemned by a lack of formal training, it has depressed me to read such things. ... I have been employed or self-employed all my working life and, like many people without formal skills, have worked in rewarding, well-paid jobs. ...

Those who would put the unskilled on the trash heap seem to have forgotten the millions of people who create their own jobs and future through their vision and tenacity, rather than depending on others to provide it for them. I'm not only talking about self-made (and formally unskilled) successes such as Paul Keating, Bill Gates and J.K. Rowling, but the legions of small and large business-owners, artists and old-school journalists. ... my local mixed business is owned by a prosperous businessman with no qualifications at all.

... All people should be encouraged to find their niche in life and develop the qualities, not just the qualifications, that lead to rewarding work, rather than being filled with fear and written off for lacking vocationally oriented skills.

6.1.2 Fred's story

Boatbuilder, retailer, National President, lifeboat coxon, father, left school with no qualifications.

Fred is an exemplary lifelong learner. He is 73 and is married with two daughters. When he was younger, he was a boat builder, but he now manages a shop which sells diesel, paint and plywood for boats and deals with boat repairs. During his career he was also involved in many other activities. For example, he was National President of the Institute of Boat Builders, he was coxon of the lifeboats and he was involved in rewriting the vocational education modules for boat building. He left school at 13, just after the second world war in 1946. Although he had the required grades to stay on to senior secondary school, he decided "it wasn't for me" and was happy to leave at that time. Fred feels that as a result of leaving formal education so early, he had to learn the hard way. He says "I didn't have much schooling so I'd to do it all uphill". He had learned the basics of course. Indeed he was good at writing, reading and basic arithmetic. What he did not have was a credential with any exchange value and that is what he meant by "having to do it the hard way". He has managed perfectly well to keep up to date with changes in information technology, such as use of the internet for advertising, receiving orders for his shop and keeping his accounts, without attending any formal courses. As he put it "I just shopped around, asked lots of questions and tried it out. My accountant knows someone who is very good if I can't work something out for myself."

6.1.3 Frank's story

Writer, artist, actor, journalist, performer, odd job man, left school without qualifications.

Frank is proud of his many identities. He has become each of them through informal learning. He told us that he had a "poor formal education" and that he doesn't "have a single qualification to my [his] name", but he seems unconcerned about this as he believes that "self-education is the best education".

Frank came from a working class background and feels that this affected his education and what he had the desire to do in life. He says "if you are in the wrong group your chances in life are limited as a consequence ... working class people, they're kind of brain washed into not searching or seeking anything better".

After Frank left school he did a variety of things and by chance when he was 22 or 23, he "found a bookshop". He explained "this opened my mind, to how ignorant I was, how uneducated I was" and as a consequence he "began to read wildly" about all kinds of things. He sees this as a critical turning point in his life and compares it to the "road to Damascus" experience. Frank feels that formal learning is over emphasised in today's society. He asks "today is it not absolutely essential to get any kind of reasonable job in life you have to have a degree? … When I was younger I managed to get a job running a local newspaper despite having no formal qualifications". Frank believes, however, that having a degree is "no guarantee of intelligence". He says that "often, I believe that an intelligent person, regardless of their birth and their upbringing they'll crave knowledge and they'll seek it out and they'll learn themselves to their own ability". He believes that people who learn informally often have certain qualities and this is why he, and he believes many others, do not fit neatly into the "normal" university education, "they are very informal, flexible… individualist, challenging, questioning, they're not the products of an orthodox education".

6.1.4 Carol's story
Factory worker, bus clippie, nursing auxiliary, cost clerk, garden nursery worker, seamstress and more. Left school at 14 without qualifications.

Carol is now retired after a very varied career and a life full of travelling. She writes many letters to newspapers and magazines and enters competitions. She left school at 14 as her mother was ill and went to work in the rubber mill, then left there to work at a factory soldering condensers to put in radios for bombers during the second world war. She then applied to work in a biscuit factory away from home as she knew this was an opportunity to "spread my wings and travel". From then on she did a variety of jobs, learning them all through informal means. Yet in her forties she went to evening classes to gain some "'O' levels, including English language" as she felt that she "had missed out through leaving school at 14 and … wanted to catch up". Carol comments that she has always had an interest in writing and that English was her "best subject at school". When she was younger she would have liked to be a journalist, but she was raised in a working class family and at this time "you didn't have a choice" as everyone either worked in a factory, so she thought "who am I to think about that, it really was unheard of I thought oh that's for the rich people not for the likes of me". When she looks back now she wishes she had pursued this, as she feels she would really have enjoyed this type of job. At 81 she would like to become a professional writer.

6.1.5 Jennifer's story
Factory worker, mother, typist, bookkeeper, home help, left school without qualifications.

Jennifer dislikes formal learning because such learning always "seems to involve examinations which I hate". Throughout her life she has had many jobs, been through marriage break–ups, new relationships, witnessed serious illnesses of her children and she has managed them all without formal learning. Recently however, her present employer insists that she attends courses on information technology which "are pretty simple really". Although she feels the knowledge required for the exam was there, she couldn't "cope with the exam situation" and it took her four attempts to pass one of the modules. She says "it began to get soul destroying; I think that's when it really came home to me that I didn't really enjoy the exam situation". Jennifer told us that in school she had problems with exams as well, although she didn't really realise this at the time. She says "I didn't really enjoy exams as I got terribly nervous and as a result it tended to make me shy away from formal education". It is for this reason that Jennifer feels she learns more efficiently in an informal situation. She reflects however that when she is under pressure in her normal work situation, she has no difficulties. The rise of what Collins (1979) calls the credential society has accompanied what we argue is an undesirable shift towards formal learning. Cases such as Jennifer's illustrate a further difficulty with this shift. Performance in one supposedly standard context serves to limit opportunities for learning across a range of other contexts.

6.1.6 Marjorie's story
Dressmaker, shop owner, factory worker, left school without qualifications.

Marjorie now owns an alterations and dressmaking shop. She is unable to carry out any of the alterations herself any longer as she has rheumatoid arthritis. Marjorie's only experience of formal learning was at school. She learnt her trade informally when she left school and worked in a factory aged 15. She explains "I had no interest in sewing at all, I just had interest in earning a wage, ... when you left school you just went out and got a job, any job really ... the only reason I chose to work in that particular factory was because my sister worked there".

There, however, she feels that many of the essential skills that were needed for her future career were learned. As she put it "that was the learning curve, I learned everything in the factory. ... It was a bit trial and error. No-one really showed you what to do ... you got on with it, you just picked it up as you went along, if you made a mistake you turned to the person that was closest to you and said how do I get out of this". She provides an easy illustration of what we mean by developing the ability to make contextually sensitive judgments. The button hole that did not come out quite right, the stitch that was uneven, and so on, prompted the kind of reflective view of activities that we argue enables learning. She developed the ability to judge in a contextually sensitive way.

6.1.7 Reg's story
Retired maths teacher, hill walker, wildlife enthusiast, campaigner.

Reg is a retired mathematics teacher. Since he has retired he has pursued other interests such as hill walking and wildlife. For the last nine months he has been a member of a group which is campaigning against the construction of a wind farm.

Reg has "always been interested in wildlife". He used to be a bee keeper and through this he developed his interest in wildlife further. "My interest in botany and flowers in particular developed through my experience as a bee keeper. ..... Of course you learn a great deal about plants through having bees, but I've always been interested in wildlife really. ... I don't go home and read wildlife books every night, usually I'll see something and if I don't know what it is and I don't know anything about it, then I'll go home and look it up and I'll learn about it that way".

Reg's interest in wildlife also ties in with his interest in hill walking. He enjoys the views and the scenery but now also looks for "other things of interest" such as plants and animals in the surrounding area. He feels that "it adds a lot to the walk if you know a bit about what's happening around you". Part of what was happening around him was the development of wind farms which Reg is now campaigning against. He knows a lot about wind farms. He can tell you much of what you could possibly want to know about their efficiency, sustainability and so on. Through this he has learned to speak out at meetings, to write letters and a host of other things that other members of protest groups are interested in.

6.1.8 Mark's story

Parent, fireman, martial artist, Open University student.

Mark is a fireman, but also participates in many other activities such as martial arts, yoga and meditation. He has two degrees which he acquired through the Open University. He comes from a poor background and feels that this has shaped how he interprets his experiences. He says "I love the brutality and the honesty of the working classes which is my background...but I hate their lack of ambition. ... I can't understand anybody who's born in poverty who wants to grow up in that – I just, I can't relate to that...the way I was raised made me unhappy so I wouldn't want to do that to my family, I don't want that".

Mark likes his job because it gives him financial security and the satisfaction that comes from doing something obviously worthwhile. At the same time it has allowed him to develop other interests and to gain two degrees through distance learning. He gives his reasons for following the Open University courses as follows: "there's two main reasons – one was because in a capitalist society you just need to prove things to people. If I was injured in a fire, at least I've got a fall back and you need to prove that intellectually you're capable of learning at an advanced level. It doesn't mean you're intelligent, but it means you're capable of taking in a lot of knowledge. Secondly there was a great thirst for knowledge I always did want to learn more...it's just a burning desire within me to learn...I had a thirst for knowledge". Mark wanted "to prove to himself and to others that [I] he could do it despite [my] his background".

6.2 Younger People

The people featured in the following cases are younger. They have been brought up at a time in which the minimum school leaving age is 16 and in which it is becoming increasingly normal to undertake further or higher education. Not surprisingly formal learning has featured more strongly in their lives to date. Nevertheless these cases illustrate the significance of informal learning too.

6.2.1 June's story

June is a 22 year old, qualified speech and language therapist in her first full time permanent job. She left secondary school after sixth year and continued on to university to study speech and language pathology. While at university, she also worked part time as a home support and day carer for Social Work Services. To date her life appears to have been dominated by formal learning and she does not regret this.

Significantly though June feels that it was the work placements that best prepared her for her job. She knew that experience and knowledge gained within placements would inevitably be beneficial when she was qualified and "working for real". June feels that "there is no real substitute" for the learning that takes place when having constantly to assess the needs of the client during therapy and readjust therapy in order for it to be more specific to the client's needs. The time available did not allow the readjustments to be completely planned as they had to be made "on the spot".

June's other care jobs required many skills, although she have received no formal training for these jobs. She has worked as a home support and day carer (involving work with both mainstream and special needs children) for approximately four years. She now works as a relief care worker in a residential and respite home for children with special needs, and in a residential flat for adults with special needs. June feels these jobs have developed her skills significantly in dealing with others and adjusting to meet their needs.

6.2.2 Barbara's story

Barbara is 24 and qualified as a primary school teacher three years ago. In this time she has worked in three different schools. Barbara told us that she was motivated to learn at school as she knew she needed to get the required grades in order to pursue her chosen career as a teacher. She comments "the motivation then is from knowing you've got exams, if you've got a focus and you know why you want a purpose to your learning, then you are learning things and you are actually rote learning a lot of time, you're memorising at that stage to get through an exam...a lot of which is forgotten after the exam". Barbara explains this point further "the things that you remember, you know, that you really learn and remember for life are things that somehow mean something to you I suppose, that you can relate to". Like many other students, Barbara feels that she learned more meaningfully on placements. She comments "I definitely think the practical learning that we did, you know, going out on placement to schools was more beneficial". While Barbara was still a student, her responsibility increased throughout the years. Yet there was always a teacher who was ultimately responsible for her and for the class. However, when she fulfilled the role of teacher herself, she had to cope on her own.

She explains that she tends to ask "tons of questions", research issues herself and find an "ally on the staff...who's kind of mutually supportive and doesn't mind your questions". Asking other staff questions tends to be a very unstructured process by simply "grabbing a minute...it's difficult to get the chance to sit down formally".

6.2.3 Susan's story

Susan is 22. She has lived on a farm all her life and through doing so has learned many skills relevant to farming. She explains "living on a farm you get to know about quite a lot of things, it's not just looking after the animals, I mean there's the, there's the paperwork and there's the machinery and I mean there is quite a bit that you learn, you just don't actually realise you're learning it...it's nothing really I've thought about before, it's just part of life really, it's not something you think about in great detail. She is also currently studying for a degree in microbiology.

She says "uni is more structured anyway, you specifically have to do things and specifically have to learn things, whereas like at home, you don't really realise you're doing it and you just get on with it". Susan tells us that she made the decision to go to university because it was the normal and expected thing to do. She says "I just decided to go into uni because it's just something that you kind of got put towards when you are at school, I mean, if you had good grades that's what you did, you went to uni ... to be honest I wanted to do something in agriculture, but I just thought, I'd got these unconditionals so I just, I went for them...I kind of forgot all about that really to be honest, sometimes I do wish I had just kept with that, but the course I'm doing I can kind of go back towards farming because microbiology will be what I get my degree with honours in so I can go back towards farming with that". Susan is also unsure about what she will do when she finishes university, she says "I don't know to be honest, I've no idea, I just really think about getting uni over and done with and then get a job, probably when I finish it'll just be a job no matter what as long as I can get one and then I'll be a bit more specific once I've actually got a job ... I think I'd like to go into farming really but there are complications there". Susan did not want to explain these to us.

6.3 Commentary

The group of older people agreed to tell us about their informal learning and in the process about their lives because they share with us the view that too much attention is focused on formal learning, whereas for them and us, informal learning is just as important if not more so. The older people may be taken to be representatives of a generation when it was common to leave school early. They are intelligent, paradigmatic lifelong learners, who the currently popular picture of lifelong learning simply does not fit. In some cases, they have taken courses of formal learning as and when appropriate, but they have all suffered as a result of the front end model of formal learning that is currently dominant. In some cases this has driven them to take formal qualifications in an attempt to prove themselves in an academic way. Many people of their generation are good informal learners. The arguments that they need formal learning because of ever increasing changes in technology or because learning is not possible without formality simply do not fit.

   The group of younger people also recognised the significance of informal learning. The ways that such learning affects and is affected by formal learning is more complex than in the case of the older people simply because of the increased time that they have spent in formal learning situations. We will pick up on their stories in later chapters. For now it is perhaps worth noting the view that it is on practical placements that many of these younger people feel they have learnt most significantly. We may wonder what advantages are to be gained from formalising these placement experiences rather that leaving them, as in the cases of older people, simply as part of work.

CHAPTER THREE

ORIGINS OF A MISTAKE

We saw in the previous chapter some of the contradictions that emerge when an account of lifelong learning is promoted which pays undue attention to economic considerations and suggests that these are causally linked to formal learning. We conclude this present chapter with a broadly Foucauldian account of how a belief in such causation leads to a panopticon society, within which people have reason to believe that they are controlled increasingly through formal learning. To reach this conclusion we examine the metaphysical and epistemological bases which support current polices towards lifelong learning and we attempt to situate such policies in wider societal concerns. These concerns include the tension between, on the one hand, fitting learners into society so that they may contribute to the proper functioning of that society including its economic functions – enculturation. On the other hand there is the desire to enable learners to decide for themselves the societal parts they want to play – individuation. It is hard to see how this latter desire could be met unless learners were formally initiated, at least to some extent, into some of the options available to them.

We do not want to argue that all formal learning is bad, nor that economic considerations are irrelevant to learning. Ours is not a nostalgic thesis in which we hanker for an imaginary past where children went to school for the love of learning alone, taught by progressive educators concerned only with some romantic notion of intrinsic goodness or student interest. For us, just as it is mistaken now to overemphasise the instrumental aims of formal learning, so it was also a mistake to attempt to formalise the informal through schemes of progressive education, as if there could be exclusive access to some notion of an intrinsic good. We are content to accept a balance between formal and informal learning as between instrumental and intrinsic values.

1. A QUEST FOR INCLUSION

The liberal idea that a central purpose of education is to promote individual autonomy may be seen to have informed British and Australian educational policy during much of the post-war era. It was believed by many commentators that such policy is not only morally justifiable but also instrumentally justifiable as the means to achieve greater social cohesion – it was expected that individuals would develop common frames of reference within which conflicting values could be articulated and resolved. It was also expected that individuals would have an equal opportunity to gain the economic rewards that were on offer through a sort of open competition within the traditional liberal arts curriculum.

67

Many came to wonder whether this educational policy failed as a social policy (e.g. Ball 1990, Marginson 1993). Existing inequalities were largely perpetuated and social cohesion was not promoted and common standards of evaluation did not evolve (Adonis & Pollard 1997). Instead there appears to have been something of a disjuncture between those who achieved material prosperity and security through their success within the liberal arts curriculum and those who did not. The disjuncture was all the greater because those who succeeded tended to value democratic citizenship and the means of resolving conflicts through discourse, whereas those who failed had neither the means nor the common values to be able to resolve their disputes in this way. So it is hardly surprising that many of these 'failures' (who were in the majority) were inclined to look to the certainty of maximising material rewards as a neutral arbiter when deciding their priorities and values. After all, if someone feels that they have been excluded from a winning team, not on grounds of ability but on the grounds of less fair factors, such as the club of which they are a member, it is hardly surprising that they should look to some objective means of determining criteria of selection in the future. Hence among this majority materialistic values became embedded within common sense, not only because such values ensure survival, but also and crucially because they were seen as the means to a fairer society through the notion of objectivity.

This ideal of social cohesion based on economic success, and personal well-being remains strong. As the English Department for Education and Skills (DFES) put it recently (2003: 4):

> Education and Skills Policy has a big impact on both economic well-being and social inclusion.

Through education people are supposed to become richer, healthier and more moral.

> High quality learning is strongly linked with higher earnings, lower chances of becoming unemployed, better health and reduced crime. *(DFES 2003: 4)*

The preponderance of these materialistic values may be seen to have led to the idea that curricula should be designed to prepare people for particular occupations through which they gain those materialistic rewards. It may seem obvious that economic success both for individuals and for the state is most likely when education policies and later policies to promote lifelong learning put economic considerations to the fore.

As Halliday (1990: 23-31) argues, however, the problems with a liberal philosophy of education were inherent in the way it was interpreted by certain educational philosophers in the 60's. The ground for a narrow and instrumental conception of vocational education was being prepared by philosophers such as Hirst (1974), who promoted a version of a liberal education which looked suspiciously like a version of the then and now popular academic curriculum. It was as if a liberal education should be concerned with the development of personal autonomy through cerebral engagement in abstraction from the practical contexts in which people actually exercise their autonomy. Moreover it was as if it was possible to learn to be a plumber, for example, in abstraction from the real contexts within which plumbers actually work. Hirst (1993) has acknowledged his (1974) mistake and it would be wrong to suggest that one philosopher could have had such an effect. Pring (1993) gives a detailed account of how others came to be attracted similarly.

The mistake was made however. As a result the distinction between the vocational and the academic, and the related distinction between facts and values, became further entrenched to serve as just two of the false dualisms that Dewey (1966) and, recently, Pring (1995) have sought to attack. It seems obvious in retrospect that a vocational education was no less loaded with values than any other type of education. Who for example wants to employ someone who is solely concerned with the monetary rewards their work can bring? Equally who wants to live alongside someone who is incapable of recognising even the simplest of practical requirements such as how to sort rubbish or cook a meal. Everyone is involved in practices concerned with work and leisure to some degrees. A problem was and remains however that an academic education continues to have higher status than its vocational counterpart and this differential is widely regarded to be undesirable (Young 1993).

The 1990's saw a continuing series of reforms in Australia, Britain and elsewhere in attempts to reduce these differentials. Almost without exception however, these reforms were concerned with vocational education and training (VET). In all cases we can think of, a concern with VET arose either as a result of a perception of poor economic performance or as a result of the political need to appear to be doing something about increasing unemployment. In that way VET reforms may be seen as reactions to a deteriorating situation. Moreover such reforms have been most often concerned with so-called low level occupations. Occupations such as those of bishop, politician and company executive have been conspicuously absent from the list of those to be analysed.

2. EMPIRICISM

The mistaken idea that a vocational education could ever be free of intrinsic values may be seen to be based on the epistemology of empiricism. According to this epistemology there is a world external to us that can be known through our senses. The better we know this world, the more efficiently we can move around within it. What we can never know, according to this epistemology is what we ought to do in the world. Thus we get the idea that values are essentially subjective preferences and that there will always be conflicts that are not resolvable according to epistemic criteria. Rather the view develops that they can only be resolvable by elitism – that is to say by membership of a community that happens to have the power to enforce its preferences over outsiders. We thus begin to lose our notion of objectivity. In order to try to prevent such loss we might appeal to the idea of a market. A market provides the ultimate test for empiricists in that observable preferences are used to settle conflicts of value. If customers do not purchase a product then the producer goes out of business. New producers emerge to satisfy demand whether that be welfare, education or learning demand.

In order to institute a market it is necessary to have similar items for sale arranged alongside each other. The notion of an occupation's competence may be seen to provide the framework necessary to support the idea of a market in the provision of learning outcomes (Hyland 1994: 30). If it is possible to specify what is to count as competent performance in each occupational area then different 'providers' can compete to determine which can 'deliver' the 'competencies' at the cheapest rate. It would be wrong however to imagine that what has come to be referred to as 'the competence revolution' (Hyland 1994: 1) is driven by materialistic values alone.

The competence revolution may also be seen to have been driven by what might be regarded as liberal values such as those that are evident in the attempt to facilitate mobility of labour between states (OECD 1994) and to make professional activities more accessible to public scrutiny (Eraut 1994: 5). In addition some Union Leaders have seen the 'revolution' as a means of fixing their members conditions of service and salaries to national and internally recognised criteria (Marginson 1993: 153).

In Australia and the UK the notion of competence is broken down into 'elements' which are supposed to be 'evidenced' in terms of performance criteria. The requirement for objectivity is supposed then to be met through intersubjective observations of appropriate behaviour which is entirely in line with the epistemology of logical empiricism. Everyone wants competence, of course, but determining competence is not as straightforward as checking off someone's behaviour against performance criteria. The 'competence revolution' prompted much debate. David Carr (1993: 18) put one main difficulty with the competence revolution in the following way:

.... [it] makes the mistake of construing the moral evaluative and motivational aspects of education as separable from or additional to the technical and craft dimensions in a way that wholly distorts the logical, normative and psychological relations between them.

So for example it is hard to imagine a competent teacher who was not enthusiastic, honest and fair. A second problem with the competence revolution was recognised by Hager at the time. It is highly problematic to make the move from observing just some performances in some contexts to the ascription of a human quality or capability that appears to guarantee competent performance in all future contexts. So:

Valid assessment of attitudinal factors will also be assisted by longitudinal and multiple assessments that gather evidence of attitudes and values from a variety of sources. *(Hager & Beckett 1995: 20)*

While this is true, it does not avoid a problem inherent within the adoption of an empiricist epistemology which relates to context. Recall that the competence revolution was an attempt to make transparent what is involved in different sorts of occupation. It was an attempt to set out in one context this involvement to cover its application in a variety of future contexts. Application needs guidance and guidance needs further guidance until we end up in a regress ended only by the appointment of people with power to penalise those who do not apply the performance criteria in the ways that they do.

It can be argued, therefore, that what the competence revolution actually achieved was not to make occupational competence more transparent and its assessment more objective. Rather what it did was to shift the power of determining competence away from the practitioners themselves to their managers who were supposed to have the expertise to apply these criteria in an objective way. It was the supposed value-neutrality of the manager that became the guarantor of objectivity. Thus as Halliday (1990) argued consumerism, managerialism and vocationalism all cohered within an epistemology which privileged a mistaken notion of objectivity based around technical rationality.

There are significant differences in the ways that such shifts occurred in the UK and in Australia (Hager & Beckett 1995, Gonzi, Hager & Palmer 1994). In Australia managerialism did not gain such a hold. The power for judging competence within credentials remained within the professional practice. Moreover not all practitioners have managers. A more holistic view of competence prevailed. Nevertheless in both countries the language used to describe education and learning shifted. The learning as product and qualification with exchange value metaphors came to replace previous metaphors concerned with process and objectivity through judgment. This happened to the extent that it is now difficult, if not impossible, to avoid talking about education without reference to delivery of a product, and educational evaluation without reference to some means quantifiably of balancing causal effects against one another.

Gradually 'skills' came to replace 'competence' as the master concept for expressing that which people need to acquire. As we have seen, the English government department name was changed to include the term 'skills' to take account of this new emphasis. That has not prevented the appearance of 'cracks' in the suitability of this empiricist epistemology for the conditions of postmodernity. We have already mentioned the seemingly endless series of reforms to which VET was subjected, in an attempt to make the demand and supply side of the employment equation match. It could be surmised that policies to promote lifelong learning serve as further paper to cover the cracks.

'Skills talk' (Johnson 1998) in the 1990's tended to suggest that education was a kind of investment that is subject to cost benefit analysis in a similar way to any other kind of investment. This suggestion coheres with the discourse of globalisation because that discourse depends upon the rapid transmission of digitised capital. So there is a mutually reinforcing set of discourses and arguments trading on the idea that programmes of learning enable the development of skills which form investments for a prosperous future.

Others argue that the unpredictability of postmodernity has increasingly rendered conventional programmes of compulsory schooling less important, founded as such schooling often is on the so-called Enlightenment meta-narrative (Usher & Edwards 1994: 159). An idea derived from that meta-narrative persists, however, and this suggests that the world of work is changing so rapidly that individual prosperity and enhanced national economic performance can only be secured if the rate and frequency at which people learn changes rapidly too. The rewards of such performance are supposed by some governments to enable further and more widespread learning. This in turn encourages further improvements in economic performance and so on into a virtuous circle of investment in learning (Giddens 1998: 108) leading to increases in real, human and social capital (Bourdieu 1986). What is needed is a new term for investment in learning that takes account of the rapidly changing global environment within which economies and individuals must compete.

3. POLICY

The term 'lifelong learning' seems to capture that sense of dynamism. No longer should individuals expect to undergo a vocational preparation for a lifetime's employment. Rather they should expect to undergo a series of vocational preparations for a rapidly changing series of employments and they should be prepared to invest in such preparations themselves. It is worth noting that this capture does not dispense with logical empiricism nor technical rationality. Rather it attempts to harness these in order to cope with one aspect of postmodernity concerned with globalisation

   Typical accounts of the capture can be found in many places (Commission of the European Communities 1994 and 1997, OECD 1973, Delors 1996, Department for Education and Employment 1998, World Bank 1996). One such is given in the Green Paper *Opportunity Scotland* (Scottish Office 1998) and this paper is quoted as an exemplar of the genre.

> Lifelong Learning is a feature of modern life and will continue to be so. Change is everywhere and we need to learn to cope with it in different aspects of our lives. Jobs are changing with continually developing technology and pressures to keep up with foreign competitors. Daily life is changing with faster communications and more technology in our homes. ... *(Scottish Office 1998: 4)*

Here interest in lifelong learning is coupled with the belief that, in the midst of change, there is a need to

> ..... update continually the skills of the workforce and better equip people to manage their own future. ... people at all levels need to use learning opportunities to keep pace in the jobs market and to ensure that Scotland is equipped to compete in the global economy. *(Scottish Office 1998: 4)*

But how do people at all levels use learning opportunities to keep pace in the jobs market? Only it seems by investing in their own skill development. The paper goes on:

> People who update their skills and learn new ones will get better paid jobs and achieve more success in their chosen fields of work. *(Scottish Office 1998: 28)*

But of course they do not choose their fields of work in this presumed rapidly changing jobs market, their fields of work are chosen for them by economic considerations beyond their control. The discourse of investment in skills is retained however through the idea that there are core and transferable skills.

> It is clear that Scotland needs a workforce which is highly proficient in both core transferable skills and specialised sector based skills. *(Scottish Office 1998: 28)*

This is not the place to rehearse the by now familiar arguments against the idea that there are core transferable skills, nor that industrial sector based skills are any less transferable than any other sort (Jonathan 1987, Johnson 1998). Suffice to say that the metaphor of a vocational product is sustained through the idea that skills may only be acquired through some sorts of investment. It seems however that some Scots are not convinced by these ideas.

> Involving adults in lifelong learning is our greatest challenge. ... Some people perceive difficulties and barriers relating to their personal circumstances or previous low attainment at school. Others simply never think about learning at all. *(Scottish Office 1998: 8)*

Are these people ignorant and/or misguided or is there something wrong with the conception of lifelong learning presented in the Green Paper? In Britain, at any rate, there is a degree of uncritical acceptance of this conception. Although as Coffield notes:

> Behind the high flown rhetoric, lifelong learning, the learning society and the learning organisation are all being propounded to induce individuals to become more or less willing participants in learning for life and to bear an increasing proportion of the costs of such learning. *(Coffield 1998: 11)*

He goes on to argue that lifelong learning can be seen as the latest form of social control. If he is right then it is hardly surprising that people resist such control even though they might be induced to learn in approved ways through schemes such as Inn tuition, cybercentres and electronic villages (Chisholm 1997: 45). These are all British government-funded schemes designed to encourage people, who are said to be excluded, to learn formally. None of these schemes are cheap. They all involve generally well-paid professionals trying to enrol generally less well-paid people into formal learning.

Braverman (1976) argues that one of the main purposes of formal education is to provide many thousands of jobs for generally middle class people supposedly training working class people for jobs for which training is not really required. It is not necessary to concur entirely with Braverman to question whether money is well spent on schemes such as the above. Nor is it necessary to keep a straight face when reading that the criteria for successful completion of a Scottish National

Vocational Qualification in cleaning includes the ability to distinguish in writing between dirt and dust (Scottish Qualifications Authority 1997). It is, however, necessary to question whether much current rhetoric of lifelong learning serves to reinforce an instrumentalist conception of education in which learning is seen as the acquisition of qualities of dubious value which are then supposed to serve as the means to fulfil someone else's aims.

4. GLOBALISATION

One way of challenging such an instrumentalist conception is to question the economic argument based on globalisation that is often put in support of it. It seems obvious that transnational corporations will seek to increase their profitability by relocating to those parts of the world where the rate of return on their investment is maximised. The production and consumption of goods and services is becoming increasingly globalised. Capital now flows round the world almost instantaneously, in digital form without regard for national boundaries. Information too flows round the world via the Internet. Even though there is a reaction against it, there is an increasing homogeneity in global culture towards such institutions as fast food outlets, supermarkets and shopping malls. As a result of these trends there is a tendency to discuss globalisation as if it was something new and all embracing. Yet all of these trends, except for the digitalisation of information and capital, were features of colonial expansion in the late 19th century too.

Certainly it is now easier and cheaper to move materials, people and information around the globe than ever it was. This means that there is no longer such a competitive advantage to be near human, physical or economic resources of any kind. Therefore it is easy to appreciate the argument that the key to economic advantage must be the value that can be added to these resources and the assumption that more skilled people are best able to add value. Hence increasing investment in education and training are seen as the only hope for economically advantaged nations to maintain that advantage and less advantaged nations to improve (Field 1998: 10).

One problem with such a strategy is obvious. If every nation, group of nations or individuals adopt it, then there will be no competitive advantage, merely better educated or trained people engaged in an ever-increasing spiral of ingenious schemes to manufacture demand and then satisfy it. A further problem is that it neglects the importance of traditional, though perhaps unglamorous, forms of work to many areas of economic life. Yet another problem with this strategy is that it assumes that those possessing most knowledge or skills should be paid to educate those having less knowledge and skills (Macrae, Maguire & Ball 1997: 500). Within the discourse of rapid change through globalisation however, such skills and knowledge must be obsolescent.

What is going wrong with this argument is something to which Hartley (1998) among others has drawn attention. There is a constant tension between government attempts to control learning and cultural forces that make such control counter-productive. For example at a time in which post-fordist modes of organising industrial and commercial activity suggest that there is a need for flexible working practice, some governments pre-specify through national curricula what individuals should be able to do long before those individuals ever have to perform in the way specified. It is easy to see why this mistake might be made. First, it gives an illusion of control, as if national governments could anticipate the effects of global capitalism and local contingency to plan to fill the job vacancies that are going to arise in the future. Second, the strategy involves a minimal shift in thinking and practice from what has become conventional within formal education. Nevertheless, if the argument of this chapter is correct, the mistake should be rectified on economic grounds alone. That is quite apart from the dire social and personal consequences of trying to enforce the view that learning should be a preparation for work or life, when for many people it turns out to be no such thing.

5. CONSEQUENCES

There is an increasing body of literature, often based on Foucault's (1977) work, that suggests that formal education might be turning into a normalising induction into procedures of surveillance and control (Falk 1998). Students are compelled to go through this induction in order to have a chance of earning a living and securing an identity in an increasingly fragmented society. If they fail at school then the increasing formalisation of what was previously informal through schemes such as the accreditation of prior learning and those listed above maintains the normalising process into a form of social control (Edwards 1997, Hargreaves 1997, Usher & Edwards 1994). It is easy to see how policies to promote lifelong learning are mere extensions to this normalising process. The process may be seen to be all the more coercive because now all the resources of people's private lives may be brought under the control of the State

In the developed world, Hillage *et al.* (2000: 6) report that there is a shift in government thinking coming about as it realised that:

..... less formal learning opportunities [are] a way of encouraging people alienated through school or other learning experiences to engage in learning activities [and, hence, there is] ... recognition of the important role informal learning can play in contributing to community development and regeneration.

Such alienation might be explained through the quality and quantity of formal education that is provided, but it could also be explained through a putative lack of interest in the types of learning that are formally encouraged. As it is impossible for informal learning to take place without some degree of interest in what is learnt, it is hardly surprising that Governments would see informal learning as a means of overcoming alienation brought about through lack of interest of what is on offer in formal educational institutions.

It is perhaps a mistake to generalise too readily here. Rather than to suggest that there is general alienation from all kinds of learning, it might be preferable to argue that, while some people are uninterested in learning those things typically on offer in schools, they are nevertheless fully engaged in learning other things. A major study of student literacy levels within British Further Education has found that students whose levels of literacy as measured within further education appeared low, actually had quite high levels when measured outside of formal contexts. (For more on this research project see Edwards & Smith 2005 and http://www.lancs.ac.uk/lflfe/publications/publications.htm). This prompts a series of questions concerned with precisely why such measurements might differ and why one might be preferred. For Governments concerned with accountability, the measurement of participation rates in learning is deeply problematic, however, because estimates of participation levels depend upon a separation of learning from doing that is not plausible in all contexts, and certainly not in informal contexts. An emphasis on participation suggests that it is participation in formal learning that is important.

Hillage *et al.* (2000: 97) conclude their study with the claim that 'there remains a significant group of non learners' as if this were an obvious problem. To be sure it is widely accepted that the more formal education that an individual participates in, the more likely it is that that individual will continue to participate. Yet in a comparative study, Field and Spence (2000:32) found that low levels of participation in formal education and training may also mean that people have found that informal learning is a better way of achieving the goals they set themselves. They suggest that "the existence of networks, norms and levels of trust that promote collective action between members of a given social grouping" – characterised as social capital – may influence both what is acceptable in terms of participation in formal learning after school, but also what is desirable in that informal learning is cheaper, less hierarchical and promotes social cohesion.

According to Rees *et al.* (1997:11):

> Those who failed at school often come to see post school learning of all kinds as irrelevant to their needs and capabilities. Hence not only is participation in further, higher and continuing education not perceived to be a realistic possibility, but also work based learning is viewed as unnecessary too.

Yet it is not as if these people have stopped learning. Rather as Eraut (1997) found, large amounts of learning arise informally. Hence a reassessment of lifelong learning as being exclusively concerned with target setting, formal courses and qualifications is required. Yet governments do not seem overly concerned to conduct such a reassessment, leading to the suspicion, as Coffield (1998) argues, that the prevailing orthodoxy within the UK actually serves to promote a model of lifelong learning as social control. Foucault (1977) is perhaps our best guide here.

In *Discipline and Punish: the birth of the prison,* Foucault (1977) argues that formal educational institutions share with such instuitions as hospitals, prisons and asylums, the function of enculturating individuals into certain ways of doing things that are regarded as normal. Enculturation here is not so much concerned innocuously with social practices that are obvious, but into aspects of social practice that enable the means of the subject's government and control. Whereas once it was acceptable to discipline and punish overtly through public torture and execution of the deviant member of society on behalf of a sovereign power, now these methods of discipline and punishment are not acceptable. In their place, learners may be regarded as deviants in the sense that they cannot function as accomplished practitioners. Moreover they may be required to attend institutions in order to remedy their deviance and make them properly functioning members of society. Through such requirements they are normalised into such activities as responding to bells which signify the end of a lesson, remaining quiet when they are told, accepting that they will be punished in some way when they transgress, accepting the judicial verdicts of their peers in this process, accepting that they must occupy a particular space at a certain time and so on. They come not so much to be enculturated into the practices themselves, but into a selection of activities which enable them to accept that they will be controlled in other social practices – at work for example. Whereas informal enculturation may be seen to pay attention to a practical tradition within which control does not feature strongly, formal learning may be seen to ignore that tradition in favour of a reification of practices that enables control.

A model is provided by the panopticon. In a panopticon the inmates of a prison can be observed at all times to check that they are behaving normally, but the prisoners cannot tell whether at any time they are under observation nor by whom. Hence the panopticon is a very efficient means of maintaining control. It is the possibility that someone might be watching and that they have the power to punish deviant behaviour that provides the panopticon with its power. Within formal learning the possibilities of panopticon power are formidable. Not only are learners observed as they learn but they are regularly examined and selected. Moreover the private life of the learner can be rendered publicly visible through progressive teaching methods. The specification of curriculum products that was described earlier leads learners to conceptualise themselves as consumers. While many learners accept a transmission model of learning as normal and succeed in achieving the products through success in examination, others do not. They fail to be engaged by the formal learning curriculum. For these deviants, more progressive teaching methods are offered. They are encouraged to 'confess' what they are really interested in and the power of confession is used to re-enter them into the normalising process. Perhaps now they wontedly pursue their interest, under the supervision of a skilled teacher able to harness those interests to the prescribed curriculum. All the time, however, they become enculturated to activities that will serve the interests of others. If all this fails, then programmes of further and higher education are offered, and if those fail then there is always lifelong learning. Just as the prison system may be seen to reform criminals into docile and obedient workers, so too policies to promote lifelong learning may be seen to reform the residual deviants in a more economic way than prison. Or so the story goes. Usher and Edwards (1994) offer a compelling account of this story concerning the relationship between Foucault's work and post-compulsory education.

It would be wrong to conceive a Foucauldian notion of power as hierarchical. While it is true that a panopticon is hierarchically controlled, its power comes from the fact that the inmates can observe each other and no one knows who is reporting what to who nor what they will believe. Power thus circulates around the activities that the inmates undertake. At any time, however, examination may take place through which the inmates may be tested, rewarded or punished according to the norms that are established 'objectively'. And there is not just one sort of examination, there are many and especially so within possibilities for lifelong learning. Wain (2004: 285) refers to a Foucauldian account of learning as the 'panopticon learning society'. He goes on:

> Panopticon power is not however the only kind the modern state has developed to render its citizens more governable ... efficient government is obtained as much, if not more, by encouraging a discourse to proliferate as by repressing it.

A panopticon learning society would be an example of what Foucault calls 'a technology of domination'. It works by classifying learners according to some scheme which is legitimised through social scientific theory. It is hard for the present work to avoid the charge that it is part of such theory. Essentially a body of theory has built up around learning which serves to legitimise the idea that there are 'experts' within it. There are technical terms used which make up professional discourse within which it is possible to make sense of the idea that some theories of informal learning are preferable to others. For Foucault (1980), a discourse is a body of knowledge which fabricates what is perceived to be real by naming and signifying experience in particular ways. This allows the compartmentalisation and evaluation of different aspects of experience rendering them amenable to interventions of one kind or another. Discourse and power therefore go together. Power is not top down so much as networked. Power is enmeshed with discipline and regulation. Discourse comprises an ensemble of practices that involve both representations and action. The calculated supervision and administration of people may be termed governmentality. Strategies of resistance themselves form capillaries of power that go to support regimes of truth. If governmentality is part of an exercise of power then there will be resistance to it. Resistance will involve counter discourse but both discourse and counter discourse will appeal to some regime of truth in order to legitimise their representations. There is no neutral vantage point from which to critique policy – the vantage point itself will be caught up in the object of critique. As Edwards et al. (2004) put it:

> Critics as well as policy makers are mongers in rhetoric.

Mongering can be highlighted and challenged. Foucault helps us to unmask these technologies of domination to show how the notion of practice is not as innocent as it might seem, but, rather, how it comes loaded with power relations. Hence enculturation into social practices is not so straightforward either. Even more problematic from a Foucauldian perspective is individuation. The idea that there could be a self that is formed in such a way that it comes to have individual autonomy has pervaded liberal educational thought for some time. Foucault's work radically challenges such an idea as Marshall (1996), Olssen (1999) and others have shown. In particular the idea that there might be an 'inner self' to be formed in some way is deeply problematic. Foucault shows how such an idea originates through the religious idea of confession, but also how selves are formed anew through practical engagement.

On the face of it such a conception of self and, later, the notion of 'care for the self' fit well into the idea of a learning society. It is attractive to think of people forming their identity on a continuous basis, rather than according to the idea that they achieve a state of rational autonomy which then enables them to function effectively as lifelong learners. The idea that there is a self to be discovered forms the basis of a technology of self which makes citizens more governable. In essence citizens learn to govern themselves through an appropriate moral code which they are encouraged to adopt through looking deep into themselves for appropriate guidance on what they should do.

To put this in a different way, what a Foucauldian reading of formal learning does is to highlight the way that practical traditions have become lost or disguised. In their place certain background activities have come to the fore to enable governmentality.

It is not necessary to follow Foucault in all details to see the importance of his work. Nor is it necessary to see everything as a conspiracy theory in order to see how what Wain (2004) calls 'the politics of suspicion' shed light on the increasing formalisation of what was previously informal through the idea of a learning society. Foucault shows us that it is naïve to envisage a learning society free from power where knowledge is available to all on an equitable and transparent basis. It is naïve to imagine that knowledge can then be used to guide practice in a rational way and that people's private lives can be utilised to make their learning more efficient. As Wain (20004: 314) puts it:

> Foucault cautions us against blanket optimistic messages like Dewey's that living together educates. While insisting that living together is living relationships of power, he reminds us that not all agendas of power are agendas of education: many are agendas of domination, suppression or manipulation and that we should approach them all, all learning agendas, with care and suspicion.

And so we should. We are all now familiar with the video cameras, the speed traps, the mobile phone records, and so on, that enable panopticon surveillance of our lives. We should be suspicious of any attempts made on behalf of the system world to invade the life world (Habermas 1987) in the interests of anything sounding good like lifelong learning. We are aware of the ease with which governments have used the incidence of terrorist attacks to limit our personal freedoms and to invade still more aspects of what was previously regarded as our private lives. It is attractive therefore to champion that cause of informal learning which seems resistant to some of these unattractive trends. Caution is needed in such championing however. As we explained earlier, there is no logical reason why informal learning could not become a cheap panopticon. No need to pay teachers when people could learn themselves under the watchful gaze of the administrator carefully monitoring the books and equipment they borrow and the groups they join. Perhaps those lacking in confidence could be given a credential to mark their achievement in such learning. In the exemplar given below we note the extent to which what was previously regarded as the outcome of informal learning has been credentialised.

6. EXEMPLARS

6.1 Formalising the Informal

We have already noted the trend towards credentialism (Collins 1979) in the supposed interests of the economy. What is perhaps new is the way that increased credentialism has also been driven by a desire for social inclusion. The following are taken from the Scottish Qualification Authority (SQA) catalogue of modules (available from www.sqa.org.uk). Similar examples can be found in New South Wales (see http://www.tafensw.edu.au). In what follows the titles of the so-called units and modules are underlined and commentary is given in italics. We aim to illustrate the Foucauldian notions of normalisation, surveillance and control through our commentary. For us these units and modules illustrate nicely the mistake that we argue is currently being made.

Basic communication in a familiar setting
This unit is designed principally for candidates developing basic skills in a supported learning environment. The unit focuses on the following basic aspects of effective communication in a familiar setting; carrying out dialogue on a one-to-one basis, and recognising information signs, for example, EXIT sign or floor numbers in Braille. Candidates should be allowed to use their normal mode of communication while undertaking this unit.

Outcome
Communicate effectively at a basic level in a familiar setting.

Performance criteria

(a)   Responds effectively to a communication from another person.
(b)   Delivers effectively a communication to another person.
(c)   Identifies two information signs associated with the familiar setting.

Associated with the chosen setting, there will be information signs with words and/or symbols which are understood and used frequently by the public. These signs may include:

   –   bus stop
   –   pedestrian crossing

- emergency exit
- entrance
- toilets.

Commentary:
Plainly this unit is intended only for certain types of people and those people are unlikely to be able readily to access the unit descriptor which is not available in Braille for example. We may wonder what purpose it serves other than as part of a process of normalisation so that all can be said to be included. What the student here is being included within and what is likely to be left unnoticed by her and her no doubt well-intentioned instructor are abstractions of practice. She is to be included within a society in which only some have access to and control of the application of criteria by which her normality can be determined. Moreover it is the expert who determines the contexts that are important to her. She learns that quantification is important – just two signs are to be identified for normality. After all – no one is perfect! She 'delivers' a communication in the interests of performativity and her response is judged 'effective' by a stranger.

Basic health care needs
This module is designed to help the student to develop an awareness of the importance of living in a healthy environment and the basic skills required to promote personal health and wellbeing.

Outcomes

1. Describe the principles of basic health care in the home and their application in daily life.
2. Assist with promoting recovery from minor illness or injury.

Commentary:
The prevalence of technical rationality is apparent here. It is supposed that once the principles can be described then they can be applied or at least their application can be described. Nothing in practice is left to chance. It can be described and after all, the student can always assist in practice or at least it is hard to know what they could do to hinder recovery so long as they have normal human sensibilities. Adequate description is supposed to be the key to successful practice.

Dealing with money
This module is designed to develop basic competence in handling money in everyday situations.

Outcomes

1. Pay for goods and services;
2. Receive payment for goods and services;
3. Use a range of banking services;
4. Budget income and expenditure.

Commentary:
This module appears to make money handling transparent. Arguably however it is when things go wrong that an ability to deal with money is best tested. There is no unit on seeking legal redress when one is short-changed.

Dealing with holiday problem situations
This unit will prepare the candidate for situations where things can go wrong before, during and after the holiday and how to cope calmly and effectively with them. It should also help them to develop the skills necessary to interact effectively with those who work in the travel and tourism industry.

Commentary:
Presumably those who work in the travel and tourism industry or at least those involved with the so-called package holiday are not inclined to pay compensation to those who experience problems. It is one thing to interact – quite another to gain compensation. In any case at what stage did it become normal formally to learn how to go on holiday with the expectation that problems will arise? It is tempting to comment that there is something desperate about this unit. It is desperate in the sense that there is nothing subtle about the normalising process. All aspects of life are to be brought under the normalising gaze.

Finding and keeping a job
Developing the competence necessary to demonstrate the basic skills and knowledge required to find a job and the interpersonal skills required to obtain and keep a job.

Outcomes

1. Identify the major sources of information and support in job finding;
2. approach employers about jobs;
3. undergo a job interview;
4. identify basic job keeping skills.

Commentary:
The emphasis here is all on the potential employee. There is no equivalent module for the employer. The module reinforces a power imbalance within the workplace so that the employee learns that if she loses her job it is her fault. She lacks the

required skills and must retake the module so that it does not happen again. Throughout these exemplars the emphasis is on potential defects in the student and not the structure within which she is supposed to work.

Participating in leisure time activities
This module is designed to develop personal and social skills through participation in a range of leisure time activities.

Outcomes

1. Identify a limited range of leisure activities;
2. participate in a limited range of leisure activities;
3. use interpersonal skills when participating in leisure activities.

Commentary:
Formal learning is now necessary for some people to participate in leisure! This is an exemplary instance of the increasing colonisation of the lifeworld. In the following example, such learning is also necessary to avoid being dirty or smelling!

Personal Care
Enhancing personal image and self confidence for employment and/or social interaction through the application of standard hygienic practices.

Outcomes

1. Demonstrate acceptable standards of personal hygiene.
2. Identify acceptable modes of dress for formal, informal and professional use.

6.2 Learning to Survive

In this exemplar we illustrate some of the dangers associated with our main thesis. All too easily, informal learning could become a cheap panopticon. The very opportunities for informal learning are all too easily closed down by those given the formal responsibility to enable others to learn informally. We are concerned here particularly with what is termed community education. Our subject, Anna, describes how she and her friends learn informally how to manipulate the social security system to their advantage. She then goes on to explain how such learning is less possible now that she has become a community worker, even though such learning would be highly advantageous to members of her community. The professionalisation of practice does not encourage this for good reason. Our point is not to take sides in a debate about the ways that social security benefits are administered. Rather by analogy we seek to illustrate some risks in making the argument in favour of informal learning. What was previously open becomes closed. Attempts to encourage informal learning by professionals may actually close down the possibility of such learning.

Anna feels that it is important to learn informally throughout life. She says "it has a better impact on you, a stronger impact because you're forced to, you know it's a survival thing, if you don't learn you don't survive, usually it's not as serious as that, but you do have that kind of impression". Anna became pregnant at 16 when her "learning curve really shot up". She married the father with whom she had another baby but unfortunately they split up after the birth. It was at this time she moved to the village where she now lives and works. At that time, as now, there were many single mothers in the same situation as her. They used to travel together to a nearby town to pick up their social security benefits, but when the bus fare increased they all decided to walk. One would stay at home to watch the children and the others would walk together. Anna says "it was like a team effort, it was brilliant". Moreover the team members shared their experiences of how to claim, when to claim, what to say to the officials and so on. They learned, it could be said the practice of social security claims handling and they became experts in it. While it might be imagined that systems of social security are means of increased surveillance and control of those regarded as deviant, such systems could be manipulated by those in the know, at least they could back then to some extent. When her two children were still relatively young, Anna met another man who moved in with her and eventually she had her third child. However he had Motor Neurone Disease and died, leaving Anna grieving with no money to support herself or her children. She faced the social security system again. This time, she says "things were much tighter … I really found it difficult then to go back to getting a lot less…there was so many changes in the benefit system … I was on my own now .. and I couldn't hack it … I said I need a job I can't cope with this".

She got a job in a restaurant in a motorway service area. She participated in some job training, but was bored as she saw most of it as simply "common sense". She is well aware of her predicament and that of those like her. She explains that these systems "social security, job training and the like are all designed to control you. … You learn to duck and weave. … You learn a lot just by bringing up your own children, for example, when to help them and when to let them figure things out and learn for themselves. … That's something you wouldn't learn at college – you don't, you don't pick up those kind of instincts, when to back off and when to be there and when to defend them and when to shut up. … It's all those kind of things and it's a fine balance and getting it right is really difficult. … Don't ask me how you know, you just have a rough idea of when you step in and when to step back. If you get it wrong then you just have to try again. … Mastering the social security system is like that – you need to judge just how far to push it, when to shut up, when to challenge … of course it helps if there's a group of you all on the same side". This is an example of what we call making judgments with ever increasing contextual sensitivity and this view of informal learning is as applicable to mastering the social security system as it is to learning how to build a boat.

As previously mentioned, Anna now works for a Community Group. She explains that "the idea of the community group is to get things going and increase participation in the village, whether it is the young ones, old ones, any kind of age group". When pressed Anna explained that while her job is supposed to be about getting people to accept their lot, she sees it more as an attempt to get people to see beyond their lot. "For me now, survival well it's about getting qualifications really, and I try to encourage the youngsters to stick in there and get some".

Anna left school at 16, and although she comments that she had "good enough O levels", she says that she had "no inclination to stay on" to pursue more formal qualifications at that time. However, she went back to college in 1999 to do an HNC, followed by an HND, then finally a degree in Psychology. While Anna feels that informal learning often taught her more throughout her life, one of the main benefits of formal learning is that it "gives you a bit of prestige". She says "anybody could do what I'm doing and what I have done, but now you need a degree before you're allowed to do it".

Here we see recognition of what has been said before about academic drift and the credential society. She feels that her skills haven't increased substantially as a result of her degrees as many skills had already been built up in an informal basis within a real context. She says "it was just a bit of paper and a bit of extra reading at the end of the day". Anna feels that there are many people who have built up skills on an informal basis, but these skills are not recognised. "I think it's quite shocking that the people without formal education don't get the chance to show or to use the skills that they do have to their full, because there's hundreds of them who didn't take the opportunities when they were at the school, because it just didn't interest them and they don't have the time or the ability or the will to go back, or even the confidence to go back". We could have pressed Anna on the way that her job actually discourages the kind of community that previously she had so much admired and benefited from. We chose not to do this for there would have been no practical point, and we think our theoretical points have been adequately illustrated.

We began this chapter by recalling how only a few years ago, researchers had missed the significance of informal learning for notions of lifelong learning and learning societies. We have tried to explain how this came about through a deep seated empiricism and dualist metaphysics that pervaded discourse in this area. We tried to show how the consequences of this deep-seatedness led policy makers into a formal cul de sac, and we concluded by outlining some of the unattractive features of this cul de sac. At the same time we have highlighted some of the risks involved in writing a book such as this, which attempts to redress a balance in favour of the informal. Put simply, it could encourage yet more colonisation of the lifeworld and yet more formalising of the informal. We begin the next chapter by looking more closely at what such colonisation might involve and what sense can be made of the notion of a private life in postmodernity.

CHAPTER FOUR

OPPORTUNITY AND CONTINGENCY

In the Introduction we described ourselves as working within a liberal humanist theoretical framework. A commonly accepted feature of such a framework is that it is based on a separation of public and private spheres. Put simply people may do as they like in private so long as they do no harm to others. The existence of a public sphere is commonly supposed to enable objective decision making through the temporary suspension of private interests in favour of some notion of a common good. As we illustrated in the previous chapter an imbalance towards formal learning within lifelong learning leads to increasing invasion of what was previously considered to be private by the 'system world' (Habermas 1987). We concluded that chapter with an outline of what lifelong learning is likely to become if that imbalance continues and if the epistemological and metaphysical assumptions upon which the imbalance is based remain unchallenged.

In this chapter we argue that the notions of public and private are nothing like so clear as might be imagined. Nor, therefore, is it clear precisely how a balance in learning could be shifted from what might be imagined as the public formal sphere to the informal private sphere. While there is an essential contingency involved in the determination of opportunities for informal learning, we argue that such opportunities can be grasped with increasing degrees of sophistication by good informal learners. Good informal learners not only know how to learn but also what to learn. Indeed we see method as subservient to content. Learning how to learn is not best conceived as a technique to be applied, but as an appropriate selection of what to learn in a context that will enable future learning of what is presumed worthwhile. On this view the problem of curriculum, which has troubled formal curriculum designers, is equally applicable to informal learning. Moreover what is learnt formally is affected by what is learnt informally and vice versa.

It is commonly supposed that the formal curriculum may be, or at least ought to be, determined according to some notion of public interest or common good, whereas private interest may determine what is learnt informally. Rawls (1971) for example puts justice to the fore in the determination of what ought to be done in the public interest and in the interest of personal freedom. In our view this supposition cannot be entirely correct. For us there are similar guides to what should be learnt both formally and informally, which we develop in future chapters. Clarification of the concepts of public and private is therefore crucial to our argument and we attempt such clarification in this chapter. We argue that the meanings of these concepts are context dependent and that it is not possible to set out criteria to distinguish between them once and for all. Rather we modify Rawls' (1993) notion of an overlapping consensus to take account of this contextuality. Put simply, we argue that what is in the public sphere shifts according to collective interests that are themselves sensitive to the many different ways that networks are formed and reformed. In this we are influenced by Castells (1996, 1997, 1998). The picture that emerges from his accounts is of society in its widest international sense comprised of an overlapping series of networks, sharing some things in common but not all things in common. According to this picture, opportunities for learning depend crucially on the networks within which people are situated. Institutions for formal learning can provide access to some of these networks, but such access is not necessarily, nor even likely, to be most advantageous for many people.

Of course the idea of a networked society within which the concepts of public and private are fluid, makes the work of national governments difficult. Hence, it is easy to see why governments might be tempted increasingly to formalise opportunities for learning. According to the argument presented in this chapter however, the growth of a networked society is likely to continue. What is needed, and what we begin to outline in the next chapter, is a new account of learning that pays attention to the inherent contextuality within a network society. The idea that there is just one master concept such as justice that may be used to determine curriculum content in the public sphere is no longer appropriate.

1. PUBLIC AND PRIVATE

We begin with Habermas (1989: 47), who argues that the separation of public from private was crucial for there to be a possibility for rational argumentation in the public sphere. Later he came to see that such a separation was not only impossible in an age in which the State increasingly took responsibility for such things as the education of the young, child protection within families, and so on, but also that the separation was undesirable. He (1992) also came to acknowledge that there was not one public sphere within which rational debate might take place, but several. It was mistaken to suggest that the public was more valuable than the private or *vice versa*. In this he came to align himself with Dewey (1927: 13) who wrote:

> The distinction between private and public is thus in no sense equivalent to the distinction between individual and social, even if we suppose that the latter distinction has a definite meaning. Many private acts are social ......

He goes on:

> There is therefore no necessary connection between the private character of an act and its non-social or anti-social character ......

And concludes:

> ..... the argument has not carried us far, but at least it has warned us against identifying the community and its interests with the state or the politically organised community.

This is significant for our argument. However much it might be convenient to claim that publicly provided formal learning is somehow necessarily in the community interest, that claim must be false. Equally, however much as it might be convenient to claim that informal learning in private cannot be in the community interest, that claim is false. Indeed the very idea that there is but one public is false. Rather there are a variety of forms of association. These are more or less stable over time, they cut across each other to some extent, as for example with people of different racial groupings who join together for the sake of some interest or pastime. It cannot be assumed that they share the same overall goals or values. Nevertheless they can co-operate in the interest of some shared project, however temporary that might be.

Across the world, ensuring that children and increasingly adults spend some time in formal educational institutions is considered to be both in the public and private interest. Moreover individual interest in learning depends upon there being some public social practices into which learners can be initiated. Yet, as we have argued, the increasing formalisation of what was previously informal learning for adults is not obviously a good thing. Moreover what is learnt informally crucially affects how well formal learning proceeds. What is learnt informally is contingent upon the opportunities people have and the way that they contextualise those opportunities.

This account of learning runs counter to a dominant view of rationality and reasonableness that has come to underpin educational policy. Roughly this view is based on the idea that what is intended to be achieved through learning must be set out in advance of learning, along with the rules that govern the achievement. An example of this has already been given in the previous chapter. There we argued that learning is much more opportunistic than policy would suggest. We also argue that learners increasingly recognise this, and that the dominant view of rationality and reasonableness as an underpinning of educational policy is no longer appropriate to the conditions of late modernity.

The meanings of public and private are contested and historically situated (e.g., see Elias 1982). Habermas (1989) sees the association of individuals who join together in community as enabling the possibility of rational critical debate. This serves as a counter to the illegitimate use of power by individuals. He sees formal education centrally concerned with fostering the conditions for such debate, yet he laments that rational critical debate is being replaced by the world of the mass media, which provides a cheap and powerful way of manipulating and creating senses of community where none in reality exists. In this way consensus can be manufactured, even though such consensus very often is formed around trivial issues such as commonly watched television programmes. Against such a powerful and cheap way of communication and engendering a sense of shared interests, formal educational institutions seem bound to fail.

As a result of this replacement, there is a crisis in the public sphere which manifests itself in part by the widespread retreat from politics which we see in increasing voter apathy during political elections. At the same time we see massive voter interest in such programmes as 'Big Brother' which now has a massive global presence. Putnam's term, 'bowling alone' (1995) has wider applicability than the United States. There is a declining capacity to form new and lasting associations and a widespread belief that wide ranging consensus is no longer possible. This capacity can be seen as fundamental to the reduction of trust upon which 'social capital' depends (Fukuyama 1995). What contemporary writers often refer to as the "new individualism" (Giddens 1998) is displacing the public realm, and even coming to construct that realm.

Within formal educational institutions, for example, we see a proliferation of agencies concerned with self-esteem, personal development plans, guidance, counselling and consumer choice. Such agencies have pretensions to control informal learning too, as we have seen. Yet it has not been possible entirely to clear such institutions of the remnants of a public interest. Paradoxically, participation in the work of these agencies has not been left to individual choice, but has become part of the requirements for participation in learning activities of many kinds. Cynically, we may speculate that that is because these agencies need something to develop, guide and choose from. Alternatively, we may speculate that these agencies represent a last desperate attempt to hold on to some notion of public interest guiding private learning and an associated view of what is rational and reasonable.

A further interpretation is provided by Furedi (2004: 22), who argues that the new individualism is so widespread that it constitutes a 'therapeutic culture' and that this culture is readily appropriated for the purposes of social control. According to this interpretation we should not be surprised at increasing government interest in formalising what was previously informal. As Furedi puts it:

> Therapeutic Culture is often characterised as a retreat to the inner world of the self. In fact the orientation to the self has the paradoxical effect of opening up the sphere of private life to therapeutic management.

According to Furedi (2004: 95), political authority has embraced therapeutics because 'it helps governments forge points of contact with an otherwise fragmented public' and 'provides authorities with a potentially important instrument of social control'. Informal learning, conceived as learning for its own sake without regard to rewards and punishments, end points and methods, evades such control. Small wonder then that learning authorities might want to bring it within their control through mechanisms such as the ones outlined above. There is a danger in doing this. The techniques of therapeutic control can free learners from any requirement to exercise critical judgement or accept moral responsibility for their actions.

More optimistically, we may speculate that these therapeutic techniques support a tradition that holds that through rational critical debate, people with differing substantive values can live together and work out collectively the kind of policies that should be set to guide them. It seems obvious that policies for formal learning should be guided by publicly endorsed values. Yet, while that may appear to be obvious, it is not likely that such public endorsement could be formalised or widespread. Rather substantive values cannot obviously be separated from those modes of reasoning and forms of understanding that are themselves subject to constant revision in the light of conversations that people have with one another.

Substantive values are always revisable and so the notion of publicly endorsed values guiding formal learning is deeply problematic. Yet, as we have seen, liberal democratic governments across the western world have sought to guide with ever increasing specificity not only what people should learn, but also how they should learn.

In common usage, liberalism embodies the idea that individuals should be free to do as they please providing their actions do no harm to others. The state therefore may only limit an individual's right to self-determination in so far as there is agreement among all citizens about what is harmful to others. On this view the state has a legitimate interest in encouraging three aims through public education:

- to enable agreement to be reached on what is harmful to others;
- to encourage people to avoid doing such harm; and
- to encourage individuals to realise their potential for self determination.

Some liberal educators of a neutralist persuasion have interpreted this latter aim to mean that above all else learners should become personally autonomous. Autonomy enables them to reason in a way that is disengaged from their immediate interests and from what others tell them should be their interests. Autonomy is also supposed to enable them to attain a level of individuation that transcends the particular effects of enculturation (Wain 2004: 138). According to this interpretation, people should learn to enable the determination of what actually does conduce to human harm and what each person should do in the light of that knowledge. We argue that this form of neutralist liberalism is mistaken.

For one thing, the matter of what actually does conduce to human harm either collectively or individually is not at all straightforward. For example Bohman (1995: 258) points out that there are many substantive cases where what is good for all (less pollution for example) is not what is good for each (cheap gasoline). In addition there are many other substantive cases where what is good for one of us (progressive taxation) is not good for others (high earners). Moreover, the idea that substantive values could be publicly endorsed presupposes the notion of public reason, since there are plainly some substantive values that will be the subject of prolonged controversy. Again, as Bohman (1995) points out, there is not one accepted form of public reasoning. Rather there are many modes of public reasoning and those modes shift dynamically, as people try to convince each other that their moral convictions are worthy of attention.

That means that public endorsement of values to guide formal learning is much more temporary and fragile than would be necessary for the formulation of a statement of agreed values that could guide either educational or societal development. While any attempt to educate will involve the communication of some values over others, it is a mistake to extrapolate from this and claim that the state or states must have validated those values in some way. Nevertheless it is clear that an education for liberalism must go beyond a damaging and ultimately futile individualism to pay some regard for the common good.

Liberal educators typically distrust what Bailey (1984: 20) calls 'the tyranny of the present and particular'. The notion of personal autonomy captures a sense of the desirability of freedom from habit and tradition, as if traditions were obviously restrictive and as if habitual behaviour was unintelligent. For many liberal educators it is as if people through reasoning could disengage themselves from those public social practices that give some meaning to their private expression and form themselves anew as it were. What underpins the idea of disengaged reason is the distinction rooted in logical empiricism between a knowing subject and an objective world to be known. Plainly the more that a subject knows about this world, the more she will perceive possibilities within it for herself and indications of what actually does harm others. Hirst (1993: 185) explains his earlier attraction to disengaged reason in the following way:

> ...... the central function of cognitive capacities is the formation of the conceptual schemes in which judgements of truth can be made and that thence can be achieved bodies of justifiable or rational beliefs, rational actions and indeed rational emotions. Grounded in knowledge and understanding, human beings can thus aspire to live in conformity with what is the case, what is objectively and naturally given in human nature and in the environment in which human beings find themselves. Such a form of life was further seen ...as the good life to which all should aspire.

Fundamentally, however, empiricism is mistaken and, as we have seen, Hirst came to reject this view of the good life. Public language and practice always mediates what is presumed private. There is a dialogic relationship between private deliberations and public stories. The world cannot be interpreted in a value-free way because it can only be interpreted in a public language which comes ready loaded with all kinds of evaluative presuppositions. Far from there being just six or seven public forms of knowledge that hold the keys to private understanding of a wide range of social practices as Hirst (1974) used to believe, people's pre-engagement in such practices both enables and limits their ability to know and reason in many other ways. There is no one form of public reasoning available to which all can have access in order to establish collective substantive values, and it is deeply damaging to some people to base public education around the idea that there is. That is because those who do not have opportunities to practise widely the supposed public form of reasoning are bound to be disadvantaged. Finally, the empiricist distinction between a knowing subject and an object to be known dissolves once it is realised that in a social sense the knowing subject is part of the object to be known. We develop this dissolution in the next chapter.

2. POLITICAL LIBERALISM

Neither is there just one vision of the good life that is shared by all citizens. A modern democratic society is characterised by many incompatible yet reasonable views of the good life. This characterisation gives rise to the question that Rawls (1993: xviii) among others is concerned to answer.

> How is it possible that [free and equal citizens] deeply opposed through reasonable comprehensive doctrines may live together and all affirm the political conception of a constitutional regime? (*sic our amendment in brackets*)

Rawls' (1993) answer to this question is to separate comprehensive liberalism from political liberalism. That is, to argue that questions about what is truly good can be neglected in favour of questions about political justice and to accept that people will hold quite different accounts of what is truly good. Political justice is ensured for Rawls through an 'overlapping consensus' of reasonable doctrines based on the moral principle of justice as fairness to which all citizens subscribe and to which the state can appeal in order to justify its coercive power. Thus citizens are bound to disagree about what is truly good, but they may nevertheless share certain doctrines and values that enable them to coexist peacefully. An appeal to this overlapping consensus can be made in order to resolve conflicts where those conflicts threaten social stability. An appeal to this consensus could also be made to help to determine which substantive values are publicly endorsed.

It is clear, when Rawls refers to an overlapping consensus of reasonable comprehensive doctrines which all citizens endorse, that he intends this to be an inclusive consensus based around general statements upon which all reasonable people might be expected to agree. It is also clear that Rawls intends this consensus to be based on a moral sense of fairness. Of course, there may never be precise agreement on such general statements as those that guide the curriculum, for example. In a liberal democracy, the values of compromise and tolerance are supposed to enable people to accept statements with which they might not entirely agree and to go along with things that they might not be entirely enthusiastic about, in the interests of societal harmony. In turn they expect others to be tolerant and to compromise their views on other occasions. In this way a sense of fairness is maintained.

A Rawlsian curriculum ought to give priority, therefore, to the inculcation of political values such as tolerance and compromise over any comprehensive values held by individuals. That is because those comprehensive values will always be rejected as unreasonable by those who do not share them. Hence such a curriculum should convey and inculcate

> just those virtues and capacities required for taking on the rights and responsibilities of citizenship ... in ways that abstain as far as possible from embodying or implying judgements about the relative worth of the competing comprehensive doctrines to which citizens might commit themselves. (*Mulhall 1998: 165*)

As Mulhall points out, however, the problem with such a curriculum is that many reasonable people, who would agree on the priority of political values in most circumstances, would nevertheless want to make exceptions for certain deeply held beliefs to which they might hope to persuade others to accept. In order to distinguish the reasonable from the unreasonable, Rawls has to be appeal to the comprehensive value of reason that is embodied within his version of political liberalism. Hence the distinction between political and comprehensive liberalism begins to dissolve. The conclusion Mulhall draws is that it cannot be assumed

that a conception of citizenship to which all can happily assent is either available in the
public political culture or the only concept suitable for the task in hand. *(Mulhall 1998:
174)*

3. *MODUS VIVENDI* OR CONSENSUS?

Rawls distinguishes an overlapping consensus from a *modus vivendi* (Rawls 1993:
147). The former is based on universal acceptance of the moral value of justice as
fairness whereas the latter is merely an arrangement of convenience between two
or more parties fulfilling their own different interests. Just as the distinction between comprehensive and political values cannot be tightly maintained, so too the
distinction between an overlapping consensus and a *modus vivendi* cannot be
tightly maintained either.

As Ackerman points out (1989: 17) a *modus vivendi*

> .... may be the best liberals can realistically hope for under one or another extreme set
> of conditions – where allowing the serious political consideration of the power that
> comes from property or whatever will tear the place apart, and lead only to the destruc-
> tion of a polity that might otherwise have generated productive political dialogue on
> other issues.

In other words there may well be limiting conditions under which it becomes impossible to examine in detail the meaning of justice as fairness and there may be
nothing wrong with a *modus vivendi*. Indeed as argued earlier, the fact that people
simply go along with some things without submitting them to critical examination,
actually enables critical examination of other cases. The values of compromise
and tolerance suggest that in limiting cases a *modus vivendi* may be the most morally desirable state.

It cannot be assumed that radical re-thinking is always better than leaving
things alone. It is not clear whether greater justice or stability results from working
within an existing mode or attempting to overthrow that mode. That is a further
reason why the distinctions between political and comprehensive liberalism,
modus vivendi and overlapping consensus cannot be tightly maintained. Where a
particular group appears to negate a preferred comprehensive value, it might be
perfectly reasonable for an individual holding that value to try to break the group
up. It might also be perfectly reasonable for others to try to hold on to it. The dilemma is similar to the one that Kuhn (1962) describes between normal and revo-
lutionary science. As Habermas (1971) reminds us, in these times politics become
increasingly conservative and differences presented increasingly as if they were
technical in nature. If Habermas is correct then it looks as if the value of justice
will most often be trumped by the value of stability. Rawls' retreat from comprehensive to political liberalism may be seen to be his best hope that political philosophy has to defend "reasonable faith in the possibility of a just constitutional
regime" (Rawls 1993: 172). A further retreat may yet be necessary however.

We may now have to accept that a political conception of justice is more dynamic and localised than Rawls supposes. People continue to reformulate such a

conception on the basis of a series of what might be called moral compromises. Values that could comprise an overlapping consensus are nothing like so static and substantive as they would need to be for such a consensus to guide direct prescriptions for political action. Moreover the reasoning that people use to establish compromises is not free of their shifting evaluative commitments. Rather such reasoning shifts with those commitments. The task for theorists is not to be nostalgic about social planning on the basis of shared values but to encourage the development of practical judgement in educational and social institutions that enable the democratic exercise of such judgement on an ongoing basis. As Smith (1997) points out, there is an essential indeterminacy about moral life which implies neither moral objectivism nor relativism but confidence to make room for the development of moral judgement. The idea that institutionally sanctioned statements of general values can guide individual behaviour in all cases is wrong.

On our view, recent government attempts to try to formalise informal learning suggests an almost obsessive distrust of the role of judgement through agency. It is as if community can only be manufactured through public educational provision which develops an overlapping consensus of commonly acquired values and principles. It is as if informal learning risks fragmenting such a consensus when people pursue their individual learning interests to acquire privately held values and principles. Underlying these attempts is a deeply held belief in certain forms of rationalism and reasoning. These forms hold that unless an interest is specified in some way in advance of its achievement and unless the rules governing judgement can be set out in a way that make them applicable in all contexts, then social chaos will ensue as a result of a deeply fragmented consensus. According to these forms, standards of public reasoning underpin the only viable conception of rationality which makes it always possible rationally to reconstruct a series of judgements with reference to a set of publicly endorsed rules. Formal learning should initiate people into this form of reasoning.

We need a looser view of rationality and reasoning than this. The concept of reasoning as an ongoing fusion of horizons (Gadamer 1975) emphasises the temporal nature of many achievements. The more that prejudices are risked, the more likely it is that understanding takes place and senses of what is worthwhile shift. Thus it makes no sense to argue that substantive values to guide societal and educational development can be decided once and for all, in an overwhelmingly important hermeneutic encounter such as an election, referendum or policy forum. Instead our understanding of our own and the values of others is itself located in the stream of an on-going series of fusions of horizons with people who to a greater or lesser degree share our values.

In some limiting cases a *modus vivendi* might be accepted as the only way of avoiding what might otherwise be a bloody conflict where individual and collective interests clash and such an acceptance may be perfectly rational in those cases. An example here might be the acceptance that some issues are best settled by means of election even though there seem to be good reasons for preferring one course of action over another irrespective of peoples' voting behaviour. In another case it may be perfectly reasonable to hold on to a moral commitment even when that risks a bloody conflict. The separation of comprehensive from political values

is based on a notion of public reasonableness that is undercut by the realisation
that reason and comprehensive value commitment are bound together. Certainly
some commitments are more enduring than others but all have the potential to
shift. If things were different from this, it would be pointless to talk to people
other than those who are known to share similar views. But of course we could not
know the extent to which others do share our views unless we are prepared to take
risks in conversation with them.

There is not room here to review further the considerable amount of comment
and criticism that Rawls work has initiated (Mulhall & Swift 1992, Mulhall 1998,
Jonathan 1997). Perhaps the best summary of this criticism is given as follows:
'Rawls cannot avoid overstepping the bounds of the purely political' (Mulhall
1998: 174) in favour of a particular conception of reasonableness that looks increasingly flawed.

4. REINTERPRETING AN OVERLAPPING CONSENSUS

Let us suppose that we reinterpret an overlapping consensus as much more transitory and shifting than Rawls suggests. Suppose that policy makers were encouraged to give up trying to work out and communicate a common set of values
through formal education. Suppose that political thinking was more concerned
with the resolution of disputes locally and in contexts in which their resolution
makes a difference. Suppose that a good life is conceived not so much as one that
is dominated by what appears to be big issues, such as the formation of moral
codes and the ways in which such codes are applied to a range of circumstances.
Rather, that emphasis is placed on the local resolution of differences, when resolution is necessary, and the private attempt to convince others of the wisdom of
holding certain comprehensive beliefs, when people care about those beliefs and
the people they are trying to convince. In short, suppose that emphasis in formal
education was placed on engaging everyone in at least some of those public practices that enable people to resolve conflicts in contexts in which the resolution has
a point for them.

Suppose the notion of an overlapping consensus is reinterpreted as a 'family resemblance' type of notion. Wittgenstein (1953: PI 65-67) explains how there is
nothing in common between uses of the same word or group of words, but that
there is a "complicated network of similarities overlapping and criss-crossing:
sometimes overall similarities, sometimes similarities of detail." He characterises
these similarities as "family resemblances; for the various resemblances between
members of a family: build, features, colour of eyes, gait, temperament, etc. etc.
overlap and criss-cross in the same way". Suppose that an overlapping consensus
of doctrines is interpreted in a similar way to the one described by Wittgenstein
for concepts. According to this interpretation of an overlapping consensus, consensus is much more localised and transitory than Rawls supposes. Indeed the
consensus consists not so much in doctrines as in beliefs about what ought to be
done in particular circumstances.

On the face of it such a reinterpretation suggests a limited role for formal education. If all that could be said to unite the members of society is a series of localised agreements with no explicit values uniting them, then it is hard to see how the
state could justify any attempt tightly to legislate about what ought to be learnt
within formal education, let alone what ought to be learnt informally. It is interesting to note that the communitarian thinker MacIntyre seems now to accept that
"the nation state is not and cannot be the locus of community" (MacIntyre 1994:
303). Rather the locus of community "has to be a relatively small scale and local
form of political association" (MacIntyre 1994: 302)

The picture that is suggested here is a series of localised transitory agreements
sharing no one thing in common, but a series of family resemblances between different agreements made by neighbours and groups of neighbours in contingent association with one another. Such resemblances overlap one another. Let us com-
plicate the picture still further by imagining that no one is a member of just one
group, but that everyone is a member of a number of groups. On such a picture,
conflicts between groups and individuals are accepted as a normal part of ordinary
life. In most cases it is neither useful nor possible to appeal explicitly to what
might have been learnt as common ground between all members of society, because there is no such common ground, merely shifting sands of agreements to
which appeal can be made on a transitory basis.

Ackerman (1989) illustrates the notion of conversational restraint with the aid
of a Venn diagram. He supposes society to be made up of many groups. P1, P2,
P3... Pn represent the set of moral propositions the members of each group affirm
in conversation between themselves. L is the area of overlap between the propositions affirmed by particular groups that members of those groups might use to settle disagreement between them. For most purposes, conversation should be re-
strained to the search for L, what might be called, following Lakatos (1978),
'touchstone'. In the case of scientific theory preference, Lakatos suggests that the
proponents of two rival theories must establish some common ground or 'touchstone' by which the rival theories are to be judged, before judging can commence.
Similarly for Ackerman, neighbours need to establish some common ground between them before any conflict can be settled. They do not, of course, have to settle differences over their religious beliefs or the justice of unequal distribution of
property. Nor do they have to agree on touchstones for all time. Rather they have
to be able to take part in a wide variety of public practices, so that they maximise
their opportunities to secure touchstones with their neighbours at particular times.

It is not that thick, general and somewhat vague statements of value are entirely
useless. Such statements may serve a variety of purposes such as the starting point
for productive argument or a rallying cry to what is believed to be desirable. The
mistake is to imagine that such statements are *necessarily* more important than any
other kind of statement. Certainly there are occasions when people need to talk
about their deepest moral disagreements or about injustices that are strongly felt.
For example Coombs (1997: 186) worries that through taking account of "the diversity of moral traditions represented in school populations, educators will attempt to carry out moral education by engaging students in 'conversational restraint'". For Coombs this would be an impoverished form of moral education.

Conversational restraint is not a principle to be applied at all times however. A responsible citizen can neither cut herself off from political practice, nor from explorations of her private morality in conversation with others. Responsibility of this kind can be encouraged in schools and other contexts, without imagining that fundamental moral concerns need to be to the fore in all contexts, or that school provides the only or main context for fundamental moral deliberation.

This reinterpretation allows us to dispense with some of the devices introduced by Rawls to sustain the idea of a just political regime, but that have been the subject of much controversy. The distinction between primary and secondary goods, the burdens of judgement, the original position and the veil of ignorance are less important if it is simply accepted that justice is context bound and not transcendental (Taylor 1994). According to this interpretation of an overlapping consensus, there is no need for people to pretend to draw a veil of ignorance of proceedings, when their immediate interests are threatened in some way, in order to determine what is just. Arguably the most intractable struggles are over the allocation of material resources and opportunities for social advancement. It is hard to imagine that a veil of ignorance can be drawn over such allocation, as if people could behave as

> ..... the hyper-Kantian agent, capable of living by rules which utterly leave out of account his or her own advantage and which thus could be agreed by everyone, since they are not designed for anyone's good in particular. *(Taylor 1994: 38)*

As Taylor points out, the intuition of rightful distribution by desert among associates does not figure in Rawls's work. The question of balance of indebtedness in a particular community is more easily addressed if references to transcendental goods are dropped.

While Rawls uses the device of the original position to try to strip away all those life experiences that make disagreements so important in the first place, many critics reject this device. For example, Ackerman rejects the original position as a hopeless attempt to get a view from nowhere that must be a view from somewhere, however well disguised. Similarly, Ackerman rejects Habermas's device of an ideal consensus as an attempt to provide a roughly similar vantage point. Both attempts are subject to similar objections which Neurath summarises through the analogy of a boat. There are no neutral foundations that can be used to adjudicate between different views of what is good. Rather there are occasional glimpses of what is good and bad, for example when people bleed, show characteristic reactions to pain and happiness, and so on. Apart from these glimpses, talking to one another is all that we have to help us to determine what we ought to do.

Ackerman puts it this way:

> The ongoing political dialogue looks very different from the kinds of conversation idealised by critical theorists such as Jurgen Habermas. Most importantly, liberal citizens do not feel free to introduce any and all moral arguments into the conventional field. Instead of looking to ultimate conversational victory in some far distant ideal speech situation, their energies are focussed on the formidable task of governing *this* world through political dialogue that does not require participants publicly to renounce their deepest moral beliefs. *(Ackerman 1989: 19)*

He suggests that we ought to talk to strangers as well as soul mates, because such talk does help us to live in this diverse world. We come to value disagreement, as well as agreement, as part of a process of maximising political capital, which helps in the resolution of potential conflicts. According to Ackerman, the possibility of a just constitutional regime rests not so much on talk about moral principles or principles of justice. The possibility rests on acceptance that practices contain their own set of moral principles and the maximisation of social and political capital (Rawls 1993: 157). In that way people are inclined to listen to the views of those with whom they disagree, to tolerate those views and, sometimes, to accept them even though they conflict with self interest. The more that people have genuine opportunities to understand and solve differences with strangers, the more social and political capital is accumulated within a community. The more people know about the practices in which others engage, the more likely it is that conflicts can be settled without recourse to legal and bureaucratic procedures. They come to see their common humanity, without taking part in what might be a debilitating attempt to describe what is common to all of them.

This latter point illustrates some reasons why a form of education based on the idea that there could be disengaged reason is damaging. Such reason is bound to be more engaging for some than for others. A form of education based on the fantasy of disengaged reason is bound to disenfranchise many students, who are neither adept nor inclined to deliberate in the ways favoured by supporters of that kind of education. Their immersion in other kinds of social practices, which favour engaged reasoning, does not prepare them well for participation in what Pring (1993) following Oakeshott calls 'an educational conversation'. The point is that there is a multitude of practices through which people can join in or strike up a conversation. Politically and educationally these can be just as important as those practices that guide utterances in mathematics, physical sciences, human sciences, history, religion, literature and the fine arts and philosophy (Hirst 1974: 46) or whatever practices are felt to hold the key to a preferred and supposedly public conception of disengaged reason.

Hirst is surely right to hold on to the view that everyone should be inducted into those modes of reasoning and forms of understanding that constitute current standards of rational thought and enquiry. Where he earlier went wrong was in suggesting that there are only a very limited number of such modes and forms, and that individuals' induction into them can somehow be disengaged from their practical interests. In that way Hirst gave support to those curriculum designers who believed, in the interests of equity, that a tightly prescribed state curriculum would ensure that everyone had equal access to those educational and social goods that are deemed to be desirable.

5. PRACTICAL ENGAGEMENT

In his 1993 publication, Hirst acknowledges some of the mistakes made in his 'liberal education and the forms of knowledge thesis'. First, he acknowledges that reason is inherently practical and interested. Second, he acknowledges the primacy of know how over propositional knowledge and concludes

> .... the good life as the rational life is conceivable only as a life personally and progressively built from possibilities available within the social groupings we can and do inhabit. ...the content of education must therefore be conceived as primarily initiation into certain substantive social practices. *(Hirst 1993: 194)*

Once the search for transcendental conceptions of justice, rationality and public reason is given up. Once it is accepted that it is not possible to track in advance the trajectory of changing and contextually-bound conceptions of reason, rationality and justice, then a much more indefinite account of public education is suggested than that which is current in England or Australia, for example. The idea that there could be a national curriculum based around an overlapping consensus in the Rawlsian sense, or disengaged reason, in the early Hirstian sense, is given up in favour of a fluid curriculum structure, in which people learn some of the many different ways that are available for reasoning with and understanding one another. They also learn to swim as it were in a current of productive disagreement, without deference or need to access any supposed lifebelts of transcendental or objective realities.

What we are suggesting here is that our response to the realisation that there is no one proper form of reason, justice and rationality should not be nostalgia for lost illusions of certainty, but full embrace of contingency and contextuality. Practically, we need to encourage the devolution of power right down to the places in which the exercise of power can make a real difference to peoples' lives. If that means that people choose to learn things informally and find what is on offer in formal educational institutions irrelevant, then so be it. If some public resources can be redirected away from formal educational institutions to provide them with the facilities to learn informally, then that is what should be done. We need also to stop conceptualising learning as a preparation for a social life, but more as an essential part of social life. In that way people learn from one another as they live with one another. We are only part of one another at the times in which we need to act together. More correctly we are only part of one another in relatively small scale associations of our choice. An ethical liberalism need not involve the formation and transmission of an overlapping consensus through formal education. Rather it could involve an ethics of openness to difference that only approaches closure when people show signs that they are being hurt.

6. VICTORIA'S STORY – A CAUTIONARY TALE

The UK government has set up a University for Industry which exists in part to encourage people to return to formal learning. It does this in part through its brand 'Learn Direct' (accessed via world-wide web). At the time of writing, one of these sites contained a number of exemplars with photographs of people who had supposedly benefited from visiting that site. We have ethical concerns about the way this was done, not least because there was no attempt at anonymity – just the reverse, but also because the stories were crucially incomplete. They suggested that there was a tidy story to be told as if a victim had been cured by a visit to a web-site. Moreover they suggest that the victim is only interested in things that can be made explicit. There is no mention of those qualities that are hard to define, but which are essential parts of the human condition. In chapter seven we attempt to illustrate an imbalance towards formal learning which shifts attention away from these qualities in unhelpful and unrealistic ways. In our commentary we suggest that not only is the story misleading but also it is yet another example of the current mistake to which Furedi drew our attention. The victim is encouraged to tell a private story. Through engagement in a government funded public programme, she comes to be cured. The message is supposed to be clear. Private confession is good for you, especially when it is combined with a programme specially structured for you and people like you. We quote the story below in its entirety but without the photographs and more personal details.

The future looks bright
A few years ago, Victoria's future looked bleak – she was stuck in an abusive relationship, lacked confidence and had no motivation to do anything about it.

Today, however, Victoria's life is back on track and nothing is holding her back. For the 33-year-old lone mother of two has not only managed to overcome her personal difficulties, but has summoned up the courage to acquire the skills to get a better job.

Victoria said: "I was thoroughly fed up being stuck in a dead-end job and an abusive relationship and knew I had to do something about it. I am also dyslexic which makes it hard for me to learn some things. I had also lost a lot of confidence because of the relationship with my ex-partner.

Still, I knew it was up to me to sort things out. When I was at the job centre, it was suggested to me that I try to update my computer skills so that I could get a better job.

I was worried, though, that this would be impossible as I have two young boys to look after and no money to spend on getting new skills. However, the lone parent advisor at the job centre explained that if I did a course at a learning centre, I could fit in learning around my children.

What was even better was the fact that I could acquire the computer skills I needed for a better paid job for free! This was great, considering I didn't even know how to switch on a PC."

Victoria was worried that her dyslexia would cause her some difficulty, but found this was not the case when she went along to the learning centre. She explained: "Because I could study at my own pace, I didn't have to worry that my dyslexia was slowing me down – I could learn at my own speed.

As I learned all about the Internet and gradually worked my way through all the different modules of the European Computer Driving Licence (ECDL), I felt so proud of myself. My confidence has improved so much and nothing can stop me now. I'm currently trying to find a job where I can use my new computer skills, and I hope to go back to the learning centre to take the advanced ECDL course soon."

6.1 Commentary

The first point to note here is that Victoria's problems seem little related to a lack of learning. Moreover she still has not actually obtained a new job. What she does have is a qualification that has given her confidence. What is misleading about this is the suggestion that life consists of a series of problems. Once these problems are confronted and made public in some way, then formal provision of something can help solve them. No doubt this is true in some cases, but in contrast, let us flesh out some of the contextual details that might have been missing in the example above. Once context is fleshed out however, the case begins, we suggest, to look much more plausible. Here is our revised story:

The Future Looks Complex and Unpredictable
A few years ago, Victoria's future looked bleak – she was stuck in an abusive relationship, had a dead-end job, lacked confidence and appeared to have no motivation to do anything about it. She did however, with the help of her friend Sheila, come to recognise these conditions and be determined to do something about them. First, she ended the abusive relationship. Second, she reflected on the kind of jobs that were not 'dead end' and she applied to do them. Eventually she secured a job in the office of a joinery firm where they offered to train her in the use of computers in which they were interested. She didn't find it too difficult and learned these new skills rather quicker than she anticipated. Her confidence began to increase. She was lucky because of the help that she was given by her colleagues and the supervisor of her training. This job was not 'dead end', because there was always something new to learn. She dealt directly with customers who expected their requirements to be considered on an individual basis. There was no manual that she could follow to help her deal with this. Sometimes the customers were angry and she had to learn how to deal with this too. Moreover, the skills that she needed to stock take on the computer were in need of updating as different packages were installed on the machine. Sometimes she had to liase with the joiners who generally worked from their homes and vans. She came to understand something about joinery through conversations with them and through liasing with their customers. She does not know where her life is going at the moment – only that it is a lot better than it was. She supposes that it will all depend on opportunities and luck – and recognising difficulties as they arise. To be sure she feels she has learnt a lot of new interesting things – most, though not all of them, concerned with people.

We suggest that this latter account is more realistic and believable than the former. It pays attention to the contingency and opportunity that we have highlighted. Most importantly, though, it pays attention to the human condition in which few problems are solved in an easy one off intervention. Nor do problems arrive one at a time, nor solutions present themselves in that way. There is no one obvious source of advice provided by government, nor can there be. Rather, as in the cases of the older learners featured at the end of chapter two, people learn as they go along. They come to accept the contingency of such learning. Certainly they seek out opportunity, but there is no linear path, and certainly not via a web site, or at least not often. At a local level and at a national level opportunities are dependent on luck, timing and openness to possibilities. Such openness, we argue, is vital for informal learning. Regrettably many instances of formal learning tend to close down such possibilities, through a preoccupation with explicit outcomes.

7. A NETWORK SOCIETY

Castells (1996) explains this idea of contingency through the concept of a network society in a way that is reminiscent of Wittgenstein's notion of a family resemblance. The picture that emerges from his explanation is of society, in its widest international sense, comprised of an overlapping series of networks, sharing some things in common but not all things in common. Castells gives a number of examples to illustrate this idea. Why, he asks, "were discoveries of new information technologies clustered in the 1970's and mostly in California?" (Castells 1996: 50). At this time, he argues, a number of important technological advances, such as communications switching, processing and genetic technology, began mutually to enhance one another, to become a source of powerful new ideas and metaphors. For example, the idea of neural networks seemed to parallel the idea of networked microcomputers made possible through the laying of optical fibre cables, digital switching and the project to map the human genome. The reason was not because of any emphasis on applied research by government. Nor was it a response of capitalism to new internal contradictions. Rather, Castells notes a number of fortuitous events: the hiring of particularly talented and visionary individuals to key posts; the flexibility engendered by a number of emerging structures within international companies rather than the rigid and moribund thinking in parts of the US. There was:

> ..... a milieu of innovation when discoveries and applications would interact and be tested in a recurrent process of trial and error of learning by doing; these milieu required and still do in the 1990's, (in spite of on-line networking) spatial concentration of research centres, higher education institutions, advanced technology companies, a network of ancillary suppliers of goods and services and business networks of venture capital. *(Castells 1996: 56)*

From this example it is clear that networks do not exist apart from the large markets developed by the state, but that such markets do not create them either. The location of basic services and products such as transport, food and restaurants are important to the existence of networks, but it is clear too that there can be no blueprint for the generation of innovative networks in the future. That is because networks exclude as well as include. They also exclude by default. Markets in many commodities are far from being fully integrated or open. Capital flows are not totally fluid. Labour is far from being mobile, because people have attachments to each other and to places at particular times that will transcend a perceived economic advantage. Multinational corporations keep most of their assets and strategic command centres in home countries. The nation state persists and forms the legislative centres and controls of spending, taxes and natural resources that influence the structure and dynamics of a network society. As a result of all these considerations it will remain the case that:

> Space and time are the fundamental variables of human life. The standards of their coordinates allow events to be quantified, rules to be made and case law established. All of these facilitate the regulation and control of societies around spatially determined groupings. They facilitate the formation of national laws and policies. *(Castells 1996: 376)*

To be sure, standardised methods of coding and decoding languages and of translations of languages provide the means globally of publicising, what was previously national or local, without delay. Advanced services, including finance, legal, insurance, marketing and others, can plausibly be reduced to information generation and flows. It might be expected that there would be an increasing homogeneity in work and culture through communications in virtual space. Yet this has not happened. For most people particular physical locations and human relationships remain the most important variables. While it might be expected that information processing power will continue to increase, it is not likely that it will ever increase to such an extent that the particularities of places and events will be irrelevant considerations in the phenomenology of work or learning.

If societies are viewed as comprising overlapping networks not free from physical space and subject to globalising tendencies, then there can exist within very short distances quite remarkable disparities of wealth and influence. The nodes at which networks do or do not overlap determine which physical places are economically and culturally prosperous and which are not. Nowhere is this more obvious than in cities, where areas of wealth and poverty seem to exist in close proximity without any obvious rationale for this spatial relationship.

All this makes the work of national governments difficult. The burdens of a collective lack of identity and civil society are placed upon them and this induces what Habermas (1973) has called a legitimation crisis. The introductions of national curricula, programmes of lifelong learning and courses in citizenship may be seen as a vain attempt to hold on to the idea that the members of a nation can share a set of common values. Such values might be supposed to enable people to live peacefully with one another, even though quite disparate levels of wealth and influence are apparent to them. But people have multiple identities and may have more in common with foreign nationals than their neighbours. Certainly people retain something of a sense of identity through the places they inhabit and the work that they do, but those places and that work may have more in common with places and work in quite distant locations than those that are near. The authors of this book provide an exemplar of precisely how a different kind of community is now possible that cuts across national boundaries.

8. PERSONAL STORIES REVISITED

Let us return now to some of the stories begun in chapter two to illustrate the roles that opportunity and contingency play in learning.

8.1 Fred's Story Revisited

It will be remembered that Fred is 73, has no qualifications, has attended no courses of formal learning since leaving school at 13. He continues to run a successful business as a yacht chandler. His story illustrates how by chance a lifelong interest in boats began, and how this sustained him in all senses throughout his life.

When Fred was 9, family difficulties led him to move to live with an Aunt for three months. His Aunt lived near a shipyard which Fred came to visit regularly. "I had a wonderful time there", he says. "I could sit in the yard until the Master of Arms came up for the mail and he took me down through the yard, so I'd get days to spend on the ships...I spent three months playing on a cruiser". He became "daft on boats". He joined the sea cadets. He became an apprentice boat builder. He became coxon of the lifeboats, he built wooden and fibreglass boats, he became president of the boat builders federation, he worked without a break in this area all his life.

The opportunity for learning so much began through chance events, unexpected family difficulties, a chance encounter with a friendly master at arms, the opportunity to "play", as he put it, on a cruiser. No doubt such a learning opportunity could not arise today in the light of safety regulations and the increasing systematisation of all aspects of practice. Yet it is worth noting that such systematisation does not open up possibilities for learning, it closes them down. It is easy to see how increasing systematisation has come about and, perhaps, to speculate on the injuries and loss of life that might have ensued without regulation of learning opportunities. However it is possible to speculate, too, on the number of injuries and losses of life that Fred has prevented through the learning that he acquired informally.

We will return to this story in chapter 7 to fill in more of Fred's story. For now we think it worth noting that Fred's business involves him in the use of the internet, in corresponding with people overseas, in discussing topics of interest across the world. As explained in our discussion of Castells, Fred may be said to be connected into a global network of yacht chandlers, selling similar and often the same products for the same applications. In that way he shares more in common with someone on the other side of the world than he does with his near neighbour.

8.2 Frank's Story Revisited

Frank came from a working class background and feels that this background affected his education and what he had the desire to do in life. He thinks that people who are born into the type of class that he was born into are more likely to turn to "criminality and drug taking", than those who are born into a middle class culture. He says "if you are in the wrong group your chances in life are limited as a consequence". Without opportunity, learning is unlikely, or, more correctly, learning can only be based on the practical activities in which people can engage. For Frank and others, those activities are limited and limiting. For some reason which he cannot explain Frank wanted to get out of that. He left school and emigrated to Montreal where he "found a bookshop". There was no reason specifically for choosing Montreal but as he says "I just had to get out somewhere ... it was by chance but it opened my mind, to how ignorant I was, how uneducated I was" and as a consequence he "began to read wildly". He sees this as a critical turning point in his life and compares it to the "road to Damascus" experience.

8.3 Marjorie's Story Revisited

Dressmaker, shop owner, factory worker, left school without qualifications, yet Marjorie now owns an alterations and dressmaking shop. She learnt her trade informally when she left school and worked in a factory aged 15. She explains "I had no interest in sewing at all, I just had interest in earning a wage, ... when you left school you just went out and got a job, any job really ... the only reason I chose to work in that particular factory was because my sister worked there".

When she had children, she left the factory but still continued to use her skills doing alterations for herself, friends and family. This allowed her to work from home, so that she had some income while she was looking after her children. She says "I did do odd jobs, things about the house, sewing for friends, for family". This carried on for 12 years before she returned to work on a part time basis. She worked for an alterations company and while she was working there, the owner decided to sell up. Three of the workers saw this as a good opportunity to go into partnership and so decided to apply to let the shop and start their own business. However, when the time came only Marjorie had sufficient finance saved up, or at least the other two women were not prepared to take the risk.

8.4 Susan's Story Revisited

Susan is one of the younger learners we first met in chapter 2. She has lived on a farm all her life and is currently studying for a degree in microbiology. We make only one obvious but key point from her story, one which is related to the point Frank made. Learning depends upon there being an opportunity actually to work with characteristic materials, tools and people. Without such opportunity, learning some things is simply not possible, however much governments might try to suggest otherwise through the offer of courses. Farming is such an example. Moreover as Susan told us "living on a farm you get to know about quite a lot of things, it's not just looking after the animals, I mean, there's the paperwork and there's the machinery and I mean there is quite a bit that you learn, you just don't actually realise you're learning it...it's nothing really I've thought about before, it's just part of life really, it's not something you think about in great detail". In common with many people whom we spoke to 'informal learning' does not capture the richness of practice into which they have been initiated. For us this is because the term 'learning' has now become so attached to the notion of 'formal learning' that informal learning is simply seen as something that happens "naturally". Farming is a rich practice, which connects with many others, in a way that what Frank described as "working class practices" do not. Unfortunately, many practices require considerable investment to sustain themselves, yet the rewards from such practice can be large. The extent to which governments have been successful in breaking into that circle in the interests of social justice is, as we have seen, limited.

Susan made the decision to go to university because it was the normal and expected thing to do. She says, "I just decided to go into Uni. because it's just something that you kind of got put towards when you are at school, I mean, if you had good grades that's what you did, you went to Uni.". Here formal learning is seen not as opportunistic, but as expected and limited. Our point is that government only has the funds to provide certain learning opportunities. In many cases such opportunities are dominated by the tools of paper, pens and computers because those tools are cheap. Hence the characteristic activities that go to make up the practice involve talking, listening and writing.

Susan went on to tell us that she really hoped that one day she would marry a farmer, but not a chauvinistic one, and of course it is often through the people that we happen to meet that we come to learn different things. For example if her future husband does turn out to be chauvinistic, then no doubt she will learn much about the legal system and family law. It is not possible to legislate for such learning – it is contingent upon meeting people at opportune times. Of course, Susan's formal learning may well help her further her farming interest. We are not arguing that informal and formal learning are necessarily unconnected, but what we are arguing is that in coming to see the connection, it is necessary to have the opportunity to learn things that can never be replicated in a formal learning institution. This is a point John Dewey (1966) made some time ago.

In this chapter we have attempted to elucidate the complex inter-relationship between formal and informal learning, public and private interest, and learning as an instrument of social policy. The meanings of public and private are underpinned by particular views of what is rational and reasonable. These views and meanings are historically situated. We have argued that the idea that greater social justice and economic efficiency can be brought about by increasing formalisation of the educational system is no longer appropriate, if it ever was. The idea that policy outcomes and rules to govern the achievement of those outcomes can be set out in advance of the attempt to achieve is mistaken. It leads to a seemingly endless series of policy interventions in learning that necessarily privilege the formal in ways that turn out not to be justifiable in the majority of cases.

We have argued that learning is far more opportunistic than many curriculum planners and policy makers imagine. We have seen how the meanings of public and private have shifted to such an extent that certain rationalistic views of what is in the public interest are no longer plausible. We have seen that we need a much looser account of what is rational and reasonable, one that pays attention to the way that people contextualise what they do in different and shifting ways, depending upon the trajectory of where their learning interest takes them. And this conclusion is as applicable to formal learning as it is to informal learning. What we need is a fresh account of learning that pays attention to its inherent contextuality, as has been described at the political level in this chapter. That account needs to respect the quality of openness to possibilities that we described. In the next chapter, we attempt to develop just such an account. For us a single account of learning is unlikely, not least because learning is a contested term, one which reflects different political values. There is no reason to suppose that many of these are held in common across time and space.

CHAPTER FIVE

RETHINKING LEARNING

At the end of chapter one it was argued that the vital relationship between informal and lifelong learning needed to be looked at afresh. It was suggested that this should serve as a stimulus to reconceptualising learning itself. Subsequent chapters have outlined and critiqued the various ways that lifelong learning, formal education provision and economic wellbeing have become entwined in recent educational policy and practice. We argue that this has resulted in an undesirable imbalance between formal and informal learning, one in which there is too much focus on the former and unwarranted neglect of the latter. To correct this, it is clear that we need to think of learning as something much wider than schooling and formal education. We need to rethink learning itself. That is the task of this chapter.

We begin by considering why a single account of learning is unlikely to be feasible. The main reason is twofold. Firstly, that we seem to be unable to think about learning without resorting to the use of metaphor, and various rival metaphors are available for this purpose. Secondly, all learning is contextualised and different contexts favour different metaphors. Hence, all attempts to provide an overarching account of learning are inevitably contested. Quite simply, for any proposed general account of learning there will be learning contexts where the theory and its accompanying metaphors are not particularly applicable. Thus, after considering why humans cannot think about learning in metaphor-free ways, this chapter outlines various metaphors and clusters of metaphors that are prominent in attempts to understand learning. There are several distinctive metaphors employed in relation to learning, each one involving its own epistemological and ontological assumptions, as well a series of subsidiary metaphors. Each of these distinctive metaphors and their attendant assumptions and subsidiary metaphors will be outlined in detail. (For the sake of brevity, the term 'metaphor cluster' will be employed hereafter to refer to a 'learning metaphor, together with its attendant assumptions and subsidiary metaphors'). This chapter will then consider how one metaphor cluster, the propositional learning one, has been elevated to the position of 'single, preferred account of learning'. Crucial problems for common understandings of learning, that have been created by this ascendency of a single, preferred account of learning, are identified and discussed. From this critique, a different, more inclusive and pluralistic, account of learning emerges. Our account of key instances of informal learning, as a developing capacity to make context-sensitive judgements, provides but one kind of learning that fits under the broader account of learning that is proposed here. Finally, in this chapter, a number of exemplars will be outlined and discussed so as to give flesh to some of the key ideas discussed up till then, as well as in subsequent chapters.

1. WHY A SINGLE ACCOUNT OF LEARNING IS UNLIKELY TO BE VIABLE

Part of the reason why a single viable account of learning is unlikely is that humans seem to be unable to think and talk about learning without resorting to metaphor. And various alternative metaphors are available. By itself, this would still leave open the possibility of a viable single account of learning, since one particular metaphor might be claimed to be superior to all others. However, the inescapable contextuality of learning excludes this possibility since different metaphors are conducive to different contexts, as we will see. Thus we begin this chapter with an extended discussion of metaphor and its past and ongoing role in educational thought. We then consider the basis of the links between metaphor and learning.

Metaphor can be thought of as "the transfer of a name or descriptive term to an object different from, but analogous to, that to which it is properly applicable, e.g. 'abysmal ignorance'" (*Oxford Companion to English Literature*). (The related notion of analogy is, of course, concerned with "likeness in certain respects"). Scheffler (1960: 48ff), in a discussion of the centrality of metaphorical language in educational theory, noted that metaphors indicate

> .... that there is an important analogy between two things, without saying explicitly in what the analogy consists. Now, every two things are analogous in some respect, but not every such respect is important.... the notion of importance varies with the situation.....

Scheffler added that every metaphor has limitations, "points at which the analogies it indicates break down" (1960: 48). For dominant metaphors he suggested we need to determine their limitations, thereby "opening up fresh possibilities of thought and action." (Scheffler 1960: 49). Nevertheless, it has been a common view in philosophy that metaphor is not part of ordinary language, and that when used in extraordinary language such as poetry or rhetoric, metaphor is a "characteristic of language alone, a matter of words rather than thought or action." (Lakoff & Johnson 1980: 3). So a widely accepted view has been that metaphor is something extra that we don't need and should avoid, especially if wanting to express ourselves clearly and precisely. Hence, metaphor has frequently been seen as something to avoid by philosophers. (Though this outlook has changed recently – see entry on metaphor in Honderich 1995). Because there has been a strong tradition in philosophy that is adverse to metaphor, we begin with a series of pertinent quotations about metaphor from a range of philosophers who think otherwise. These quotations have been selected in order to presage a number of the issues that will recur throughout the chapter.

Iris Murdoch:

> The development of consciousness in human beings is inseparably connected with the use of metaphor. Metaphors are not merely peripheral decorations or even useful models, they are fundamental forms of our awareness of our condition: metaphors of

space, metaphors of movement, metaphors of vision. *('The Sovereignty of Good Over Other Concepts' (1967), in Murdoch 1997: 363)*

.... we naturally use metaphors to describe states of mind, or to describe 'thought processes', in those cases where a sentence giving the verbal content of the thought is felt to be inadequate. In such a context metaphor is not an inexact *faute de mieux* mode of expression, it is the best possible. Here metaphor is not a peripheral excrescence on the linguistic structure, it is its living centre. *('Thinking and Language' (1951), in Murdoch 1997: 39-40)*

Bryan Magee:

When human beings try to voice the deepest experiences of all ..... they almost always resort to metaphor. Why? Is it because it is possible to *say more* in metaphor than in direct utterance?
.... Yet the whole point of an image is that it means something other than what it ostensibly says. A particularly puzzling thing about this is that although the meaning conveyed is not the one apparently stated, in practice this does not usually create confusion: we all, in normal circumstances, understand immediately what is meant, and understand it in the same sense. *(Confessions of a Philosopher, 1998: 154)*

George Lakoff & Mark Johnson:

Metaphors are the very means by which we can understand abstract domains and extend our knowledge into new areas. Metaphor, like any other embodied, imaginative structure, is not a philosophical liability. Rather, it is a remarkable gift – a tool for understanding things in a way that is tied to our embodied, lived experience. Identifying philosophers' metaphors does not belittle them. Instead, it helps us understand the power of philosophical theory to make sense of our lives. *(Philosophy in the Flesh: The Embodied Mind and Its Challenge to Western Thought 1999: 543)*

Ian Hacking:

Metaphors influence the mind in many unnoticed ways. *(The Social Construction of What? 1999: viii)*

There are some suggestive preliminary ideas about learning that might be inferred from these quotations. If human inner states are fertile ground for metaphors, then an association of metaphors with learning talk is predictable. *Pace* the behaviourists, there is an inherently inner quality to human learning. But, while some human learning undoubtedly belongs to Magee's "deepest experiences of all", much of it is clearly not in this category. Yet, as will be argued, there is little we can say about learning without resorting to metaphor. According to Lakoff and Johnson this is not a weakness, but a necessary part of making sense of our experiences of learning. But, as Hacking warns, although metaphors can help us to understand, they can also impede understanding by channelling our thinking in ways that might go unnoticed. Murdoch's noting of the crucial roles of 'metaphors of space, metaphors of movement, metaphors of vision' as 'fundamental forms of our awareness of our condition' anticipates the Lakoff and Johnson argument outlined later in the chapter.

1.1 Metaphors in Historical Accounts of Learning

The history of educational thought is awash with metaphors concerning teaching and learning. In Plato's *Theatetus*, learning is analogous to childbirth, with the teacher's role being that of a midwife. For Plato learning is a matter of bringing to conscious attention what is already latent in the mind. As the metaphor suggests, the bringing of knowledge to consciousness may be a difficult and painful process. Nor is what is brought to consciousness always sound. In this account, what is brought to consciousness, knowledge, is a thing or substance of some kind. As Bowen & Hobson observe:

> To this day we find ourselves using physical metaphors to explain what are still ob-
> scure mental processes: our mind conceives, we get fertile thoughts; in universities
> we deliberately call some kinds of classes 'seminars'. *(Bowen & Hobson 1974: 26)*

In Plato the physical metaphor for learning presents a substance moving from a state of latency to one of being consciously entertained. In direct contrast to Plato's 'inside-out' movement of substance, in the 19th century, prominent theories of learning employed the metaphor of external substances being incorporated into the learner's mind when learning occurs ('outside-in' movement). For instance, in Herbart's theory of apperception (see, e.g., Curtis & Boultwood 1970), newly presented ideas are assimilated or not depending on how well they relate to existing 'apperception masses' in the learner's mind. Ideas that are assimilated in turn increase the size of the apperception masses to which they belong. These apperception masses then sink below the threshold of consciousness until recalled to the surface by the next suitably related idea that is presented to the learner's mind. The teacher's role is thus primarily to arrange the presentation of suitable sequences of ideas so that their assimilation into the learner's existing apperception masses is most favourably assisted. According to Herbart, new ideas should only be presented when the mind contains an appropriate apperception mass to absorb and reinforce them. Herbart's physical metaphor views the mind as a kind of mental reservoir with floating massed clumps of learned ideas operated according to hydraulic principles.

A further influential metaphor in the 18th and 19th centuries likened education to the cultivation of plants. Proponents of this metaphor included Pestalozzi, Rousseau and Froebel (see Curtis & Boultwood 1970). As was the case with Plato, on this metaphor teachers are charged with bringing to actuality something that is latent in the learner ('inside-out'). In this case, the aim is the proper development of innate biological potentialities. Usually proponents of this type of horticultural metaphor favour broader all-round development of human potentialities, rather than a too narrow emphasis on the education of the mind. Once again we have a physical metaphor in which learning is contingent on appropriate conditions and resources being supplied (water, soil, nutrition, etc.).

In contrast, 20th century attempts to develop scientific accounts of learning saw new versions of the 'outside-in' movement of substance metaphor. Behaviourists talked about learning being the 'stamping in' of conditioned responses. Skinner's operant conditioning was a variant in which the environment was specially arranged to reinforce selected responses that were already inherent in humans. As well, the 20th century produced its own distinctive versions of learning as the development of innate biological potentialities, most notably in the work of Piaget. Piaget's focus is on the staged development or construction of cognitive structures, which are themselves real but unobservable. According to Piaget, it is the staged development of these structures which makes progressively richer learning and thinking possible. The key explanatory terms employed by Piaget to account for the development of these putative structures are paradigmatically metaphorical – e.g. schemata, accommodation, assimilation, and equilibration. A standard criticism is, of course, that Piaget has not really explained the various facets of learning. Rather, he has simply renamed them in metaphorical terms (e.g. Phillips & Soltis 1998). For instance:

> What does it mean to say that a cognitive structure has been put out of equilibrium? It is clear that a physical structure – say, a model made of building blocks, or a house of cards – can lose equilibrium, but a cognitive structure is *not* physical. It cannot topple over. This is just a misleading figure of speech. So, when Piaget asserts that a learner's cognitive structure changes because it is out of equilibrium, is he saying anything more than that it is changing? And if so, then he has not explained why change occurs. ...... Similar problems beset the notion of accommodation. *(Phillips & Soltis 1998: 47-48)*

Sfard (1998) argued that two basic metaphors – learning as *acquisition* and as *participation* – have underpinned much educational thought. As the discussion so far suggests, the acquisition metaphor has long been influential. In all of the examples discussed, whether 'inside-out' or 'outside-in', learning (knowledge, skills, attitudes, values, behaviour, understanding, etc) is some *thing* that is acquired, a thing akin to a physical substance. Sfard contrasts this acquisition metaphor with the increasingly influential participation one, claiming that neither metaphor by itself is adequate to understanding of the full complexities of learning. The participation metaphor is prominent in approaches to theorising learning that, influenced by developments in sociology and psychology, have become particularly prominent in the last decade or so. One such approach is based on sociocultural theories (e.g. Lave & Wenger 1991, Wertsch 1998). This approach focuses on processes rather than entities or structures, and stresses the inseparability of the individual and the social. Learning is, broadly speaking, a process of participation in particular social settings. Equally influential but different theoretical approaches have been developed from activity theory, which was originally inspired by the work of Vygotsky and Leont'ov, and developed by Engeström (2001) and others. Activity theory produces dynamic accounts of human activity that emphasise its mediation by tools (understood in the broadest sense). Also crucial for this kind of theorising are the differences between internal and external activities and the transformative links between the two. Learning results from appropriate participation in activity systems.

Amongst philosophers of education, the participation metaphor for learning would likely resonate with those inspired by Wittgenstein's later philosophy (see, e.g., Williams 1994, Winch 1998). Likewise, Peters' education as initiation (Peters 1965) seems to have strong affinities with the participation metaphor. The educated person travels with a different view rather than arriving at a destination, because education is an ongoing process rather than the acquisition of a set of specific products. The initiated participate in a type of exclusive club, as Peter's other favoured metaphors ("keep the barbarians at the gates", "lure suitable learners into the citadel") suggest. The right to participate in the exclusive club of the educated is contingent upon possession and development of the appropriate attributes and capacities. Peter's exclusionary metaphors suggest that it is not open to just anybody to acquire these attributes and capacities. Nevertheless, in principle, it should be possible that someone might both acquire the attributes and capacities, and thence become a participant in the club of the educated. This illustrates Sfard's claim that both metaphors have important roles in understanding learning. This kind of point is also implicit in Scheffler's earlier quoted claims about metaphorical language in educational theory.

1.2 Metaphor in Current Educational Ideology

According to Bereiter (2002) there is a widely accepted 'folk theory' which views learning as 'adding more substance' to the mind. This is in line with what Lakoff & Johnson (1980) call the 'common sense' account of the relation between knowledge and minds. This 'common sense' account has the mind as a 'container' and 'knowledge as a type of substance' that is placed in the container. Thus, the acquisition metaphor clearly dominates popular thinking. As Bereiter comments:

> Under the influence of the mind-as-container metaphor, knowledge is treated as consisting of objects contained in individual minds, something like the contents of mental filing cabinets. *(Bereiter 2002: 179)*

Likewise, as Rooney and Solomon (2004) point out, metaphors associated with the consumption of food abound in everyday popular talk about learning. However, if the primary learning metaphor in the public mind is learning as acquisition of substance, it would be reasonable to expect something more sophisticated from those charged with running formal education systems. If this is too much to expect from politicians, surely policy makers have something to offer? Apparently not, since the mind as a container and learning as acquisition metaphors dominate common educational nomenclature that is routinely used in formal systems. We talk of *acquisition* of content, *transfer* of learning, *delivery* of courses, course *providers*, course *offerings*, course *load*, student *load*, etc.

Of course, Lyotard (1984) and other postmodern writers (e.g. Usher & Edwards 1994) have argued that the recent neo-liberal marketisation of education results in a commodification of knowledge, in which knowledge is equated with information. Such information can, for instance, be readily stored and transmitted via microelectronic technology. Students become consumers of educational commodities. All of this is grist to the learning as acquisition of substance mill. However, it needs to be emphasised that learning as acquisition of substance was the dominant mindset long before the rise of neo-liberal marketisation of education. This is reflected in the standard educational systems nomenclature just discussed. This universally used educational nomenclature clearly predates the economic rationalist 'turn' in educational systems.

The economic rationalist 'turn' has seen education become a market, as noted in previous chapters. In this market, students become consumers, and teachers salespersons whose role is to supply a product for money.

> It follows logically that what is exchanged must be material and quantifiable; it is not something which is intangible or immaterial. *(Ozolins 2003: 4)*

The knowledge society is one in which education is judged by its capacity to directly provide for the economic well-being of the state. Ozolins (2003: 4) suggests that the ever more rapidly creeping credentialism springs from the commodification of education.

So, while the learning as acquisition of substance metaphor has been prominent for a long time, the economic rationalist 'turn' has helped it to run riot. There seems to be little room for the learning as participation metaphor either in current formal educational ideology or in the general public's understanding of education.

1.3 Why is Learning Conventionally Conceptualized in Terms of Metaphors?

The beginnings of a possible answer to this question lie in Murdoch's idea that metaphors of space, metaphors of movement, and metaphors of vision are 'fundamental forms of our awareness of our condition'. Lakoff and Johnson (1980, 1999) take this Murdochian idea much further. Rejecting the hostility to metaphor in much philosophy, that was noted above, Lakoff and Johnson take the contrary view that:

> ..... metaphor is pervasive in everyday life, not just in language but in thought and action. Our ordinary conceptual system, in terms of which we both think and act, is fundamentally metaphorical in nature.....
>
> ..... the way we think, what we experience, and what we do every day is very much a matter of metaphor. *(Lakoff & Johnson 1980: 3)*

In brief, the basic argument that Lakoff and Johnson advance for the conclusion that our "conceptual system ..... is fundamentally metaphorical in nature" is as follows:

i.   Human reason is embodied in our sensorimotor system. (The sensorimotor apparatus enables us to perceive, move and manipulate).

ii. This embodiment of reason in the sensorimotor system is contrary to the canon of Western philosophy which has celebrated the supposed autonomy of reason.

iii. Since humans are basically sensing objects moving through space, our sensorimotor experience is expressed in terms of concepts relating to such things as location, movement, and interaction with objects and forces.

iv. Hence, because of the embodiment of reason, reason inevitably employs metaphors that derive from concepts relating to location, movement, and forces. The "very structure of reason itself comes from the details of our embodiment" (Lakoff & Johnson 1999: 4).

According to Lakoff and Johnson cognitive science has been through two waves. The first wave assumed most of the fundamental tenets of traditional Anglo-American philosophy. The second wave rejected most of these tenets on empirical grounds. The three major findings of second wave cognitive science that underpin their book are:

1. The mind is inherently embodied.
2. Thought is mostly unconscious.
3. Abstract concepts are largely metaphorical.
(Lakoff & Johnson 1999: 3)

If Lakoff and Johnson are right about these three "results", each of them has a major implication for how we think about the notion of learning. They suggest that:

1. Learning is an inherently embodied phenomenon.
2. Much learning is unconscious.
3. Learning, being an abstract concept, is largely metaphorical.

Although Lakoff and Johnson see their work as a major challenge to much analytic philosophy, these three theses about learning are not, we suggest, particularly surprising to contemporary philosophy of education. Certainly, the first two theses are widely accepted (see, e.g. Winch 1998, Beckett & Hager 2002). The plausibility of the third thesis should be evident from much of the content of this chapter.

According to Lakoff and Johnson (1999: 45ff), the cognitive mechanism of (what they call) *conceptual metaphor* enables human subjective experience to be commonly conceptualised in terms taken from the domain of sensorimotor experience. For example,

..... we conceptualize understanding an idea (subjective experience) in terms of grasping an object (sensorimotor experience) and failing to understand an idea as having it go right by us or over our heads. *(Lakoff & Johnson 1999: 45)*

"Conceptual metaphor" is the name Lakoff and Johnson give to the cognitive mechanism that enables such conceptualizations, the mechanism that enables us to use the physical logic of grasping to reason about understanding. They claim (Lakoff & Johnson 1999: 45) that conceptual metaphor is "pervasive in both thought and language". Important examples of subjective experience that are claimed to be commonly reasoned about in terms derived from sensorimotor experience are:

- Subjective judgments about "such abstract things as importance, similarity, difficulty and morality" (1999: 45), and
- Subjective experiences of "desire, affection, intimacy and achievement." (It seems that learning, knowing and understanding are examples of Lakoff & Johnson's 'achievement').

They observe (1999: 45) that it "... is hard to think of a common subjective experience that is not conventionally conceptualized in terms of metaphor." If they are right, since learning is a subjective experience, we have an answer to the question: why is learning conventionally conceptualized in terms of metaphor? In that case learning is inherently metaphorical like time and other key notions discussed by Lakoff and Johnson. Of course, all of this is controversial. As Lakoff and Johnson emphasise (1999: 254), widely accepted principles of Anglo-American analytic philosophy exclude the very possibility of *conceptual metaphor*. In turn, they offer detailed critique of the account of metaphor inherent in recent Anglo-American analytic philosophy (Lakoff & Johnson 1980: 195ff.). There is no space to pursue these arguments further here. Instead, we will turn to an outline of how some of the Lakoff & Johnson work does shed light on the apparent centrality of metaphor in educational thought.

In their detailed analysis of the metaphors that pervade human reasoning, Lakoff & Johnson single out what they call "event-structure concepts" (1999: 170). These concepts include events, causes, changes, states, actions and purposes – all central concepts in philosophy. Of these concepts, Lakoff & Johnson assert:

> The concepts of cause and event and all other event-structure concepts are not just reflections of a mind-independent reality. They are fundamentally human concepts. They arise from human biology. Their meanings have a rather impoverished literal aspect; instead, they are metaphorical in significant, ineliminable ways. *(Lakoff & Johnson 1999: 171)*

They then embark on a detailed analysis of event-structure metaphors. A key point is that event-structure metaphors are *duals*, i.e. "metaphors that overlap in content but differ in figure-ground orientation" (Lakoff & Johnson 1999: 194). For instance, the two spatial metaphors for time are duals. There is the moving time metaphor (in which time – the figure – moves and the observer – the ground – is stationary) and the moving observer metaphor (in which the observer – the figure – moves and time – the ground – is stationary). The dual event-structure metaphors are what Lakoff and Johnson call respectively the Location Event-Structure Metaphor and the Object Event-Structure Metaphor. This duality is illustrated by the following example, which also points to the relevance of these ideas for understandings of learning:

Harry has reached trades-person level. (Location Event-Structure Metaphor)
Harry has got a trades-person's skills. (Object Event-Structure Metaphor)

In the first sentence of this equivalent pair, the state of achieving learning or becoming skilled is metaphorically represented as arriving at a location. This is an instance of the Location Event-Structure Metaphor, which Lakoff & Johnson

identify as a key instance of conceptual metaphor (1999: 179, see also pp. 52-53).
They characterise the main features of this metaphor as follows:

- States Are Locations (interiors of bounded regions in space)
- Changes Are Movements (into or out of bounded regions)
- Causes Are Forces
- Purposes are Destinations

Drawing on this key metaphor to describe learning, we could infer that:

- Learning (product) is located in specific locations that learners need to strive to reach.
- Learning (process) is movement of the learner to the desired location.
- Teaching is a force that moves learners from their present location to desired locations.
- Learning is complete when the desired location is reached.

It is not difficult to link these to some of the traditional educational metaphors outlined earlier. The Location Event-Structure Metaphor is also closely connected to the participation metaphor discussed earlier in the chapter.

In the second sentence of the Harry pair above, learning or becoming skilled is metaphorically represented as acquiring entities (knowledge or skills). This is an instance of the Object Event-Structure Metaphor, which Lakoff and Johnson also identify as a key instance of conceptual metaphor. They characterise (1999: 198) the main features of the Object Event-Structure Metaphor as follows:

- Attributes Are Possessions
- Changes Are Movements of Possessions (acquisitions or losses)
- Causation Is Transfer of Possessions (giving or taking)
- Purposes are Desired Objects

Drawing on this key metaphor to describe learning, we could infer that:

- Learning (product) is accumulation of items kept in an embodied mind or other container.
- Learning (process) is movement of items to the embodied mind or other container. Decay of learning is loss of such items from the embodied mind or other container.
- Teaching is a force that transfers desirable items to the learner's embodied mind or other container and removes undesirable items from such containers.
- Learning is complete when the desired possessions are acquired.

Once again, it is not difficult to link these to some of the traditional educational metaphors outlined earlier. The Object Event-Structure Metaphor is also closely connected to the acquisition metaphor discussed earlier in the chapter. In addition, the work of Lakoff & Johnson offers a possible supporting rationale for Sfard's claim that both the acquisition and participation metaphors have important roles in assisting understanding of learning. According to Lakoff & Johnson, it is because of the dual nature of event-structure metaphors that both types of metaphor are commonly employed.

1.4 Alternative Metaphors for Learning?

An obvious question is whether Sfard's two metaphors exhaust the possibilities, or are there other significant or theoretically fertile learning metaphors? If there are, how do they relate to the Lakoff and Johnson analysis of conceptual metaphor? Sfard does not mention other possible metaphors, but Elkjaer (2003), drawing on Dewey, suggests that *inquiry* is a more suitable metaphor for thinking about organisational learning. In support of the idea that inquiry is a more potent metaphor than acquisition, Elkjaer illuminatingly quotes Dewey:

> ...... thinking is a process of inquiry, of looking into things, of investigating. Acquiring is always secondary, and instrumental to the act of *in*quiring. It is seeking, a quest, for something that is not at hand. *(Dewey 1966: 148)*

While being sympathetic to Elkjaer's Deweyan perspective, we suggest that an even better metaphor for capturing Dewey's learning as a process view is *development* (*construction* or *re-construction* are other possible alternatives. However, given our focus in this book on the kind of informal learning that involves the *development* of an evolving capacity to make context-sensitive judgments in changing contexts, we will stick with the development metaphor). Development is also a Deweyan idea, but is, we argue, superior to the inquiry metaphor for suggesting the rich scope of the changes that are implicated in Deweyan learning, an idea that will be pursued in detail in chapter six (see, e.g., Dewey & Bently 1949, Emirbayer 1997). The development metaphor encapsulates the construction/re-construction of the learning, of the learner's self, and of the environment (world), which includes the self.

Thus, the argument is that the development metaphor captures the various dimensions of change, which are so crucial to Dewey, much better than the participation or inquiry metaphors do. Even some well-known sociocultural theorists, whose work has brought the participation metaphor to prominence, seemingly recognise its limitations. For instance, Rogoff (1995: 139) proposes viewing learning and development within a community in terms of three ".... inseparable, mutually constituting planes comprising activities that can become the focus of analysis at different times, but with the others necessarily remaining in the background of the analysis." The three planes of analysis are:

Apprenticeship (community/institutional)
Guided participation (interpersonal)
Participatory appropriation (personal)

It is the third of these that particularly involves development processes, since appropriation of a personal kind clearly implies something stronger than mere replication. So Rogoff in effect proposes that participation needs supplementation. How all·of this relates to the Lakoff and Johnson analysis is a matter for further work.

In summary, it seems that we are unable to talk about learning without resorting to metaphors. This claim has been discussed and illustrated with examples from the history of educational thought and from current educational ideology. The philosophical question is why this strong link between learning and metaphor? Various philosophers have begun to take metaphor seriously. But as far as we are aware, the work of Lakoff and Johnson offers the most complete answer to the question of why learning and metaphor are so closely related. However their work is also controversial. But, if we reject their account, what other explanations are available of the learning-metaphor nexus?

2. METAPHOR CLUSTERS

If, as has been argued, metaphors are inescapable for thought and talk about learning, then a single account of learning is unlikely simply because, reflecting different kinds of contexts, various different metaphors can be employed to think about and explain human learning. This section will consider a variety of these different metaphors and the contexts in which they are commonly deployed to provide an explanatory account of some kind(s) of learning. As noted earlier, each distinctive metaphor includes a set of attendant assumptions and involves the use of subsidiary metaphors. These will be delineated in this section. (Recall that the term 'metaphor cluster' will be employed to refer to a learning metaphor, together with its attendant assumptions and subsidiary metaphors).

Far from a favoured metaphor emerging from this discussion, it will become apparent that there is an unavoidable multiplicity of disparate, and even conflicting, metaphors that surround our thought and talk about learning. Perhaps this multiplicity of metaphors reflects a situation that there really are many different kinds of learning? As Winch has argued, there are many and diverse cases of learning, each subject to "constraints in a variety of contexts and cultures" which precludes them from being treated in a general way (1998: 85). Thus each metaphor cluster offers understanding of some kinds of learning better than it does others. This means that to rely exclusively on one particular metaphor cluster for understanding learning is in effect to limit understanding in advance. Yet precisely this has been the prevailing tendency in educational literature, most of it based on the transfer and acquisition metaphors.

The main strategy in this section will be to flesh out these ideas by identifying some of the very significant and different metaphor clusters that are available for understanding learning. The assumptions and subsidiary metaphors that accompany these different metaphor clusters will be outlined, together with the types of learning that each metaphor cluster illuminates best, as well as those types of learning that it is less successful in explaining. The assumptions and subsidiary metaphors that accompany each major learning metaphor include ideas about what it is to be human and how society should be organised. These epistemological and metaphysical assumptions that are a, mostly invisible, part of different understandings of learning, constitute one important sense in which learning is contextual. Because epistemological and metaphysical assumptions underpin any understanding of learning, it is inevitable that understandings of learning will be contested. If, as will be demonstrated, distinctly different kinds of learning, each important in their own right, are best explained by different metaphor clusters each with their own assumptions and subsidiary metaphors, this will serve to solidify the claim that there is no single general account of learning. It will also serve to drive home the vital point that, when it comes to understanding learning, it is futile to rely on one or a few central metaphors.

2.1 Types of Metaphor Clusters for Understanding Learning

2.1.1 The propositional learning metaphor cluster
One very influential and common metaphor cluster for understanding learning is the propositional learning cluster. This centres on explaining the learning of facts, concepts, propositions and the like. Here the *dominant metaphor* is *acquisition* with *transfer* being a ubiquitous associated metaphor. This metaphor cluster has become the 'common sense' account of learning. It invokes such further metaphors by viewing the mind as a 'container' and 'knowledge as a type of substance' (Lakoff & Johnson 1980). This links to Bereiter's 'mind-as-container' metaphor referred to above. Acquired knowledge becomes entities in a container, entities that can be transferred to and from the container as required (cf. Freire 1972 on 'banking education'). Another possible link here is with empirical realism, with its focus on a world of common sense objects that are the focus of knowledge. Though it seems that what is acquired by the mind cannot be the objects themselves, but some kind of photo-real representation of them.

Thus 'adding more substance' to the mind, preferably as 'bite-sized' chunks, has become the 'folk theory' of learning (Bereiter 2002). Note that it emphasises the accumulation of learning products. It says little about how processes of learning might occur. The metaphors of acquisition and transfer are silent on actual processes.

Fundamental assumptions underpinning this metaphor cluster for understanding learning are:

- What is learnt is a thing or substance that is independent of the learner.
- Learning involves movement of a thing or substance from place to place.
- What is learnt is separate from and independent of the context in which it is learnt.

The first assumption that what is learnt is something that is independent of the learner is a pervasive part of a whole network of common sense ideas that surround learning. For instance that learning can be stored in various receptacles other than minds, such as books, libraries, CDRoms, etc; and that in principle it is possible for every learner in a group to have achieved identical learning, i.e. that their minds have each acquired the same something that is independent of any one learner. Later in this chapter, it will be argued that there are kinds of learning where this first assumption does not apply. The assumption that what is learnt is something that is independent of the learner also raises questions about what it is that has entered the mind of the learner. Attempts to explain this have led to a series of subsidiary metaphors including representation – a representation (or imitation or copy) of what is learnt is supposed to be present in the mind of the learner. These ideas of course raise complex ontological issues.

The second assumption, that learning involves movement of a thing or substance from place to place, is at the heart of the acquisition and transfer metaphors. The most naïve view is that a commodity or substance is literally moved from place to place, e.g. in cases of 'movement by the learner', we learn 'x' in location 'y'. We then take it to location 'z' and use it (or not). The case where there is transfer of knowledge from a teacher to a learner ('movement to the learner') is presumably more complicated, since the teacher also retains what has been transferred to the learner. Here there is a multiplication of what it is that is learnt – a new instance of the object of learning is created in the learner's mind. Platonists, for example, regard this new instance of the object of learning as an imitation or copy of the genuine object that exists in the world of forms. This more sophisticated idea that what is learnt is multiplied as more or less exact representations of it are formed in the minds of learners, leads, of course, to a version of the traditional problem of universals.

The third assumption, that what is learnt is separate from and independent of the context in which it is learnt, has strong roots in Western and especially enlightenment thought. The basic image is of an individual human mind as a spectator that is not itself in the world, but is able to represent the world to itself via propositions. As this solitary human mind becomes steadily stocked with propositions, it could, potentially, recapitulate the course of human learning. This solitary spectator is aloof from the world, as is the knowledge accumulating in the spectator's mind. Thus, the learning is separate from and independent of the context in which it is learnt. Of course, the notion that what is learnt is context-free sits very well with the propositional learning metaphor cluster for understanding learning. This is so since true propositions are in some sense unchanging and enduring. They exhibit a kind of generality that stands apart from changing contexts. However, later in this chapter, it will be argued that there are important kinds of learning that are significantly and inescapably contextual. An over-reliance on the propositional learning metaphor cluster for understanding learning results in these important kinds of learning being overlooked.

Of course these basic ideas about propositional learning require further elaboration and discussion to do them anything like proper justice. For instance, propositional learning involves not just knowledge of the truth of isolated propositions, but also knowledge of how they are related to one another, how they are validated, etc. (see Winch 1998: 16). This task is beyond the scope of the present chapter. One interesting outcome of carrying it through would be that it would serve to introduce further metaphors, such as identification of central, key, basic or fundamental concepts; the surface learning/deep learning distinction.

Formal education systems have, of course, traditionally been closely aligned with the propositional learning metaphor cluster. Propositional learning has dominated curriculum at all levels to the extent that it has been regarded as the highest form of learning. Thus the general implication has been that able students should focus on traditional theoretical disciplines and that less able students should combine more elementary versions of these disciplines with the study of more practical and applied subjects. Likewise educational assessment has been dominated by a focus on assessing propositional learning, partly because reliance on the various kinds of pen-and-paper tests that cater most readily for assessing propositional learning is more economical than the alternatives. One result of the ubiquity of pen-and-paper tests is that, because formal education has been largely compulsory for well over a century, the public has been 'schooled' to regard propositional learning as the 'natural' kind of learning (Hager 2005a). Hence, as noted above, we have the public or common-sense view of learning – that it essentially consists of accumulation of propositions and a capacity to accurately recall them on demand.

This common-sense view of learning underpins the public perception that successful performance in quiz shows is a measure of learning. This common-sense, quiz show view of learning carries with it a series of associated assumptions, each of which can be related closely to the transfer metaphor:

- All questions have a correct answer.
- The height of learning attainment is to be able to answer all questions.
- The degree of learning can be accurately quantified (e.g., as % of correct answers).

However, it does not take much thought to realise that the quiz show view of learning is a very limited and partial one. Consider, for example, a discipline such as chemistry, which is replete with factual propositional knowledge. There are literally millions of chemical compounds each with their own formula, colour, boiling point, melting point, freezing point, etc. These millions of chemical compounds fall into a huge number of classes, each with distinctive properties and types of reactions they take part in. Now suppose that someone became a quiz show champion by unfailingly answering correctly whatever factual questions on chemistry were asked of them, no matter how difficult or obscure the questions might be. Would we describe that person as an expert chemist? At the very least we would have some doubts about the kind of person who would furnish their mind with such minutiae. Expert chemists certainly do not fill their minds with this multiplicity of facts. Rather, they know what factual information may be useful in a given situation, where and how to access this information as needed, how to use it in suitable situations, etc. So their understanding (*not* acquisition) of the immensity of chemical knowledge is contingent on a range of know how that is not itself purely chemical nor codifiable as a series of true propositions. For this reason, expert chemists might not perform as well as expected in a quiz show on the subject area 'chemistry', especially if the questions were pitched at a level significantly beyond the elementary.

If the knowledge of an expert chemist does not conform very well to the quiz show ideal, this is even more so for experts in artistic fields of practice. In Australia, there was once a quiz show champion whose special subject was 'Verdi operas'. He had an encyclopaedic knowledge of plot and scene details, names of characters, details of first performances, singers who performed particular roles, etc. But was he really an expert on Verdi operas? From the evidence of his knowledge displayed on the quiz show we cannot really tell whether he appreciated and was moved by performances of Verdi operas. Certainly specialists on performance of Verdi operas have quite other learning and knowledge than that required by the quiz show. Whereas the quiz show can only deal with questions where there is an indisputably correct answer, the practice of performance of Verdi operas is one in which important matters are very much open to interpretation and contestation. Different opera directors will have varying interpretations and approaches to performance of Verdi operas. Questions like 'who were the three greatest Verdi tenors?' do not have clear-cut answers precisely because different people have different background assumptions, beliefs and experiences which reflect their responses to such questions. In a word, the 'contexts', which have shaped their approaches to such questions, differ markedly.

2.1.2 The skill learning metaphor cluster
The skill learning metaphor cluster is a second and common cluster for understanding learning. Its conceptualisation in many ways parallels the propositional learning metaphor cluster, although its focus is on skills rather than propositions. Main assumptions underpinning this metaphor cluster for understanding learning are:

- What is learnt is a thing or substance that is independent of the learner.
- Learning involves movement of a thing or substance from place to place.
- What is learnt is separate from and independent of the context in which it is learnt.

The first assumption, that what is learnt is something that is independent of the learner, is reflected in the idea that skills can be *passed on* from one generation to the next. It is also suggested by the caveat about skills that 'you either use them or you lose them'. However, unlike propositions, which are thought of as entering the mind of the learner, skills are independent somethings that enter or are formed in the body of the learner. The independence of skills is demonstrated by the fact that various learners can all master the same skill. As with the propositional learning metaphor cluster, the skill learning metaphor cluster implies that what is learnt is a thing or substance that is located within the learner, whilst at the same time being independent of the learner. This raises some interesting ontological puzzles. Here, echoing Scheffler as quoted earlier, we are at the point at which the metaphor is starting to fail. Treating what is learnt as analogous to an independent entity may mislead more than it enlightens.

The second assumption, that skill learning involves either movement of (e.g. transfer of the skill from a teacher to a learner) or multiplication of what it is that is learnt (e.g. a new instance of the skill is created in the learner's body), raises the same issues as were discussed above for propositional learning. Once again, Platonists might regard the new instance of the skill as an imitation or copy of the perfect skill that exists in the world of forms.

The third assumption, that skills that are learnt are separate from and independent of the context in which they are learnt, commonly underpins attempts to specify occupations in terms of a list of competence statements. Such competence statements have proliferated in recent years, but the results of their use have been mixed at best. It seems that skilful practice of occupations is both holistic and significantly contextual, rather than atomistic and context-free, as is assumed by naïve use of competence statements. It is not too far-fetched to suggest that uncritical adherence to the acquisition and transfer metaphors lies behind the naïve uses of competence statements. However, there is also an important difference between propositional learning and skill learning that makes the acquisition and transfer metaphors even more problematic in the case of skill learning. The fact is that we cannot specify skills with anything like the precision with which we can specify propositions. Widespread impressions to the contrary typically confuse outcomes of performance (which can be specified accurately) with descriptions of human skills, abilities, and capacities (the specification of which is inevitably a matter of contestation – for reasons set out in Hager 2004b). But the acquisition and transfer metaphors apply to the skills, abilities, and capacities needed for performance, not to the outcomes of performance. So it follows that the favoured metaphors about learning fail to connect to those aspects of skilled performance that can be specified accurately, and instead deal with underlying skills, abilities, and capacities that are inevitably imprecise. No wonder the skill learning literature is in such a sorry state, and that skill learning is a poor relation of propositional learning!

However, despite the fact that skills are not transparently specifiable in the way that propositions are, there is increasing recognition of the importance of such non-transparent types of learning. The basic claim is that dispositional learning, which is non-transparent, is presupposed by other more highly valued forms of learning. Passmore (1980) offers an account of the abilities or capacities that are presupposed by propositional learning and other forms of learning. For example, reading and writing require the successful development of a range of capacities and dispositions whose specification is contested (in the sense discussed in the previous paragraph). For similar reasons, Winch (1998: 19) argues that knowledge is largely dispositional, thereby taking the central focus firmly away from transparent propositions in minds. So the skill learning metaphor cluster parallels the propositional learning metaphor cluster in many ways, but it also provides fresh grounds for strongly doubting the overall value of the acquisition and transfer metaphors.

2.1.3 The learning through participation in human practices metaphor cluster
A third important and common type of metaphor cluster for understanding learning is the learning through participation in human practices cluster. This metaphor

cluster focuses on the initiation and education of people into performance of human practices of all kinds. The performance may involve a variety of levels from novice through to expert. The emphasis is on successful action in the world as against the capacity to understand and recall propositions. The *dominant metaphor* for this metaphor cluster is *participation*. Subsidiary metaphors include notions such as 'finding your way around' the field of practice and terms that designate either level of attainment (e.g. 'second year apprentice', 'journeyman') or degree of acceptance within the community of practitioners (e.g. 'legitimate peripheral participation' (Lave & Wenger 1991)). If the propositional learning metaphor cluster could be seen to have connections with empiricism, the learning through participation in human practices metaphor cluster suggests a rejection of empiricism. Rather than entertaining a split between the knower and the known, this metaphor cluster suggests that the knower is a part of what is known, as a participant in it.

Fundamental assumptions underpinning this metaphor cluster for understanding learning are:

- What is learnt is a complex social construction that is independent of the learner.
- Learning involves movement of the learner from insignificance to greater prominence as they engage in the practice to be learnt.
- What is learnt is significantly shaped by the context in which it is learnt.

The first assumption, that what is learnt is a complex social construction that is independent of the learner, continues a prominent feature of the first two types of metaphor cluster for understanding learning, but with a difference. While the claim that what is learnt is independent of the learner continues to be a pervasive part of the ideas that surround this third type of metaphor cluster, the nature of what is learnt has changed. Rather than being a thing or substance, what is learnt is a set of more or less complex practices, i.e. a social construction that is susceptible of more or less continuous change. Although the learner might possibly be an agent of this change, that is not the usual situation. One way in which what is learnt is more complex than was the case with the first two types of metaphor cluster for understanding learning, is that here it is clear that what is learnt cannot reside fully within the learner. For example, in communities of practice there is the possibility, indeed the likelihood, of communal learning, i.e. learning by teams and organisations that may not be reducible to learning by individuals. As Toulmin has pointed out, the assumption that learning is located in individual minds creates the problem of accounting for collective knowledge (Toulmin 1999: 55). He adds that understandings of learning centred on individuals as the unit of analysis offer no "convincing account of the relationship between 'knowledge' as the possession of individuals and 'knowledge' as the collective property of communities of 'knowers'..." (Toulmin 1999: 54). So, according to this third type of metaphor cluster for understanding learning, human practices have a scope beyond any individual practitioner.

The second assumption, that learning involves movement of the learner from insignificance to greater prominence as they engage in the practice to be learnt, also provides an interesting difference from the corresponding assumption for the first two types of metaphor cluster for understanding learning. In them, movement was imputed to what was learnt. Here it is the learner that moves rather than what is learnt. The learner engages actively in a practice, something that is 'there' before the learner comes along. In doing so the learner moves within the practice from novice to, hopefully, proficient performer, i.e. from legitimate peripheral participation to, eventually, full participation.

The third assumption, that what is learnt is significantly shaped by the context in which it is learnt, contrasts sharply with the corresponding assumption for the first two types of metaphor cluster for understanding learning. Both of them seek to de-contextualise learning, though with mixed success, as was argued. However, the metaphors of acquisition and transfer gain a major part of their purchase from the idea that learning transcends context. With its assumption that learning is significantly contextual, the learning through participation in human practices metaphor cluster can be seen as challenging the explanatory worth of the acquisition and transfer metaphors. Of course, acceptance of the idea that learning has contextual features does not rule out the possibility, indeed likelihood, that the learner might modify and adapt the original learning when dealing with a related situation in a somewhat different context. This is a common happening in human practices of all kinds. However, this is a situation that is already more complex than the 'acquire it and transfer it' model assumes.

¶ However, if anything, the participation metaphor may err on the side of locating the learning so fully with the particular context that it is silent on exactly how learners are reshaped (another metaphor) by their learning. It could be argued against participation theories that their account has little to say about the learning by the individual learner that underlies the reconstitution of their personal identity from that of novice to full participant. Various writers have noted this deficiency in the Lave and Wenger account (e.g. Elkjaer 2003, Guile & Young 1999). As Elkjaer argues, the Lave and Wenger participation metaphor deals with learning at the organisational level, but

> .... at the expense of a description of the actual learning process – *how* does learning come about through participation? *(Elkjaer 2003: 488)*

There is, of course, a wide literature relevant to understanding and explaining learning to participate in human practices – literature on learning from practice, experiential learning, reflective practice, etc. However, the learning through participation in human practices metaphor cluster is probably not used as much as it should be to think about formal education systems. The most obvious examples of its applicability are higher education and vocational education courses that aim to prepare graduates for careers in practices such as law, medicine, plumbing or carpentry. But this metaphor cluster is also applicable to courses based on traditional disciplines. For instance, literature courses often have a strong emphasis on the practice of literary criticism, particularly at the honours level. Likewise philosophy courses usually encourage the ablest students into the practice of philosophy. Yet the propositional learning metaphor cluster discussed above is the one commonly invoked to think about such courses (see Bowden & Marton 1998). In recent decades, professional and vocational education courses have often been criticised for lacking 'workplace relevance'. Hence there has been a spate of attempts to improve the credibility of such courses by adopting problem-based learning, innovative practicum arrangements, etc. (see, e.g., Beckett & Hager 2002: chapter 6). These innovations have involved concomitant changes to curriculum and assessment. Yet the success of these endeavours has been rather mixed, most probably reflecting the tensions resulting from employing simultaneously both the propositional learning metaphor cluster and the learning through participation in human practices metaphor cluster.

   How does the learning through participation in human practices metaphor cluster relate to the common-sense view of learning? One might think that widespread respect for what is useful or practical would mean that the common-sense view of learning would have close connections with the learning from human practices metaphor cluster. However, the power of schooling is such that the propositional learning metaphor cluster holds sway in the arena of the practical. Having learnt to do X, is equated with acquisition of a something followed by the transfer of it as needed. Hence the atomistic approach to skills which has plagued both the competence agenda and generic skills policies. Not surprisingly, then, in the popular mind learning to perform in human practices is thought of as a series of discrete acquisition events followed by transfer as circumstances warrant it. Surely a better view of learning to perform in human practices is that it is a developing capacity (i.e. a process, something that evolves over time). The learning through participation in human practices metaphor cluster achieves this to some extent. The next section suggests further ways to enrich this understanding.

   The earlier examples of the learning involved in becoming a chemist or an opera director can be used to illustrate the range and variety of knowledge needed by expert practitioners, that goes beyond the scope of the propositional learning metaphor cluster. As suggested, the good performer in chemistry is not necessarily, or even likely, a quiz show star in chemistry. While a certain level and understanding of propositional knowledge is necessary, such knowledge does not need to be encyclopaedic, nor does it all need to be available to short term memory. It is more a matter of being able to access and use technical guides, books, texts, etc., as appropriate. This repertoire of propositional knowledge is only a part of the make-up of the good performer in chemistry. A major focus is on what one can do in the practice of analytical chemistry – a multi-facetted set of practices that greatly exceeds any store of propositional knowledge. It includes judging how to proceed in situations where there is not always a right answer. This practice know how is not readily codifiable into discrete techniques, much of it is learnt from practice, and much of it is tacit. These kinds of points are even truer of the practice of performing Verdi operas. As suggested earlier, this is an even more open practice in that there is legitimate dispute and divergence of opinions over interpretations.

   The learning through participation in human practices metaphor cluster can be seen as heralding the breakdown of uniformity in what is to be learnt. The crucial role of local practices, novel situations, etc., mean that contextuality starts to be an issue. Just because someone is good at producing or singing in Verdi operas does not mean that the same goes for all operas. Likewise success in the practice of analytical chemistry in (say) a pharmaceutical manufacturing company may not entail similar success in the laboratory practices of a metals-based resource company. Thus, for all of the reasons discussed in this section, transfer and acquisition are starting to look rather threadbare as general explanatory concepts. Participation in a continually evolving process looks better for both the practice of analytical chemistry and the practice of performing Verdi operas.

The learning through participation in human practices metaphor cluster implies a very different kind of ontology from the two previous metaphor clusters. For the first time, learning is something that extends beyond the individual learner. It is a set of more or less complex practices, i.e. complex relational structures that presumably include both particulars and universals. Moreover these structures are social and are susceptible of more or less continuous change. So an ontology based on processes would be one possibility here.

2.1.4 The learning as development (or transformation) metaphor cluster
A fourth important metaphor cluster for understanding learning is the learning as development (or transformation) cluster. This involves the *dominant metaphors* of the *development* or *transformation* of the learner and/or of their environment. This type of learning leads to the emergence of new entities, encompassing both the learner being changed as well as alteration in the environment in which they are immersed. Since the learner is not totally separate from their environment, the overall effect is a change in that part of the world. Hence, the common subsidiary metaphor that this type of learning creates new 'worlds'. When the focus is on the development or transformation of the environment, *world-making* is the favoured subsidiary metaphor. When the focus is on the development or transformation of the learner as part of that environment, *auto-poesis* or *identity change* are favoured subsidiary metaphors.

Fundamental assumptions underpinning this metaphor cluster for understanding learning are:

- The learner is an integral part of the learning, of what is learnt.
- Learning is an evolving process that includes the learner evolving.
- Learning involves emergence of novelty as new contexts are formed.

The first assumption, that the learner is an integral part of the learning, confronts the corresponding assumption of the three previously discussed metaphor clusters for understanding learning, that the learner is independent of what is learnt. According to the development (or transformation) metaphor cluster, what is learnt is significantly shaped by the context in which it is learnt, whilst at the same time the context is reshaped by the learning. The learner, as a part of the context, is an aspect of this context shaping and reshaping. This holism is a feature of recent accounts of performance that have been influenced by the work of Dewey and Vygotsky (see Hager 2005b). Whereas the propositional learning metaphor cluster had the learner and the learning separate from the world, here the learning develops (transforms, or reconstructs) the world including the learner. This continuous re-making of the world leads to the important subsidiary metaphor of *creating new worlds*. Whereas the propositional learning metaphor cluster focused on the solitary individual learner, the development (or transformation) metaphor cluster views learning as an integral part of social practice. So learning, like practice, entails participation and belonging. However, learning operates at many 'contextual' levels, so that changing of contexts is rarely a change at all levels.

The second assumption, that learning is an evolving process that includes the learner evolving, underlines the idea that in principle there is no finality to learning. This is not inconsistent, of course, with learning outcomes being specified and assessed for particular stages of the learning process. For the development (or transformation) metaphor cluster, learning is embodied and encultured, and is therefore integral to learner dispositions and identity. The link between learning and personal identity is a major theme. In these circumstances, the notion of transfer of learning loses its point. What 'transfers' is the person and their learning into a new context.

The third assumption, that learning involves emergence of novelty as new contexts are formed, challenges the traditional emphasis (evident in the previous metaphor clusters) on the reproductive, a-contextual character of learning. The development (or transformation) metaphor cluster stresses that learning is an emergent process, with the learning having the character of a complex relational web in which the learner is enmeshed. This conception has clear implications for how we might conceptualise lifelong learning.

There is a growing literature relevant to this approach to understanding learning (see, e.g., Horn & Wilburn 2005). It has been a particular focus of literature on learning that has appeared in the last fifteen years or so. However, the development (or transformation) metaphor cluster is usually not as closely associated with formal education systems as were the first, second and third metaphor clusters for understanding learning discussed above. The most obvious place in the formal education system to find aspirations to develop (transform or reconstruct) learners is in the macro aims of such systems. As such they are statements of hope about what (say) seven or twelve years of formal schooling might achieve. To this extent, formal education systems can be said to pay some lip-service to this fourth type of metaphor cluster for understanding learning. However, when the day-to-day activities of such systems are scrutinised, they are found to focus almost exclusively on the earlier types of learning, especially those favoured by the first and second metaphor clusters. In contrast, the literature on the fourth metaphor cluster for understanding learning, that has appeared in the last fifteen years or so, focuses on the day-to-day educational activities that develop (transform or reconstruct) learners. Informal learning as development occurs naturally as part of practice. As we have argued at various places in this book, this vital type of informal learning has become less visible as the policy balance has swung too far towards formal provision.

It is not surprising, then, that the kinds of day-to-day educational activities, activities that this literature claims develop (transform or reconstruct) learners, do not fit closely with typical educational activities in formal systems. For instance, this literature recognises that much important learning is tacit. Formal systems focus on and valorise overt, public learning. Likewise such developmental or transformative learning flows from learners' constructive responses to particular, even unique, learning opportunities that arise in their own individual learning context. As such, developmental or transformative learning is not easily captured in generic curriculum documents. It requires something akin to an individualised curriculum for each learner. As well, such learning takes places in contexts in which oftentimes there is no single correct or even precise answer available. Sometimes the exact nature of the problem that engenders learning is a matter of dispute.

Because of its holism, the ontology of the development (or transformation) metaphor cluster is necessarily complex. It would appear that some kind of process ontology would serve the case best. It would need to account for ongoing identity change in learners as their abilities, dispositions and skills evolve, whilst at the same time accounting for concomitant environmental change and development.

In summary, it has been argued that there are multiple metaphor clusters through which we can view learning. Each metaphor cluster features its own distinctive assumptions and metaphors. Because learning is diverse, no single metaphor cluster is adequate to capture all learning. Perhaps there are other important metaphor clusters for understanding learning that have not been considered in this section. Transfer and acquisition are metaphors that have been over-used in relation to learning. They conceal more than they reveal, and make it difficult to explain crucial learning that occurs when people learn to work and live in new contexts. Alternative metaphor clusters, with their associated assumptions and metaphors, will enable us to ask better questions about these matters.

3. DOMINANCE OF THE PROPOSITIONAL LEARNING CLUSTER

As was noted in the earlier discussion of the propositional learning metaphor cluster, it has become the 'common sense' account of learning, centred on the metaphors of acquisition and transfer, with the mind as a 'container' and 'knowledge as a type of substance' being common associated metaphors. Around all this, there is a common story about learning that goes something like this. The best learning resides in individual minds not bodies; it centres on propositions (true, false; more certain, less certain); such learning is transparent to the mind that has acquired it; so the acquisition of the best learning alters minds not bodies. Subsidiary threads of the story include: the best learning can be expressed verbally and written down in books, etc.; the process and product of learning can be sharply distinguished; and, though residing in minds and books, the best learning can be applied, via bodies, to alter the external world.

A number of basic assumptions about learning underpin this story. Chief amongst these is the following major assumption:

There is one best kind of learning, the furnishing of minds with true propositions.

Thus, though it is recognised that learning comes in distinct kinds, according to this assumption, the relative worth of all types of learning is to be judged against the best, viz acquisition of propositions by minds.This major assumption centrally underpins the above story. Closely related to it are a number of other assumptions as follows:

Learning is best studied scientifically. Hence the search for *the* correct, comprehensive theory of learning, e.g. by psychologists.

Learning is essentially an individual activity. Hence the focus on individual persons or minds by almost all learning theories.

Learning that is non-transparent is inferior. Since minds have self-reflexive access to the propositions they contain, the best kind of learning is transparent to the learner.

Learning centres on the stable and enduring. Since true propositions are in some sense unchanging and enduring, the best kind of learning remains relatively stable over time.

Learning is replicable. If the best kind of learning is something that is stable and enduring, then the learning of different learners can be literally the same or identical.

The main purpose of this section is to further delineate and then to challenge each of these basic assumptions about learning. The main implication of challenging these basic assumptions is that a somewhat different philosophical understanding of learning emerges.

3.1 The Basic Assumptions Expounded

3.1.1 There is one best kind of learning
As noted already, this is the central basic assumption that connects with and supports in various ways the other assumptions. Hence this key assumption will be discussed in some detail; then the others will be treated more briefly. The prominence in educational thought of the assumption that there is one best kind of learning can be traced to the abiding influence of Greek ideas, particularly those of Plato and Aristotle, a prominence preserved by the later equally significant influence of Cartesian ideas. If humans are essentially minds that incidentally inhabit bodies, then development of mind remains the focus of education. Likewise, if thinking is the essential characteristic of minds, it can be treated in isolation from non-essential characteristics like emotion and conation. For example, according to Aristotle, theoretical knowledge is superior to both practical and productive knowledge. Aristotle associated theoretical knowledge with "certainty, because its object was said to be what is always or for most part the case" (Hickman 1990: 107). As Aristotle saw it, theoretical knowledge thereby shared in the divine. For him practical (or ethical) knowledge was ranked below theoretical knowledge

because it involved "choice among relative goods" (Hickman 1990: 107-8). But productive knowledge was ranked even lower because it involved "the making of things out of contingent matter" (Hickman 1990: 108). This Greek hierarchy of theory/practice/production was not only epistemological, but also social in that the kind of knowledge that was a person's daily concern correlated closely with their role and standing in the city state.

As this discussion suggests, a striking feature of the assumption that there is one best kind of learning is the foregrounding of a series of dualisms such as mind/body, thought/emotion, theory/practice. The mind/body dualism underpins the notion that all mental events and activities are *essentially* interior to the mind. As Toulmin (1999: 56) puts it, common understandings of learning assume that ".... the supposed *interiority* of mental life is an inescapable feature of the natural processes in our brain and central nervous system". On this view, human sense organs are instruments that can add content to mental life, but are themselves part of the 'outer' world of the body, not of the 'inner' mental world. As Winch (1998) points out, modern cognitivism rejects this interiority of the mental, but still persists with the assumption that the most valuable form of learning is focused on thinking (what minds do), rather than on action in the world (what bodies do, or, more exactly, what embodied minds do).

Though the contents of minds were often characterised by the vague term 'ideas', concepts and propositions as objects of thought are central to the common story about learning set out above. According to this story, meanings of concepts are established via the activity of individual minds. Concepts in turn are combined in propositions that represent things and states of affairs in the world (see, e.g., Winch 1998: 63ff). So the individual solitary mind becomes a spectator that is not itself in the world, but is able to represent the world to itself via propositions. Since this mind is in effect in a different world, the same is so for the propositions. This may be a step on the way to viewing propositions as timeless universal entities. But it is clearly not the full story since the mental world is not timeless or abstract, as propositions are usually supposed to be.

Likewise, learning is seen as a change in the contents of an individual mind, i.e. a change in beliefs. Knowledge is then viewed as a particular kind of belief, for instance, justified true belief. Since belief is a mental state or property, learning is a change of property of a person (mind). So for the mind to have acquired particular learning is for it to have the right properties. But properties, like propositions have been regarded as universals, i.e. the same in each instance. Hence we link to the notion that knowledge centres on universal, true propositions, the traditional focus of education according to the common story about learning. So a lot of important implications are clustered around the notion of the essential interiority of mental events.

As the above discussion suggests, the prominence in educational thought of the assumption that there is one best kind of learning, centred on the acquisition of favoured propositions, can be traced to the ongoing influence of certain philosophical traditions. Perhaps one reason for the enduring influence of these ideas on learning both within philosophy and beyond it is that, according to these assumptions, learning of philosophy itself becomes something of a paradigm of learning.

Of course, there has been a long tradition that the primary focus of philosophy is how to live one's life well. But it is an ongoing legacy of the influence of mind/body dualism that the essential first step is for the mind to acquire the right sorts of propositions, usually by formal study.

The ongoing influence of this rationalist bias as regards what learning should be most valued is evident in well-known work in philosophy of education. For instance, Hirst and Peters (1970) recognised that it follows from their two logically necessary conditions for learning that there is a wide variety of kinds of learning. The two necessary conditions for learning are: that it have an object; and that some standard of achievement or success has been met (1970: 75). Because of the seemingly endless diversity of objects of learning, there are very many different kinds of learning. However, some of these are to be valued more highly than others.

> The value criterion for education clearly implies that much which can be learnt must
> be excluded from education either as undesirable .... or as trivial ..... *(Hirst &*
> *Peters, 1970: 76)*

It is because "education is taken to centre on developing desirable states of mind involving knowledge and understanding" (Hirst & Peters, 1970: 85), that, for example, learning Newton's laws of motion is valued above learning of physical skills of whatever kind, or even above learning of highly useful interpersonal skills such as the capacity to empathise with the feelings of others.

A similar tendency to elevate the more rational forms of learning is found in Hamlyn. He takes the line that less rational forms of learning can be assimilated to the more rational ones. In attempting to define 'learning' he proposes

> .... that learning must at least involve the acquisition of knowledge through experi-
> ence and that changes of behaviour due to learning must be the result of the new
> knowledge. *(Hamlyn 1973: 180)*

Hamlyn then considers the objection that there are various kinds of learning that appear not to centrally involve the acquisition of knowledge. He instances learning to love someone, but suggests that even here "my love follows upon and exists in virtue of what I have come to know", though he admits that how this happens is too "complex" to "enter upon here" (Hamlyn 1973: 180). Thus, without going into the complexity, Hamlyn maintains that such instances of learning ".... are parasitical upon those cases of learning which do involve the acquisition of knowledge *simpliciter*" (1973: 180). In fact the problem for Hamlyn is that in making knowledge acquisition a necessary condition for learning, his analysis covers the very many diverse kinds of learning only at the cost of broadening the notion of knowledge so as to include the full range of know how, much of which is tacit or implicit. This contravenes the requirement that the best kind of learning is explicit and transparent, as will be discussed further below.

Having discussed the central assumption in some detail, the subsidiary ones will now be considered more briefly.

3.1.2 Learning is best studied scientifically
If, as the common story holds, there is one best kind of learning against which the worth of all other kinds is to be judged, this encourages the notion that there should be a single preferred theory of learning to cover the best learning. Or the theory might even be entertained that lesser kinds of learning are somehow reducible to the kind that exemplifies *the* correct, comprehensive theory of learning (e.g. Hamlyn above). Such tendencies to parsimony of explanation have encouraged the idea, e.g. amongst psychologists, that the study of learning is a science. However, adoption of the scientific method for studying learning has not so far resulted in any widely accepted general theory of learning. As well, there has been substantial criticism of the 'scientific' study of learning and the resultant 'psychologising' of education (e.g. Usher, Bryant & Johnston 1997: 73-82). Despite this, the idea persists that all learning is at bottom the same kind of thing.

3.1.3 Learning is essentially an individual activity
The common story about learning involves the basic image of an individual human mind steadily being stocked with propositions. This implies that each individual mind can potentially recapitulate the course of human learning. Hence, on this view, in theorising learning, the individual is the appropriate unit of analysis. Thus, the focus of learning as a *process* is on circumstances that favour the acquisition of ideas by individual minds. The focus of learning as a *product* is on the stock of accumulated ideas that constitute a well-furnished individual mind, the structure of those ideas, how various ideas relate to one another, and so on. In emphasising learning by minds as the most valuable form of learning, not only does the common story about learning favour a mind/body dualism, it makes learning an essentially solitary process, an individualistic even narcissistic process, where the learner becomes a spectator aloof from the world.

3.1.4 The product of learning should be transparent to the learner
For the common story about learning, to have successfully learnt in the best sense, is to know what it is that you have learnt.. Learning that is non-transparent is inferior. Winch puts this point as follows:

> It is natural for us to talk about learning as if we recognise that we have both a capacity to learn and a capacity to bring to mind what has been learned. *(1998: 19)*

This second capacity trades on the image of the mind as the home of clear and distinct ideas. If we have really learnt well, we will be able to bring the learning to mind. An inability to do so is a clear indicator that learning has been imperfect or unsuccessful. Once again propositions are the model. If we really understand (have learnt) a proposition then we will be able to 'bring it before the mind'. Inability to do so indicates ineffectual or inferior learning. This also implies that for the common story about learning, non-transparent learning, such as tacit knowledge, informal learning, and the like, is either an aberration or a second rate kind of learning.

3.1.5 Learning centres on the stable and enduring
Another presupposition of the common story about learning centres on the idea
that products of the best kind of learning are relatively stable and enduring.
Traditional understandings of the nature of propositions have reinforced this
presupposition. Stable products of learning can be incorporated into curricula and
textbooks, be passed on from teachers to students, their attainment be measured in
examinations, and the examination results for different teachers and different institutions be amenable to ready comparison. Thus formal education systems are set
up to deal with assessment of learning that is stable, familiar and widely understood. Engeström puts this assumption of what he calls "standard theories of learning" as follows: "a self-evident presupposition that the knowledge or skill to be
acquired is itself stable and reasonably well-defined" (Engeström 2001: 137).

3.1.6 Learning is replicable
This can be thought of as a corollary of the stability assumption. As noted above,
the practice of comparing assessment results for students across different class
groupings and different institutions involves the stability of learning assumption.
In fact, the everyday practice of comparing the learning of different students also
requires an even more fundamental presupposition, the replicabilty assumption.
This is the assumption that the learning of different learners can be literally the
same or identical. The sorting and grading functions of education systems require
the possibility of this kind of foundational certainty of marks and grades. These
matters are reflected in the common term used to denote replicabilty of learning –
different students are said to have the same 'attainment'.
　　As a check of several English dictionaries confirmed, **'to attain'** means 1. to
arrive at, reach (a goal, etc.), or 2. to gain, accomplish (an aim, distinction, etc.).
In either case, conscious development or effort is often involved. The noun **'attainment'** has two distinct meanings reflecting the process/product distinction:
1. the act or an instance of attaining, or 2. something attained or achieved; an ac-
complishment. Thus, when applied to learning, the verb to attain introduces metaphorical connotations – learners have arrived at or reached a place or gained an
object. This is consistent with the Latin derivation from 'attingere' – to touch.
　　These metaphors associated with attainment appear to fit very well with various
aspects of the common story about learning. For a start they encompass the proc-
ess/product distinction. Attaining learning, stocking the mind with contents is akin
to arriving at a goal or gaining an object. The learning that has been attained is
akin to the mind having 'touched' the relevant propositions. Recall that propositions were sometimes viewed as timeless, unchanging entities located in a world
of ideas. Students with the same level of attainment can be thought of as mentally
'touching' the same range of universal propositions. Inside their individual minds
each has completed the same mental journey, on the way calling at the prescribed
places or destinations.
　　These, then, are the basic assumptions that underpin the common story about
learning. Each one of them has attracted cogent philosophical criticisms.

3.2 The Basic Assumptions Challenged

3.2.1 There is one best kind of learning

Because this central basic assumption connects with and supports in various ways the other assumptions, it was discussed above in more detail. Similarly, the various grounds for challenging this key assumption will be treated now in some detail. Then objections to the other basic assumptions will be presented more briefly.

Two major challenges to the claim that propositional learning constitutes the one best kind of learning come from its reliance on dualisms such as mind/body and its narrowly rationalistic quarantining of thinking from other important human characteristics like emotion and conation.

Problems with dualisms

As noted earlier, the assumption that there is one best kind of learning foregrounds a series of dualisms such as mind/body, thought/emotion, theory/practice. However, these basic dualisms have created intractable problems of their own. An example is the theory/practice account of workplace performance/practice. If the most valuable learning resides in minds that are essentially passive spectators, then this must be the starting point for understanding performances of all kinds that are significantly cognitive. Hence the claim that such performances are somehow applications of the valuable learning that derives from spectator minds. Long ago, Ryle (1949) pointed out the futility of this view, which effectively seeks to reduce practice to theory. However, such theory/practice accounts of performance remain common today, though they are increasingly seen to be implausible. These increasing doubts have been fuelled by research on expertise and the rise of the knowledge society, both of which emphasise the creation of valuable knowledge during the performance of work, i.e. not all valuable knowledge is the domain of the passive spectator. Nevertheless, the elevation of theoretical knowledge over practice has strongly shaped the front-end model of vocational preparation. This model views the main business of vocational preparatory courses as supplying novices with the stock of theoretical knowledge that they will apply later on to solve the problems that they encounter in their workplace practice. Not surprisingly, the current era has been marked by an increasing breakdown of the front-end model of occupational preparation, including various attempts to renovate or reconceptualise it (Beckett & Hager 2002: chapter 6).

Narrow rationalism

As we have seen, the common story about learning, influenced by Plato, Aristotle, and later, Descartes, ensures that knowledge is quarantined from emotion and will. If humans are essentially minds that incidentally inhabit bodies, then development of mind remains the focus of education. Likewise, if thinking is the essential characteristic of minds, it can be treated in isolation from non-essential characteristics like emotion and conation.

As Hirst (1998: 18) summarised it, this rationalist view of learning

> .... is based on seeing the exercise of reason as necessarily the use of our cognitive powers, independent of all other capacities, to achieve propositional knowledge and understanding to which all other aspects of human life must then conform.

However, Hirst adds, contemporary philosophical work has severely challenged this account of "the operation of reason in the living of a rational life" with important consequences for philosophy of education. In particular it rejects the idea of

> .... education as centrally the acquisition of propositional, or abstracted, detached theoretical knowledge and understanding. *(Hirst 1998: 18)*

In its place, Hirst proposes that:

> The central tenet here is that social practices and practical reason are the fundamental concerns of education, not propositional knowledge and theoretical reason. *(Hirst 1998: 19)*

Dewey, of course, is one noted philosopher of education who rejected both the dualisms and the narrow rationalism inherent in the assumption that propositional learning constitutes the one best kind of learning. He was a noted critic of dualisms, such as the mind/body dualism, and of spectator theories of knowledge. For Dewey (e.g. 1966, 1938) learning and knowledge were closely linked to successful action in the world. While Dewey did not deny that concepts and propositions were important, he subsumed them into a wider capacity called judgment which incorporates, along with the cognitive, other factors that are omitted from the essentially rationalist common story about learning such as the ethical, the aesthetic and the conative. Some idea of the scope and significance of Deweyan judgment can be gleaned from the following quotation:

> Dewey's view also differs from mainstream theories of logic in terms of what it is that judgment accomplishes. It is a commonly held view that the point of judgment is to make a difference in the mental states or attitudes of the judging subject. But Dewey thought that this view yields too much to subjectivism. According to his own view, the point of a judgment is to make a difference in the existential conditions which gave rise to the inquiry of which the final judgment is the termination. Changes in wider existential situations may involve alterations of mental states and attitudes, to be sure, since mental states and attitudes are also existential. But to ignore the wider existential situation and to focus exclusively on mental states and attitudes is to open the door to the prospect of pure fantasy. *(Hickman 1998: 179-80)*

Note that Dewey is not totally discarding the explanatory items of the common story about learning. Rather propositions are part of his larger explanatory scheme.

Passmore is another philosopher of education whose account of learning takes us well beyond the learning of propositions. He draws attention to the capacities presupposed by learning. According to Passmore (1980: 37) capacities are a major, perhaps the major, class of human learning. For Passmore in normal cases ".... every human being acquires a number of capacities for action ..... whether as a result of experience, of imitation or of deliberate teaching....". Examples that he gives are: learning to- walk, run, speak, feed and clothe oneself; in literate societies, learning to- read, write, add; as well, particular individuals learn to- drive a car, play the piano, repair diesel engines, titrate, dissect, etc.

However, not all human learning consists in capacities, according to Passmore. He gives as examples (1980: 37) development of tastes (e.g. for poetry), formation of habits (e.g. of quoting accurately), and development of interests (e.g. in mathematics). However, Passmore has each of these depending on capacities: to understand the language; to copy a sentence; to solve mathematical problems. So the argument is that capacities are basic for other kinds of learning. That is, the mental enrichment seen as basic in the common story about learning, actually depends on the exercise of learned capacities.

That capacities are much more than mental in their scope is evident from their definition and characteristics (Honderich 1995: 119):

'capacity' – A capacity is a power or ability (either natural or acquired) of a thing or person, and as such one of its real (because causally effective) properties.

Honderich goes on to describe natural capacities of inanimate objects, such as the capacity of copper to conduct electricity. These are dispositional properties whose ascription entails the truth of corresponding subjunctive conditionals. But the capacities of persons, the exercise of which is subject to their voluntary control, such as a person's capacity to speak English, do not sustain such a pattern of entailments and are consequently not strictly dispositions. Thus capacities are vital features of human learning.

Passmore (1980: 40) further distinguishes two different types of capacities – open and closed. He characterises them as follows:

Closed capacities: "A 'closed' capacity is distinguished from an 'open' capacity in virtue of the fact that it allows of total mastery." Examples include playing draughts, starting a car, etc.

Open capacities: "In contrast, however good we are at exercising an 'open' capacity, somebody else – or ourselves at some other time – could do it better", e.g. playing the piano.

As Passmore's range of examples of capacities, such as titrating, dissecting, healing, makes clear, their exercise often closely connects with the kind of judgment emphasised by Dewey.

Passmore's capacities are "capacities for action". This raises the role of action in learning. How important is action to learning? Consider a recent standard definition of learning: "The acquisition of a form of knowledge or ability through the use of experience" (Hamlyn in Honderich 1995: 476). (It is worth noting that since his 1973 account of learning, discussed above, Hamlyn has expanded the scope of 'learning' to include ability as well as knowledge). At first sight this definition suggests learning is an active process, as the 'use of experience' implies. However the passive spectator featuring in the common story about learning can be seen as using experience in order to furnish the mind, so it seems that activity other than mental activity may not be required by this definition.

A learning theorist who subscribes to a stronger notion of activity is Jarvis (1992). He argues that "learning is intimately bound up with action" (1992: 85). He views learning as a "process of thinking and acting and drawing a conclusion" (1992: 84). He suggests that it occurs when presumptive (almost instinctive) action is not possible. Thus, for Jarvis the norm is for learning to involve an action component. Learning that lacks this action component, such as contemplative learning, is abnormal learning – "the other learning processes involve a relevant and important action component" (1992: 85). So Jarvis upends the common story about learning that privileges contemplative learning at the expense of all other kinds of learning. He holds the common story responsible for the phenomenon of people rejecting as learning what does not fit under its assumptions (the 'denial of learning' syndrome) (Jarvis 1992: 5)

As noted earlier, one implication of the common story about learning was a sharp separation of the processes and products of learning. This distinction is plausible whenever learning is separated from action. However, when learning is closely linked with action, the two are not sharply distinguished at all. The process facilitates the product which at the same time enhances further processes and so on. Further critique of the rigid separation of process and product is found in the work of Wittgenstein which is considered next.

Wittgenstein's later philosophy provides an abundance of arguments for rejecting the view that propositional learning constitutes the one best kind of learning. As expounded in detail by Williams (1994), the following insights into learning are central to Wittgenstein's later philosophy:

- The basic case of teaching (training) is not about mentalistic concepts being connected to objects (as in ostensive definition and rule following). Rather, it is about being trained into pattern-governed behaviours, i.e. learning to behave in ways that mimic activities licensed by practice or custom, "learning to act on a stage set by others".
- Genuinely normative practices (i.e. ones not causally necessitated, but structured by, and admitting of evaluation by reference to a standard, norm, or rule) are social. So a period of training or learning is necessary to become a practitioner.
- All use of concepts presupposes a background technique for using the concept, a technique that cannot be expressed as a set of concepts or rules. So the concept (rule) is not foundational of all else. Technique is not reducible to concept (practice is not reducible to theory).
- Training in techniques creates the regularities of behaviour necessary for any judgement of sameness, in this way the process of learning is constitutive

of what is learned. So judgements of sameness are based on practices, not on mental states as such.

It follows from the above that meanings are not established internally by individual minds, rather meanings emerge from collective "forms of life" (Toulmin 1999: 55). As Toulmin (1999: 58) argues:

> All *meanings* are created in the public domain in the context of *collective* situations and activities.

The central social dimension of learning that is being stressed here is closely related to the "social practices and practical reason" that Hirst (1998) claimed to be "the fundamental concerns of education". Though meanings emerge from collective forms of life, Toulmin adds that once they are created in this way, they can, of course, be internalised by individuals. But the point is that, contra the common story about learning, meanings are not essentially internal. He refers to Vygotsky's work in illustration of this (Toulmin 1999: 58). According to Toulmin, two key points follow from this:

- There are various kinds and cases of internalisation:

Far from being a single clear-cut procedure, internalisation therefore embodies a *family* of techniques that make mental life and activity more efficaceous in a number of very different ways. (Toulmin 1999: 59)

- Learning begins with interaction in the public domain, i.e. some form of action is basic to learning with internalisation of the learning coming later.

In his major philosophical study of learning (Winch 1998), Winch further expounds the implications of these Wittgensteinian themes. Winch focuses on the ineluctable normativity of human learning/life and the consequent crucial role that training plays in this. Thus, Winch argues, training is essential to teaching. He proposes that training for humans invariably involves language use and rule following. Far from being anti-educational, as some have mistakenly supposed, for Winch training in normative practices opens up options and flexibility in human behaviour. He concludes that those who see a paradox in the notion of being trained in ways that promote independence and autonomy have confused training with conditioning. The distinction is that training leads to capacities for overt rule following whereas conditioning merely results in behaviour that accords with a rule. So, for Winch, flowing out of normativism is an essential role for teaching. According to him, the rules need not be overt. They can be implicit so long as they have the characteristics of normative activity. For Winch part of the flexibility of 'trained' behaviour comes from the fact that rules can be interpreted.

What emerges from the above discussion is an acceptance that there are ineliminably many different kinds of learning, at least several of which are central to education and its associated learning. Against this, the claim that propositional learning by individual minds constitutes the one best kind of learning is seen to be intellectually threadbare. It could be dismissed as merely naïve were it not for the untold damage that it and its associated assumptions have wreaked on the theory and practice of formal education delivery over centuries. Of course, none of this is to deny that propositional learning is an important type of learning. It's just that this is no longer a plausible standard against which all other types of learning should be judged.

3.2.2 Learning is best studied scientifically
As noted previously, there has been substantial criticism of the 'psychologising' of education that has resulted from scientific approaches to the elucidation of learning, approaches that have encouraged the quest for a single general theory of learning. Of course, the denial that there should be a single preferred theory of learning to cover the best learning, still leaves open the idea that scientific approaches are the best way to understand the diverse types of learning. Such ideas have been influential in attempts to provide scientific accounts of learning, e.g. by psychologists. Though it has been a growing trend amongst psychologists themselves to accept that the diversity of types of learning means that a 'one theory fits all' approach is unlikely to be successful (e.g. Bruner 1996, Bereiter 2002). Winch goes further in maintaining that "…..the possibility of giving a *scientific* or even a *systematic* account of human learning is ….. mistaken" (1998: 2). His argument is that there are many and diverse cases of learning, each subject to "constraints in a variety of contexts and cultures" which precludes them from being treated in a general way (Winch 1998: 85). In what he views as a futile attempt to achieve generalisability, learning situations are studied in experimental conditions that aim to be context-free. But Winch sees two problems with this. Firstly, the experimental setting is itself "highly culture specific" and, therefore, not "context-free" (Winch 1998: 85). Secondly, the settings in which learning occurs are nearly always different contexts from what pertains in the experimental setting. Hence, "… grand theories of learning …. are underpinned … invariably … by faulty epistemological premises." (Winch 1998: 183). Clearly, Winch agrees with the position advanced in this book, that all learning is significantly contextual.

Influenced by Wittgenstein, Winch recommends that we focus on description and understanding of various instances of learning viewed as distinctive cases: "….we have been obsessed with theory building at the expense of attention to particular cases…." (Winch 1998: ix). It might be inferred from this that Winch views 'learning' as a family resemblance concept. In fact he never goes this far, although he does discuss family resemblance concepts in his book (Winch 1998: 110-111). Certainly, viewing learning as a family resemblance concept caters for the diversity of cases of learning while recognising that there may be no single feature common to all of them. This more inclusive approach is arguably a conceptual advance over the assumption of the common story about learning that cases of learning are to be valued according to how closely they approximate to propositional learning by minds.

So Winch stresses that he does not wish his book to be seen as advancing an alternative theory of learning, rather he is content to focus on description of particular cases. Overall, he sees himself as providing "a philosophical treatment of the concept of learning as it applies to child-rearing and education", a project necessitated by "the distorted way in which learning has been treated by many psychologists and those educationists who have been influenced by them." (Winch 1998: 1).

3.2.3 Learning is essentially an individual activity

As noted earlier, a virtually universal assumption, central to the common story about learning, is that the individual is the correct unit of analysis. This assumption about the individual has been variously challenged. It is claimed that it is founded on a faulty view of the individual self (Usher, Bryant & Johnston 1997: 97-100). Crucially, however, this assumption discounts the possibility, indeed the likelihood, of communal learning, i.e. learning by teams and organisations that may not be reducible to learning by individuals. Understandings of learning centred on the individuality assumption offer no "convincing account of the relationship between 'knowledge' as the possession of individuals and 'knowledge' as the collective property of communities of 'knowers'..." (Toulmin 1999: 54). Likewise the assumption that meaning is established via individual minds creates the problem of accounting for collective knowledge (Toulmin 1999: 55). Adopting the individuality assumption has wide-ranging implications for vocational education, e.g. human capital theory incorporates this assumption. This is evident from a typical definition of human capital: '[T]he knowledge, skills and competences and other attributes embodied in individuals that are relevant to economic activity' (OECD 1998: 9).

However, as Winch stresses, the implications of the social nature of learning go far deeper than remedying a failure to account for collective knowledge. In crucial senses we need to recognise "the necessarily *social* nature of learning" (Winch 1998: 183). Normative learning of all kinds, including the important case of learning rule-following, presupposes the prior existence of social institutions. "No normative activity could exist *ab initio* in the life of a solitary" (Winch 1998: 7). Clearly, when considering learning, the isolated *individual* is often not the appropriate unit of analysis.

3.2.4 The product of learning should be transparent to the learner

The transparency assumption is challenged by the increasing recognition of the importance of non-transparent types of learning, one of which, dispositional learning, is presupposed by other forms of learning. Passmore's (1980) account of abilities or capacities that are presupposed by other forms of learning was discussed earlier in this chapter. Winch (1998: 19) argues that knowledge is largely dispositional in Rylean terms, thereby taking the central focus firmly away from transparent propositions in minds.

3.2.5 Learning centres on the stable and enduring

A narrow concentration on learning of propositions encourages the assumption that what is learnt is relatively stable and enduring. However, as will be argued at length in later chapters, once the wide diversity of *kinds* of learning is recognised, together with the significant *contextuality* of most kinds of learning, change rather than stability is the norm. As Dewey recognised, learning to live in a more or less changing environment never stops. Such learning is not *stable* as contexts continually change and evolve. In many occupations people with just the expertise of a decade ago are no longer employable. Much work requires practitioners to develop open capacities (in Passmore's sense) in an ongoing way. Of course, this does not necessarily mean that what they learned a decade ago is now irrelevant. Only that this earlier learning needs to have been supplemented, and perhaps transmuted by, current or recent successful practice.

So, once the focus shifts from the learning of propositions to the diversity of kinds of learning the metaphors associated with attainment seem to fit much less well. Perhaps 'attaining but never quite' is a more suitable metaphor here since learning becomes a process as much as a product. In fact, the process/product distinction is less applicable, reflecting that finished products of learning are not so readily identifiable. In workplaces, typical learning involves developing the gradually growing capacity to participate effectively in socially-situated collaborative practices. This means being able to make holistic, context sensitive judgements about how to act in situations that may be more or less novel. As well, these judgements are often developed at the level of the team or the organisation. So in these circumstances the propositions acquired by individual minds may be of limited interest.

3.2.6 Learning is replicable
Nor, once the wide diversity of learning is recognised, together with the significant contextuality of most kinds of learning, does the replicability assumption stand up to detailed scrutiny. As noted already, formal education systems have their own reasons for not questioning the replicability assumption. However, in the wide world of learning beyond the classroom, replicability has little purchase. Quite simply, the learning histories of workers, for example, will rarely if ever be the same because of the contextuality and particularities of their different work experiences. Hence it makes little sense to look for exact *replicability* of learning histories across individual workers. Of course, there will be some commonalities. For instance, all proficient workers in a particular field will need to be able to recognise certain basic patterns. But even here differences in learning histories and/or pattern recognition capabilities might well lead to subtle differences in how a given situation is read by different workers.

4. THE KEY ROLES OF JUDGEMENT AND CONTEXT

4.1 An Emerging Understanding of Learning

Increasingly prominent in educational thought of the last hundred or so years is an alternative conception of learning that views it as a process (or, more accurately, as a dialectical interplay of process and product). Viewing learning primarily as a process rather than as a product enables different features to be emphasised. Learning becomes a process that changes both the learner and the environment (with the learner being part of the environment rather than a detached spectator – see Beckett & Hager 2002: section 7.9). This view of learning underlines its contextuality, as well as the influence of cultural and social factors. It is holistic in that it points to the organic, whole person nature of learning, including the importance of dispositions and abilities. This view of learning aligns fairly closely with the development (or transformation) metaphor cluster and the learning through participation in human practices metaphor cluster; it is much less congruent with the propositional learning metaphor cluster or the skill learning metaphor cluster.

The following definitions highlight the contrasts between the two views of learning – product vs. process. According to the *Oxford English Dictionary*, learning means: "To acquire knowledge (of a subject) or skill (an art, etc.), as a result of study, experience or teaching." Besides portraying learning as a product, this definition is in danger of limiting learning to propositions and skills. The more holistic emerging view of learning is captured in Schoenfeld's (1999: 6) definition: "... coming to understand things and developing increased capacities to do what one wants or needs to do ...".

What are some main features of a more inclusive understanding of learning? The following is a preliminary outline (see Beckett & Hager 2002: 150). Learning of many different kinds produces knowledge which:

* is integrated in judgements, which reflect a capacity for successful acting in and on the world;
* underpins choices of how to act in and on the world since such choices flow from the exercise of judgement;
* includes not just propositional understanding, but cognitive, conative and affective capacities as well as other abilities and learned capacities such as bodily know-how, skills of all kinds, and so on. All of these are components conceivably involved in making and acting upon judgements;
* is not all expressed verbally or written down;
* in the process of its acquisition, alters both the learner and the world (since the learner is part of the world).
* resides in individuals, teams and organisations;
* may be significantly particular and contextual, rather than general and abstract.

Taking note of Winch's cautions about purportedly general theories of learning (discussed above), the emerging understanding of learning is not presented as a general theory. Rather it attempts to understand and explain a major sort of learning that occurs in many life activities, including much work, yet is largely overlooked by common understandings of learning. Our account of key instances of informal learning, as a developing capacity to make context-sensitive judgements, provides but one kind of learning that fits under this broad emerging understanding of learning that is proposed here. Likewise it is not being claimed that the notion of making judgements is all there is to workplace practice, nor even that judgements are central to all workplace activity. So it needs to be clear that the kind of informal learning that is the focus of this book, is but one kind of informal learning. We are not claiming to cover all cases of informal learning. Examples of informal learning that fall outside of our present scope would include things like learning by trial and error to use an automatic ticket machine, or learning where particular items are located in an unfamiliar supermarket. Likewise, we are not offering an account of animal informal learning. However, though we are considering a restricted kind of informal learning, we believe it to be a very important kind, especially for richer notions of lifelong learning and the learning society.

4.2 Judgement and Learning

The above features of the emerging understanding of learning can be further clarified by expounding the general ideas on which it is based. It has a holistic, integrative emphasis that aims to avoid dualisms such as mind/body, theory/practice, thought/action, pure/applied, education/training, intrinsic/instrumental, internal/external, learner/world, knowing that/knowing how, process/product, and so on. The argument is that judgements, as both reasoning and acting, incorporate both sides of these ubiquitous dualisms. Thus, this understanding of learning does not reject as such any pole of these dualisms. For instance there is no rejection of propositional knowledge. Rather, propositions are viewed as important subcomponents of the mix that underpins judgements – though the range of such propositions extends well beyond the boundaries of disciplinary knowledge. What is rejected is the view that propositions are timeless, independent existents that are the epitome of knowledge. By bringing together the propositional with the doing, the emerging understanding of learning continually judges propositions according to their contribution to the making of judgements. Because the judger is immersed in the world, so are propositions. So they lose their classical transcendental status. On this view, learning becomes a developing capacity to make sound context-sensitive judgments as contexts continually change and evolve. As Lakoff and Johnson argued earlier in this chapter, metaphors should provide "understanding [of] things in a way that is tied to our embodied, lived experience" (1999: 543). The development metaphor used here seems to be well-suited to the holistic, integrative character of our account of judgement.

In all of this, judgement is the key theoretical idea. Some particular features of judgement will now be outlined and discussed. According to Beckett and Hager (2002: 185) six major features of practical judgements at work are:

1. Judgements are holistic
2. Judgements are contextual
3. Judgements denote
4. Judgements are defeasible
5. Judgements include problem identification
6. Judgements are socially shaped

Judgements are holistic: practical judgements are highly integrative of the full gamut of human attributes. The cognitive, the practical, the ethical, the moral, the attitudinal, the emotional, and the volitional are all integrated in such judgements. All of these are seamlessly present in embodied, holistic performance. Inevitably, the "right" judgement will involve some balance of these.

Judgements are contextual: practical judgements are contextual in several senses, which will be discussed in detail in the next chapter. One sense in which they are contextual is that they are often part of a holistic nest of intermediate judgements leading to the final or culminating judgement. For instance, the final judgement could be the diagnosis of a patient's condition. To reach the diagnosis, there will have been many intermediate judgements, such as the significance of the patient's self-reported symptoms, the significance of the patient's previous medical history, tests to be carried out, etc.

Judgements denote: practical judgements connect with the wider world, as they determine action in the world and the consequences of that action. Hence, judgements denote. For better or worse, they usually make a difference. This explains why practical judgement can only really be learnt from the experience of actual practice.

Judgements are defeasible: practical judgements are rarely made to produce learning. They have other purposes such as solving a crisis, meeting a client's needs, satisfying a deadline, etc. Such practical judgements are usually not final in that they can be modified if things are not working out as hoped. So they are defeasible or fallible. Our judgements will not succeed every time. They will be more or less satisfactory or effective, and further understanding or information might lead to a change of judgement.

Judgements include problem identification: practical judgement often begins with working out what the problem is. As Schön (1983) famously pointed out, it is typical of real life practice that ready-made problems do not simply present themselves to the practitioner. Rather, a major task for practitioners is to identify what might be the problem or problems in a given situation. As well, the problem or problems may have no unique solution. Nor might all of the data needed to solve the problem(s) be available, nor might suitable procedures be clear. Thus a major aspect of developing workplace practical judgement is to learn to reliably identify and deal with problems as a fairly autonomous practitioner. "This is informal workplace learning *par excellence*." (Beckett & Hager 2002: 188).

Judgements are socially shaped: practical judgement is often made within a community of practice, or at least according to the norms of such a community. Thus judgements inevitably have inherently social, cultural and political dimensions. The collaborative and collegial nature of much practice only enhances this. These social, cultural and political norms and values also evolve over time, giving a temporal dimension to practical judgements. For instance, in the construction industry, occupational health and safety rules and procedures are now more stringent than they were a decade ago. (For more details on judgement see Hager 2000, Beckett & Hager 2002).

This section has outlined an emerging understanding of learning, one that will be developed further in later chapters of this book. The capacity to make context sensitive judgements is central to this understanding of learning and some central features of such judgements have been outlined in this section.

5. EXEMPLARS

In this section we provide some exemplars/case studies of learning in order to illustrate some of the key ideas from this and earlier chapters. In this book we have stressed that we are focusing on informal learning of a particular kind that takes place during the performance of practices. We have also stressed that we accept that there are many different kinds of learning – this includes informal learning. So, we are not asking 'what is informal learning in general?' Accordingly, as this book proceeds, we will be presenting a series of exemplars and case studies of many and varied instances of 'informal learning'. These will serve to illustrate main points in our argument, as well as challenging it on some issues. We hope that the sheer variety of exemplars and case studies will demonstrate that there really are many different kinds of informal learning. As well, these exemplars and case studies will show that informal learning is richer than theorisations of it often suggest. It will also become apparent that received theories of learning are of limited use in explaining these exemplars and case studies.

5.1 Charles' Story

5.1.1 General work and education history
Following being 'headhunted' Charles, who describes himself as a 'self-motivator', has been in the position of Survey Manager for the Infrastructure Operating Unit of a large construction group for 8 months. He describes himself as a 'hands-on' man and still goes onto sites to do surveys when he can, so as to keep himself in touch. The responsibilities of his current position are the development and control of survey staff and equipment to ensure that the group remains an industry leader. A major focus of his work is the planning of the future surveying needs of the construction group in terms of both human and physical resources.

Charles has been in surveying all his working life, moving from being an assistant to a surveyor, to field party leader and on to a surveyor. Then in 1980 into a managerial position as project surveyor and foreman, with the specific task of streamlining the use of software packages, survey equipment and lines of communication with surveyors on various jobs. Although he is not a registered surveyor, he tells of a broad experience in positions within a number of major construction companies including project manager, foreman, project surveyor, senior surveyor and chief surveyor.

Looking back he says he was rather shocked when he 'fell on his face' at the end of his schooling because he 'spent year 12 in the surf'. As he was not then eligible to go to university, Charles decided he wanted to be a surveyor and enrolled in and successfully completed a 4 year part-time Certificate in Surveying at a Technical and Further Education (TAFE) college, while working as a survey assistant. Failure of earlier plans to take a university course motivated him to do very well in the TAFE course. He then worked as a young surveyor in a variety of positions, including the Lands Department (cadastral surveying) and in maritime surveying, before moving to large construction companies.

5.1.2 Changes in job skills in surveying
Charles views construction surveying as a service industry, whose purpose is to formulate methods to set out a project and to calculate the relevant data and quantities. While this basic purpose has not changed, Charles across his career has seen the way that it is carried out change, and continue to change, dramatically as technology has evolved. The scope and extent of the major revolution in surveying is reflected in comparisons like the following:

- When he began in surveying, Charles calculated survey data with log tables or small calculators and did well if he surveyed 10-15 property blocks in a day. Now with Global Positioning Systems (GPS) he might do anything from 600-10000 shots a day on site, with the calculations of the data being done in the office using sophisticated PC software.
- Charles' first surveying calculator had a memory capacity of twenty-five program steps; now he uses software that can deal with a million survey points.
- The early Modeling software used in the 1980s would run overnight to process survey data, but now it does the same calculations in 'about a few seconds'.

Charles summarizes briefly these enormous changes in surveying as follows. 'Broadly speaking, there was the introduction of the computer, followed by an electronic survey equipment revolution, then a software revolution. Now, as an example, all three are being merged to control and drive sophisticated machines that in the future may not require an operator'.

5.1.3 Acquiring work skills and keeping up with the continual changes
Essentially, Charles believes he has learnt his job skills, both technical and managerial, from experience on-the-job and personal research as he has gone along. He claims that, basically, there is no training whatever for construction that can replace actual on-the-job experience. So he sees his learning as having been self-developed gradually over the course of his career, including gaining the knowledge and skills to perform in higher positions. Thus, as Charles sees it, the role of formal training in his moves to higher jobs has been negligible.

The rapid computer innovations in a small field such as surveying are such that there are not a lot of worthwhile courses available. Charles works with the software writers to understand and assist in directing the latest innovations. For Charles and most software users they either pay for training or work it out for themselves. In doing the latter, Charles has become used to 'pushing himself to the limits'. Survey equipment manufacturers run some training sessions and there are university workshops available from time to time. He is about to attend an intense 3-day workshop at a university on GPS. These workshops run at universities or TAFE colleges are the result of organizations combining to give a more structured training alternative to that of manufacturer organized sessions. He comments that this is better than manufacturer's sessions as they feature more intensive learning. Another benefit is that you come away from these workshops with not only the course literature, but also your own set of reference notes for applications and procedures experienced.

Charles compensates for the lack of suitable courses in these specialized areas through personal research. A common instance of self-teaching for him is venturing into the software to try out what it can do. If he makes a mistake, he just starts again. Charles keeps in touch with software package writers by conducting trials of their products and providing feedback and advice. He does the same with prototype survey instruments. He also belongs to a software user group made up of people from all sections of the industry. A software company technical support manager runs the group. Charles' company pays him to attend this user group. The user group talks about the problems experienced, the needed innovations or applications and the overall directions for the industry. He sees this as invaluable as no university or TAFE course can possibly keep currency with the speed and cost of the equipment being developed. This applies also to the use of survey instruments.

There is no specific construction sector training as such in Australian surveying degrees, but at the University of Newcastle surveying and civil engineering can be merged, which Charles sees as a logical combination of skills. Charles learnt and developed his skills on the job by working extremely long hours. Summarizing his development and maintenance of up-to-date technical surveying skills, Charles sees some of it coming from formal off-the-job learning (e.g. a short course on a technical innovation), some of it coming from formal on-the-job learning (e.g. training on how to use a newly purchased machine), but by far the vast majority of it is from informal off-the-job reading, research and testing, that he does for himself. (Note that in this analysis of his learning, Charles does not mention informal on-the-job learning. This was because he was one of the minority amongst our interviewees who thought of learning as something different from working, so that when you were working learning was not happening as well. He thought that his informal learning about work occurred when he organised various learning activities for himself. Though elsewhere in the interview he stressed his actual on-the-job experience as the main source of his current capacities and abilities).

The other area where Charles has had to gain and maintain skills is in his role as a manager. As with his technical surveying skills, Charles sees experience on-the-job as the significant source of the management skills that he has acquired. He describes the management roles he has performed as centering on running smoothly operating teams, structured surveying methods and clear company policies. He describes his first experience of management evolving from frustration at the rather ad hoc surveying methods at the firm. He approached his manager with procedures to improve and streamline survey methods for better efficiency. He was encouraged to implement his ideas and manage them.

Until this job, his role as manager occurred at all hours of the day. This was due to the fact that Charles was required to provide site survey services to one or more large construction sites, using junior surveyors and, simultaneously, assisting surveyors all over NSW at other sites with methods and procedures, this invariably by telephone. The on site management was 'hands-on' in which he could gather his team to show them something when needed, whereas the telephone assistance to other sites Charles believed to be restricted and difficult. Charles' new management role is not tied to a site and allows him more time for face to face assistance, time to solve problems and provide solutions to sites and surveyors. Regular visits to sites also helps to maintain quality and motivation. This role structure also allows Charles time to assist with head office tenders and variations.

5.1.4 Plans for the future
Charles' one big regret is that he didn't go to university. Although he has held responsible positions and was headhunted for his current management role, he feels he would have had a much easier road to his present employment standing, if he had attended university. He is highly motivated and has a thirst to do more courses. Charles would like to progress to a Construction Manager's position in the future, and management courses, particularly courses in managing large employee groups would be an advantage. He would also like to teach in the field of survey software. However with the long hours of work (12 hour each day for 6 days a week) it is difficult to have time for formal study.

5.1.5 Commentary
Charles' story connects with and illustrates several main themes of this chapter. We have defined informal learning generally as learning not under the control of a formal education institution. The informal learning from the practice of work, which is a main focus of this book, has been characterised as the development of an evolving capacity to make context-sensitive judgments in changing contexts. This definition can be expanded via the six key features of informal learning at work, identified by Beckett & Hager (2002: 115), which were outlined above. Charles' story will be considered against these six features.

1. Informal learning is organic/holistic
Charles is passionate about his ongoing learning. He is not just a detached observer focusing on furnishing his mind with information and understanding. Rather Charles as a whole person is engaged in the ongoing learning. His enthusiasm for 'hands on' leadership, and trial and error learning, reflect his view of himself as a highly skilled, practising construction worker. He is definitely not just someone with a lot of theoretical knowledge about construction surveying.

2. Informal learning is contextual
Charles' passion for his area of specialty gives his learning a sharp focus. Some might view his specialty as narrow. However, his knowledge gains some breadth from his keen interest in the history of surveying. The highly contextual nature of Charles' learning is evident, in part, from the rapid nature of the changes that characterise the field of surveying. No formal course can keep up with these changes. At best, formal courses can give people a preparation to become highly self-directed learners like Charles.

3. Informal learning is activity- and experience-based
This is a major feature of the general mix of Charles' learning activities. Even the formal short courses that he occasionally attends, centred on recent innovations or new types of equipment, are in part activity- and experience-based. The informal learning that he arranges for himself, such as the software users' group and the collaboration with software writers, are heavily activity- and experience-based.

4. Informal learning arises in situations where learning is not the main aim
As noted above, Charles was inclined to view learning as something that happens in situations set aside for learning. Although, somewhat contradicting this, he described his on-the-job experience as one of his main assets. Presumably even when participating in the software users' group, or when testing software for writers to see how well it works, Charles learns in ways that he had not intended.

5. Informal learning is activated by individual learners rather than by teachers/ trainers
Charles' self-direction is very evident. He values some formal off-the-job learning, and some formal on-the-job learning. But by far the vast majority of it is from informal off-the-job reading, research and testing, that Charles organises for himself.

6. Informal learning is often collaborative/collegial
Collaboration is part of the construction work ethos, especially for the large projects that are Charles' company's specialty. Collegiality and collaboration are distinctive features of the informal off-the-job reading, research and testing, that Charles organises for himself. Examples are trialing software package for their writers and providing feedback and advice; and participation in the software user group.
    Overall, Charles' mix of learning, most of it informal, is ensuring the development of his evolving capacity to make context-sensitive judgments in changing contexts.

5.2 Anne's Story

Anne is an experienced nurse who had become an ambulance officer. In the past, ambulance culture had privileged the most senior officer present with the decision making. More recently, this has been giving way to a newer norm whereby, of the two officers in the ambulance, the non-driver has primary patient responsibility. (Officers normally take it in turn to drive the ambulance, thereby taking turns to have primary patient responsibility). Anne has concluded that one of the qualities of sound ambulance practice is a capacity to tactfully suggest to fellow officers that their proposed procedure may not be the best one in the circumstances, this needing to be done in ways that do least damage to officers' egos.

Anne described an instance where she broke prevailing norms to achieve better patient outcomes. As a new ambulance officer, who had qualified quicker than usual because of significant recognition of prior learning for her nursing work, Anne was assigned to work with a fairly senior partner. This situation created some tensions as the experienced officer recognised that in certain areas of prac- tice she probably had more experience and know-how. Sure enough they were called to a fairly rare case for ambulance officers, one where a young child was in cardiac arrest and resuscitation was the likely option. Though there was existing tension between Anne and her more senior partner, a tension which she was wary of exacerbating, they both knew immediately that she had easily the more exten- sive experience in child resuscitation. Anne unhesitatingly and spontaneously took over care of the patient from her senior partner. The roles of rank and seniority in procedural rules and norms within the ambulance service, were no doubt intended to advance good outcomes for patients. But it is clear that if adhered to too rigidly they can diminish such outcomes.

Here we have Anne making a spontaneous judgement to risk a senior officer's wrath in the interests of achieving optimum patient outcomes in a serious emer- gency. Her judgement was *holistic* in that her full gamut of attributes were inte- grated in the judgement. These included the:

- cognitive (she knew that this case was urgent and that she had more rele- vant experience than did the senior officer);
- practical (she had the manual skills needed for child resuscitation):
- ethical and the moral (she followed processes that recognised the parents' rights in this situation);
- the attitudinal and the emotional (she was sensitive to the senior officer's feelings as the situation unfolded); and
- the volitional (she was determined to try to save the child, even at the risk of offending her senior colleague).

Her judgement was *contextual* in that it involved a unique combination of factors, including an emergency case rarely encountered by ambulance officers, her senior colleague having primary patient responsibility, yet her having vastly more ex- perience of dealing with such a situation.

Her judgement certainly *denoted* for the young patient in that it was literally a life and death situation. Likewise, her judgement was *defeasible*, e.g. she might have turned out to be wrong in her estimation that the senior colleague had virtu- ally no experience of an emergency situation like this. Anne's judgement included *problem identification* on several levels. Because of her nursing experience, iden- tifying the patient problem was straightforward. However, her position vis-à-vis the senior officer complicated the problem situation. Fortunately, all concerned viewed optimum patient care as the overriding consideration. Finally, Anne's judgement was *socially shaped*. The factors are many. But here we have the unusual situation where practice in one domain (nursing) had a major role in shaping practice in a different, but related, domain.

Anne reported that her learning from this situation was some of the richest in her ambulance career. Her holistic judgement in this situation and its aftermath have proved to be pivotal in her sense of herself as a highly proficient ambulance officer. Her learning in this situation does not connect readily with characteristics of formal learning outlined earlier in this chapter. But her judgement making sits very comfortably with the theory of informal learning presented in this book. This learning may not fare well against formal criteria, but we accept Anne's estimate of its pivotal contribution to her career as a successful ambulance officer. In later chapters we will pick up other facets of Anne's story.

5.3 Alison's Story

The suggestion that personal values and beliefs of the practitioner are likely to shape significantly the internal goods of their practice has figured to some extent in the above discussion. A case study that shows this very clearly concerns Alison, who is a training and development consultant running her own practice, which is "to make education and training work better for client corporations". Her corporate consultancy addresses gaps between strategic needs of the organisation and its existing training and development arrangements. Essentially what Alison does is to make judgements about how best to close that gap. Her success or otherwise is demonstrated by its impact on the bottom line. So the external goods of her practice are pretty clear. But it is also apparent that Alison's own distinctive values and beliefs strongly shape her practice and its internal goods. These key values and beliefs include:

- Opposition to 'slash and burn' and 'downsizing' approaches. She finds that her consultancies can usually make a satisfactory difference without shedding staff.
- A preference for consultancies that focus on longer-term strategies and allow time for partnerships to be built (say over two years with the consultant being paid according to results).
- Scepticism about the value of 'off-the-shelf' training packages. Rather she advises on selecting and designing training (often from external providers) suited to the particular needs and context of the organisation in question.

During her practice, Alison reported that she commonly makes a variety of judgments, such as: What are the main limitations of the current education and training arrangements? What arrangements would be significantly better? How much of the knowledge she had gained about the organisation should she report to the senior people who employed her services? How much should she hold back? Is the organisation mature enough to change its current training system? In making these and other judgements, Alison's recommendations are heavily influenced by her personal beliefs and values. Clearly the organization could hire other consultants with very different values who would, no doubt, come up with very different recommendations. So whatever, the internal goods are that underpin the practice of training and development consultants, they will reflect significantly the particular beliefs and values of those chosen to carry out the consultancy.

6. THE INFORMAL LEARNING AND LIFELONG LEARNING CLUSTER

The remainder of this book will centre on the arguing for the vital relationship between the emerging view of learning and the notions of informal and lifelong learning. This congruence has already been reflected in relation to discussion of the development (or transformation) metaphor cluster for understanding learning, as well as the learning through participation in human practices metaphor cluster. If, as we have argued, educational policy and practice have shifted too much towards formal learning while neglecting informal learning, there is a need for wider adoption of learning metaphors that favour informal learning. The acquisition and transfer metaphors and associated assumptions fit formal learning assumptions like a glove, while also acting to render informal learning invisible. As Hacking observed near the start of this chapter, "metaphors influence the mind in many unnoticed ways". Perhaps because of this invisibility, there is no widely used and accepted metaphor for informal learning.

As was noted in chapter one, there has been much scepticism about the concept of lifelong learning within the educational literature. But many of these critiques reflect their author's unstated acceptance of a version of the common story about learning. If learning is centrally about minds acquiring propositions, lifelong learning is potentially about perpetual enrolment in formal accredited courses. The individual learner is in danger of being condemned to learn all subjects/disciplines. In this respect, part of the common story about learning is an acceptance of a 'quiz show' view of what it is for someone to be learned. As well, the focus is firmly on the individual learner. Illich was right that we have been schooled to accept a 'consumer of formal courses' view of knowledge acquisition. However, as the above features of the emerging understanding of learning suggest, much learning, including informal learning at its best, is accurately described as a form of lifelong learning. Changing social and contextual circumstances may be creating conditions in which the concept of lifelong learning is potentially a fruitful one. Note also that, influenced perhaps by the common story about learning, much literature on lifelong learning assumes that the individual learner is the appropriate unit of analysis. It may however be useful to view entities such as communities and organisations having a lifetime over which they can learn. In Kuhnian terms, it might be argued that in the present era the formal learning paradigm with its accompanying metaphors is in crisis and nearing the end of its useful life. So far the details of the emerging replacement paradigm are less than clear. A rich understanding of lifelong learning may well point the way to a viable replacement paradigm.

Because work is a main arena for informal learning, workplace examples will figure prominently in the discussion in the remainder of this book. There is no doubt that many contemporary work arrangements discourage learning, let alone lifelong learning. This is reflected in much research that addresses issues such as work structures, workplace power and gender relations, workplace culture, etc. Nevertheless, there are also work situations in which significant learning occurs. Our own research (e.g., Beckett & Hager 2000, 2002, Hager, 2001, 2004a, Buchanan *et al.* 2001) has identified many such instances, including some where the learning is sufficiently rich to pass as lifelong learning at work. In all of these cases, a common factor is that workers place high value on the satisfaction they obtain from their work. It provides them with a strong sense of personal development. This personal development is something that is an internal good to the work itself. For these workers, work is much more than paid employment. We need an account of work that locates this satisfaction and distinguishes it from work that is essentially alienating.

Dewey (1966) was well aware that much work is alienating and maintained that unless workers see the social and political point of their work and the ideas that underpin it, then the educative potential of experience at work is negated. For Dewey work should assist workers to develop a capacity for judgement applicable beyond their practice at work. This requires their practice to be informed by some overall notions of purpose and intention that link to practices that are not obviously related to work at all. Thus for Dewey, work and lifelong learning can coalesce.

Dewey's predilection for "occupation as becoming" and the importance of productive learning at work finds a resonance in more recent writers. According to Standing (1999: 3), work is

> .... rounded activity combining creative, conceptual and analytical thinking and use of manual aptitudes – the *vita activa* of human existence...... Work involves an individual element and a social element, an interaction with objects – raw materials, tools, 'inputs', etc. – and an interaction with people and institutions.

Standing goes on to contrast labour sharply with work: "Labour is arduous – perhaps *alienated work* – and epistemologically it conveys a sense of 'pain' – *animal laborans*." (1999: 4). Thus, for Standing, labour is "activity done under some duress, and some sense of *control* by others or by institutions or by technology, or more likely by a combination of all three."

The economic rationalist labour market policies that have dominated Western countries in recent decades treat individuals as mere economic units ('labour), rather than as "aspirants with personal and professional goals" (Waterhouse, Wilson & Ewer 1999: 22). For economists, labour is merely that which is expended in production. The alienation associated with labour reflects an impoverished work context "..... that uses only a narrow range of physical or mental attributes, or that restricts the development or renewal of physical, intellectual or psychological capacities ....." (Standing, 1999: 7). Whereas the complex set of relationships that characterise work on Standing's account, requires a rich and varying context. Clearly, ".... wherever possible, policy should encourage work and not merely labour." (Buchanan *et al.* 2001: 25). Such possibilities are more widespread than previously thought, if Murphy (1993) is correct in his conclusion that economists, including both Adam Smith and Marx, have typically overestimated the technical restrictions that efficiency of production places on work organisation. On Murphy's account, it appears that "[m]any social divisions of labour are compatible with different (but equally technically efficient) configurations of tasks." (Buchanan *et al.* 2001: 25).

So for those like Dewey and Standing who support an understanding of work as creative action that is productive of human growth and development, lifelong learning at work is a viable possibility. It is interesting to note that contemporary workers' views on what they themselves want from work are closely akin to Dewey and Standing. In 2001, the NSW Labor Council (in Australia) commissioned a comprehensive study of employees' views about working life. A key question was: 'What would you say is the most important factor to you making your work a positive experience?'. Twenty nine percent of respondents nominated 'Interesting and Satisfying Work', while twenty six percent nominated 'Co-Workers Getting Along'. All other factors received much less support, with 'Fair and Reasonable Pay' scoring seven percent, 'Recognition of Efforts' seven percent, and 'Control Over the Way You Do Work' five percent, with lesser factors making up the remaining twenty six percent (Buchanan *et al.* 2001: 23). Quite clearly, "the content and immediate social setting of work are very important for people enjoying paid employment." (Buchanan *et al.* 2001: 24).

Although the global flourishing of capitalism and the unbridled profit motive gives us cause for pessimism, it seems that in some sense, lifelong learning at work may still be possible. However, even in instances where work arrangements are more favourable for learning, there does not seem to be wide recognition that this is the case. Why is this so? Our diagnosis is that learning is widely misunderstood in our present society. Traditional understandings of learning give learning in general a bad press, let alone lifelong learning.

Throughout the discussion of the emerging understanding of learning, and, indeed, throughout this chapter, context has been a vital consideration. Learning is inescapably contextual. We regard this matter as so important that to do it proper justice, it needs a chapter of its own. Accordingly, the next chapter considers the crucial role of context in a richer understanding of learning.

CHAPTER SIX

THE IMPORTANCE OF CONTEXTUALITY FOR LEARNING

> Most educational theorists and researchers recognize that all knowledge and inquiry are context-dependent. In spite of this recognition, the exact definition of context remains unclear. *(Garrison 1997: 86)*

To say that informal learning is contextual can seem like a pretty bland statement. For one thing, it can seem like stating of the obvious. Of course, all learning, indeed all human activities, occur in a context, so what is new? As well, context can seem to be a catchall idea for something that is too complex to unravel. The fact that we have a single general word to represent context suggests that it is a single thing. Yet, when looked into more closely, context is something that is multi-facetted, very diverse and very complex. Hence the feeling of blandness induced by blanket and undiscriminating applications of the term 'context'. In this and the next chapter, we establish some of the multiple bases for viewing learning as inescapably shaped by context, and we elucidate the diversity and complexity of context. We then introduce the key notion of 'nesting of contexts' as a way of dealing with this diversity and complexity.

In its simplest formulation, context refers to the surroundings in which learning occurs and the possible influences that these surroundings have on what is learnt. As this chapter develops, it will become apparent that there is much more to context than this simple formulation suggests. However, relying on this simple formulation, much literature on learning leaves only a secondary role for context, thereby denying that it significantly affects learning. The various arguments can be appreciated by considering the following, three views of context (drawn from Hager & Smith 2004). The role of context in shaping learning gradually becomes more influential across these views.

1. UNDERSTANDINGS OF CONTEXT

1.1 Context as Minimally Influential

The view that allows the weakest influence for contextual factors regards them as relevant only when they prevent learning from being optimally achieved. That is, context is seen as having a negative effect on learning only if, for instance, it distracts the learner from the task at hand. This kind of thinking presupposes

the basic or common metaphors of learning, such as that learning involves acquisition of products by the mind of the learner. These products are taken to be independent of context. So the only influence of context is in cases where it might interfere in the process of acquisition by the learner. On this view, as long as
distractions are absent or minimised, context is irrelevant.

1.2 Context as Influential but Controllable

This view allows more influence for context, but still consigns such influence to a
secondary role. It treats contextual factors as mere data that can be organised and
manipulated to promote or enhance learning. On this second view, context plays a
more important role in determining which learning processes or arrangements are
best, but only relative to a set of learning content that is not itself context-
dependent. Context only determines how the learning outcomes should be optimally achieved, but does not help to shape the learning outcomes themselves. It is
up to teachers to arrange and rearrange the learning so as to optimise learning.
This puts a focus on such contextual factors as quality of teaching aids, variety of
teaching and learning activities, strategies for arousing student interest in the
learning, etc.

1.3 Context as Decisively Influential

Stronger contextualist views argue that *both* learning processes and learning content are significantly shaped by contextual influences. According to these views
the notion of *context* is itself very complex. It is seen as including a multiplicity of
diverse factors. This complexity and diversity of context will be addressed in detail in the rest of this chapter and in the next. However, the main feature of this
stronger sense in which context can influence learning is that context is seen to
shape the *outcomes* of learning as well as the learning processes themselves. Thus,
on this view, what is learnt is marked or altered by details of the particular learning context. This challenges various cherished beliefs, for instance the belief that
learning outcomes can be fully specified in advance. In this book we favour this
third interpretation of the influence of context. As we will see, the influence of
context on informal learning is crucial.

Although context is very complex, there are ways of approaching and thereby
understanding it. Before we embark on this, it will be useful to consider briefly the
main reasons for so much educational thought and tradition having treated learning as being context-free.

2. REASONS FOR NEGLECTING CONTEXT

There are several bases for treating learning as context-free. Firstly, it is thought
that what is learnt is apparently the kind of thing that can be independent of its
context. Propositional knowledge is an archetypical and ubiquitous example of

something that is learnt. The very abstractness of propositions seems to mark them as context-free. Likewise, turning to another kind of thing that can be learnt, different people appear to possess the same psychomotor skills suggesting that such skills are something above and beyond the people that possess them or the contexts in which they might be deployed. Thus typical kinds of things that can be learnt appear to exhibit a generality that frees them of particular contexts.

A second basis for treating learning as context-free, is that it is apparently located in spaces that are separate from the contexts in which it was learnt or is to be applied. Paradigmatically, propositional knowledge is located in learners' minds or heads. (Or, in a more sophisticated account, minds are in contact with an abstract Platonic realm of propositions). Psychomotor skills are somehow lodged in learners' bodies. These cranial or whole body locations are thought of as quarantining the learning from the various environments or contexts that the host learner successively occupies. In nearly all educational thought the individual learner is viewed as the unit of analysis. If learners are thought of as being relatively free of surrounding contexts, *a fortiori* the learning that they acquire is context-free. Both of these bases, in turn encourage and underpin a third basis for treating learning as context-free. This is the range of familiar metaphors that are automatically and unthinkingly deployed in thought and talk about learning (as was discussed in chapter five). Learning is paradigmatically thought of as a substance or thing (Saljo 2002), hence the ubiquitous acquisition and transfer metaphors. The substance or thing assumption about learning is ingrained into our language. So much so that it renders difficult the expression of the alternative understandings that we attempt in this and subsequent chapters.

We will use the term 'abstract rationality' for the view that learning is paradigmatically abstract propositions located in individual minds that are independent of their surrounding contexts. (Or, in the Platonic variant, minds in contact with abstract realms). A close relative of our 'abstract rationality' is Winch's (1998: 5) 'mentalistic individualism'. When the abstract rationality account seems to work best, it is for cases involving 'pure', universal propositions, such as the use of multiplication tables. But, we want to insist, the great bulk of learning is not like this. Certainly informal learning in its many manifestations, which is a central concern of this book, is not at all like that. The cluster of assumptions that constitute abstract rationality in turn lead to other assumptions that commonly shape educational measurement procedures – that learning consists of a series of discrete items, each item showing the stability of things, and, thereby, able to be learnt in the same way by all learners in a group (replicability of learning). While many, when pressed to think about it, would claim that they reject the bald metaphors of learning, we claim that there still remains a widespread implicit acceptance amongst educators of abstract rationality's learner as an independent spectator in the world.

3. INFORMAL LEARNING IS SIGNIFICANTLY CONTEXTUAL

There are a range of reasons for rejecting abstract rationality and the understanding of learning associated with it. Three of these reasons have been chosen for particular discussion here. The order for discussion of these reasons has been chosen to enable ideas from the earlier ones to be drawn upon in the later ones.

1. We can dispute whether propositional learning is itself context-free. Here, just for the sake of the argument, it is accepted that learning is essentially propositional learning. However drawing on writers such as Brandom and Dewey, the claim that propositional learning is context-free is disputed.
2. We can question whether propositional learning is itself a good place to start for developing an understanding of the nature of learning processes. The claim here is that propositional learning is not representative of learning in general. There are many important kinds of learning that are not propositional. It will be argued that these other kinds of learning are even more clearly contextual than is propositional learning – though we maintain that the latter is contextual in crucial ways. It will be suggested that holism of various kinds is at the basis of the contextuality of most kinds of learning.
3. We can dispute whether learning, when viewed as product, can be plausibly thought of as occupying spaces that are free of context. It will be argued that, not only does learning not reside in minds or crania, it is not even restricted to human bodies. Rather, learning ranges between and beyond individual learners. Hence the spaces it occupies are not separate from their contexts but are part of them.

Each of these will now be considered in some detail.

4. PROPOSITIONAL LEARNING AND CONTEXT

As noted above, we are using the term 'abstract rationality' for the view that learning is paradigmatically about abstract propositions located in minds that are independent of their surrounding contexts. (Or minds in contact with abstract realms). What the work of Brandom and others does is to undermine the view that propositions and the concepts that comprise them are independent of everyday contexts. The relative objectivity and stability of certain concepts and propositions encouraged theories that sought to ground them individually as representations of specific discrete features of the world. The gist of Brandom's argument for present purposes is that it offers an account of the use of concepts and propositions that rejects representational views. Instead Brandom replaces such theories with an account of conceptual understanding that bases it on inference and judgement. Rather than the items of understanding being relatively independent of one another as postulated in the representation accounts, for Brandom's inferentialism, concepts are mutually dependent upon one another in chains of inferences. This means that they are constantly revisable as understanding develops further. Drawing on Sellars' (1956) rebuttal of 'the Myth of the Given', Brandom takes Sellars to show that

> ..... even the non-inferentially elicited perceptual judgments that the empiricist rightly appreciates as forming the empirical basis for our knowledge can count as judgments (applications of concepts) only insofar as they are *inferentially* articulated..... To apply any concepts non-inferentially, one must be able to apply concepts inferentially. *(Brandom 2001: 83)*

Thus, Brandom develops an account of conceptual objectivity that locates it not in a formal, abstract, universal realm, but in the normative context of the human social practice of "giving and asking for reasons" (Brandom 2001: 83).

> Grasping or understanding a concept is simply being able practically to place it in a network of inferential relations: to know what is evidence for or against its being properly applied to a particular case, and what its proper applicability to a particular case counts as evidence for or against. Our capacity to know (or believe) *that* something is the case depends on our having a certain kind of know-how: the ability to tell what is a reason for what." *Brandom (2001: 82)*

So for Brandom

> .... concepts are broadly inferential norms that implicitly govern practices of giving and asking for reasons. *(Brandom 2001: 84)*

As Derry (2000: 2) suggests:

> .... the realm of reasons, (the normative context) that makes knowledge possible, exists outside individuals in the world itself, that is the social world which individuals inhabit.

This approach denies that knowledge is grounded in direct access by individuals to bedrock experiences and the propositions that correspond to them. Nor does it licence the unbridled discursive freedom of choice of fashionable postmodernists. Rather, knowledge and concepts derive from the human practices of inference and judgement set in a space of reasons that is independent of individual learners. These practices are social thereby having a history, one which with hindsight can be interpreted and reconstructed as rational in the Hegelian sense.

So Brandom's account, inferentialism, replaces both foundationalism and anti-foundationalism. For him, our understanding of concepts is contextual in that what a concept means is contingent on the inferences and judgements that it allows in relation to clusters of many other concepts. In chapter two it was argued that the development (or transformation) metaphor for learning has a number of advantages over its two main rival metaphors, acquisition and participation. Work by Beckett (2001, 2002) and Mackenzie (2000) establishes close links between the development metaphor and Brandom's account of understanding. Beckett argues that "embodied actions are the very source of the generation of understanding something" (2002: 3), with knowledge needing to be understood as a "process of construction (i.e. as a series of inferences), rather than as a state of arrival (i.e. as a set of representations)" (2002: 2).

A related cluster of ideas about concepts and mearning can be found in Wittgenstein's later philosophy. For Wittgenstein meanings are not established internally by individual minds, rather meanings emerge from collective "forms of life". As Toulmin (1999: 58) puts it:

> All *meanings* are created in the public domain in the context of *collective* situations and activities.

Though meanings emerge from collective forms of life, Toulmin suggests that once created in this way, they can, of course, be internalised by individuals. But the point is that, contra abstract rationality, meanings are not essentially internal.

A somewhat different account of the contextuality of propositional learning can be derived from the work of John Dewey. Here we will focus on considerations drawn from Dewey's conception of logic. In the section after this, the account will be enriched by a consideration of Dewey's theory of learning. In his work Dewey tried to develop a "naturalistic and ecological conception of logic" (Burke 1994: 2) with a focus on action and inquiry, as against mainstream formal logic with its focus on abstract propositions. The major differences between Dewey's conception of logic and the mainstream can be summarised as follows. Mainstream formal logic centres on abstract, necessary propositions and the deductive relations between them. Historically, these characteristics came to represent the ideal for theoretical knowledge. So much so, that the more knowledge claims departed from this ideal the more dubious they seemed to be. One early example of this was the ancient Greek hierarchy of theoretical knowledge placed above both practical and productive knowledge. As was noted in chapter five, for Aristotle, theoretical knowledge was linked "to certainty, because its object was said to be what is always or for most part the case" (Hickman 1990: 107). According to Aristotle it thereby had a share in the divine. He held that practical knowledge was inferior to theoretical knowledge because it involved "choice among relative goods" (Hickman 1990: 107-8) and productive knowledge was even more inferior because it involved "the making of things out of contingent matter" (Hickman 1990: 108). Thus formal logic came to be seen as representing the ideal form which sound theoretical knowledge ought to take. The knowledge involved in everyday workplace practice and production was thereby viewed as epistemologically uninteresting except to the extent that it represented an application of sound theoretical knowledge.

In contrast to formal logic and its close connection to theoretical knowledge, Dewey's focus was on a logic of action which repudiated the theory/practice dichotomy (and similar cognate dichotomies). It also distinguished propositions from judgements. As Burke (1994) argues, with the development of artificial intelligence, robotics, etc. the field of logic is finally turning its attention to the logic of action and Dewey's ideas are starting to receive serious scholarly attention. In a logic of action, vocational (or professional) knowledge is no longer placed at the periphery of knowledge. Such a logic does not simply invert the order of traditional logic and privilege the particular over the universal and the practical over the discursive. Rather it incorporates all of these and rejects as false dichotomies theory/practice, universal/particular, discursive/practical, etc. (Hickman 1990). Thus the Greek hierarchy of theoretical knowledge/ practical knowledge/ productive knowledge is rejected.

For classical views of learning, e.g. abstract rationality, learning becomes a one way process in which discrete items of learning, such as propositions, are transferred to the mind. The items of learning are thought of as discrete, mirroring the classical correspondence between propositions and facts. They are also abstract and independent of the world. (Of course, once such propositions are transferred to a mind, ideally they subsumed and reinforced into prior learning, i.e. their various connections with other propositions are appreciated). Later, determined by the learner's particular beliefs, desires, etc., learned propositions are marshalled to plan and underpin action on the world. That is, they are applied. This puts them at one remove from action in the world, thus preserving their supposed independence of context. In contrast, Dewey's logic of action makes propositions inherently contextual. As Burke (1994) shows, Dewey's logic features a much more sophisticated account of the kinds and characteristics of propositions that are relevant to knowledge. Dewey firstly argues that the universal/particular distinction is not the same as the generic/specific distinction. He then identifies seven sorts of propositions, only one of which is particular and two of which are universal. The other four share characteristics of both the particular and the universal. However, in terms of the generic/specific distinction, three of the seven sorts of propositions are specific and four are general. Dewey further provides an account of the roles of these assorted kinds of propositions in judgements.

Unlike formal logic with its focus on propositions, in Dewey's logic of action, propositions are subordinate to judgements in a "hermeneutic helix" of inquiry (Burke 1994: 229). Burke expresses it thus:

> ..... for Dewey, propositions are the *means* by which the subject matter of an inquiry is described and subsequently made determinate; and though it is not entirely meaningless to say that they may be true or false in what they say about the world ....., that is not what distinguishes them as *propositions*. What is more relevant to characterizing propositions is their 'validity value' (to coin a phrase) as means to instituting warrantably assertible judgment. This involves not truth values but things like relevance, salience, coherence with other propositions, persistence in the face of ongoing inquiry (i.e., failing to be disconfirmed by ongoing experience), and so forth. These are existential factors which an inquirer has a direct handle on... *(1994: 206)*

So for Dewey propositions are significantly implicated in everyday contexts. Hence propositional learning cannot be free of context. In the next section, the importance of this will become even clearer as Dewey's theory of learning is considered in more detail.

In this section, for the purposes of the argument, we have accepted the common assumption that propositional learning is representative of all learning. We have argued that there are important senses in which propositional learning is not itself context-free. We have considered philosophical arguments about the nature of concepts and understanding to suggest that common assumptions about propositional learning, as well as their widespread use to endorse 'common-sense' accounts of learning are both very dubious. If the 'context-free' assumption is dubious for propositional learning, this is even more so for other familiar types of learning, as will be made clear in the next section.

5. WHAT'S SO IMPORTANT ABOUT PROPOSITIONAL LEARNING?

The argument of this section is that there are many kinds of learning and that most of them are more clearly contextual than is propositional learning. So taking propositional learning to be representative of learning in general has had the effect of masking the contextuality that is actually an important feature of learning. (Of course our own position is that even propositional learning is significantly contextual, but we accept that the contrary view is more plausible in this case than it is for other kinds of learning). To establish the plausibility of the claims that there is much more to learning than propositional learning, and that, incidentally, all learning is inherently contextual, we will first examine Dewey's theory of learning in some detail. This will be followed by some ideas from other authors including Wittgenstein, Passmore, Winch, and Lakoff and Johnson, ideas that will extend and support the main points derived from Dewey's work.

5.1 Dewey's Account of Learning and its Inherent Contextuality

Dewey draws attention to a distinction between learning as a process and learning as a product. He argues that the latter (product) sense has come to dominate the meaning normally attributable to learning, such that learning is mistakenly likened to a kind of mental state – that of understanding or knowing. The former (process) sense however implies that learning is a lifelong process within which means and ends are dialectically related. This mistake is related to *"the* philosophic fallacy". Dewey characterised this fallacy in *Experience and Nature* as "the conversion of eventual functions into antecedent existence" (Dewey 1925: 34). As Garrison expresses it: "the greatest philosophical errors arise from confusing the *consequences* of linguistic meaning making and logical inquiry with *antecedent* metaphysical existence" (1999: 291). For Dewey, knowledge and inferences are the "eventual functions" of inquiry. As such they "bear the marks" of the processes by which they were produced (Garrison 1999: 292). Hence, they cannot be timeless, perfect forms or some such. This means that the product/process dualism is dissolved since the process inescapably shapes features of the product.

For Dewey, inquiry is initiated by the disruption of an habitual function. Inquiry is set in train by the individual being put into a state of what might be called bodily need from which it needs relief. This contrasts with traditional educational thought in which inquiry is the outcome of an intellectual puzzle or cognitive doubt. Therefore, for Dewey all inquiry is contextual in that it "is controlled, in part, by the constraints placed upon the inquiry by the context (situation) it seeks to ameliorate." (Garrison 1999: 293). Thus "inquiry is always practical reasoning that seeks means for securing desirable consequences in a given context." (Garrison 1999: 293). This leads to Dewey's definition of rationality:

> Reasonableness or rationality is .... an affair of the relation of means and consequences. .... Rationality as an abstract conception is precisely the generalised idea of the means-consequence relation as such. *(Dewey 1938: 17)*

It follows that for Dewey "[a]ll reasoning is practical means-end reasoning, or contributes to it ...." (Garrison 1999: 291).

If means-consequence reasoning is at the heart of Dewey's practical reasoning, the desirable end or consequence is a return to a state of smooth habitual functioning such as preceded the triggering of the inquiry. However it needs to be stressed that for Dewey means-ends or means-consequences are not so readily separable:

> Ends always *emerge* in the course of inquiry. Means are indistinguishable from the end in a given context until the process of inquiry is complete... *(Garrison 1999: 295)*

Therefore, ends should not be given the transcendental status accorded them in much traditional metaphysics. Rather ends are contextual and revisable, apt to transmute into means for redirecting action. To capture this continuity between means and ends, Dewey introduces the notion of "ends-in-view" (Dewey 1925: 88). Ends-in-view are distinguished from ends in that they "are foreseen consequences that pre-interpret events and provide possibility. They allow us to act intelligently in the present." But while guiding present action they "require constant reinterpretation" (Garrison 1999: 296). However, once "achieved, ends-in-view become means or 'pivots', for directing, and redirecting, further action; they provide new beginnings.... Ends-in-view are the pivots or fulcrums for creative redirection within action" (Garrison 1999: 296).

Dewey expands his account of the philosophic fallacy by characterising it as the "neglect of context" (Dewey 1938), that is, committing the philosophic fallacy involves ignoring part of what is needed to understand a phenomenon, namely its context. Something like this happens when we analyse a phenomenon, such as reasoning, into various components as we attempt to understand, improve and predict it. The danger is that mere conceptual distinctions, which Dewey accepts are useful for enhancing understanding, become concretised into fixed dualisms, which create delusion. For instance the Aristotelian separation of theoretical and practical reasoning leads to the two being viewed as distinct entities. According to Dewey, the result is that:

> .... [r]easonableness or rationality has ..... been hypostatized. One of the oldest and most enduring traditions in logical theory has converted rationality into a faculty which, when it is actualised in perception of first truths, was called *reason*.... *(Dewey 1938: 18)*

This hypostatisation creates the problem of how, when attempting to understand and explain a holistic phenomenon like practice at work, the various hypostatized parts might relate to one another. A common strategy is to attempt to explain the phenomenon solely in terms of the most favoured of the parts. This results in thin, implausible accounts, such as "practice as application of theory". But for Dewey this difficulty is due to neglect of the context in which the original phenomenon occurred. Quite simply, the parts devoid of the context will not add up to the original phenomenon. Thus Dewey offers a different way of understanding reasoning and its role within practice. As Garrison puts it:

> For Dewey, all reason is practical reason; he denied the existence of a realm apart from human action wherein we might complete the quest for certainty and find eternal rest. *(Garrison 1999: 294)*

The holism and contextuality of a Deweyan approach can be summarised as follows:

> Reason itself is a contextual achievement according to Dewey who writes: 'For reason, let it be repeated is an outcome, a function, not a primitive force.' ...... The meaning of reason itself is something that emerges and continuously evolves in the process of conducting inquiries. Reason evolves much as species evolve... *(Garrison 1999: 306)*

According to Tiles, Dewey takes a distinctive approach to context reflecting

> .... a different attitude to the parts and wholes found in reality and ... a correspondingly different method. Dewey always starts with the inclusive and the connected, and considers the process of differentiation. His opponents assume the task is to assemble wholes out of isolated elements. *(Tiles 1988: 22)*

In short, Dewey starts with context, others tend to ignore it.

A most obvious, way of distinguishing contexts is in terms of the social practices that give judgements meaning. Thus it is appropriate to judge the connection of wires to terminal blocks within the practice of electrical installation, and that practice provides the context for understanding the activity of connection. We have seen however the limitations of attempting to suggest that social practices which include both internal and external goods are self-contained and not overlapping and nested.

If we focus on the individual learner from a Deweyan perspective, then both holism and contextuality are important for understanding learning. For Dewey, learning is associated with the learner's activity within its environment. Learning employs a holistic complex of cognitive, conative and affective capacities as well as other abilities and learned capacities. This complex of reasoning, precognitive awareness, habitual reactions, and feeling (the learner) is involved in the ongoing reading of changing situations, and is itself reshaped by further activities. Thus, personal identity shapes responses and is itself continually reshaped by responses.

However, this account still leaves the focus firmly on the individual set against a surrounding context. But in Dewey there is an even more important sense of holism that extends the learning beyond the individual. The individual is located within an environment which actually incorporates the individual. Here holism entails the individual being subsumed into the context of learning. Learning involves a change in this broad context. Some of the change can be thought of as happening to the learner, some of it as happening to the environment that surrounds the learner. In the widest sense of the term context is all there is, so learning only takes place in the context. This is the most profound sense in which learning is contextual. However, for analytical and practical purposes, understanding of learning is usually best served by distinguishing individual learners or groups of learners from the contexts in which they operate as learning takes place. However, in making this distinction, it is crucial to not bring in the trappings of abstract rationality whereby the learner and what is learnt are both viewed as things independent of the environment, and what is learnt is somehow wholly located within the learner. Abstract rationality can be seen as the extreme opposite for the Deweyan position that in the widest sense learning only takes place in the context.

Dewey's means of distinguishing individual learners or groups of learners from the contexts in which they operate as learning takes place is his theory of transactional processes (Dewey & Bently 1949, Emirbayer 1997, Garrison 2001). Dewey and Bently contrast *transaction* with *interaction*. In interaction, substances or things interact but remain the same entities following the interaction. What has changed as a result of the interaction is the relations between them. In transaction, substances or things interact and become different entities following the interaction. What has changed as a result of the interaction is both the substances or things and the relations between them. That is, everything has changed. In thinking about learning, on the interaction approach, learner and context remain the same separate entities, with the relations between them being altered. On the transaction approach, both learner and context change, as do the relations between them. Hence, the situation as a whole is changed. From this whole we can distinguish learner and context for the purposes of advancing understanding, just as in his earliest work Dewey argued that we can distinguish stimulus and response, but actually they both aspects of a whole, the reflex arc (Dewey1896). So, on this account, learning is a transactional relationship in which both learners and their environment change together. In the broadest sense, the overall context changes, and of course continues to change as time passes. This account renders learning inherently contextual.

In chapter five we argued that the development (or transformation) metaphor for learning captures the various dimensions of change, which are so crucial to Dewey, much better than the participation or inquiry metaphors do. We concluded that the development metaphor encapsulates the transformation or reconstruction of the learning, of the learner's self, and of the environment (world), which includes the self. The above discussion provides a strong substantiation of these claims.

So far in this section we have provided a detailed account of Dewey's theory of learning, one which highlights the inherent contextuality of learning. Now we turn more briefly to a consideration of various other writers, each of whom in their various ways adds to the evidence for the inherent contextuality of learning.

5.2 Other Proponents of Diversity of Kinds of Learning

As was argued in the previous section when considering work by Wittgenstein and Toulmin, learning begins with interaction in the public domain, i.e. some form of action is basic to learning, with internalisation of the learning coming later. Certainly, Wittgenstein's later philosophy provides an abundance of arguments for rejecting the view that propositional learning constitutes the one best kind of learning. As was discussed previously in chapter five, as expounded in detail by Williams (1994), the following insights into learning are central to Wittgenstein's later philosophy:

- The basic case of teaching (training) is not about mentalistic concepts being connected to objects (as in ostensive definition and rule following). Rather, it is about being trained into pattern-governed behaviours, i.e. learning to behave in ways that mimic activities licensed by practice or custom, "learning to act on a stage set by others". (This would appear to apply alike to both propositional learning and non-propositional learning).
- Genuinely normative practices (i.e. ones not causally necessitated, but structured by, and admitting of evaluation by reference to a standard, norm, or rule) are social. So a period of training or learning is necessary to become a practitioner. (Here normative practices would cover discursive practices, such as conceptual reasoning as well as all other normative practices that are less clearly centred on discursive activities).
- All use of concepts presupposes a background technique for using the concept, a technique that cannot be expressed as a set of concepts or rules. So the concept (rule) is not foundational of all else. Technique is not reducible to concept (practice is not reducible to theory). So, once again, we have important learning that goes beyond propositional learning.
- Training in techniques creates the regularities of behaviour necessary for any judgement of sameness, in this way the process of learning is constitutive of what is learned. So judgements of sameness are based on practices, not on mental states as such.

As was also noted in chapter five, Winch has argued for the ineluctable normativity of human learning/life and the consequent crucial role that training plays in this. However, far from viewing training as being anti-educational, as some have mistakenly supposed, Winch maintains that training in normative practices opens up options and flexibility in human behaviour. He concludes that those who see a paradox in the notion of being trained in ways that promote independence and autonomy have confused training with conditioning. Stickney (2005) agrees.

Bringing together a careful reading of Wittgenstein's diverse texts on training and a consideration of the training/teaching cases alongside of the anthropological cases and thought experiments, Stickney finds that this:

> ..... points to how the pupil can also overcome this training. Gradually the pupil comes to operate within the norm independently, no longer requiring the instructor's direction; the further possibility exists of coming to question some of the rules absorbed in, and the fundamental *bedrock* deposited during, the training.... Together these cases show: (a) how training constitutes subjects in collective, normative ways of acting, *seeing-as* and judging (that is, initiation into *forms of life* and *world-pictures*); and (b) the extent to which these shared forms of agreement and judgment are arbitrary and open to renegotiation.... *(Stickney 2005: 299)*

Winch and Stickney both find training in norms important in the development of human agency. In the previous section Brandom supported the importance of training in norms for being able to deploy concepts. Such training in norms that are both social and historical would seem to be a crucial feature of many kinds of human learning. Contrary to some opinions however, such training does not imply narrow and unthinking adherence to acquired habits.

The central social dimension of learning that is being stressed here is closely related to the "social practices and practical reason" that Hirst (1998) claimed to be "the fundamental concerns of education". As we saw in chapter five, Hirst coupled this position with a rejection of the view of

> .... education as centrally the acquisition of propositional, or abstracted, detached theoretical knowledge and understanding. *(Hirst 1998: 18)*

As was also noted in chapter five, Passmore argued that most learning is dispositional. This, of course, takes the scope of learning well beyond the learning of propositions. Passmore particularly draws attention to the capacities presupposed by learning. According to Passmore (1980: 37) capacities are a major, perhaps the major, class of human learning. So the claim is that the having of various capacities is presupposed by other kinds of learning. That is, the mental enrichment commonly seen as the basic sort of learning, actually depends on the exercise of previously learned capacities, capacities that are much more than mental in their scope. Likewise, Winch (1998: 19) argues that knowledge is largely dispositional, thereby taking the central focus firmly away from transparent propositions in mind. For present purposes, the differences between capacities and dispositions are unimportant. Both Passmore and Winch are reminding us that there is vastly much more to learning than propositional learning. Already discussed in chapter five, were Winch's arguments for there being many and diverse cases of learning, each subject to "constraints in a variety of contexts and cultures" which precludes them from being treated in a general way (1998: 85). As we saw, influenced by Wittgenstein, Winch recommends that we focus on description and understanding of various instances of learning viewed as distinctive cases: "....we have been obsessed with theory building at the expense of attention to particular cases...." (Winch 1998: ix).

Finally, as yet another extension of the scope of learning way beyond propositional learning we can recall the claims of Lakoff and Johnson, in chapter five,
that most learning is unconscious. Since a hallmark of successful propositional
learning is that it is transparent to the learner, the Lakoff and Johnson claim entails
that most learning is not propositional learning.

In this section we have drawn on various writers to argue that: firstly, there are
many and diverse kinds of learning, with most of these kinds being very different
from propositional learning; and, secondly that most of them are clearly located in
and shaped by the context in which they occur. Traditional accounts that seek to
quarantine propositional learning from influences of context are not plausible if
extended to these diverse kinds of learning.

6. LEARNING, SPACES AND CONTEXTS

We have seen that there are many diverse kinds of learning. If we forget this for a
moment and focus only on propositional learning, it is at least plausible to see the
product of learning as being located in the learner's mind or brain, and in this
sense divorced from context. However, once we attend to the diversity of kinds of
learning, learning is no longer so clearly located. Nor is it so obviously divorced
from context. In fact, this section will argue that we need to jettison the common
sense idea that learning is somehow located within learners. Rather, it will be argued, learning is located outside of learners.

We can start this section by noting that the widespread acceptance of abstract
rationality and its attendant metaphysics leads almost inevitably to the conclusion
that in some important sense learning must be located in the mind (or brain).
Likewise, since the mind or brain can do various things with the learning (recall it,
analyse it, apply it cleverly or inappropriately, etc.), it is almost inevitable that we
postulate that the mind or brain possesses a range of specific 'mental powers' that
the individual person deploys. So endemic and influential has been the 'common
sense' account of learning (discussed in chapter five) that almost all research and
theorising around learning has centred on the existence of mental powers, with the
main agenda being how to elucidate them. Yet, as Davis (2005) and others have
argued, the existence or otherwise of mental powers is a conceptual rather than an
empirical matter. Increasingly, on conceptual grounds "the very existence of some
supposed mental powers is open to challenge, at least if these powers are conceived of in an individualist fashion". (Davis 2005: 637). More broadly, this
would imply that how we view learning itself is in important respects a conceptual
rather than an empirical matter. Increasingly, as the significance of context for understanding learning is appreciated, the appealing common sense idea that learning resides in the mind or brain is under question.

Discussing the many conceptual confusions that arise from blending the findings of neuroscience with 'common sense' accounts of minds and learning, Bennett
and Hacker (2003) argue that:

.... brains cannot be said to be knowledgeable, ignorant, learned, untutored, experts or charlatans – only human beings can be such things. *(2003: 152)*

According to Bennett and Hacker, it is simply wrong to think that knowledge and information can be recorded in the brain in the same way that they can be recorded in books, card-indexes and computers. Regarding knowledge they state:

We may say of a book that it contains all the knowledge of a lifetime's work of a scholar, or of a filing cabinet that it contains all the available knowledge, duly card-indexed, about Julius Caesar. This means that the pages of the book or the cards in the filing cabinet have written on them *expressions* of a large number of known truths. In this sense, the brain *contains* no knowledge whatsoever. There are no symbols in the brain that by their array express a single proposition, let alone a proposition that is known to be true. Of course, in this sense a human being *contains* no knowledge either. To possess knowledge is not to contain knowledge. *(Bennett & Hacker 2003: 152-3)*

We can add that learners' possess their learning, but that does not mean that they contain it. This is the normal situation for human possessions. We can possess a car, a block of land, or a stamp collection. But none of these possessions are located inside of us. Why should possession of knowledge be any different? As we will argue below, learning is typically a kind of relational complex that includes learners and their surroundings.

Bennett and Hacker go on to argue that the same considerations apply to the idea that information can be recorded in the brain:

A great deal of information is contained in the *Encyclopaedia Britannica*. In that sense, there is none in the brain. Much information can be *derived* from a slice through a tree trunk or from a geological specimen – and so too from PET and fMRI scans of the brain's activities. But this is *not* information that the brain *has*. Nor is it *written in* the brain, let alone in the 'language of the brain', any more than dendrochronological information about the severity of winters in the 1930s is written in the tree trunk in arboreal patois. *(2003: 153)*.

So the commonly accepted idea that in propositional learning propositions are transferred to the mind or brain is dubious. *A fortiori*, it is even more dubious to try to locate the many kinds of human learning within the cranium. While there are still those who dream that neuroscience might accomplish just such an account (e.g. Clark 2005), the weight of recent work seems to be pointing in other directions. Even Howard Gardner appears to be retreating somewhat from his well-known mental powers approach:

It makes sense to think of human cognitive competence as an emerging capacity, one likely to be manifest at the intersection of three different constituents: the 'individual', with his or her skills, knowledge and aims; the structure of a 'domain of knowledge' within which these skills can be aroused; and a set of institutions and roles – a surrounding 'field' – which judges when a particular performance is acceptable and when it fails to meet specifications...a new assessment initiative should acknowledge the effects of context on performance and provide the most appropriate contexts in which to assess competences, including ones which extend outside the skin of the individual being assessed. *(Gardner 1999: 99-100)*

If recognising that learning is significantly implicated in its context is a precondi-
tion for developing satisfactory conceptual understandings of learning, then we
need to reconsider the locations in which common wisdom has placed it. One of
the consequences of much of the discussion in this chapter is that learning, both as
process and product, extends well beyond individual minds or even the skins of
individual learners. Rather, learning is typically a kind of relational complex that
includes learners and their surroundings. This is a clear implication of many of the
ideas discussed in earlier sections of this chapter. For instance, Brandom's normative space of reasons is public, rather than private to individuals. It is one that
changes learners as they learn, but is itself subject to change by learners, in
Deweyan transactional fashion. Similar considerations apply to Wittgenstein's notion of training in communal norms and practices. As well, Dewey's transactional-
ism (Garrison 2001, Vanderstraten 2002) is a rich source of argument along this
line. For Dewey, not only is learning contextual, but so is thought in a strong sense
that takes it well beyond the cranium. According to Dewey, thought and learning
do not even take place entirely in the agent:

> Thought, in the most general sense of the term, does not even take place solely within
> the agent but rather is a kind of agent/world interaction. Thought takes place in the
> interactive interface between agent and world. *(Burke 1994: 164)*

Thus, for Dewey, learning is thoroughly implicated and located in its context and
needs to be viewed as a complex web of relations that transact over time.

Note that there is nothing in the above discussion that would prevent us from
focusing on the learning by an individual. It is just that learning in general has a
somewhat broader scope. Thus, Bereiter (2002) differentiates between 'learning
for individuals' and 'knowledge-building' for groups or organizations. Both ideas
can be useful for understanding learning so long as we realise that minds and organizations have somewhat different roles in the complex web of relations that
constitutes learning.

7. SOME EXAMPLES TO ILLUSTRATE THE CONTEXTUALITY
OF LEARNING

7.1 Charles' Story Revisited

Charles' story, of a surveyor educating himself to remain at the forefront of technological developments in this rapidly changing field, was set out in chapter five.
The highly contextual nature of Charles' learning was evident in part from the
rapid nature of the changes that characterise the field of surveying, and in part
from his own focus determined by his senior role in a major construction company. Charles observed that no formal course could keep up with these changes.
At best, formal courses can give people a preparation to become highly self-
directed learners in the particular contexts of their practice.

7.2 Anne's Story Revisited

Anne the ambulance officer (who we met in chapter five), provided the following rich example of the contextuality of judgements. A frequent occurrence for ambulance officers is to attend the scene of vehicle crashes. These are often quite horrific. A very common scenario is the need to extract injured passengers from wrecked vehicles. There are guidelines for extracting injured passengers trapped in wrecked vehicles so as to minimise the possibility of further injury. But as Anne observed:

> .... Every time you go to an accident, the car will be in a different position and the people in the car will be in a different position. So we're taught the fundamentals of how to get them out, but you can't possibly know all the different ways that people are going to wreck themselves and what position they may be in.

Thus emergency situations commonly require interpretation and contextualisation of protocols and guidelines by ambulance officers. Disagreement about the best way to proceed is not uncommon. This can lead to tensions around what the crucial decision should be and, even, who should make it. (Interestingly, Anne claimed that ambulance work provided much greater responsibility for creative decision making than did her former career, nursing, which she described as "a much more controlled work environment"). So, guidelines and protocols can be minutely specified, but in the end practitioners need to contextualise them, a process that requires professional judgement and, possibly, professional disagement.

7.3 Jack's Story

Jack, a senior manager, is responsible for delivery of child support services within a large region of Australia. His segment of the organisation is characterised by the very high commitment of staff to the policies that they administer. Jack is a stream leader who definitely sees himself as a leader rather than a manager. He knows the business intimately and sees himself very much as a hands-on person, one who aims to lead by example. Overall, Jack has found that his kind of leadership can motivate the work team to achieve extremely difficult goals. Jack also has a very high commitment to business outcomes. So much so that he finds that he sometimes has to remind himself that a single-minded focus on outcomes can occasionally be counter-productive. These business outcomes provided a very clear articulation of the external goods flowing directly from the practice. There is a well-developed team-work philosophy operating in this segment of the organisation. Although staff have a one-to-one relationship with clients, there is a strong culture of the team providing a much valued support network. (Due to the nature of the work, there is seldom a day when there is not someone in tears). Another aspect of this team culture is a 'buddy' system for inducting new staff into the job.

Procedures to be followed for the various kinds of cases are highly standardised. These procedures can be accessed on the computer simply by clicking on the 'quality' icon. However, a difficulty with these standardised procedures is that many cases have distinctive features that resist easy classification. There is a danger of the procedures protocols encouraging a narrow approach to categorisation of cases. In effect, the quality assurance system can in some instances work against quality outcomes being achieved. Therefore, Jack encourages the staff in his branches to exercise judgement so that cases are thought through in terms of the spirit of the legislation, rather than in terms of procedures to be followed for their own sake. Quite simply, child custody staff need to learn when and how to break the rules. So, performance as outcomes can be specified closely, but performance descriptors that are taken too literally as guides for action can interfere with good practice. Novice staff begin with the standardised procedures, but part of the functions of the buddy system and the team-work culture is to enable novices to develop flexibility in their use of these standardised procedures. Similar movement away from reliance on formulaic protocols occurs in other occupations, Novice doctors are provided with a stepwise protocol for arriving at diagnoses. Experience fairly quickly leads to diminishing reliance on the protocol, together with increased facility to make reliable diagnoses. Likewise, beginning teachers employ well-tried formulae to develop suitably structured lessons. With experience the need for such guidance tends to vanish.

When asked about the abilities that staff needed to perform their child support work to a high standard, Jack mainly focused on interpersonal capacities and the ability to make sound judgements about the best way to proceed in a given case. He also emphasised the importance of values, such as caring and a commitment to justice for clients. Otherwise, based on what was elicited in this case study, the internal goods of child support work remain somewhat tacit.

Here we have illustrations of various major points about informal learning from practice and the making of context sensitive judgements. For instance, the holism of judgements is clear (cognition, emotions, volition are all involved in the judgements). Likewise the unique features of each case serve to emphasise the contextuality of these judgements.

8. AN INFORMAL RECOVERY PROGRAMME

This chapter has challenged traditional and common sense notions of where learning is located. Csikszentmihalyi (1996: 23-28) asks where creativity might be located and concludes that

> ....creativity does not happen inside people's heads, but in the intersection between a person's thoughts and a sociocultural context. It is a systemic rather than an individual phenomenon.... Creativity is any act, idea or product that changes an existing domain, or that transforms an existing domain into a new one.

One could make the same point about learning.

The last two chapters have provided an account of various important aspects of the type of informal learning that is the central concern of this book. A key fact about this informal learning is that it happens during the course of practice. Hence, in the next chapter we continue our investigation of this sort of informal learning, by turning to an examination of practice. We aim to recover the informal, so as to shift the balance from the current one-sided concentration on the formal. This 're-covery of informal learning' is the chief focus of the remainder of this book.

CHAPTER SEVEN

THE IDEA OF PRACTICE

So far we have used the term practice without attempting any detailed clarification of its meaning. We are not alone in this as Biesta (2005: 344) explains:

> The magic spell cast by Jean Lave and Etienne Wenger's situated learning has led many to believe that education is a process of participation in 'communities of practice' ... If there has ever been a time in which we need a critical re-examination of the idea of 'practice' in order to counter its conservative and conserving connotations, it may well be now.

It is Alisdair MacIntyre (1981) however who arguably has made the term 'practice' philosophically interesting and educationally useful. As already argued activities are located within practices which provide one context for their understanding. MacIntyre extends such nesting to include traditions. According to Mulhall and Swift, (1992: 90):

> A tradition is constituted by a set of practices and is a mode of understanding their importance and worth: It is the medium by which such practices are shaped and transmitted across generations.

This gives more sense of the widening nests that constitute MacIntyre's moral theory. For MacIntyre the narrative of an individual life is to be understood against the background of the wider social context that the individual finds herself within. This wider social context consists of sets of practices which serve to exemplify virtuous conduct, and those practices, in turn, are situated within traditions. Traditions are the repositories of standards of rationality. People are not trapped within traditions however. In a passage that is strongly reminiscent of Lakatos's (1978) account of degenerating research programmes, MacIntyre (1990) points out that all traditions from time to time experience their own internal contradictions and tensions. When these become serious, the adherents of a tradition may look to other traditions for the conceptual resources to enable them to make progress, perhaps within an emergent new tradition or an altered version of the old.

It is clear that there are degrees of complexity involved in practices that make bricklaying, for example, more likely to encourage the development of the virtues than brushing teeth, and that building is more likely to develop them than bricklaying. It is also clear that some practices may have become so dominated by external goods that the contexts for understanding their purpose may best be found

179

within the tradition to which they are related. In summary, the interpretation of what humans do is related to the context that gives sense and purpose to what they do. These senses and purposes can be nested according to the interests of the interpreter. Moreover they often overlap. The more complex the activity, the wider the range of contexts within which the activity can be interpreted. Such activities are more likely to lead to productive learning. In addition, those practices in which internal goods predominate are more likely to lead to productive learning than those in which external goods predominate. That is because virtue depends upon the realisation of internal goods and such realisation is most likely when it is easiest to detect what MacIntyre (1999b) acknowledges as instances of 'appearing to be virtuous'.

In this chapter, we attempt to develop MacIntyre's work in the light of the previous discussion of contextuality. We aim to show how contextuality and practice are related. We aim to illustrate that practices form part of a nest of concepts, which range from the particular to the more general, and that practices are layered in the sense that they overlap to differing extents. One practice is located within one nest. At a particular level, there is an activity which is nested within a practice at another level, which is nested within a tradition at another level which is nested within some narrative unity of a life overall. An activity may also be nested within alternative practices and traditions. In that sense, activities and practices are layered. For example, when asked why we knocked a nail in a piece of wood, we may respond by focusing on a number of levels within a nest – the activity itself, or the practice of joinery, or the tradition within which joinery has meaning, or some overall sense of what we are trying to achieve. The activity of nailing also forms part of the practice of building, so the practices of building and joinery may be said to be layered.

The notions of layering and nesting are important because they help explain how it is, that by learning one activity, we are enabled to do and become interested in other activities. They also help us to explain how we come to develop a critical perspective on what we do through engagement in layered practices. They thus help us to avoid the worry of Biesta (2005), that an account that suggests learning is enculturation into practices, is necessarily conservative. Our argument is that people are not inducted into just one practice, but into a number, and through such induction they come to see their practical engagements from alternative perspectives. They come to be able to stand back from those engagements and evaluate at a distance, as it were. While tradition is important, traditions evolve as practices evolve. Evolution occurs, in part, because people can stand back from their practical engagements and examine them from alternatives.

1. MACINTYRE

MacIntyre (1981: 187) famously describes a practice as:

> Any coherent and complex form of socially established co-operative human activity through which goods internal to that form of activity are realised in the course of trying to achieve those standards of excellence which are appropriate to, and partly definitive of, that form of activity.

On this account, the game of chess is a practice. It is not hard to imagine the game being played only for the sake of an appreciation of the elegance of the moves internal to the game, for example, and not for the sake of any external goods such as money.

Practices are contrasted with institutions that 'are characteristically and necessarily concerned with external goods' (MacIntyre 1981: 194) such as money and power. For example, it is possible to imagine people pursuing activities at work for no purpose other than the acquisition of private wealth. In most cases work practices, such as farming, involve both external goods, in the form of commercial considerations, and internal goods, such as care for animals and the environment. MacIntyre acknowledges that practices cannot survive for any length of time unsustained without institutions. So practices and institutions exist in symbiotic relationship. What is alluded to here is the distinction between pursuing something for its own sake and pursuing it for the rewards that pursuit can bring. According to Higgins (2003: 280):

> A good is something we judge to be worthwhile to have, achieve, attend to or participate in. As such goods are what provide us with reasons for acting ... we desire them because they are good and not the other way round ...

Rightly, MacIntyre notices that both internal and external goods are important, but that while it is possible to be concerned with both, internal goods are always under a kind of threat. He (1981: 194) writes:

> Indeed so intimate is the relationship of practices to institutions – and consequently of the goods external to the goods internal to the practices in question – that institutions and practices characteristically form a single causal order in which the ideals and creativity of the practice are always vulnerable to the competitiveness of the institution. In this context the essential function of the virtues is clear. Without them, without justice, courage and truthfulness, practices could not resist the corrupting power of institutions.

It is not clear how practice could resist in this way. What we think MacIntyre has in mind is that practitioners need to resist the power of managers, who are necessarily concerned with the maximisation of external goods and who place employees under some pressure not to pay too much attention to the internal goods of their work practice. While such maximisation is important, so too is respect for the internal goods of practices, for without such respect many are worse off as workers complete a job with minimum regard to internal goods. This normative view of practice is not restricted to work of course. Similar considerations may apply in any practical endeavour. Selfish or narrow pursuit of external good for personal reward is always likely to conflict with virtues as MacIntyre describes.

Hence, for MacIntyre (1981: 190):

> external goods are essentially someone's property, internal goods are goods for the whole community.

On the face of it internal goods are those goods that can only be obtained through a particular practice. For example, well-built walls as a prime outcome of brick-laying are internal goods, but they are also someone's property, so in this case internal goods are also external. It might appear as if "those who lack the relevant experience are incompetent thereby as judges of internal goods" (MacIntyre 1981: 189). Plainly however, it is not only good bricklayers who can judge a well built wall, though obviously such people would be more attuned to the nuances of practice than a customer, for example. Yet an even spread of mortar, a uniform level, and so on, are much more obviously internal goods than the money that is paid for the wall, which is more obviously an external good.

We do not therefore believe that clear criteria can be set out once and for all to distinguish internal and external goods in all contexts. That does not make the distinction useless however. To be sure external goods can be obtained through a variety of social practices. Internal goods can only be obtained through the particular practice. Very often such goods take the form of knacks and feels or the ability to contextualise judgements without regard to written criteria. It might be imagined that both internal and external goods focus on characteristics of the work, not characteristics of persons doing the work. However, while the internal goods might be distinctive within a practice, they are also embodied in some sense in the practitioners. Diligence, for example, enables bricklayers to build good walls with consistent application of mortar, regard for levels etc. Such criteria have historically developed standards of excellence which require practitioners to accept the judgement of an expert and ultimately to act with regard to others. Hence it is vital that there are such experts and the means of recognising their authority. How else could their authority be recognised other than through the virtues that they display in their work? The internal goods of bricklaying are in part well built walls but they are also those typically human capacities of various kinds that are difficult to put precisely into words, things like knacks and feels and sensitivity to them. In that sense internal goods can refer both to the process and the product of a practice. When an adequate description of the product cannot be set out, very often reference is made to the process and characteristics of the person engaged in the process. As Higgins puts it:

> MacIntyre understands the virtues as acquired excellences of persons, as dispositions to act for the good ... since the virtues are partly constitutive of our well being they themselves constitute goods. *(Higgins 2003: 280)*

For MacIntyre (1981: 191):

> A virtue is an acquired human quality the possession and exercise of which tends to enable us to achieve those goods which are internal to practices.

By virtues MacIntyre does mean moral qualities, but not in a restrictive sense. For example, in performing well at work, people do display moral qualities of various kinds and, following Dunne (1993) and others, it is not always or even ever possible to separate moral from technical qualities. There is a caricature of the person who talks a good, concerned, moral game about care for others, but when it comes to actually making sure that he drives carefully, hangs the door correctly so that fingers don't get trapped, etc., he fails. A problem with much moral philosophy is that is seems to locate morality mainly within the spheres of debates (about abortion, for example). What MacIntyre does is to locate morality firmly within the realms of practice, and good technical ability within practice does have moral force, whether at work or elsewhere.

So while it is true that these distinctions between internal and external, practices and institutions can be problematised, it is clear, as MacIntyre (1981: 188) points out, that people may practise solely by the desire for external goods such as money. It is also clear that people practise because they seek to excel in whatever ways the practice itself demands. Moreover, as he writes (1981: 196):

> Although we may hope that we can not only achieve the internal goods of certain practices by possessing the virtues *and* become rich, famous and powerful, the virtues are always a stumbling block to this comfortable ambition. We should therefore expect that, if in a particular society the pursuit of external goods were to become dominant, the concept of the virtues might suffer first attrition and then perhaps something near total effacement, although simulacra might abound.

MacIntyre's account of practice forms the basis of a moral theory that emphasises that

> .... the kind of recognition of authority and of achievement, the kind of respect for standards and the kind of risk taking which are characteristically involved in practices demand for example fairness in judging oneself and others – and willingness to trust the judgements of those whose achievements in the practice gives them an authority to judge which presupposes fairness and truthfulness in those judgements. *(MacIntyre 1981: 193)*

He goes on

> ..... to enter into a practice is to enter into a relationship not only with its contemporary practitioners but also with those who have preceded us in the practice particularly those whose achievements extended the reach of the practice to its present point. *(MacIntyre 1981: 194)*

There is therefore something stable and enduring about practices. Practices develop however as practitioners learn. Those practices that do not develop simply die out. In a similar way those people who do not come to understand the history of the practice cannot be said to be practitioners. Hence there is nothing necessarily conservative about practices. Practices do develop over time as a result of critical debate within them. Moreover there are practices such as philosophy through which it is possible to theorise development in other practices and to form a critical perspective on them.

From this discussion it might appear as if all that there is to learn can be captured in combinations of practices. Yet we maintain that this appearance is deceptive. At the beginning of *Philosophical Investigations,* Wittgenstein describes what might be thought of as a simplified practice of building. One builder shouts orders such as 'slab' and another builder fetches a slab. In a commentary on this, Rhees (1970: 77) suggests that it is "as though Wittgenstein has described a *game* with building stones, and not the sort of thing people would do if they were actually building a house". In the latter case it would be necessary to deal with unforeseen circumstances, it would be necessary for one builder to be able to ask the other what he meant when the 'slab' did not fit in the place where it was required, and so on. Rhees goes on to make the point that while we can imagine language games in which speaking words and actions are combined in some determinate way, those games could not comprise language. It is part of the richness of language that to speak it cannot be detached from the possibilities for explaining things in different kinds of ways, of envisioning possibilities, of judging with respect to a variety of contexts. In short, there is a need to 'find sense' in what we are doing in a variety of ways and this presupposes a 'common understanding'. For Rhees (1970: 84), a common understanding

> ..... has to do with what is taken to make sense, or with what can be understood; with what it is possible to say to people: with what anyone who speaks the language might try to say.

For Rhees it seems that practices can only be understood in relation to other practices and traditions within which practices are located, and within which people make sense of their lives as a whole. While it might appear as if the notion of practice is elastic without limit, the limits in reality are provided by the way people actually act and the way they describe what they do. In this way language limits the possibilities both for action and for its own development. Moreover language also enables the possibility and indeed necessity of contextualising activity and judgement in ways that go beyond one practice.

Famously MacIntyre (1981) declared that building was a practice whereas bricklaying was not, and recently he declared that physics is a practice whereas teaching physics is not. Such practical elitism suggests that the question of how practices are constituted carries some importance for him. In contrast Paul Hirst has come to the view that so long as practices are 'successful' (Hirst 1999: 130), it does not matter much how they are described. By 'success' Hirst (1999: 132) means those practices "that have emerged progressively in our society as relatively distinct areas."

Clear distinctions are not readily forthcoming however. Moreover, as the example from Wittgenstein's builders was meant to illustrate, it seems impossible to isolate learning one practice from others and from some overall sense of what is worth doing and why. There is a related hermeneutic problem here. It seems impossible to interpret a part of practice without some understanding of the whole and it seems impossible to interpret the whole without some understanding of the parts. This hermeneutic problem suggests an interpretation of practice as something not only enduring but also as encompassing a way of life. MacIntyre (1994) describes the lives of the members of a fishing community. Here the practice of fishing forms the central core of their community. Other practices are subsumed within it. It is fishing that provides the ethical orientation of the whole community and the relations of the people within it. Such a community seems to function as a kind of ideal for MacIntyre, yet it is hard now to imagine within western liberal democracies where to find such a community. That is because the rigours of market competition have led, in many cases, to both a reduction in the numbers of owners of fishing vessels and of owners who actually put to sea with those people they employ. MacIntyre might respond to this observation with the argument that within liberal democracies the language of morality is deficient and some return to premodernity is required. For us however, there are sufficient instances where it is possible to distinguish internal and external goods that some moral orientation can be discerned. Hence, for us, practices and institutions in MacIntyre's sense are merged into the generic term 'practice' simply because we think that the use of this generic term now coincides with people's ordinary use. Moreover it is more economical to write 'practice' rather than 'practice/institution' which seems to us to be the next best alternative.

MacIntyre's notion of a practice appears unrealistic. No doubt MacIntyre (1994: 284) intends it to be so for his purpose is not to set out a theory of informal learning. Rather, he is a moral philosopher working within a tradition of virtue ethics. Unlike us he seems to see the tradition of liberalism as hopeless. He (1981: 11) describes the moral philosophy of liberalism as emotivism which is

.... the doctrine that all evaluative judgements and more specifically all moral judgements are nothing but expressions of preference.

Not surprisingly, MacIntyre (1987) in his most pessimistic writing, believes that emotivism renders education impossible. That is because there are no ways of determining what is most worth learning. Moreover there is no educated public with sufficient broad practical experience to provide the basis for any kind of enculturation that is desirable. One practice seems as good as any other. In his less pessimistic moods (e.g. MacIntyre & Dunne 2002), MacIntyre does seem to think that education might yet be possible and that not all is yet lost, despite the years of liberal emotivism. Whatever problems there might be with outlining an account of practice that further elucidates our theory of learning, the idea of practice seems likely to remain as a central educational concept for some time (Smeyers & Burbules 2005). As Biesta notes, the idea has been made famous within the field of social psychology through the work of Lave and Wenger. Wenger has developed this work further in a way that invites comparison with that of MacIntyre (McLaughlin 2003).

2. LEGITIMATE PERIPHERAL PARTICIPATION

While Wenger's (1998) notion of practice is similar to MacIntyre's notion in that for Wenger (1998: 124-126) "practice is neither a specific, narrowly defined activity or interaction nor a broadly defined aggregate that is abstractly historical and social", there are important differences, as we go on to explain. Throughout we have tried to make clear the sense in which we use the term practice. In the absence of any qualification to the contrary, we use 'practice' as defined in the introduction as any coherent and complex form of socially established collection of human activities that is identifiable by a single word or phrase. Through this form goods are realised in the course of trying to achieve those standards of excellence which are appropriate to, and partly definitive, of the form with the result that human powers to achieve excellence, and human conceptions of the goods involved, are systematically extended.

This is an adaptation of MacIntyre's work because, as we explained, it seems to us that MacIntyre draws too sharp a distinction between goods that are internal and goods that are external to practices so that it is difficult to imagine any form of practice as defined by MacIntyre (1981: 187). The idea that young people are initiated through learning into the practices of a community seems attractive. In this way, learning is equated to a kind of socialisation. Indeed, as we pointed out in chapter one and in the introduction to this chapter, this idea has all but taken over the field of workplace learning. The questions of what constitutes community and how such practices are determined are rather more problematic, however, because human activities and associations can be classified in a variety of different ways. Plainly activities overlap to some extent and they can be combined in a variety of ways and labelled as different practices. Hence, for example, when an additional electrical socket is added to a kitchen, this may be contextualised within the practice of electrical installation. Alternatively, since this addition involves chiselling some plaster work, the practice of building might provide an appropriate context, or perhaps there is an overall practice of home improvement within which the addition can be contextualised. Perhaps however the addition is best contextualised in some other way, such as the means to cook using a piece of electrical equipment.

Some common theories of learning, with which trainee formal educators have to grapple, are outlined by Phillips and Soltis (2003). They include the behaviourism of Watson, Thorndike and Skinner and the psychological constructivism of Piaget. In these theories, the learner is 'depicted as a lone investigator' (Phillips & Soltis 2003: 53). What is missing from these theories is the idea that learners are associated with various groups and that they learn from those more proficient in the business of the group. Perhaps the most famous recent account of such learning is that given by Jean Lave and Etienne Wenger, which was introduced earlier. In essence these writers argue that the social world is made up of communities of practice. Learners become full participants in the community of practice through apprenticeship.

Guile and Young (1998: 176) summarise this as follows:

> The view of learning implicit in the traditional concept of apprenticeship involves four main elements – the apprentice as learner, the idea of a trade or craft knowledge

as fixed and unproblematic, the master as teacher and the idea that learning in workplaces is a form of context-bound understanding not conducive to transfer.

A community of practice does not embody a fixed or static conception of knowledge. Rather, what is to count as knowledge develops as the community develops.
As Lave and Wenger (1991: 51) put it:

> Participation is always based on situated negotiation and re-negotiation of meanings
> in the world.

Lave and Wenger (1991) accept that learning is contextual with 'communities of
practice' being their version of the context in which learning occurs. Hodkinson
and Hodkinson (2004b, 2004c) argue that there are at least two different kinds of
context that are covered by Lave and Wenger's notion of 'communities of practice'. While these two are clearly different, each is important in its own right.
Hodkinson and Hodkinson take this further by drawing on Bourdieu to argue that
a third context or level needs to be added to the two drawn from Lave and
Wenger. Their advocacy of this tripartite version of learning contexts is bolstered
by the claim that only a complex account of context can make sense of empirical
evidence on learning at work that they have gathered from a range of recent research projects. Their conclusion, that at least these three different levels of context are needed to make sense of learning at work, provides a fine illustration of
our concept of the nesting of contexts.

Hodkinson and Hodkinson (2004b, 2004c) identify both broad and narrow
senses in which Lave and Wenger use the term 'community of practice'. They
claim that these cover two quite different kinds of context. The broad sense of
'community of practice' seems to be very far-reaching, as is evident from the following definition proposed by Lave and Wenger:

> A community of practice is a set of relations among persons, activity, and world, over
> time and in relation with other tangential and overlapping communities of practice.
> *(Lave & Wenger 1991: 98)*

This definition resembles our account of tradition following MacIntyre. For Lave
and Wenger, participation in this broad sense of 'community of practice' seems to
be a pre-condition for attaining knowledge of the particular practice:

> A community of practice is an intrinsic condition for the existence of knowledge.
> ....Thus, participation in the cultural practice in which any knowledge exists is an
> epistemological principle of learning. The social structure of this practice, its power
> relations, and its conditions for legitimacy define possibilities for learning.
> *(Lave & Wenger 1991: 98)*

However, Lave and Wenger slide to the narrower sense of community of practice
whenever they discuss specific examples. As Hodkinson and Hodkinson note,
their illustrative examples are always "a close knit group of workers sharing
knowledge, tasks, activities and a common physical location" such as a tailor's

workshop or a particular Alcoholics Anonymous group (Hodkinson & Hodkinson 2004c: 7). Certainly, Hodkinson and Hodkinson have focused on important general distinctions for understanding communal dimensions of learning. An engineer, for example, typically works with an immediate group of colleagues, some of whom are not engineers. At the same time this engineer is located in wider communities of practice, such as 'electrical engineers' or even 'all engineers'. Hodkinson and Hodkinson maintain further that understanding of learning also requires some consideration of individual activity – always viewed as socially formed – but still a necessary component of an adequate account. So here we have widening nests of context being invoked in the explanation of learning. No doubt various activities, narratives, and traditions would all be relevant in such explanation. Other such examples of nesting of contexts abound. For instance Rainbird, Munro and Holly (2004b) researched effects of employment relation on learning. They found effects at three levels: the immediate working group, the organisation and the state (through policies and practices around education and training provision). Here, only one factor amongst many that shape vocational learning is being considered, yet it involves widening nests of contexts.

Wenger (1998: 45) develops the idea of a community of practice in a more instrumental way than Lave. He writes:

> We are constantly engaged in the pursuit of enterprises of all kinds, from ensuring our physical survival to seeking the loftiest pleasures. As ... we interact with each other ... we learn.

> Over time, this collective learning results in practices that reflect both the pursuit of our enterprises and the attendant social relations. These practices are thus the property of a kind of community created over time by the sustained pursuit of a shared enterprise. It makes sense therefore, to call these kinds of communities *communities of practice*.

As Hobsbawm (1994: 428) points out however:

> Never was the word 'community' used more indiscriminately and emptily than in the decades when communities in the sociological sense became hard to find in real life.

Nor we might add has the word practice been used more indiscriminately in education than in the decades when learning to actually do things, as opposed to write about things, was less and less common. Delanty (2003: 1) suggests that the appeal of the idea of community might be related to the search for belonging in the insecure conditions of modernity. The appeal might also be related to the need to find consensus in the fractured conditions of postmodernity in which the main forms of social involvement are 'associations' (Hirst 1994) or 'networks' (Castells 1996, 1997, 1998), usually for the achievement of external goods of one sort or another.

The idea of community may suggest some justice in the distribution of external goods, against a background of what is in reality a society deeply divided in its means of access and control over such goods. This division serves the interest of capital accumulation but not the interest of community. Whereas capital can now flow round the globe almost instantaneously and companies are now freer to move to cheaper sources of labour than ever they were, most people are not. Whereas companies can be run by an elite of managers and shareholders able to function in any location through the technology of communications, those who are managed tend to be tied to one location. The latter have neither the resources nor the inclination to move. As Bauman (1998) points out, such technology tends to detach a managing elite from the majority of the work force. It cuts the elite off from what previously would have been their obligations and duties towards those they control. As he puts it:

> Capital can always move away to more peaceful sites if the engagement with 'otherness' requires a costly application of force or tiresome negotiations. No need to engage, if avoidance will do. *(Bauman 1998: 11)*

For theorists such as Bauman (1998), Harvey (2000), Castells *et al.* (1999), the closing off of public spaces, the fencing in of managerial locations, the formation of global networks, are necessarily destructive of community. MacIntyre would take an even more pessimistic view. For Wenger (1998), however, that is not the case. For Wenger community involvement can be for the sake of some external goods, such as money, and for him what primarily may bind the members of a community of practice together may be precisely the shared quest for external goods, not the goods internal to that practice.

It is not surprising then that Wenger so enthusiastically endorses Saint-Onge and Wallace's 2003 book, the very title of which, *Leveraging Communities of Practice for Strategic Advantage*, would be an oxymoron for MacIntyre. As Wenger writes on the back cover:

> Fantastic. We have been waiting for a book like this: the unabridged story of building a strategic, web-based community of practice … a must read for anyone serious about building strategic capabilities in organizations.

Broadly, the thesis presented in the book is that organisations have 'intangible assets' that are held both individually and collectively. For example, individuals have 'mindsets' or dispositions to act in particular ways. "Culture reflects collective mindsets" (Saint-Onge & Wallace 2003: 5). Where the culture can be characterised as:

- a desire to collaborate with colleagues
- a commitment to learning and generating new capabilities
- a need to find a solution for issues of problems related to those of practice.
  (Saint-Onge & Wallace 2003: 40)

Then, communities of practice may flourish. For management, it is necessary to 'align' the community with a strategic purpose so that it can "make a significant contribution to creating an organisation's competitive advantage" (Saint-Onge & Wallace 2003: 42).

For Wenger, McDermott & Snyder (2002: 4) communities of practice are:

> Groups of people who share a concern, a set of problems or a passion about a topic, and who deepen their understanding and knowledge of this area by interacting on an ongoing basis.

According to this definition:

> ..... we all belong to communities of practice ... we belong to several communities of practice at any time. *(Wenger, McDermott & Snyder 2002: 6)*

And, according to Saint-Onge and Wallace, work needs to be organised in such a way as to leverage the communities of practice in the workplace for the competitive advantage of the employer. According to them, the key to doing this is to establish a level of trust within the organisation, trust that members' contributions to the community will be recognised and rewarded – that the external goods will be distributed on a fair and equitable basis. Part of that basis must be constituted by respect for the internal goods of the practice. Even in the case of insurance claims handlers, which Wenger cites as a community of practice, it is clear that the practitioners have some idea of what good practice consists in – they do not perform at the lowest level consistent with them being paid. For example, Wenger reports the way that an employee Ariel "types and writes impressively fast" (Wenger 1998: 23) and how

> .... you are good at claims processing when you can quickly find legitimate ways to get the charges reimbursed to a reasonable extent. ... You have to develop a good sense of how much is reasonable, juggling the whole thing to produce quickly a reasonable story. What makes a story 'reasonable' can't be taught during the training class. *(Wenger 1998: 31)*

Wenger gives fourteen indicators that a community of practice has formed. For example, he cites

> ..... absence of introductory preambles as if conversations and interactions were merely the continuation of an ongoing process. ... Mutually defining identities,... local lore, shared stories, insider jokes, ...jargon and shortcuts .... *(Wenger 1998: 42)*

For Wenger these kinds of characteristics indicate that three dimensions of a community of practice are present. Such an approach would be far too instrumental for MacIntyre and would illustrate precisely the dangers of liberal emotivism in which the only reason for pursuing anything would be instrumental.

We can expand our critique of Wenger's notion of a community of practice by a detailed examination of three of its proposed dimensions:

(i) A community of mutual engagement
By mutual engagement Wenger means such things as working in the same location, being able to talk while working, or being able to talk on the telephone. This

does not mean that communities are homogeneous – far from it. For him diversity keeps communities going – diversity provides interest within a community of practice. But there is a problem here for Wenger – if we accept that community survives and prospers because of some synergistic relationship between sameness and difference, then precisely what does this synergy consist in? At what stage do the members of a community become so diverse that the community may be said to no longer exist? Alternatively at what stage does a community become so consensual that it is so boring that it falls apart? As Wenger (1998: 77) explains:

..... in some communities of practice, conflict and misery can even constitute the core characteristic ... In real life, mutual relations among participants are complex mixtures of power and dependence, pleasure and pain, expertise and helplessness, success and failure, amassment and deprivation, alliance and competition, ease and struggle, authority and collegiality, resistance and compliance.... Communities of practice have it all.

This final phrase is telling. If communities of practice have it all, what characteristic could there be that would limit the indiscriminate use of the term? Unfortunately Wenger does not answer this question. Likewise, his discussions of the other dimensions of a community of practice are also epistemologically vague.

(ii) A negotiated enterprise
Wenger oscillates between two apparently opposing positions suggesting again that communities of practice can 'have it all'. As he (1998: 78-79) writes:

..... the enterprises reflected in our practices are as complex as we are. They include the instrumental, the personal and the interpersonal aspects of our lives ..... communities of practice are not self-contained entities. They develop in larger contexts ... even when the practice of a community is profoundly shaped by conditions outside the control of its members ... its day to day realities are nevertheless produced by participants within the resources and constraints of their situations.

It seems then that communities of practice are all-inclusive and nested within other communities. Their purpose may be constituted by those not involved in the community – managers for example. Yet the way that people deal with their situation is sufficient for Wenger to enable us meaningfully to talk about a community. For example, no manager could nor would want to specify every aspect of the work of employees. Those that are not specified must be negotiated in some way. Wenger is correct to point out that the way that these negotiations take place is crucially important to the overall success of the community as measured both by members and managers. He is also correct to note the ambivalent position of managers in this respect. When Wenger goes on to refer to a 'repertoire' of shared resources, he clearly means these to be in the service of some aim that is not negotiated.

(iii) A repertoire of negotiable resources
As might be expected from the preceding such a repertoire "remains inherently ambiguous" (Wenger 1998: 83). This prompts the question of the sense in which these resources could be said to constitute a repertoire. The ambiguity is supposed

to enable new meanings to be created within the community and for members of the community to have a tacit understanding of what is going on. The height of a pile of papers on a particular desk indicates a state of processing as things stand, but it could mean something else as new arrangements are negotiated. The possibility of misunderstanding is unproblematic for Wenger (1998: 84):

> ..... agreement in the sense of literally shared meaning is not a precondition for mutual engagement ... mismatched interpretations or misunderstandings need to be addressed and resolved directly only when they interfere with mutual engagement.

Much of this section of Wenger's work continues to suggest that communities of practice can 'have it all'. He (1998: 85) goes on:

> ..... the local coherence of a community of practice can be both a strength and a weakness. ... Communities of practice are not intrinsically beneficial or harmful ... Yet they are a force to be reckoned with for better or for worse.

What all this seems to mean is that people will make the best of whatever circumstance they find themselves in and that the language they use and the actions in which they engage will not, nor need not, match exactly the desired purpose of the powerful. As Habermas (1984, 1987) might say, the lifeworld will always distort the system world in unpredictable ways. Following Habermas, we might suggest that the term 'community of practice' is a kind of consolation for the powerless in an age of increasing systematisation of the lifeworld – a response to a condition that Nietzsche (1994) drew our attention to some time ago – a further chapter in the genealogy of morality.

Let us summarise these difficulties with Wenger's account of 'community of practice':

- What is the minimum number of people needed for a community to be formed?
- How complex does a practice have to be for it to be possible both for insiders and outsiders to distinguish good from bad practice?
- What distinguishes insiders from outsiders given that communities are nested in some way?
- How long does a group have to be together for it to be clear that a community has formed?
- What has to happen for a community to disintegrate?
- To what extent do the values of community members have to coincide and in what ways?
- What minimum condition with regard to internal goods needs to be satisfied before it makes sense to refer to a community rather than an association or even a group?

We think that we escape these difficulties by avoiding the term communities of practice. For us networks and associations are more helpful terms now. The determination of level is contextual as is the determination of insider and outsider. The matter of exiting and entering communities does not arise because for us people are practitioners of different sorts and to different degrees at different time. It is not necessary, or possible, to distinguish internal from external goods in all contexts in order for the distinction between internal and external goods to be useful.

3. PRACTICES AND CONTEXTS

It might be imagined that our theory of learning as developing the ability to make contextually sensitive judgements is circular. As has been noted, one obvious way of making sense of the notion of context is through the practice within which a judgement is located and that itself is a matter of judgement. There can be no algorithmic account of how best to contextualise a particular judgement in terms of the general or particular. People are familiar with the situation in which they appear to have made the wrong choice only to find that 'it turned out well in the long run'. Yet our theory needs to avoid regressive claims that all judgements could be good because things could turn out alright in the long run.

Such a regress is avoided through the notion of recursion. It is always possible to contextualise judgements in a variety of ways and at a variety of levels. It is therefore possible to evaluate judgements in a number of ways which potentially, at least, may conflict. Such conflict may give rise to a further series of recursive possibilities for resolving the conflict. What prevents the infinite regress is the interest of the actor or interpreter at any particular time, not possible interest – there is no way of knowing in advance what this might be. The solution of a particular practical problem may be the only interest that counts in many cases. In other cases problems may seem more complicated. While it is possible to problematise indefinitely and to engage in a seemingly endless series of recursive reflections, our common understandings are based on the fact that most of us do not do that for most of the time. To take one obvious example, many forms of work would become impossible if workers continued recursively to reflect on whether they did the right thing at any particular time. To take another example, while it may not be immediately apparent that a decision is a cleverly designed attempt to further powerful interests, upon reflection the design may become apparent. The judgement may be contextualised in a different way and at a different level.

3.1 An Example – Learning to Fix a Computer Fault

Suppose the screen with which I (one of the authors) am now working suddenly goes blank. No amount of pressing keys or switching on and off brings an image back. Suppose I endeavour to fix the problem myself and in so doing learn a little more about how the computer works. What steps might I take?

First I might seek to identify the practice or level of practice most relevant to the problem – is it a problem with the operating system, the hardware, the drivers or some software conflict? These diagnostics suggest that I already have some knowledge of the way that the computer works, but even if I did not, I might begin my search for a solution by getting hold of some books on computers and computer fault finding. In order to make sense of these books I would need perhaps to understand the meaning of terms such as software, display, keyboard and so on. I might need to do further research which identified these components in ways that I could recognise. Terms such as display feature in practices other than computing, of course, so I might understand their meaning from my knowledge of the practice of shopping where displays are common.

In consulting books in this way, I would perhaps be taking the next step which is to recognise the source of authoritative help. Again, from my participation in a range of other practices, I might consult books because I know that a book is likely to have undergone most critical scrutiny in its production, that it will have been reviewed by those more knowledgeable than I and that, in short, while there is no guarantee, there is a reasonable likelihood that much of what I read will be accurate and useful.

Through participating in other practices I might also have learnt that search engines such as Google are sometimes useful in identifying sources of authoritative help. I might know, for example, that Google works by foregrounding those sites that have overall been found to be useful to those seeking help on a particular topic or activity. Finally, I might see what those who earn their living through fixing computer faults advise, on the grounds that they would go out of business if they were useless and offering false advice is not in their long term interests. After all, if I get stuck, I might have recourse to take the machine in to them for a professional repair and I know again from knowledge of other practices in which commercial interests are important that firms use telephone contacts as a way of advertising both their expertise, their reasonableness and their business. However, a firm that is desperate for business is unlikely to be an authoritative source of advice.

Now in sifting through all these potential sources of advice, I am drawing on my knowledge of other practices that overlap in different ways with what might be called the practice of computing, and I am making judgements about what to accept and what to reject. How do I make these judgements? Well it seems to me that I make them through an immensely complex series of recursive attempts to make sense of the problem at hand, with regard to what has worked for me in the past.

And here is the point, my judgement is likely to be better the more that I have attempted to solve these problems for myself, rather than reverting to 'safer' but less problematic formal sources. In the former cases the outcome is uncertain, I have to be prepared for failure and to take a long time finding out that I have failed. I have to be prepared to attempt systematic trials and I have to be prepared to switch the angle or focus that I use to frame the problem.

In this way, perhaps, the most difficult of these is identifying the practice or level of practice that is involved, and judging when it is appropriate to switch levels of focus. The matter goes beyond fixing the computer, of course, because that is not the only, nor necessarily the most important, problem that I face and I need to judge just how long to persevere with that problem before leaving it for another to fix. But then if I do this, I lose confidence. Many of the other problems that I face are truly intractable and it will never be clear that I have reached the proper solution. I need to cope with this uncertainty and I am hardly prepared for doing so if every problem that I face, even those with a definite solution such as restoring the screen on my computer, ends in failure. So the way that I handle this overall complexity of my life also calls for judgement about which I cannot be certain.

4. PRACTICAL INVOLVEMENT

As we have seen the key difference between MacIntyre's and Wenger's account of practice concerns the latter's inclusion of external goods as the prime focus of practical concerns. In addition to the problem of a lack of clarity, a main problem for the latter account is in determining how community can survive without some sense of justice in the distribution of external goods? Just as a common pursuit of external goods may serve to bind a group together in some way, a recognition that membership of the community brings unjust differential rewards may serve to destroy a sense of community. This, we believe, is part of the thrust of Saint-Onge and Wallace's (2003) book. Wenger (1998) seems to present a rather romanticised view of a group of claims handlers somehow satisfied with their distributive lot in life. The members seem content to gain recognition through their part in the negotiation of micro aspects of practice, such as where to put the pile of claims forms, and so on. No need to worry about deep senses of injustice over a communal cup of coffee!

In contrast there is a rather bleaker idea of community outlined by Delanty and attributed to Honnett, Bourdieu and Sennett which holds that community is no longer possible because

> .... the increase in demoralisation ... has led to a situation in which people no longer share a common language through which to communicate their experiences of ... the absence of 'recognition'. *(Delanty 2003: 69)*

More positively, according to Little (2002: 3),

> ..... communities exist where virtues such as friendship, voluntarism and care are exhibited. What this entails is a definition of community whereby individuals belong to a social group either through choice or birth and where their behaviour and status is not based on instrumental gain.

Where behaviour and status are based on instrumental gain, Little (2002:4) suggests the term 'association' is more appropriate. Yet as Hirst (1994: 51) notes, it is from:

> The right to be a voluntary member of an association [that] we derive the most basic right in an associative society, that is, the apparently paradoxical right of exit, to be able to leave an association within a relatively short and specified period of time and without a significant fine or equivalent financial loss.

An association may be a rather weaker term than community, but for both forms of grouping, it seems essential that individuals should be free to leave if they choose without financial or other sort of loss, and this is a problem for Wenger's notion of a community of practice. On Wenger's account, individuals are not free to leave many communities of practice without financial loss. That means that there is a tendency for individuals to perform at the lowest level consistent with them being paid. Such performance is plainly not in the interests of a market economy. For MacIntyre, individuals do not choose to become or not to become practitioners. The question regarding a right to exit does not arise. Nevertheless there must be a sense in which someone no longer practices in that their practical involvements come to be formed elsewhere. In these cases the question of financial penalty does not arise other than contingently, when, for example, the practitioner chooses to earn their living through the institutions associated with other types of practice. It is difficult to envisage this because, as has been indicated earlier, MacIntyre is not outlining a practice in a sociological sense, but as a normative guide to what a moral community ought to be like.

For reasons similar to this theorists such as Putnam (1993) and Fukuyama (1999) argue that communities help to establish relationships of trust in society, which in turn encourages greater social capital that facilitates the healthy working of market economies. In other words, the existence of communities in the strong sense of people who hold values in common are necessary instruments in the pursuit of economic ends. Moreover economic success helps to sustain strong communities. In contrast John Gray (1997: 18) argues that communities need to be protected from the impact of markets. Gray goes further. He argues that there can be no non–political notion of community (1997: 77):

> There is no over arching value of community to which all political movements can reasonably pay lip service. Conceptions of community, and public policies aiming to promote it, will vary radically according to the political projects they express.

A similar scepticism about depoliticised notions of community is expressed by Frazer and Lacey (1993). They point out the way that power relationships can skew the nature of community life. Of course MacIntyre would agree with this. In summary, not only is the notion of a community of practice lacking in clarity in a sociological sense, but it is also lacking in clarity in a moral and political sense. MacIntyre and Wenger use the term practice in different ways. For MacIntyre practice that is dominated by institutional considerations cannot form the basis of a morally and politically desirable society. For Wenger it can. For us, people are associated or networked into a variety of practices to different degrees at different times. That is not to deny the importance of tradition. Rather it is to note the way that traditions evolve through peoples' differing practical involvements.

5. FORMAL LEARNING

MacIntyre, Wenger and us come together somewhat in our consideration of formal learning. For Wenger the theory of legitimate peripheral participation has implications for what ought to be learnt within formal educational institutions. He acknowledges (1998: 223) that:

> ..... learning cannot be designed. Ultimately it belongs to the realm of experience and practice.

Hence, for him, communities of practice are already involved in their own learning and it is part of the very notion of a community of practice that it structures the ways that newcomers are initiated into it. Therefore there is "no division of labour between learners and non learners" (Wenger 1998: 234). Formal educational institutions cannot comprise a community which 'fully designs the learning of another [community]'. If learning is to be conceived as being initiated into a community of practice then there must be 'facilities of engagement' with those communities. Where the prime function of an institution is to maintain a number of communities of practice into which learners can be inducted, and where those communities are detached from their real point and purpose, then there is always the possibility, even the likelihood, that learners become inducted into a reified version of the practice. Such reification serves the ends of the formal educational institutions well, but not those of the community of practice

What Wenger is getting at here is similar to Engeström's (2001) point that there is no reason why theories of situated learning cannot include the role of a formal educator or trainer. However where that role is detached from practice, then newcomers must be inducted into a reified version of the practice. We may speculate that this is one reason why MacIntyre argues that teaching is not a practice. All too often teaching is reified – divorced from the contexts that would give it some pedagogical force. For example, the particular practice of claims handling which Wenger describes, gets its point from its contextualisation in the work of a particular company in a particular place, involving certain amounts of money, certain real risks, the possibility of real gains and so on. An attempt to simulate that community within a formal educational institution is bound to fail because the crucially important features of context are missing. In a simulated situation, students are initiated into a different (reified) practice. That is not to say that such initiation is bound to be useless. As Wenger (1998: 268) notes

> .... applying what one has learned in a classroom becomes a matter of moving from one practice to another. In this respect there is not that much difference between the school house and the claims processing centre. Both are local practices that have specific relations to the rest of the world.

There is however one crucial difference. In the latter case, the point of the practice is clear and there is no reason to make the nuances of practice clear. The opposite may be true. In the former case there is every reason to do so in the interests of

explaining the possible point of practices that will only become apparent in context. In formal learning, there is a requirement to try to make internal goods external whereas informally there is no requirement to do this.

From the earlier discussion, it might appear as if virtues are capacities for learning that enable the achievement of internal goods. To put the matter the other way
round, formally and informally people should do things that best enable the acquisition of internal goods, because through such acquisition they come to acquire
desirable capacities for learning. Very often, formal learning works against the
development of capacities for learning and is bound to do so. That is because formal learning is, at least to some extent, always concerned with values and values
are not always or even often communicated directly. Rather as Kelly points out in
connection with the formal hidden curriculum:

> Implicit in any set of arrangements are the attitudes and values of those who create
> them, and these will be communicated to pupils in accidental and perhaps even sinis-
> ter ways. *(Kelly 1999: 8)*

Values are not external goods. Telling people to value certain things or rewarding
them for doing so, cannot cause them to value those things. A recent case concerning institutional racism within the police force highlighted the way that direct
training to combat racism actually enabled racists to remain undetected, as they
learnt to avoid precisely those external behaviours that constitute public evidence
for racism. What such training should aim to encourage are certain dispositions to
behave in certain ways, but coming to change one's values is not often the result
of someone telling you to do so.

A similar argument may be used against the idea that the development of capacities for learning can best be learnt formally. There is no reason why certain
practices should not be supported within formal educational institutions. Typically
however such institutions do not do this. Rather they involve the teaching of reifications of practice which learners may or may not see as relevant to their practical
concerns. We are now in a position to see why MacIntyre was keen to suggest that
it does matter precisely what we regard as a practice. A main problem with teaching as professional practice is that all too often it is bound to be concerned with
external goods, if only in the interests of attempting to make something understandable to those who have never had much interest in the lesson to be taught.

Richard Smith (2003) argues that MacIntyre ignores the distinction between
self-contained practices and purposive practices. The former are those such as
chess, football and games in general that are in a sense self-contained, the latter
are those that have some end beyond themselves such as teaching. Where Smith
goes wrong, in our view, is in supposing that the assignation of purpose or function to practice can somehow be detached from the interests of the person making
the assignation. Certainly the main purpose of playing chess may be the love of
the game only, but it may also be a way of passing time, or getting to know someone. In this way the assignation of purpose is a function of context. A problem
with formal teaching is that it is far too easily contextualised in terms of external

goods and is not so easily contextualised as a part of the practice of what is actually being taught. Teaching X is rarely practising X.

In that regard the University teacher is in a much better position than her secondary school counterpart. That is because the University teacher through her research can more readily be seen as a practitioner within which she teaches novice practitioners. Of course there is nothing necessary about this observation and a shift in balance towards informal learning might help to bring about redress. As we argued in chapter five, what we need is a new conception of learning. One which pays much greater attention to that which cannot be readily described, but is still made superficially, and in many cases misleadingly, accessible to those who have no good reason to be interested.

6. EXEMPLARS

Let us now return to two of the cases of the younger people introduced in chapter two. They have had extensive periods learning formally. We will see how the above account matches their stories.

6.1 June's Story Expanded

June is a 22 year old, qualified Speech and Language therapist. While at university, she also worked part time as a Home Support and Day Carer for Social Work Services. June said that although she has always known that she wanted a career which was in a "caring and therapeutic capacity", she never really felt any "strong desire" to pursue any particular profession. She partly attributes her view of the importance of care to the fact that both her parents work within care settings. She saw school purely as the means to achieve a good career through the credentials that were on offer. She was primarily interested in external goods. It was through the reifications of practices such as Physics and Biology at school that the appropriate credentials were obtained.

Once on the University course, June felt that she had learnt most on placements. At this stage we may say that she became initiated into a set of practices related to the profession of speech and language therapy. The requirements of the University were still present in that she had to keep a journal of attempts to plan therapeutic interventions as if means ends rationality was appropriate. For June and others on her course, no matter how much planning takes place, "there is no real substitute" for the learning that takes place when having to constantly assess the needs of the client during therapy and readjust therapy in order for it to be more specific to the client's needs as therapy proceeds. She explained the way that such adjustment was always a matter of weighing different requirements based on different aspects of practice and on how a decision to do this could always be re-examined from another practical point of view.

In June's case, the lectures at University were also valuable. This is in contrast to the view of many students on other types of courses who complain "theory is irrelevant". A key reason for this may be that all of June's lecturers continue clinical practice. June saw this as resulting in an ability to "make the link between theory and practice". Theory in this context may be regarded not as a reification of practice but as part of practice itself. The lecturers were able to illustrate lectures with real examples and did not feel the need to try to render all features of practice transparent.

In her first placement in third year, June was working with two different therapists, one for two days per week and one for one day per week. Although both were experienced therapists and were both equally competent, they had very different ways of working and different views on how best to interact with patients. June found herself having constantly to adjust her therapy to suit whichever therapist she was working with on that day. While neither way was necessarily wrong, she felt this inhibited her ability to find her own way of carrying out therapy. She said "For the time being, it seemed more important to adjust to their way of working in order to please the therapists I was working with and find my own way of working once I had qualified myself". One way of interpreting this is to suggest that there is always a balance between internal and external goods and between different layers of context. To be sure there was the desire to please the therapist and the desire to do what was best for the client. It seems that June was recognising the authority of the therapists she was working with, in recognising that they were more able to make contextually sensitive judgements than she was. June admits that it's likely that even if she had disagreed with the type of therapy used for any particular client, she probably wouldn't have revealed this to the therapist, whereas if she had been working independently it would have been easier to change the therapy. She admits that initially she simply wanted a job that enabled her to live a rewarding life and she was prepared to chase external goods in the form of pleasing the teacher in order to achieve this. Through practical experience she started to come to appreciate the internal goods of the practice. Such recognition was helped, she thought, through her part time care work.

Upon reflection during the course of the interview, June acknowledged the role that chance had played in all this. Her account reminds us of Boisvert (1998: 16) who comments that Dewey acknowledges that situations very often are not clear-cut.

> Unlike the philosophers he criticises, Dewey does not begin with a prior commitment to achieving absolute certainty. Human knowing is provisional, incomplete and probabilistic. We rarely act with the absolute security that our choices are *the* absolutely appropriate ones.

While June's case does not especially celebrate informal learning, it does highlight the ways in which people weave different contexts for making judgements together in a myriad of ways that are not readily, if at all, explainable in terms of means ends rationality. It also highlights the significance of our theory of informal learning for formal learning too. That is because many courses particularly in higher education involve periods of practical experience and many lecturers retain their practical involvement so that they see themselves, as in June's example, primarily as practitioners rather than teachers.

6.2 Barbara's Story Expanded

Barbara qualified as a primary school teacher three years ago. As with June, Barbara states that she was motivated to learn at school, as she knew she needed to get the required grades in order to pursue her chosen career. She says "the motivation then is from knowing you've got exams, if you've got a focus and you know why you want a purpose to your learning, then you are learning things and you are actually rote learning a lot of the time, you're memorising at that stage to get through an exam…a lot of which is forgotten after the exam". This is a clear example of acting in pursuit of external goods alone and, as Barbara says, little of this acting counts as learning since it was soon forgotten. She goes on "the things that you remember, you know, that you really learn and remember for life are things that somehow mean something to you". It could be suggested that the learning that "means something" is that where internal goods are realised.

Like many other students, Barbara feels that she learned more on placements than while actually learning the theory at university, and similar comments might apply here as in June's case. One difference is that few of Barbara's lecturers continued to practise as Primary teachers and as a result, Barbara was less impressed with the University based part of her course. She said "although I would not slate my course, in three years being in the job you learn reality, I think definitely". Few University tutors "had the newest and freshest ideas. Often those with the most enthusiasm were the ones who still had a foot in the door of teaching to some extent. They were still in touch with children and working with children. You could sense a person's enthusiasm by the way they were talking and the way they were communicating their ideas…and there was definitely then people giving lectures where you got the impression, it's been a long time since you stepped foot in a classroom".

Barbara had not had any part time work experience and her course seemed far more concerned with technique than in June's case. For example she says "the teacher I worked with in fourth year was an inspiration, she really was, particularly in her behaviour management…her sheer presence in the room was amazing". She feels that she learned many essential strategies for behaviour management from this teacher, for example, "how to show confidence when you don't feel it, when to discipline, when to let things go, tone of voice, her whole physical presence, moving herself to where the problem was". Although, Barbara picked up many of these techniques, this was not explicit. She explains "you probably think about it when you are evaluating looking back, rather than necessarily realising you're learning it at the time, I don't know that I knew at the time I was learning all that at the time from her". When pressed about how this learning comes about, Barbara said that she feels it is a mixture of her picking up on these techniques and commenting on them to the teacher, and the teacher explaining them. She says, "you would say to her, gosh, they're so quiet for you, your presence seems to really work and she would talk about little things that she did". However, Barbara notes that it was never explicit and directed. "I can't think of any time when she actually said here's an example of a behaviour management strategy and go and try it … it is something where you have to develop your own kind of style, I don't think it's something that can be spelled out. … You do not necessarily know that you are taking on board her idea and altering it. You're are just kind of naturally doing it, so I suppose it's not that conscious the process of learning from somebody in that way". On this account, techniques look like examples of internal goods and clearly they have moral importance. That was not how Barbara was taught at University however. Rather attempts were made explicitly to communicate a series of techniques and as Barbara notes, "this does not work". Reifications of practice at University are good examples of what we think should be avoided and why we think that it is important to shift the balance in learning more towards the informal.

Barbara told us that learning opportunities very much depend upon the individual school that a teacher is working in. She says "you can be influenced by the sort of enthusiasm and commitment, to be honest of the school, the general ethos of the school and staff. I think if there's a general atmosphere of all wanting to help each other, of wanting to help improve each other, you know, willingness to learn from each other. Basically I think that's really healthy and you're not scared to take on board ideas and to give ideas as well which I think is important…you feel less threatened then I think". While she sees this as a healthy atmosphere, in schools where it is not "the norm" to be open to learning from each other, it can be perceived as quite threatening and can "affect your openness and willingness to learn from each other". This is a reflection of her own experience of teaching within different schools as, since she has qualified, she has worked within three different schools. The Newly Qualified Teachers in Williams (2003) study also felt that in schools where staff work in a collaborative fashion the learning opportunities are increased. This feeling is also supported by Fuller and Unwin's (2004: 130) theory of expansive learning environments where we might say there are simply more opportunities to contextualise what you do differently and more possibilities for accessing the views of an authority. In a restrictive environment, it is not possible to do these things and especially it is not possible to learn from mistakes, because mistakes are contextualised as failure. There is a lack of openness to possibilities and an ethos which wants to label, to pin down, to determine. In short external goods come to dominate to such an extent that it is not acceptable to contextualise what is going on in terms of what is unclear and possibly hidden.

CHAPTER EIGHT

THE IDEA OF JUDGEMENT

In this chapter we examine more closely the notion of judgement upon which our theory of informal learning is based. Following the work of post-empiricist philosophers of science, it is now widely accepted that there can be no judgements that are theory or context free. As Oakeshott (1933: 14-21) puts it:

> Sensation, then, as a form of experience independent of thought or judgement must be pronounced self-contradictory ... [there is no difference between say] seeing a green leaf and judging 'that the leaf is green'. ... it is impossible to discover a form of experience which is *less* than judgement.

Since experience is a homogenous whole, there are no absolute divisions of contexts within it. Potentially, therefore, there is an infinite number of ways of contextualising judgements. On this account, judgement may be regarded as an attempt to find an appropriate context. The determination of what constitutes a good judgment is a concern both for the practitioner herself and for the observer or customer, for whom the internal good of practice is also an external good. For the latter external goods are likely to be of prime concern, whereas the former is more likely to be concerned with internal goods. In determining the extent to which a judgement is contextually sensitive, there are therefore at least two possible foci of concern. In this chapter we attempt to explain how this multi focus enables us to make sense of the idea of contextual sensitivity in judgement.

We concluded the previous chapter by noting the way that there is nothing within practices themselves that enabled them to be contextualised. Rather it is the assignation of purpose and interest that enables contextualisation. We begin this chapter with an introductory section that illustrates further how it is our interests and purposes that enables us to make sense of judgments, sometimes in terms of some short term purpose and interest, but sometimes in some longer term search for meaning. We argue that it is not so much that we are members of different communities of practice which provides us with a way of making sense of judgements, but that we are practitioners of different sorts to different degrees. We cannot have a complete grasp of practice and, as the next chapter is meant to show, even when we can be considered to be a practical authority, the source of our authority is not the acquisition of certain properties. Rather it is the disposition to go on learning.

An example is provided by driving a car, an activity that requires various levels of explanation. One can offer a physical description of the working of the various components of the car during a given trip. This description will explain some aspects of the trip, but not many. One can then appeal to the rules of the road – these will help to explain some other aspects of the trip. One can then describe the wishes and desires of the occupants of the car. These will help to explain still other aspects of the trip. A description of traffic conditions (the environment) will offer further explanation. And so on. But there is no one level of description that will explain all about the trip. We think that perhaps learning is like travelling (and other basic human activities such as eating, talking, etc). Any particular example of travelling is highly situated and contextual. But in principle, we can explain/describe it. However, this will require various types of explanation, as the car journey example illustrates. No one type is *the* explanation of the travelling. Nor is there any reason to expect there to be a single, general theory of travelling. The same applies to learning. To think otherwise is, perhaps, to fall into the scientistic assumption that because there is one word for something, it refers to a single, unitary object. Explanations are different according to different interests.

We may regard car driving as a practice and regard gear changing, indicating, etc., as activities within it. All of these activities require judgement as does deciding whether to drive the car at all. There are internal goods involved in car driving most obviously connected with judging such things as width of the vehicle when negotiating a tight passage, or the appropriate speed of the vehicle when negotiating a bend and so on. Consider how the ability to make such judgements might be taught. It is possible to imagine the instructor explaining that the tighter the bend or the lower the camber, the more speed should be reduced. It is unlikely, but possible, that she might also get the learner to do some applied mechanics which would show the centrifugal forces involved, and so on. In the end, however, the learner is going to take the bend under some supervision so that she does not get things hopelessly wrong. If she hears the tyres squeal, she will contextualise her judgement according to her interpretation of tyre squeal. But how does she learn how to interpret tyre squeal? Perhaps the instructor tells her that this is a kind of warning sign that not all is well.

The practice of driving requires that she come to see the avoidance of tyre squeal as a kind of internal good. Within another layer the squeal of rubber will be an external good – made explicit when perhaps she rides a bicycle down a steep incline and the brakes start to squeal. She finds it increasingly difficult to stop and the squeal increases and energy is dissipated not in stopping the bike but in making the noise. Perhaps she learns to use the gears to avoid some of this noise, and perhaps such use may be regarded as an internal good within another practice. The point of this example is to illustrate how it is often necessary to appreciate an external good within one practice, which then serves as an entering wedge to appreciate an internal good in another. It also illustrates how within one practice an external good may be of prime concern which is an internal good in another. Moreover it illustrates how in a sense a customer more concerned with external goods in the case of a work practice, may nonetheless come to be sensitive to the internal goods involved in the work.

Another way of putting this is that implicit context can be made explicit and vice versa. When to do this is also concerned with judgement. We have seen that practices are multi-layered, that they extend from collections of activities through traditional ways of working to considerations of how, among a range of competing identities, people make sense of their lives and the lives of others. We have seen too that this layering of contexts enables us to explain how and why people learn new things.

1. MAKING IMPLICIT CONTEXT EXPLICIT

In more recent work MacIntyre (1999a) extends the notion of internal and external goods to include goods that benefit human beings in general. In this way he suggests a richer and broader notion of practice and an outline of how initiation into practice might proceed. He recognises that judgements may appear to be concerned with the achievement of external goods, but that such goods may well be instrumental in achieving some other good within a practice or enabling participation in some other practice through which internal goods can be realised. For example, someone may serve hamburgers to secure resources to enable them to pursue their hobby of sailing through which they realise goods internal to sailing. In that way the practice of sailing provides a context for understanding the activity of serving hamburgers. Alternatively, the contexts for some judgements seem obviously related to a particular practice through the internal goods that are realised through that practice. Finally, the contexts for some judgements may best be understood according to whether a practice does conduce to some overall sense of unity of purpose in life or tradition that is felt to be worth preserving.

It is never entirely clear which sort of judgement is made at any time. MacIntyre explains this as follows:

> At any particular time, I have some range of projects, of goals and of desires. ... And if I do act on a particular desire, I either make or presuppose a judgement that it is best for me here and now ... But ... if my reason for acting as I did was a good reason for so acting, it must have been ...that there was no better reason for acting in any other way.
>
> In so evaluating my desires I stand back from them. ... Most of the time deliberation does proceed and must proceed without bringing this question to mind. And if this question were raised too often and too consistently, it would paralyse us as agents. But without the ability to raise it we cannot function as practical reasoners. *(MacIntyre 1999a: 69)*

In this passage MacIntyre suggests an account of learning that resonates with that of Dewey. "Ends-in-view" are under constant review and potential revision in the light of experience. Significant learning is determined by the degree of sensitivity to context that leads learners to discern an experience as problematic in a way that will facilitate their educative growth. That does not mean that the most productive learners discern all experiences as problematic. Nowhere is this more obvious than in some workplaces where it would simply display a lack of contextual sensitivity to deliberate and refine tentative solutions to potential problems so that nothing else got done. Yet for MacIntyre it is an ability to evaluate at a distance as it were that distinguishes the good practitioner from the novice. There is a clear sense in which only the actor herself knows why she acts as she does. But there is also a clear sense in which it is only those with a wider view of what is good that are better placed to make such judgements. This suggests that novices commence their initiation into a practice by acting without reasons that go beyond personal wants and desires. They go on to be able to formulate reasons for action that relate to standards of goodness within the practice. Finally, and through participation in other practices, they come to be able to imagine a future that is in some significant ways different from the present. They come to be able to ask "what else might we have done and how better might we judge in the future?"

This ability is related to the Deweyan distinction between implicit and explicit context (e.g. Dewey 1933). Explicit context refers to those features of experience that all learners recognise. Implicit context refers to those assumptions that learners have taken for granted, but which might be problematic. Dewey explains that:

> a person in pursuing a consecutive train of thoughts takes some system of ideas for granted ... Some context, some situation, some controlling purpose dominates his explicit ideas. ... Yet the fact that reflection originates in a problem makes it necessary at some points to inspect and examine this familiar background. We have to turn upon some unconscious assumption and make it explicit. *(Dewey 1933: 281)*

It is not possible to explain or predict precisely this inspection and examination. That is because there can be no ultimate distinction between the processes and products of learning. Moreover an unconscious assumption may sometimes best be described as an expectation of a kind of feel. For example, when a joiner hits a nail, she has an expectation both of how the nail will penetrate the wood and how the hammer will rebound off it in her hand. An attempt to drive a nail into new material may be the kind of problem that Dewey describes. In judging how hard to hit a nail with a hammer, there is an expectation which can be more or less refined in experience of what will happen. For many workers, a feel for a whole range of aspects of performance becomes habitual, implicit and not obviously the outcome of a judgment. These aspects do however show that the worker has come to appreciate some internal goods of the workplace practice.

Beckett (1996) argues that it is simply incorrect to suggest that judgements are always based on reflection of possibilities for achieving some end in view. What he calls "hot action", which seems to involve multiple rapid judgements, may best be described as an anticipation rather than reflection. The notion of "ends-in-view" is related to the time frame within which an activity is interpreted. A flick of a wrist may be an unnoticed part of a particular medical operation, surgical practice in general or the projected narrative unity of the surgeon's life depending upon the time frame within which the flick is interpreted and the interests of the interpreter. It is not possible to set out in the abstract the features of context that will or will not be relevant at any time. Thus lists of the sort given by Beckett and Hager (2002: 294) have limited value and may serve to deceive some readers into believing that through a systematic analysis, precisely these abstract features of context can be set out once and for all as it were. It is even mistaken to suppose that the most compelling features of context can be set out in this way for similar reasons.

Heidegger's use of the term "ready to hand" also illustrates the way that contexts are understood. What could count as a relevant context is indeed far reaching. As Heidegger (1962: 116) puts it in connection with a hammer,

> .... with the 'towards which' of serviceability there can again be an involvement with
> this thing, for instance, which is ready to hand, and which we accordingly call a 'ham-
> mer', there is an involvement in hammering: with hammering there is an involvement in
> making something fast: with making something fast, there is an involvement in protec-
> tion against bad weather: and this protection is for the sake of providing shelter for
> Dasein – that is to say, for the sake of a possibility of Dasein's Being.

In this way any single statement or act is capable of a seeming infinite number of interpretations which anticipate patterns of familiarity. These patterns include what Searle (1995: 135) calls "scenarios of expectation" or what Beckett (1996: 140) terms "feedforwardness". An accomplished practitioner is able to judge when to call into question features of the implicit context for any judgement.

As already suggested, work practices overlap with, and are but particular instances of, societal practices in general. Moreover, it may be preferable to interpret judgement at work with regard to practical contexts that are more widely situated and not obviously concerned with work at all. In summary, initiation into the practices of a society begins simply by copying others in pursuit of what must be external goods related to basic wants and desires. By comparing the consequences of such copying within and between practices, the learner comes to discriminate between good and bad reasons for acting in certain ways. She comes to perceive similarities between and within practices that enable her to develop some overall idea of what is worth doing and what is not. Through language she is able to compare her ideas and reasons with those of others. She comes to judge when it is wise to trust those others and when it is better to trust her own independent judgments. This process depends upon there being opportunities for her to participate with others in practical activities and for the consequences of some of these activities to be sufficiently determinate for her to develop some confidence in her ability to judge correctly. According to our argument, correctness here depends upon an appropriate discrimination between levels in what turns out to be a nested series of concepts.

It is important to note, with Dewey, that the seemingly endless potential to expand context to include every possible feature of the universe is blocked by the actual experience of the learner. Moreover, the seemingly endless potential to expand interpretation indefinitely is limited by the actual interest of the interpreter, not by any possible interpretation. An example may be useful here. A joiner may develop good practice in the course of work in a variety of contexts, each of which shares some things in common with its predecessor, but which also introduces novel features. There comes a point however when the context is stretched so far that we come to identify the joiner's practice as something other than joinery. So, for example, if the joiner starts to do some electrical work following the installation of a door frame because it is convenient to do so, it is normal to talk as if he were practising as an electrician rather than as a joiner. Plainly there is some overlap between practices when it is plausible to refer to contexts of either joinery or electrical work. It is also plausible to interpret activities with reference to other practices and traditions such as those concerned with robbery or deception.

Language is not completely elastic because there are traditional ways of speaking and acting. As Blake *et al.* (1998: 33) argue:

> We can only wait and see what our language lets us do. But that is all we need to do.

It is not possible to extend the notion of practice to cover all novel contexts in which the learner might find herself. Indeed nesting suggests that some features of context are more likely to be revised than others. Thus it is normal to talk of a novel context, less likely to talk of a novel practice, and very unlikely that we talk of a novel tradition.

2. JUDGEMENT

Judgement then may be considered as one of the fundamental units of the nested concepts already introduced. Activities comprise multiple judgements, some of which may usefully be made explicit with reference to an explicit context. The reference to context enables us to make sense of judgement, to evaluate particular judgements and to suggest the sort of episodes, activities, practices or traditions that are likely to encourage productive learning. For Dewey (1933: 123), productive learning leads to the development of what he calls "good habits of thought".

> Good habit of thought lies in the power to pass judgements pertinently and discriminatingly.

He goes on:

> No hard and fast rules ... can be given. It all comes back, as we say, to the good judgement, the good sense, of the one judging. To be a good judge is to have a sense of the relative indicative or signifying values of the various features of the perplexing situation: to know what to let go of as of no account: what to eliminate as irrelevant: what to retain as conducive to the outcome: what to emphasise as a clew to the difficulty.
> *(Dewey 1933: 123)*

It is not hard to see the connection between the Aristotelian virtue of phronesis and the Deweyan term "good habit of thought", and thereby to see a putative connection between the work of MacIntyre and Dewey. Good judgements are good precisely because they include the weighing up of the features of a situation that are salient, the balancing of those features, and the ability to do all these parts with what Mulhall (1990: 200) refers to as "the quality of seamlessness". According to MacIntyre (1981: 154):

> Phronesis is the capacity to exercise judgement in particular cases. Phronesis is an intellectual virtue: but it is that intellectual virtue without which none of the virtues of character can be exercised. ... It is easy to see why Aristotle held that the central virtues are intimately related to one another.

From this we may say that phronesis is a virtue, the possession of which enables us to make wise judgements in particular cases. Judgements which take into account relevant features of a situation, rejecting those that are irrelevant. It may be seen to be acquired by:

> Long familiarity with like operations in the past. *(Dewey 1933: 123)*

But what constitutes "like operations"? The selection of the relevant features of context is important here. Davis (1998), following Goodman (1970), makes the point that such selection is "theory dependent". By this he means that "we judge actions to be repetitions depending on our purposes and interests". While these purposes and interests may be nested in precisely the ways outlined earlier, there are at least three possible interpretations of the 'we' who have an interest. In the first case there is the group of what we might call 'outsiders' who describe the practice in particular ways. Second there is the group of 'insiders' who regulate the practice through distinguishing good from bad moves within it, and, third, there is the group of practitioners who themselves describe what they do in particular ways.

While a practice might appear to have a structure that is regulated by insiders, it is clear that it cannot be completely regulated in this way. Otherwise novices could not be inducted into it. Structure only exists insofar as some activities within the practice remain constant through each recursion, not that any particular activity remains constant for all time. It is the recursive quality of human activities, made possible by a shared form of life, that enables sense to be made of the notion of "like operations". While judgement about the appropriate features of context depends upon what others deem appropriate, those others can only deem what is appropriate because collectively people do act in particular ways. Hence the possibility of change and traditions in practice are mutually dependent. Reflexivity here involves not only a monitoring of how the judgement is made, but also how others interpret the judgement and, as we have seen, that can be done with reference to any part of nested features of context. Indeed it is part of what it is to be human to be continually assessing one's judgement in relation to how others assess it, whether insiders or outsiders, and from whatever level in a nest of possible interpretations of context.

What this means is that there is no way of knowing in advance precisely what features of context are most likely to be relevant to the future interests of learners. A further example may be helpful here. To what extent does a trained hairdresser have to learn afresh her practice when she begins work in a new salon in a different part of the world from where she was trained, or even when moving to a salon within her own country that has a very different approach to the business of hairdressing. It is common to suggest that there are sufficient similarities between practice in one salon and practice in another, for it to make sense to say that her learning has 'transferred' in some way. However the notion of transfer suggests that there is a core to hairdressing that always subsumes a range of contexts within which hairdressing can plausibly be said to take place. This is incorrect according to our argument. Rather it is not possible to determine in advance which features of context will be most relevant to future practice in advance of that practice. It is this impossibility that prompts inquiry which is the first stage of learning. What has become a habitual practice is disrupted by the move to a new salon. Judgement is needed to identify those features of a new context to which she can relate through previous experience.

The only guidance that can be offered to the work-place curriculum designer or the worker herself who is hoping to prepare herself for future practice is to situate her judgements and activities in as wide a range of contexts as possible. There is an inevitable tension, however, between valuing tightly controlled behaviour and valuing the potential for making good judgements in unforeseen circumstances. There is also an inevitable tension between valuing internal goods, described earlier as kinds of feel, and external goods, described earlier as forms of status and reward. Ultimately these tensions are not resolvable exclusively with reference to learning or economic theory, but must include political theory that relates learning to work in new and creative ways. The distinction between learning at work and elsewhere turns out to be not especially significant. Work provides some additional features of context that makes judgement more complex, but the concepts of judgement, activity, practice and tradition are nested in similar ways whether or not activities count as work. The dominance of a particular view of academic learning as a preparation for work leads to an impoverished view of work-based learning as necessarily instrumental, narrowly reflective and unreliable to assess. To be sure there are good reasons for favouring the cognitively rich aspects of context, but rich cognition does not always, or even often, involve the use of pens and paper. Moreover rich cognition is not in opposition to the kind of physical expectations that form an essential part of good judgement in many workplaces.

To make learning more productive in the Deweyan sense, it is necessary both to situate it in as wide a range of contexts as possible and not to ignore the physical aspects of expectations. This implies some positive intervention in what otherwise could be most easily located within the practice that forms the prime focus of activity at work. To make work more productive in the narrow economic sense, it may well be necessary to do the opposite. That is because economically it may seem more desirable to value reliable practice within which the room for exploring the contextual quality of judgement is strictly limited. But there is a social and educational price to be paid for this. Moreover it is not entirely clear that there is not a longer term economic price to be paid too.

As Winch (2000: 181) remarks in connection with a discussion of the notion of social capital:

> Modern conceptions of social capital show a tendency to ignore its cognitive element. They also fail to take into account its civil element.

Winch here argues that the formation and maintenance of social capital both contributes to production of economic consumption and the development of productive powers. Economic consumption on its own is not enough, because it must always be narrowly focussed on the immediate needs of employers. If the logic of globalised postmodernity is accepted, these needs are bound to be subject to rapid and uncertain changes. There are, therefore, good reasons to make work productive in both senses and for governments to intervene to make it so. Even when this does not happen, it is clear according to the arguments of this chapter that workers will learn to contextualise their activities in ways other than those that relate to the immediate needs of employers.

Fuller and Unwin (2004) refer to 'expansive working environments' and have found evidence to suggest that within such environments, productive learning at work is more likely to take place in ways that benefit individuals, their employers and wider society. Their findings indicate that where employers make efforts to structure working environments so that judgements within them can be contextualised in a variety of ways, then more productive learning results. In contrast in restrictive learning environments context is limited and dominated very much by the pursuit of external goods. They have found that while it may seem not to be in an employer's interest to create expansive learning environments, that appearance is deceptive. Even though workers with increased interest in learning seem more likely to move on to seek further learning opportunities, perhaps with another company, they do not necessarily do so. Rather in the best expansive learning environments, they transform the culture within the organisation and, in many cases, that organisation becomes even more productive, leading to a virtuous circle of productivity. In contrast 'restrictive learning environments' discourage imaginative attempts to understand things differently. In those cases workers come not to see connections between their activities at work and elsewhere, but rather to see work as alienating and restricting.

3. INTERESTS AND PURPOSES

John Searle (1995) demonstrates how purpose and interest are central determining factors in a search for meaning. He also shows how contextualisation is made possible by a shared, unexamined form of life which he terms Background. It is this Background which enables our ability to see things in particular ways and to act upon them in order to bring about intended changes. Intentions are framed in terms of practices which are interdependent and judgements within those practices are understood with reference to some grasp of the way that the practices are related overall.

Searle notes the importance of function to consideration of context. For him, context is always a part of a system through which teleology is assigned. For example the context of work is always in part understandable with reference to an assigned purpose of earning money. The context of joinery is always in part understandable with reference to an assigned purpose, such as hanging a door. The function the joiner assigns to a hinge is not necessarily the same function as a cleaner assigns to the hinge. Indeed the cleaner might not notice the hinge at all. The assignation of function is dependent upon some wider notion or system within which the function has meaning.

Searle attempts to account for what he calls social reality – the fact that some things are facts by virtue of human agreement. For example, it is a fact that pieces of paper with certain marks on them are money. Such an institutional fact cannot exist in isolation but only in a set of systematic relations to other facts. Thus, for example, money depends upon there being a system of exchanging goods, a system of property ownership and so on. Institutional facts depend upon there being a network of established practices that are simply there and not questioned – at least not all the time. Searle notes the remarkable capacity that humans have to impose functions on objects. As he (1995: 19) puts it:

> ..... functions are never intrinsic; they are assigned relative to the interests of users and observers.

At certain stages in social development, it seems that users and observers simply come to agree on these institutional facts:

> ..... the key element in the move from the collective imposition of function to the creation of institutional facts is the imposition of a collectively recognised *status* to which a function is attached. (Searle 1995: 41)

But this leads to the problem of how such an imposition can avoid circularity. If the only reason that something is true is because we believe it to be true, then if we believe it to be true then it must be true. But for Searle (1995: 52) the resolution of the paradox is quite simple:

> .... the word ... marks one node in a whole network of practices ... and the fact that people practice in the ways they do supports the institutional fact.

Moreover part of practices consist in performative utterances made by the appropriate person and the fact that people speak in this way in contexts that are generally taken to be implicit, enable us to make sense of the utterance as part of the practice that supports the institutional fact. That is not to say that the status of such utterances may never be challenged. Rather it is to say that their status depends upon not challenging what Searle (1995: 129) calls the 'Background' or what Dewey might call 'implicit context'.

> ..... intentional states function only given a set of background capabilities that do not themselves consist in intentional phenomena.

The point here is that we just have to accept certain things as the things they are, in order to be able to interpret other things. At least there has to be some stability in our acceptance and we show this stability through our practices and through the fact that we are able to describe certain patterns in practices as in traditions, that are least open to revision. Tradition enables the possibility of understanding.

Searle (1995: 132) notes that it was Nietzsche who was 'most impressed' by the radical contingency of the Background and that artists generally often strive to illustrate such contingency, but language necessarily limits their efforts. In the end we can only describe their efforts in the language we have, though of course such description can have the effect of changing the possibilities for description. It is important to note that while the Background does not remain static, it is necessarily limiting. Participation in practices would not be possible if there was no Background that limits the possibilities of interpretation and judgement. For most of us for most of the time, we learn to participate in practices and we learn to contextualise our judgements with reference to those practices and others that are related through our interest.

Just as there would be no practices which include the transfer and exchange of money without there being a range of associated practices such as banking, property purchase and so on, nor would individuals be able to understand the concept of money without having learnt to participate in those associated practices to some extent. Moreover it would not be possible to judge their depth of participation, if judges themselves did not understand something of the network of social practices involved and the way that those practices are related.

We have seen how judgements may be contextualised in a potentially infinite number of ways that are limited only by the interpreter's or judge's interest at any particular time. We have seen too how in many cases contextual relationships take the form of a series of overlapping nests. Nests begin with basic activities and judgements and move upwards through traditions to include some notion of the way that people make sense of their lives as a whole, often by reflecting upon the way that they have structured these overlapping nests for themselves in contrast to the way that others have done so. A central problem that emerges again is the possibility of circularity in our explanations, which are, of course, bound within the context of a book which is intended to have explanatory power. What we are doing is attempting to articulate something that in the final analysis must remain tacit. When we have exhausted all the recursive possibilities for analysing judgement, we are left with a Background which must remain unexamined.

As Luntley (2003: 18) puts it, in connection with a discussion of Wittgenstein:

> The fundamental condition for the possibility of judgement is not capable of theoretical articulation. It consists in seeing the world aright, in taking the right attitude to the world.

For Luntley (2003: 148):

> Attitude is our take on the world. It is not justified, or supported with reasons. It is the point of view that makes reason giving possible. When I get the point of some activity, my attitude changes. I see the similarity. I get the point and then I know how to go on. I do not always give reasons for this when getting others to see as I see.

We may extend Luntley's (2003) account to explain further how it is that someone comes to select, from a range of possible contexts, the best selection for a particular purpose. On the traditional conception of expertise, someone comes to acquire capacities which function as causal antecedents of behaviour. For Luntley (2003), the expert has a set of attentional skills that enable her to focus on just those aspects of context that regulate her behaviour. Luntley describes such focusing as 'coupling' and such contexts as 'attractors'. The expert is not working to a theoretical rule in determining performance; she is working to achieve a balance to the various attractors that at any one time arise in virtue of their capacities for attending to the particularities of the situation. As Luntley (2004: 3) puts it:

> The structure of thought is not a linguistic structure; it is a structure of couplings. By 'coupling' I mean a conceptually articulated engagement with a thing or property of the environment. Couplings are relational. It takes two to couple. They are intentional states that are not capable of individuation independently of the way we are in the environment.

We may say then that an expert comes to achieve the right balance in making a judgement about the most appropriate possible contexts within which the judgement might be framed. She learns to do so in unforeseen circumstances.

4. EXEMPLARS

4.1 Back to Tyre Squeal

We can imagine someone able to drive a car, but who failed to recognise the significance of tyre squeal. On taking a bend, there may be a variety of activities taking place and a variety of considerations in the driver's mind, as we illustrated earlier. The recognition of tyre squeal may not be one of them however. In such a case it is unlikely that we would describe the driver as an expert, for she has failed to pick up the coupling of a particular sound and the driving context. Her sensitivity to context is not properly developed. How could it be developed? In the limit situation, she might be encouraged to experiment by driving progressively faster. Her attention might be drawn to the intensity of the noise produced. Still she might not come to see its significance. We may encourage her to feel the temperature of the tyres after taking a bend too fast. Still she may not understand the significance of squeal. We may then heat up rubber in a laboratory and so on. What we would be doing here is initiating her to different degrees in a range of practices connected with driving in an attempt to enable her to recognise the significance of tyre squeal. Normally however we would not do this. Rather we would simply assume on the basis of a shared tradition that she has come across situations where inanimate objects make noises when they are put under stress – creaking floorboards. Moreover we might imagine that she has seen films which include car chases and so on. In short, normally we assume that she has had certain experiences which form an unexamined background for her, so that it is hard to imagine someone having no grasp of the coupling of the sound of squealing with driving.

What this discussion of the work of Dewey, Luntley and Searle draws attention to is that at the bottom of our nests of contexts, there remains an aspect of judgement that is perspectival – that comes down to a particular way of seeing things and that accounts for our distinctive intentions. Those intentions are not detached from traditions and practices into which we are initiated, but they are not determined by them either. For the most part context remains unexamined other than in times of crisis. What this means for our theory of learning is that while we might feel inclined to be able to illustrate how people learn things and why they learn certain things at certain times, and even what kind of things they should learn at those times, these inclinations should be resisted. We have seen some of the dangers of informal learning turning into a cheap panopticon and we have seen how some of the best intentions of government towards greater social justice all too easily lead to greater systematisation of learning, which works against the recognition of internal goods that we argue is desirable. Let us return again to one of the stories introduced in chapter two to see how well it illustrates the theoretical discussion of this chapter.

4.2 Fred's Story Revisited

Fred, it will be recalled is a boatbuilder who now runs his own shop. Recall too from chapter four how it was a chance visit at the age of 9 that led to a lifelong interest and learning about boats. When Fred was 11 he joined the Sea Cadets, a voluntary organisation which exists to encourage young people to learn about various aspects of boating and themselves through practical activities of one sort or another. Fred recalls how he learned to row, to control a powerboat, to put up sails with others – to learn to care for others. When pressed, the list he recalled was extensive. We might summarise by saying that Fred's interest in boats was kindled by his opportunity to "play on a cruiser". This prompted him to wonder what it was like to move through the water, what forces are involved, and so on. It was not the practice of Physics in which he was primarily interested, although it could have been. Rather it was at that stage a series of activities such as rowing, tying a boat up, steadying it when others got into it, and so on. All of this could be said to comprise the practice of boat handling.

Even with a simple activity such as rowing, there may be seen to be complex judgements involved, including such activities as placing the oars in the rowlocks at just the right place, of pulling the oar at just the right depth, and so on. As with the example of tyre squeal, if in the end Fred had not come to feel the relevant contextual factors, it is hard to know what to say to him. No obvious external goods are involved other, perhaps, than the desire to please an adult supervisor or to gain the approval of fellow Cadets with whom Fred was working.

Fred recalls how membership of the Cadets afforded many opportunities to learn different things. It was not so much that Fred was exiting and entering practices of different kinds. Rather what he was doing was practising in different ways and at different times to different degrees. He was contextualising all this in a number of different ways depending upon purpose and interests. For example, rowing can be contextualised as a series of activities, as part of a practice or a tradition of boat handling, or as part of a wider practice of ship handling through which small boats are used to transport people to larger boats. Rowing can be and should be contextualised in these and other ways. On a larger boat, Fred learned among other things to help cook for large numbers of people, how to organise a large table, and so on. He came as we saw to reflect on the way he got on with others, how morally he ought to behave towards them, and what kinds of things he wanted to do with his life overall. What we see here is someone at an early age developing the habit of good thinking, which involves contextualising what he did in a variety of ways which lead to other forms of learning on a continuous basis.

It is perhaps not surprising that Fred became an apprentice boat builder. At that time an apprenticeship lasted for five years. Unfortunately, for commercial reasons, he was not taken on by the company that provided his apprenticeship and he had to look elsewhere. The apprenticeship was all practical work under the supervision of a master. Much of it appeared repetitive, but as Fred noted, "it wasn't really". Even such basic things as planing a piece of wood are complex. "By the time you had planed a hundred or so, you knew what it felt like, the wood, the sharpness of the blade – you knew when to sharpen it, when to lengthen the blade". It could be said that Fred had learned to couple such indicators as the size of the shavings with the smoothness and accuracy of the cut. He developed the ability to judge correctly at the level of this basic activity.

Now that wooden boats have largely been replaced by fibreglass, Fred's skills may appear to be obsolete with no practice left to sustain them or give them meaning, but the success of his shop disproves that. Why did someone past retirement age, whose craft skills seem no longer in demand, choose to support an industry that in many ways he had come to resent? First, there is a reason entirely to do with external goods. Second, within what is now a fairly institutionalised collection of activities that comprise boat building, there remains aspects that are not amenable to the quick fix, the ready made product, the helpful fact sheet. The skills of carpentry, painting and engine maintenance are still required. It is interesting that Fred devotes part of his shop to an area where he can demonstrate some of these skills, because for him teaching and selling goods are part of practice.

Fred ensures he is up to date by buying boat magazines and using these to anticipate what types of products are going to become popular. He then "reads up" on these products and finds out more about them, so that when customers start to come in asking for the products, he has the knowledge required to inform them. He has also become competent with the use of computers and communicates with people around the world who are engaged in a similar business.

Fred provides us with an excellent illustration of the way that a chance meeting leads to an interest which leads to a variety of other interests which sustain a variety of practical involvements. He also illustrates how it is possible to reflect on what he is doing and what he has done from different perspectives provided by these involvements. Finally he illustrates how a need for external goods need not even now come to dominate, and as a result and perhaps paradoxically, his business is thriving.

CHAPTER NINE

WISDOM

The current world is increasingly described as a 'risk society' (Beck 1992). The risk society is supposedly characterised by a move from structure to agency, from people gaining life meaning by giving their allegiance to large organisations and structures, to free ranging selves, individual agents having loyalty only to themselves. In the risk society, an individual's fate is bound up with the risks that they deliberately choose to take. Obviously, our notion of a growing capacity to make sound contextual judgements can be linked to this. However we are more sympathetic to the attendant social and communal factors in such judgement making, than to the rugged risk-taking individual conjured by the risk society.

Wisdom is commonly characterised as something more than just knowledge and understanding, even if these are at a superior level. The extra dimensions that wisdom is supposed to add to cognitive knowledge and understanding are usually non-cognitive qualities associated with experience and practice, such as judgment grounded in experience. For instance, *The Concise Oxford Dictionary* views wisdom as

> ..... possession of experience and knowledge together with the power of applying them critically or practically.

Webster's New World College Dictionary defines it as the

> ..... power of judging rightly and following the soundest course of action, based on knowledge, experience, understanding, etc.

In both of these definitions, experience is added to knowledge and understanding to enhance the power to act or judge appropriately in the prevailing practical circumstances. The emphasis on the role of practical experience in these definitions brings to the fore the idea that those extra dimensions that wisdom is supposed to add to mere knowledge and understanding are only developed over a suitable period of time. Thus, in a book concerned with the relationships between informal learning and lifelong learning, it is entirely appropriate to consider the connections between these two concepts and the development of wisdom.

However, it might well be thought that there is something important missing from this. What is missing from these accounts of wisdom is some recognition of its moral dimension. Our analysis of practice, drawing on the work of MacIntyre, has highlighted the moral dimensions of practice. We will argue in this chapter that the wisdom of practice takes on diverse moral features reflected in the different levels of practice, with each level being variously nested in the ways described earlier in the book.

In this chapter we firstly provide a brief account of the main approaches to understanding wisdom, with a focus on its possible connections to lifelong learning. We then examine in some detail the work of certain theorists that promises to illuminate the relations between informal learning, lifelong learning and wisdom. These include Shulman's work and his notion of the wisdom of practice; Hubert Dreyfus' work, particularly his 'stages of wisdom model', and his ideas on the nature of practice and the role of rules in practice; and Sternberg's balance theory of wisdom. Finally, we draw the discussion together by showing that it has provided us with some useful and important principles that productively link informal learning, lifelong learning and wisdom.

1. A SHORT SUMMARY OF WISDOM

Sternberg (2003) provides a critical overview of the major approaches to understanding wisdom. He suggests that there have been three major approaches: philosophical, implicit-theoretical and explicit-theoretical.

Philosophical approaches are characterised by seeking to develop a persuasive analysis of the concept of wisdom. According to Robinson (1990), Plato's dialogues offer the first such accounts, with wisdom being discussed in them in three different senses. Firstly, wisdom as *sophia*, found in those who lead a contemplative life searching for truth. Secondly, wisdom as *phronesis*, the kind of practical wisdom exhibited by statesmen and legislators. Finally, there is wisdom as *episteme*, found in those with scientific understanding of things. Although *sophia* is often translated as 'wisdom', perhaps *phronesis* is closer to the two contemporary dictionary definitions of wisdom quoted above. In any case, having three different concepts connected with wisdom suggests its somewhat elusive character. Significantly, wisdom has not been a particular topic of interest in subsequent Western philosophy (Honderich 1995: 912). (For instance, two contemporary 'Dictionaries of Philosophy' that were consulted had no entry for 'wisdom').

Implicit-theoretical approaches attempt to understand wisdom by finding out what people actually believe wisdom to be. So these approaches do not propose a prescriptive scientific or psychological account of wisdom. Rather they aim to identify people's beliefs about wisdom, without evaluating the worth of these beliefs. Sternberg's (2003: 148-149) overview of these approaches suggests somewhat mixed results. If there is one clear finding, it is that wisdom involves something more than intelligence. Not surprisingly, the most popular candidates for what that something extra might be are, broadly, experience and judgement, as suggested in the dictionary definitions quoted above.

Explicit-theoretical approaches involve the development and testing of some formal theory about what wisdom might be. Sternberg rates Baltes and his colleagues as major contributors to this strand (e.g., Baltes & Smith 1990, Baltes & Staudingerr 2000). Their work on wisdom is part of their long established research program on aging and intellectual abilities. For this reason, their conception of wisdom centres on general life-management problems, such as underage preg-nancy or mid-teens marriage. They characterise wisdom as "expert knowledge about fundamental life matters" or as "good judgment and advice in important but uncertain matters of life" Sternberg (2003: 150). They have developed and tested a five-component model that seeks to explain this kind of wisdom. The five compo-nents are:

- Rich factual knowledge (general and specific) about the conditions of life and its variations.
- Rich procedural knowledge (general and specific) about strategies of judgment and advice concerning matters of life.
- Knowledge about life span contexts and their temporal relationships.
- Knowledge about differences in values, goals and priorities.
- Knowledge about the relative indeterminacy and unpredictability of life and ways to manage this.

Baltes and his colleagues have found that wisdom construed on this model over-laps with measures of intelligence and personality, but is not identical with them. They have collected much data that they conclude supports the empirical utility of the model, e.g. human services professionals were found to outperform a control group on wisdom-related tasks (Staudinger, Smith & Baltes 1992).

Other theorists have sought to construe wisdom as a stage of thought beyond Piaget's formal operations stage. Still others, including Sternberg, have favoured 'balance' accounts of wisdom. According to Sternberg (2003: 151) at least three major kinds of balances have been put forward. These are balance among various:

- kinds of thinking;
- self-systems (e.g. cognitive, conative and affective);
- points of view.

Sternberg's balance theory will be considered below. In general, the work on wis-dom discussed in the following sections of this chapter has been chosen because it has clear connections to the kinds of informal learning that have been a major fo-cus of this book. We turn then to Shulman's notion of the 'wisdom of practice'.

2. SHULMAN AND THE WISDOM OF PRACTICE

Shulman employs the term 'wisdom of practice' to suggest that if we want to un-derstand practice, there is no better strategy than to focus on actual practice and investigate how it proceeds and why. He came to this position from his experi-ences of investigating medical problem solving (Shulman & Elstein 1976, Elstein, Shulman & Sprafka 1978). Shulman reports that he and his colleagues went into their research on how experienced diagnosticians went about solving complex cases with very definite ideas about what they would find. These expectations arose from two sources. Firstly, both standard medical textbooks and consultations with medical educators led them to have

> .... clear expectations regarding the strategies that expert physicians would use. ..... we found a clear consensus regarding how physicians ought to proceed in their diagnostic work-ups. *(Shulman 2004: 253)*

The expected strategy was a conservative inductive one in which physicians would carefully assemble a lot of data whilst keeping an open mind, and would then order the data into larger units before coming to a diagnosis.

Secondly, this expectation was supported by then current psychological research on the management of cognitive strain during information processing. This research suggested that the most likely strategy employed by diagnosticians would be found to be "conservative focusing"

> .... an inductive, step-by-step process in which the problem solver systematically reduced the field by ruling out alternatives. The alternative strategy, guessing particular hypotheses and testing them directly, was untenable. It simply placed too much strain on the fragile vessel of human memory. As soon as one tried to keep the result for more than one or two hypotheses in mind simultaneously, errors of memory increased rapidly. *(Shulman 2004: 254)*

However, the Shulman and his colleagues found that the inductive, step-by-step diagnostic process described in medical education textbooks was a myth. The 'wisdom of practice' proceeded quite otherwise. The physicians were found to be generating multiple competing hypotheses, usually two or three at a time, chosen so that the evidence that was consistent with one was inconsistent with the others. This evolving framework of hypotheses and evidence formed the basis of ongoing questioning of the patient. The research concluded that:

> In general, the clinician's competence in problem formulation and hypothesis generation was the key to diagnostic success. Both of these processes are closely related to the physician's substantive knowledge base and specific experiences in a particular domain. *(Shulman 2004: 256)*

It was later realised that the psychological research on the management of cognitive strain during information processing was not predictive for this research, since the cognitive strain research was based on tasks of which subjects had no prior knowledge or experience. However, in the case of experienced medical diagnosticians, prior knowledge or experience is at the heart of their practice. Shulman and his co-workers found no evidence of any supposed general competence in medical diagnosis – rather such competence was found to be case- or domain-specific. Although the basic problem solving strategies were very similar across all physicians, they were actually only skilled at diagnosing in domains where they had specific knowledge and experience.

Hence, Shulman's general claim that those who would seek to understand the complexities of highly skilled performance need to acknowledge the 'wisdom of practice' by studying practice itself, by "getting inside the head of the practitioner whose skills you wish to understand ...." (Shulman 2004: 257). However, this does not mean that expert practitioners are always right – there are times when they make mistakes, when their practice is unwise. So, concludes Shulman, the

> .... lesson is thus to treat the wisdom of practice with respect, with deference, albeit with careful scepticism. *(Shulman 2004: 265)*

Shulman also allows that wise practitioners may vary in their practice, more so in some types of practice than others, depending on the nature of the field of practice. The fact that the account of diagnostic procedures in medical textbooks could for so long be the opposite of how it was done in practice by experienced clinicians, illustrates for Shulman a theory-practice gap which is a key topic in his work. He posits a judgement making capacity developed from experience of practice as a way of bridging this theory-practice gap:

> The process of judgment intervenes between knowledge and application. Human judgment creates bridges between the universal terms of theory and the gritty particularities of situated practice. And human judgment always incorporates both technical and moral elements, negotiating between the general and the specific, as well as between the ideal and the feasible.
>
> .... To put it in Aristotelian terms, theories are about *essence*, practice is about *accident*, and the only way to get from there to here is via the exercise of *judgment*. *(Shulman 2004: 534)*

Shulman's use of the term 'judgment' closely parallels, of course, the account of judgement that we have expounded throughout this book.

There are a number of other features of Shulman's work as outlined above that relate closely to main themes of this book:

Firstly, the limitations of formal learning provisions in engaging with the actual processes of clinicians making diagnoses may be symptomatic of a more general failure to appreciate the extent to which informal learning in practice situations is a crucial aspect of becoming a skilled practitioner. In this process, informal learning, much of it tacit, is too often unnoticed.

Secondly, the crucial importance of domain-specific knowledge highlights the need for ongoing learning, especially in domains where knowledge changes rapidly, or in those common cases where practitioners wish to practice in a somewhat different domain from their previous practice.

Taken together these two ideas point to important links between on-the-job informal learning and lifelong learning.

3. DREYFUS AND THE STAGES OF ATTAINING WISDOM

3.1 The Seven Stage Model

Hubert Dreyfus and his brother Stuart (Dreyfus & Dreyfus 1986) developed a well-known five-stage model of skill acquisition. In more recent work (Dreyfus

2001), Hubert has extended this to a seven-stage model of which the seventh stage is called "practical wisdom". Dreyfus clearly intends his seven-stage model to have much wider applicability than just the development of specific vocational skills. He characterises it as specifying

> .... the stages in which a student learns by means of instruction, practice, and, finally, apprenticeship, to become an expert in some particular domain and *in everyday life*. *(Dreyfus 2001: 32, our emphasis added)*

Thus, Dreyfus takes his model to be describing the various stages through which learners pass as they become high level performers in the full gamut of skills, be they motor skills, intellectual skills, or, more commonly, embodied capacities for action that involve both motor and intellectual components. Dreyfus' seven stages will be described briefly. From this description, it will be evident that the role of informal experiential learning over extended time periods becomes increasingly important in the later stages of the seven-stage model.

Stage 1: Novice. This involves learning to recognise basic context-free features of the skill environment and understanding rules for determining actions on the basis of these features. So this stage is restricted to acquiring information, i.e. memorising key features and the rules that relate them. However, remaining at this level will result in "poor performance in the real world" (Dreyfus 2001: 34).

Stage 2: Advanced Beginner. This involves the learner coming to employ not just the context-free features and invariant rules of stage 1, but also taking account of "meaningful additional aspects of the situation or domain" (Dreyfus 2001: 34). This latter learning requires that the learner begin to engage with real situations, because this kind of experience is the only way that beginners can start to identify particular contextual aspects that will be vital for performance of the skill. According to Dreyfus, in contrast to the codifiable context-free features and invariant rules of stage 1, the additional aspects of the situation or domain, that are the focus of stage 2, are not codifiable. He allows that there are instructional maxims that can refer to these new situational aspects, but argues strongly that the knacks, feels, sounds, and the like, that these maxims refer to, "cannot be adequately captured by a list of features" (Dreyfus 2001: 34). Here we come up against the limitations of language for accurately describing experience. The learner comes to understand the maxims best by being coached in their import in actually experienced situations. Hence Dreyfus' claim that:

> Unlike a rule, a maxim requires that one already has some understanding of the domain to which the maxim applies. *(Dreyfus 2001: 35)*

Stage 3: Competence. This stage involves the complication that

> .... [w]ith more experience, the number of potentially relevant elements and procedures that the learner is able to recognise and follow becomes overwhelming. At this point, since a sense of what is important in any particular situation is missing, performance becomes nerve-racking and exhausting, and the student might well wonder how anybody ever masters the skill. *(Dreyfus 2001: 35)*

The learner at stage 3 achieves competence by learning to deal with this overload of cues and information. The competent performer is characterised by a capacity

> .... to devise a plan, or choose a perspective, that then determines which elements of the situation or domain must be treated as important and which ones can be ignored. *(Dreyfus 2001: 36)*

According to Dreyfus, the variety and multiplicity of situations and contexts is such that codified rules and procedures for deciding which plan or perspective to adopt are elusive, more so than the rules and maxims of previous stages.

> Students, therefore, must decide for themselves in each situation what plan or perspective to adopt, without being sure that it will turn out to be appropriate. *(Dreyfus 2001: 36)*

Because the learner decides on the plan or perspective to adopt, they become responsible for the outcome, whether it be satisfactory or not. This responsibility, Dreyfus argues, increases the involvement of learners in their practice. He views competent performers as being characterised by such responsibility and emotional involvement. He refers to empirical evidence that learners who lack this responsibility and involvement do not make the grade as competent performers.

Stage 4: Proficiency. The learner is only able to advance to this stage, according to Dreyfus, if "the detached, information-consuming stance" of stages 1 and 2 has been replaced by the whole-person "involvement" of stage 3 (Dreyfus 2001: 39-40). Only then

> ..... the resulting positive and negative emotional experiences will strengthen successful responses and inhibit unsuccessful ones, and the performer's theory of the skill, as represented by rules and principles, will gradually be replaced by situational discriminations, accompanied by associated responses. Proficiency seems to develop if, and only if, experience is assimilated in this embodied, atheoretical way. Only then do intuitive reactions replace reasoned responses. *(Dreyfus 2001: 40)*

According to Dreyfus, at this stage, "the involved, experienced performer sees goals and salient aspects, but not what to do to achieve these goals" (Dreyfus 2001: 40). The discriminating part is automatic, but not the reaction to the discrimination. Thus, the proficient performer "*sees* what needs to be done, but has to decide how to do it." (Dreyfus 2001: 41).

Stage 5: Expertise. In this stage the expert not only sees what needs to be done, but "thanks to his vast repertoire of situational discriminations, he also sees immediately how to achieve his goal" (Dreyfus 2001: 41). Thus, the expert surpasses the proficient performer in that both the seeing and the reacting become automatic. Dreyfus suggests that the proficient performer is seeing many situations as similar with respect to a plan or perspective, so needs to deliberate on how to proceed, whereas

> ..... the expert has learned to distinguish those situations requiring one reaction from those demanding another. That is, with enough experience in a variety of situations, all seen from the same perspective but requiring different tactical decisions, the brain of the expert gradually decomposes this class of situations into subclasses, each of which requires a specific response. This allows the immediate intuitive situational response that is characteristic of expertise. *(Dreyfus 2001: 41-42)*

Dreyfus goes on to consider the implications of this for course providers. Clearly professional courses that centre on theory will be in no position to produce graduates that will be anywhere near stage five of skill development. On the other hand, those courses that provide a focus on case studies that approximate to real-life situations will have more chance of achieving this level of skill development. However, Dreyfus warns that even here,

> ..... the cases must matter to the learner. ..... for the case method to work, the students must become emotionally involved. .... Provided that they draw in the embodied, emotional student, not just his mind, simulations – especially computer simulations – can be useful. *(Dreyfus 2001: 43-44)*

Dreyfus adds that the

> ..... most reliable way to produce involvement, however, is to require that the student work in the relevant skill domain. So we are back at apprenticeship. ....
> Even where the subject matter is purely theoretical, apprenticeship is necessary. *(Dreyfus 2001: 44)*

Dreyfus' main point here is that all vocations, even the more academic and theoretical ones, require new entrants to develop a range of abilities and capacities to engage in practice, abilities and capacities for which there are no codified rules. Examples include "how long to persist when the work does not seem to be going well", "style(s) of approaching texts and problems", and "just how much precision should be sought in each different kind of research situation" (Dreyfus 2001: 44). New entrants to vocations need to learn these largely tacit abilities and capacities for practice from accomplished practitioners or masters. Dreyfus maintains that in

> ..... order to bring theory into relation with practice, this sort of apprenticeship turns out to be essential. *(Dreyfus 2001: 44)*

Stage 6: Mastery. One can attain expertise by learning style and other tacit aspects of practice from an influential master. In so doing, practitioners can become slavish followers of the master, and Dreyfus regards this as ultimately stultifying. In order to become a master, it is desirable to develop to some extent your own unique style and ways of practice. Dreyfus recommends that those seeking to attain the highest levels of practice should work over time with a range of different masters. Not because, as some people think, that different bits and pieces of skill are acquired from each different master, with all the pieces being put together to complete a novel whole. No, Dreyfus has a much more holistic view of skilled practice.

Rather, one master has one whole style and another has a wholly different style. Working with several masters destabilizes and confuses the apprentice so that he can no longer simply copy any one master's style and so is forced to begin to develop a style of his own. In so doing he achieves the highest level of skill ..... *mastery*. *(Dreyfus 2001: 46)*

Stage 7: Practical Wisdom. Although mastery is the highest level of skill, Dreyfus posits a further stage of skill development. While stage 6 dealt with development of a style in a specific domain, stage 7 deals with development of the style of one's culture, which Dreyfus connects with Aristotle's practical wisdom. This cultural style is part of the taken-for-granted background:

Our cultural style is so embodied and pervasive that it is generally invisible to us ... *(Dreyfus 2001: 46)*

We can start to appreciate aspects of our own cultural style by comparing it with a very different one, e.g. Japanese culture. However, it inevitably remains somewhat elusive:

Like embodied common sense understanding, cultural style is too embodied to be captured in a theory, and passed on by talking heads. It is simply passed on silently from body to body, yet it is what makes us human beings and provides the background against which all other learning is possible. *(Dreyfus 2001: 48)*

There are a number of general points that should be made about the seven stage Dreyfus model. Firstly, as McPherson (2005) points out, the stages are *not* stages of individual psychological development:

For we can and do keep going through these .... stages at different times in life and in different areas of learning. The Dreyfus stages are, in some respects, more like ideal types in sociology. *(McPherson 2005: 712)*

Secondly, McPherson points out that in moving from five stages to seven, Dreyfus is not saying that there are literally two further stages of skill development that he now realises that he failed to notice in his earlier model. Rather,

..... the two 'new stages' make better sense if they are interpreted as concerned with features of learning already present at earlier stages, but which now need to be made more explicit....... Stages (6) and (7) involve increasing self-awareness and concern for some enhanced version(s) of personal coherence or integrity, all of which are aspects of reflexivity. *(McPherson 2005: 711)*

Thus, the two new stages might be seen as meta-stages of the earlier five stage model.

The Dreyfus model of skill development is not just a sideline within the larger body of his work. Rather it coheres closely with important themes in Dreyfus' more general philosophical work, particularly a series of theses around the notion of practice, strongly influenced by his reading of Heidegger. (Some indication of how largely the concept of practice looms in Dreyfus' work can be gleaned from its prominence in the essays in a two volume *festschrift* honouring his work (Wrathall & Malpas 2000)).

3.2 Some Key Themes in Dreyfus' Work on Practice

The primacy of practice vis-à-vis the theoretical. This means that cognition derives from practice, and not the other way around. This major theme encompasses multiple theses such as the following:

- Embodied, practical coping in a skilful way with one's surroundings is a fundamental mode of intentionality.
- Practice (practical coping) cannot be made fully explicit.
- Practice (practical coping) cannot be adequately explicated theoretically.
- Practice or skilled performance cannot be understood as rule following.

Practices are social skills. This major theme encompasses multiple theses such as the following:

- Skills have rich interconnections so that modifications in any part of the system of skills will modify the others.
- Skills being social means that there is a convergence in how people do things.
- Rather than asking how people are related to their practices, it is more helpful to say that people *are* their practices.

Practices and skills are flexible. Skilled practitioners can respond creatively and imaginatively to new, different or unexpected cases, where a routine response would be ineffective or unsatisfactory.

The informal learning, centred on judgment and practices, that is the focus of this book has been explained a number of times already in terms of six key features of informal learning at work that Beckett & Hager claim are important for understanding it (Beckett & Hager 2002: 115). These six key features are:

1. Organic/holistic
2. Contextual
3. Activity- and experience-based
4. Arises in situations where learning is not the main aim
5. Activated by individual learners rather than by teachers/trainers
6. Often collaborative/collegial

Dreyfus' work on practice can be seen to connect to these themes in interesting and suggestive ways. The embodied, practical coping that is phenomenologically basic for Dreyfus suggests an important dimension of the *organic, holistic* character of this informal learning. Another aspect of this is reflected in the way that involvement of the whole person is crucial by stage 3 of the model. i.e. relatively early in the learning process. The flexibility of skills and practices that Dreyfus emphasises is represented in stage 5 of his skill development model. This accords with the *contextuality* of the informal learning, centred on judgment and practices. All stages of the Dreyfus model are *activity- and experience-based*. What the seven stages do is suggest the range of complex dimensions involved in this key feature of informal learning. For Dreyfus, skills and practices are nonrepresentational; they are passed on through society to individuals without conscious thought necessarily being involved. The social character of skills and practices means that they can be developed through conformism. So while it is perfectly possible, and common, to teach skills and practices, they will develop naturally in situations where *learning is not the main intention*. According to Dreyfus' skill model, experts engaging in practice are very likely to learn. But usually, they are not engaging in practice in order to learn. So informal learning will commonly occur in situations that were *not initiated by teachers/trainers*. Dreyfus' insistence on the social nature and origin of skills and practices illuminates the *often collaborative/collegial* of the informal learning that we are investigating.

Overall, the Dreyfus model provides strong guidance for those wishing to teach skills and practices. However, it is only at the very start that there is any scope for traditional didactic teaching. Very quickly, the model moves towards apprenticeship as the way for teaching to advance. From the middle stages onwards, progress depends on whole person learning by the learner. Something that can be encouraged, but ultimately not ensured, by teaching. The responsibility for the learning is shifted more and more to the learner. The learning from experience of diverse cases, that becomes a feature of the later stages of the model, is closely connected to the informal learning that is the focus of this book. The reflexivity that characterises Dreyfus' final stages, points to the salience of the lifelong learning concept for his model.

4. STERNBERG ON WISDOM – THE BALANCE THEORY

Balance theories of wisdom were described very briefly in the overview account of theories of wisdom at the beginning of this chapter. We saw that balance theories proposed a balance among various entities including:

- kinds of thinking;
- self-systems (e.g. cognitive, conative and affective);
- points of view.

Sternberg has developed a balance theory that extends previous work in a number of ways. While much of the detail of Sternberg's theory is not especially relevant for present purposes, what is most striking about his theory from the perspective of the present book is that it includes a key role for tacit knowledge.

Successful intelligence and creativity are necessary, but not sufficient, conditions for
wisdom. Particularly important is tacit knowledge, which is critical to practical intelligence. *(Sternberg 2003: 152)*

It is for this reason that a number of Sternberg's general claims about wisdom
resonate quite strongly with much of the foregoing discussion in this chapter.
Some important themes in Sternberg's balance theory are:

1. Sternberg's work emphasises the crucial role of informal learning in attaining wisdom:

   .... the heart of wisdom is tacit informal knowledge of the kind learned in the school
   of life, not the kind of explicit formal knowledge taught in schools. *(Sternberg 2003:
   157)*

2. Sternberg also emphasises that the analytical reasoning that is an important
   component of wisdom arises in part at least from prolonged experience of
   the world of practice.

   .... wisdom requires analytical thinking, but it is not the kind of analytical thinking
   typically emphasized in schools or measured on tests of academic abilities and
   achievements ..... Rather it is the analysis of real-world dilemmas where clean and
   neat abstractions often give way to messy and disorderly concrete interests. *(Sternberg
   2003: 157)*

Thus for Sternberg wisdom and practice are closely connected, as suggested by
earlier discussion in this chapter:

   ...... practical thinking is closer to wisdom than are analytical and creative thinking,
   but again, it is not the same. Wisdom is a particular kind of practical thinking. It (a)
   balances competing intrapersonal, interpersonal, and extrapersonal interests, over
   short and (b) long terms, (c) balances adaptation to, shaping of, and selection of environments, in (d) the service of a common good. *(Sternberg 2003: 158)*

5. EXEMPLARS

5.1 Jack's Story Revisited

Jack's story, concerning the practice of child support administration, was introduced in chapter six. It provides a good illustration of Dreyfus' point that good
practice requires practitioners to go beyond the rules of practice. In Jack's work
there are standardised procedures for dealing with the various kinds of cases.
However, there is a difficulty that many cases have distinctive features that resist easy classification. So there is a danger that the procedures protocols might
encourage practitioners to adopt a narrow approach to categorisation of cases.
In effect, the quality assurance system can in some instances work against quality

outcomes being achieved. Therefore, Jack reports that he encourages the staff in his branches to exercise judgement so that cases are thought through in terms of the spirit of the legislation, rather than in terms of procedures to be followed for their own sake. Quite simply, child support staff need to learn when and how to break the rules. So while performance as outcomes can be specified closely, performance descriptors that are taken too literally as guides for action can interfere with good practice, as Dreyfus suggests.

5.2 Anne's Story Revisited

In chapter six, where we last met Anne, we illustrated the contextuality of practical judgement by pointing to the disparity between the general guidelines on the position of crash victims in wrecked vehicles and the reality of nearly every case being unique. This can also serve as an illustration of Dreyfus' point about the inability of a set of rules to encapsulate professional practice. Expert practice requires a practitioner to interpret the rules and sometimes, seemingly, to break the rules.

Anne also provided a useful example of the emotional involvement that becomes a feature at stage three of the Dreyfus model. The involvement of the whole person, including their emotions, is part of the holism of professional judgement. Here is the relevant extract from Anne's story:

Anne made a very interesting point about her early years in ambulance work, one that is very suggestive of important internal goods required by ambulance officers. Ambulance officers are frequently exposed to horrific and gruesome scenes. She was asked how she learnt to deal emotionally with these grim realities. Her response was:

> Through exposure I suppose and exploring how my feelings play a part .....Quite a few years ago I started doing this. Looking at what role my emotions played in it, and I found that the more dissatisfied with how I performed, I was, the more my emotions had played a less than constructive part in the job. So I don't believe – you can keep your emotions right out of it or have your emotions controlling the situation. And I think you need to have a balance somewhere in between, and so I'm getting to that point, and I'm practising it, and actually I think I do it pretty well. I find it easy to do a job now and keep my emotions right out of it, and think about it later on. And I think that's a step up for me from having my emotions play a part and affect my judgements. And that's a step up from not having your emotions in there at all.

Here Anne has described a personal quality that she has had to develop from experience, i.e. a virtue in MacIntyre's sense as was discussed above (chapter seven). Clearly, this personal quality of being able to keep a suitable reign on emotions, is closely aligned with the internal goods that characterise ambulance officer practice. Once again, we have seen that performance descriptors can specify procedures and outcomes fairly closely, but that the realities and complexities of actual practice point to the limitations of such descriptors. The internal goods of practice include dimensions that are outside of the scope of such descriptors. As well, the internal goods include capacities to creatively interpret, and even ignore, such descriptors in certain situations.

5.3 Barbara's Story Revisited

Chapter seven (section 6.2) provided an account of Barbara's transition into a
primary school teaching career. Her comments on her fourth year placement,
which was particularly significant for her development as a teacher, suggest that
Barbara's development was mirroring Dreyfus' Stage 6: Mastery. She was discussing how she learnt a lot about behaviour management from this placement.
But she thought that much of this learning was tacit. She stressed that it was no
use simply trying to imitate her mentor, the inspirational teacher who was highly
skilled at behaviour management:

> I can't think of any time when she actually said here's an example of a behaviour
> management strategy and go and try it ..... it is something where you have to develop
> your own kind of style, I don't think it's something that can be completely dictated to
> you ... you do what suits your personality because it comes across as false if it
> doesn't work, if it's not your own, if it's not your natural style.

As we saw earlier, according to Dreyfus, one can attain expertise by learning style
and other tacit aspects of practice from an influential master. But Dreyfus warns
practitioners against becoming slavish followers of the master, which he regards
as ultimately stultifying. In order to become a master, it is desirable to develop
your own unique style and ways of practice. Barbara recognises this. It seems that
she also concurs with the Dreyfus recommendation that those seeking to attain the
highest levels of practice should work over time with a range of different masters.

5.4 June's Story Revisited

Chapter seven (section 6.1) provided an account of June's transition into a career
as a speech and language therapist. Like Barbara in the previous story, June also
saw the need to develop her own particular style in practicums in the later years of
the course. However she reported problems in the third year practicums, where she
was working alternately with two different experienced therapists. She recognised
that both were competent practitioners, but they had very different individual
styles for interacting with patients. Unlike Barbara's practicum mentor, who recognised the need for novices to develop their own particular style, June's mentors
both expected her to imitate their own particular style. She ended up being com-
fortable with neither mentor. She found this practicum to be less than optimal, as
she disaffectedly copied styles foreign to her personality, just in order to obtain a
passing grade for the practicum. In other words, her attention switched to external
goods, to the neglect of cultivating the internal goods, which constitute the main
purpose of the practicum. It appears that June's mentors here had little insight into
stages of professional learning and the implications of this for the practicum. A
model like the Dreyfus one is a very useful vehicle for encouraging practicum
mentors to be much more reflective about what it is that they are supervising, and
how best to go about their mentoring work.

5.5 Charles' Story Revisited

Charles' story has already been discussed in chapters five and six. Charles is a surveyor proactively educating himself to remain at the forefront of technological developments in his rapidly changing field of practice. He does this through activities such as participation in a software users' group and by trialing innovative software for its writers. In keeping up with developments in this way, Charles has attained and is maintaining what Shulman dubs the wisdom of practice. Part of Shulman's argument is that the wisdom of practice is, at least in part, tacit. So it cannot be gained from a book or a formal course. Being a leading edge practitioner such as Charles is, and keeping up with innovations as Charles does, is the only way to attain and maintain the wisdom of practice.

5.6 Maria's Story

Maria is a private secondary school principal. Her succinct characterisation of her practice was that she was the prime manager of the school's culture. The instances that were elicited in the interviews of her exercising professional judgement in challenging or non-routine circumstances, were all cases where the outcomes, in terms of external goods, were very clear. As well, they all connected readily with the notion of managing the school's culture. Overall, Maria was very clear-sighted about the external goods of her practice.

However, when it came attempting to elucidate the components of expertise that she brought to this practice, she was much more vague. She continually referred to her intuition, which she believed she had developed over many years of experience. As well she referred to her capacity to read the culture or the situation. She also emphasised her strength of mind in taking hard or unpopular decisions and enforcing them. An example she gave of her intuition in operation was in the appointment of new staff ("some of the most critical judgements I ever make for the school"). As she puts it:

> ..... if someone walks through my door for an interview ... when I'm choosing people to come and work here, ... the CV goes out the window the minute they come through the door and instinct takes over, but also a little bit of that is feelings.

The example she gave of her taking and enforcing unpopular decisions related to school assemblies and attendance at chapel. Some girls (and teachers) wanted attendance at these to be somewhat voluntary. Maria's view was that "these are the way we transmit our culture" thereby making it "easy" for her to insist on compulsory attendance. While the internal goods of her practice were fairly vague, a range of committed personal beliefs and values that clearly had a major impact on Maria's practice and expertise were evident. It seems to be a plausible view that strongly held personal beliefs and values would be a major influence on the leadership and management style of school principals. This would certainly be the case across different types and systems of schools, but even within a single system a fair bit of variation could be expected. Whether Maria exhibits the wisdom of practice is probably unclear from the limited data provided by a few interviews.

However, what she continually referred to as her intuition, does bear some striking similarities to Dreyfus' description of stage five of his model where the expert not only sees what needs to be done, but "thanks to his vast repertoire of situational discriminations, he also sees immediately how to achieve his goal" (Dreyfus 2001: 41). So, for the expert both the seeing of the situation and the reacting become automatic, or in Maria's terms, intuitive.

The suggestion that personal values and beliefs of the practitioner are likely to shape significantly the internal goods of their practice has figured to some extent in all of the above case studies.

6. THE PARADOX OF WISDOM

What is the wisdom of practice? It is not to have attained a state of a superabundance of skills and abilities that can in no way be improved upon. Paradoxically, to think that you have attained wisdom, means that you are not wise. Rather wisdom is a disposition to go on developing and learning in a world of contingency and happenstance. The wise practitioner is somehow able to weigh up the risks of the various choices of action and then choose the right action – at least most of the time. This comes from the kind of informal lifelong learning that has been a main focus of this book. The wise practitioner is able to step back from difficult situations and arrive at a balanced view of what needs to be done. The trajectory of their professional life displays a 'narrative unity' in MacIntyre's sense of the term. Their decisions and actions serve to add to this narrative unity, a unity that will only be complete when they die. Of course, the wise practitioner will still need to engage in some trial and error, some mistakes will be made. To take no risks is not wise. Just as to take silly risks is not wise. Wisdom enables one to steer between these two undesirable extremes. Wisdom should enable the avoidance of catastrophic mistakes, such as the one Heidegger made when he elected to support the Nazis. To make an irrecoverable catastrophic mistake, as Heidegger did, is not wise.

What are the prospects for the kind of judgement making celebrated in this book leading to wisdom of a rich kind? Reading some of the writers that we have particularly drawn upon, such as MacIntyre and Foucault, one can easily become pessimist about the possibility of wisdom in the current era. Paralysis rather than wisdom looks to be the more likely outcome. However we are not as pessimistic as this. On our theory judgements are not so bounded. They can be nested in various practices and contexts. They involve various levels and layers. This variety of possibilities opens practitioners to reflexivity as an antidote to paralysis. It points to the moral dimension of wisdom and the narrative unity that they can achieve. So ultimately we are somewhat more optimistic than writers such as MacIntyre and Foucault.

In chapter ten we will draw things together, firstly, by further emphasising key points of our account of informal learning, and secondly, by applying the key points to the discussion of some kinds of learning situations that have not figured prominently in the previous chapters. This will in turn lead us to some overall conclusions and recommendations.

CHAPTER TEN

RECOVERING THE INFORMAL

In this final chapter we begin by summarising some key features of our theory of informal learning that has been developed in this book. We then illustrate these ideas by applying them to the discussion of a number of disparate learning situations. These include:

- learning through leisure – hobbies, crafts, sports, etc.
- learning while preparing for work
- learning for continuing vocational development
- learning for surviving, e.g. unemployment, dead end jobs, etc.

Finally, we present a series of conclusions and implications that follow from our arguments. These conclusions and implications are centred around the need to shift the balance from over-reliance on formal learning more towards informal learning, together with a pressing need to rethink our common assumptions about learning.

This book has argued that informal learning deserves more attention from policy makers than it has hitherto received. This is so, we claim, because informal learning covers much valuable learning, the importance of which is overlooked or downplayed when policy is skewed by too exclusive an emphasis on formal learning. We argue that only by achieving a sensible balance between formal and informal learning, will rich and productive notions of lifelong learning be developed. The alternative is to be stuck with thin accounts of lifelong learning derived from an over-reliance on assumptions about learning that are uncritically derived from formal learning. As Duke (2001: 508) so pertinently put it, ".... [l]earning is seen only in terms of provision". The results of this move are far-reaching:

> This transposition of language denies legitimacy to the kinds of learning that are not recognised in educational theory and policy-making. The scope of learning, lifelong and life-wide, mysterious, little understood and invisible, is reduced to that which the 'empire of education' can reach. *(Duke 2001: 509)*

Throughout this book we have sought to establish the importance of informal learning, mostly by conceptual argument, but also with evidential and practice-based support for the relevance of the concepts that we have proposed. This means that our writing is an unusual mix, firstly of philosophical ideas that are sometimes highly complex, and, secondly, of plain language descriptions of peoples' everyday experiences. The latter, of course, centres on the learning, both formal and informal, that is a key part of these descriptions of experience. In most cases, this experience of learning was specifically identified as an instance of learning by the people themselves, though, in a few cases, this recognition required some assistance from the researchers.

Why this unusual mix of philosophical argument and descriptions of everyday experience? It seems to us that the exemplars and case studies show very convincingly that learning is something that is much richer and more widespread than it appears to be if we focus too exclusively on formal learning in its many varieties. Yet the sway of assumptions that derive from common sense and formal understandings of learning is such that much informal learning remains invisible. To change this, we need a paradigm shift, one that is likely to involve drastic conceptual change. This is the motivation for the fairly sophisticated philosophical arguments that are deployed in this book. Our sometimes complex argument aims to challenge basic assumptions and beliefs about learning; assumptions and beliefs that are too often taken for granted. Our conclusion, that the balance between formal and informal learning needs to shift somewhat in favour of informal learning, is a simple one. But its justification requires new ways of thinking about learning. For such a shift to be effected, a new paradigm for understanding learning needs to take hold. Our philosophical argument seeks to provide and develop some key ideas for this new paradigm. So, we are urging the need for a 'Copernican revolution' in thinking about learning.

Perhaps learning as a concept, at the start of the 21st century, is in a similar position to the concept of motion at the end of the middle ages. Motion is, of course, one of the central concepts in physics, just as learning is a central concept in education, and some of the social sciences. Till the end of the middle ages and beyond, understanding of motion was limited by adherence to the Aristotelian attempt to provide a single account of all motion, based on a second-order distinction between natural and violent motions. It was the supposed 'nature' of all terrestrial bodies to have a natural motion towards the centre of the universe (i.e. the centre of the earth). But bodies were thought to be, at the same time, subject to violent motions in any direction, motions imparted by disruptive, external, 'non-natural' causes. Aristotle privileged one kind of motion as basic and accounted for others in terms of non-natural disruptions to this natural motion. This account largely accorded with 'common sense' ideas on motion, so it seemed to offer understanding of what was happening. Thus, it was difficult to think of motion in any other terms. Galileo's ideas were hindered initially, because they conflicted with this prevailing orthodoxy. Likewise, today virtually everyone has experienced formal schooling and this both shapes and entrenches the 'common sense' understanding of learning (that was discussed in chapter five). The dominance of this concept of learning has helped to render informal learning largely invisible, and has restricted understanding of the possibilities of lifelong learning. Real progress in understanding motion came when physicists departed from 'common sense' ideas and recognised that there are many different types of motion – falling, projectile, pendulum, wave, etc. – each requiring their own account. A paradigm shift ensued. Likewise, it seems there are many types of learning, including the kind of informal learning that has been a focus of this book. Understanding of these diverse kinds of learning may well require a range of theories each with somewhat different assumptions. Hence, the role of the philosophical arguments in this book is to suggest alternative ways to conceptualise learning. However, there is further problem for the strategy that we have adopted in this book. We are attempting to explain that which, by our own theory, might be best left unexplained, at least in part, in order to respect internal goods and the more tacit aspects of practice. We do not want to do what formal teachers so often attempt to do, to formalise practice, thereby turning it into something else that lacks vital features of actual practice. We are wary of being strong on explanations about practice, while ourselves having little immersion in practice. This points to the importance of our exemplars and case studies. They are not intended to be mere illustrations of our theoretical points. Rather, since we believe that the phenomenon of practice is richer than our attempts to characterise it, we hope that the exemplars and case studies will convey something of this multi-dimensionality of practice. We maintain this hope well aware that the exemplars and case studies are themselves merely descriptions of practice, albeit very different kinds of descriptors than our theories about practice.

These exemplars and case studies, that we hope will serve to show the reader the richness of practice and the vital informal learning that frequently accompanies it, have been drawn from a range of empirically-based research projects in which the authors have been involved. This work has convinced us that contextually sensitive judgement making is a very significant kind of informal learning, one that is very common, yet one that is under-acknowledged in the general literature on learning. Our account has situated contextually sensitive judgement making within practices, mostly workplace practices of one kind or another. But workplace practices are but one kind in a wider category – societal practices. Examples of societal practices include hobbies, crafts, sports and other recreational activities. We have seen that workplace practices inevitably involve a strong focus on external goods, in extreme and detrimental cases to the exclusion of internal goods. However, by shifting attention to wider societal practices, such as hobbies, crafts, or sports, we are likely to come across practices that are more firmly centred on internal goods than are workplace practices. This is so because practices such as hobbies crafts, or sports can be engaged in purely for their internal goods, though often, of course, there will be some accompanying external goods. However, in the case of workplace practices it is virtually always the case that significant external goods are involved as a prime focus.

So we begin by summarising main features of our account of this key kind of informal learning. We then discuss the implications of this account for a range of learning situations, including some examples of societal practices that have not, thus far, figured prominently in the discussion.

1. A THEORY OF INFORMAL LEARNING IN SUMMARY

While not attempting to provide a general theory that would encompass the myriad distinctive cases of learning that we believe are significant for humans, we have offered an account of a particular kind of learning that we think is widely important to human practices interpreted broadly. This kind of learning is the developing capacity to make appropriate context sensitive judgements during ongoing participation in practices of various kinds. We argue that learning of this important kind is a paradigm case of informal learning, yet, for reasons already outlined at length, to do with the dominance of formal education assumptions on thinking about learning, this ubiquitous kind of informal learning has remained largely invisible. We will here consider some of the key features of this informal learning that have been outlined and discussed at various places in the book. These key features of informal learning are that it is indeterminate, opportunistic, involves internal and external goods, and is an ongoing process.

1.1 Informal Learning is Indeterminate

Because understandings of learning have been shaped by formal education assumptions, they exhibit a tight rationalism that views learning as a kind of transparent product that can be minutely pre-specified, while being independent of learners and learning contexts. By contrast, our account makes it clear that much vital learning is less determinate than this. It is less determinate for a variety of reasons, including the following ones.

One aspect of indeterminacy is that such learning is contextual and, as has been shown in chapter six, context is a very multidimensional and fluid notion. Apart from these considerations that illustrate the complexity of context, it has also been argued that the learner is included as part of the context, thereby adding a flavour of uniqueness to the kinds of informal learning that we are considering.

A related aspect of indeterminacy is that such learning arises from practices that we saw in chapter eight are variously nested (judgements, practices, institutions, traditions, all so as to provide narrative unity to the life of the learner). Clearly, such nesting problematises attempts to fully pin down context. As well, in chapter eight, the important distinction between implicit and explicit context was developed. This related to the capacity of practitioners to constantly monitor and revise their 'ends-in-view' in the light of ongoing experience, thereby adding another dimension of indeterminacy. Our suggestion that learning be viewed as a process rather than as a product (or perhaps more accurately as a dialectical interaction of processes and products) is also pertinent here. Thus learning takes on the character of a continually evolving process rather than of a series of successively completed acquisition events.

Finally, much that is valuable in the kind of informal learning that we have been investigating is tacit. It is whole person embodied learning that cannot be fully captured in a series of propositions. The Dreyfus skill model, outlined and discussed in chapter nine, exemplified this point, as did material from various of the exemplars and case studies.

For all of these reasons, important instances of learning, such as the informal learning that we have been investigating, are much less determinate than learning is commonly taken to be by those under the hegemonic sway of formal learning assumptions. This is the basis of our rejection of restrictive vocationalism with its

key assumption that all learning is specifiable in advance. This assumption underpins marketisation of vocational learning as products, and promotes credentialism,
with efficiency being the overriding aim. But the tacit and indeterminate elude
market efficiency. In reducing learning to a suite of pre-packaged products to be
marketed, we badly misrepresent the nature of learning and its role in human living. Our account of informal learning accepts that risk and uncertainty are part and
parcel of the human condition. Living with risk and uncertainty points the way
forward beyond technological colonisation of the life-world and the panopticon.

1.2 Informal Learning is Opportunistic

We have shown that much important learning is opportunistic and contingent, both
at the individual and communal levels. It is partly because much informal learning
is indeterminate in the ways outlined above, that life continually throws up unan-
ticipated opportunities for new learning. Our exemplars and case studies have
clearly illustrated this trend. We have also argued, in chapter four, that the currently popular notion of communities of practice is often employed in ways that
are too restrictive and closed. A more realistic view of community has been suggested, drawing on Castells' notion of a network society. There are clear links between these ideas and the development of wisdom as discussed in chapter nine.
There we argued that practices develop through a network of human agreement,
with this agreement being guided by the recognition of authority, which is, in turn,
based on the recognition within that network of the human capacities which enable
good practice. We suggested that such recognition in the end forms a goal for a
lifelong learner. Within such networks, wisdom becomes an ability to go on learning in a measured way, one that enables the wise to distinguish productive lines of
enquiry and activities and to weave these into some kind of unity. This ability includes productive learning from mistakes and, also, a willingness to bring to the
surface and make explicit features of implicit context which would otherwise remain hidden at both the societal and individual levels.

1.3 Informal Learning Features Both Internal and External Goods

Rich examples of the kind of informal learning that this book has celebrated involve both internal and external goods. We have suggested, based in part on our
exemplars and case studies, that informal learning is enhanced in practice situations where there is an emphasis on internal as well as external goods. Traditionally, mainstream disciplines have been regarded as centred on internal goods (i.e.
they are worth studying for their own sake). Some well-known definitions of education revolve around this feature of learning (e.g. Peters 1965). By contrast, vocational education has often been portrayed as centred on the instrumental (external
goods), and hence dismissed as mere training. However, the grading and sorting
functions of education, which have expanded and multiplied in neo-liberal policy
agendas, have served to turn the focus of formal education systems onto external
goods. As was noted in earlier chapters, neo-liberal policy agendas have served to

entrench ideas of education as a product to be marketed like any other product. More and more, teaching seems to be aimed at surviving in a testing regime, rather than at engaging with a discipline or a practice. In vocational learning, because internal goods are closely connected with whole person know how and the tacit, they are being increasingly neglected as the focus has shifted to the marketisation of pre-specified products. So much of the present educational climate is simply not conducive to the internal goods that we argue are central to rich informal learning, as well as to learning in general.

1.4 Informal Learning is an Ongoing Process

It has already been stressed above that learning is more fruitfully viewed as a continually evolving process, rather than as a series of successively completed acquisition events. Thus, learning is about ongoing becoming rather than about attaining a particular state as a preparation for something else. Conceptualising learning as a process of becoming in this way provides a richer understanding of lifelong learning. Central to such an understanding of lifelong learning is the contribution of the kind of informal learning that this book has been investigating. A balanced mix of suitable learning over a lifetime promotes the kind of wisdom discussed in chapter nine.

2. FURTHER EXEMPLARS

2.1 Informal Learning in Leisure – Hobbies, Crafts, Sports, etc.

Hobbies, crafts, sports and other recreational activities can be major sources of learning, much of it informal, but in some cases involving formal learning as well. However, even where people are initiated into such activities in formal learning situations, significant pursuit of a hobby, craft, sport, etc. is bound to include substantial informal learning, such as learning from becoming acquainted with the work of other practitioners or devotees. Such learning, both formal and informal, will significantly shape and reshape a person's identity as a practitioner of the hobby, craft, sport, etc. Such activities also provide major examples of internal goods in operation. Hobbies, crafts, sports, and the like are often engaged in for their own sake and, at their best, offer rich possibilities for ongoing development of skills, know how and other capacities that underpin excellence in the particular activity. Of course, the balance of internal and external goods will not be the same for each participant. While some will engage in the activity essentially for its own sake, others might see it more as a way of passing the time, still others might view it as a potential source of income. However, in all cases, there is the possibility of the practitioner developing contextually sensitive judgement, i.e. the kind of learning that has been our focus in this book. There is also the possibility of a strong focus on internal goods relative to external goods.

The informal learning associated with hobbies, crafts, sports and other recreational activities can be seen to exemplify the four key features of informal learning set out above. For a start it will be indeterminate in various ways: its context will include the particular ways of engaging with the hobby, craft, sport, etc., of significant others who happen to stimulate the learner's initial interest and involvement; these practices will be nested in, e.g. local traditions relating to the hobby, craft, sport, etc. As the learner's involvement and experience as a practitioner grows, there will likely be revision of 'ends-in-view', for instance, as awareness develops of new and different possibilities. So serious engagement with the hobby, craft, sport, etc. is a continually evolving process. There will likely be opportunistic reshaping of this process, as, for example, the learner extends acquaintance with other committed practitioners of the hobby, craft, sport, etc. From such acquaintance new understandings and know how, much of which are tacit, can be developed.

Committed engagement with a hobby, craft, sport, etc. will entail an expanding focus on internal goods of various kinds, such as skills, feels, knacks, etc. Many of these will involve bodily know how of a kind that eludes precise verbal expression. The disputed language of wine tasting provides an apt illustration of the gap between bodily performance and verbal descriptors of it. For instance, names of other fruits are invoked to describe both the aroma and the taste of the wine. At best they are similes as the wine aroma and taste never quite matches that of the other fruits. Thus, the language of wine tasting is an inexact verbal supplement to the activity of wine tasting. To become proficient tasters, learners need significant experience and practice of tasting. The language of wine tasting plays a subsidiary role in this process. Likewise, cookbooks of whatever detail are inadequate to convey the full range of know how inherent in skilled cookery (Mulcahy 1996: 49-50). They are but verbal supplements to an activity that is much richer than any descriptions of it. Nor are such limitations confined to the verbal. Travel guides, for instance, often feature attractive photographs and other images of desirable destinations, yet as seasoned travellers will testify, these photos and images only make their full impact after one has gone to the location and experienced it first hand. Thus, increasing involvement in the practice of hobbies, crafts, sports, etc. opens up the learner to a diversity of internal goods that mostly elude precise verbal specification.

Of course, growing involvement or commitment to the practice of hobbies, crafts, sport, etc. also opens up the learner to an increasing range of external goods, e.g. peer acclaim, sales of outputs, public celebrity, etc. In many cases, what started as a hobby has the potential to grow into a business (see Martin's story below). Finally, significant engagement in the practice of hobbies, crafts, sports, etc., will clearly be a major contributor to a person's sense of identity. Certainly for hobbies, crafts, sports, etc. that involve any real complexity, there will be scope for ongoing development of capacity, for engagement with the internal goods of the practice. So the informal learning relating to carrying on the hobby, craft, sport, etc. will be more accurately thought of as a process of becoming rather than as arrival at a set destination.

2.1.1 Martin's story

A travel agency that specialises in quality tours that become in effect a course in the history and culture of the locality being visited, originated from Martin's (one of its founders) personal passion and love for medieval Italian history. This passion firstly led Martin to become a history lecturer in adult education courses. His next step was to complement a course on the historical workings of Italian renaissance courts with an optional study tour exploring various historical sites in Italy, with himself as the expert academic tour leader. This opportunity to gain first hand experience of relevant sites and artifacts proved very popular. The initiative was repeated for various other courses, with similar success. This encouraged Martin to co-found a travel agency that specialised in providing tours to places of suitable historical and cultural interest that featured a high level of personal learning shared with a community of like-minded individuals under the guidance of highly skilled tour leaders/mentors.

In realising this vision Martin has not only been able to use and extend his knowledge and love of ancient and medieval European history, but he has also been able to develop and run his own business. But it should not be thought that the business is centred on external goods in a way that the passion for medieval Italian history is not. The success of the business is contingent on clients being satisfied with the internal goods that characterise the specialist tours. They are paying a significant premium above mass tour rates in order to have access to this high level of internal goods. However, the ongoing success of the business is equally contingent on the external goods being taken care of as well. People will not pay premium rates if the externals such as hotel bookings, transport connections, etc. are handled poorly. So both the internal and external goods need to be attended to properly for the business to work.

There are, no doubt, other kinds of productive links between work and leisure such that practice in one can enhance practice in the other, and vice versa. Martin's story is but one instance of such a link.

2.2 Informal Learning in Preparing for Work

In this book we have argued that a new balance needs to be struck between formal and informal learning, with the crucial role of the latter needing to be acknowledged. Learning in preparation for work is one arena where this recognition is pressing. Current courses that prepare people for entry to occupations, whether they belong to vocational education or higher education institutions, tend to be dominated by formal considerations that leave little room for informal learning to play a significant part. Thus, in denying any significant and explicit role for informal learning, such courses tend to be dominated by considerations that are the opposite of the four features of informal learning that we have been highlighting.

For a start, formal courses are heavily shaped by the idea that professionalism and accountability requires learning to be pre-specified and determinate. What is to be learnt, how it will be taught, and the circumstances of assessment of learning are all carefully articulated and advertised at the beginning of the course. As economic rationalism and 'user pays' assumptions have come to dominate, course providers risk legal sanctions if these tight requirements are not met. Students become customers whose satisfaction is paramount. In this climate, anything that associates learning with the indeterminate is suspect. For instance, it is a growing mantra from employers that group work is important. However, group work poses problems for common assumptions about formal education, assumptions that insist that individuals are the unit of assessment. How to assess group projects in terms of the individual contributions? Assuming that all contributed equally creates disaffection; yet awarding the individuals marks judged as commensurate with their respective contributions seems to be impractical. The potential for an outbreak of customer dissatisfaction is high.

Faced with this dilemma, group projects are frowned upon, e.g. some institutions set an upper limit (say 10%) to the amount of group work permitted within a course. Likewise, when students undertake practicum placements to gain workplace experience, there is a perennial problem on how to assess this so as to obtain valid and reliable results. It is costly to have teaching staff visit the various sites to assess student performance. However it is also a problem to have workplace supervisors complete the assessment. Having as many assessors as student placements leads to reliability problems. Hence such placements are often graded as simply pass or fail, thereby encouraging students to think that the really important learning occurs back on campus. Though, as our exemplars and case studies show, students frequently view work placements as one of the most productive sources of learning.

Opportunistic or contingent learning is also minimised in the carefully controlled environments of formal courses. Increasingly, the formal requirements are more than enough to fill students' time. Such student initiated activities as informal study groups are the rare situations in which very keen students might learn beyond the confines of the immediate task. Likewise, in the present climate, external goods such as satisfying minimum assessment requirements or passing next week's assignment, dominate over the internal goods that enrich learning. As we have seen, many of these internal goods are tacit. This means that they are best acquired in situations such as guided observation of performance carried out by a skilled practitioner, mentoring by an experienced practitioner, and critical reflection on one's own performance. However the current climate encourages the overlooking of what cannot be minutely specified in writing in advance.

Likewise the current ethos suggests that arriving at a destination is the appropriate way to think about learning. You pay for goods, they are delivered and the contract is completed. Economic rationalist and 'user pays' policies suggest to students that learning is about finalising the delivery of goods. For this mindset, the suggestion that learning is an ongoing process beyond the formal course carries all sorts of undesirable implications, such as 'all of the goods that were paid for have not been delivered' or that 'this is a ploy to keep squeezing more money from me'.

How can we change these impressions? The indeterminate character of much vocational learning should be acknowledged. For example, students should be made aware that much practice know how is tacit, but is not thereby beyond the pale. The formal course should be presented as a helpful prelude for further vocational learning from engaging in work. Nor does all valuable learning in preparation for work come from formal courses. Currently, many vocational courses are seeking to educate students in so-called generic attributes that are thought to be crucial for effective workplace performance. Examples of such generic attributes include critical thinking, problem solving, communication, and interpersonal understandings. Such is the power of the assumption that formal learning is the source of all vocational learning, that there is little appreciation of the fact that activities unconnected with formal courses offer ideal opportunities for employing and refining these attributes. According to research by Te Wiata (2006) engagement in casual work, participation in sports and other group activities, and community participation of various kinds, are all more effective sites for developing these generic attributes, than is participation in formal education activities.

We have noted that opportunistic or contingent learning is minimised in the carefully controlled environments of formal courses. It seems that casual work, participation in sports and other group activities, and community participation all provide contingent opportunities for valuable generic aspects of vocational learning. Certainly most students engage in these kinds of activities. We need a more inclusive view of vocational learning that encompasses both formal and informal learning, one that encourages students to avail themselves of opportunistic, contingent learning. A step in this direction would be to make students more aware that all practices involve internal goods whose development requires significant experiences beyond the realm of formal courses. An appreciation of the importance of internal goods would also complement the need to view learning as an ongoing process of becoming, rather than as arrival at a destination, such as completion of the formal course.

2.3 Informal Learning and Continuing Vocational Development

Many of the exemplars and case studies that have been discussed in this book can be seen to belong to this category. But it is still worth exploring this matter further, under the headings of the four key features of informal learning that are being highlighted in this chapter. Continuing professional education has become mandatory in many occupational areas. This trend recognises that practitioners need ongoing learning in order to maintain their proficiency. However, as we found was also the case for vocational preparation courses, continuing professional education has been dominated by formal education assumptions. The result is that performance in this important area of professional development has left much to be desired. Thus continuing professional education arrangements have had a strong emphasis on imparting up-to-date information. Hence, commonly, there has been a focus on building up a mandatory number of points in a set time frame. Points are gained for activities such as attendance at approved lectures or conferences, and purchase of approved publications, audio-visual materials, etc. Commonly, there is no serious attempt to monitor what learning has resulted from these activities. So the focus is on the learning of determinate information from a variety of sources. The learning opportunities afforded by indeterminate aspects of practice are passed over. The emphasis on building up points within a set time keeps the spotlight on external goods. Professional learning becomes arrival at the requisite number of points rather than the ongoing process of becoming a wise practitioner. Instead of focusing so strongly on formal assumptions, continuing professional education needs to shift somewhat towards the informal. It needs to be more practice-based with the focus on quality practice. It needs activities that enable practitioners to share and reflect upon practice and procedures in challenging situations, in the more indeterminate aspects of contemporary practice. This would also shift attention towards the internal goods and the ongoing process of becoming a wise practitioner. In creating opportunities for practitioners to learn from one another's rich informal learning from practice, there is no rejection of more formal learning, such as gaining understanding of up-to-information. Rather, it is a matter of shifting the balance, so that the hitherto neglected informal learning from practice is used to complement and enrich formal professional development activities.

It is ironic that the professional bodies that oversee defective continuing professional education arrangements of the kind criticised above, are often themselves sites of very effective informal learning. When functioning well, they are, amongst other things, lively forums for bringing together dedicated and experienced practitioners. Inevitably practitioners share ideas and seek advice on professional matters (difficult cases and problems, understandings of new developments, etc.). So professional bodies serve as communities of peers within which professional judgement can develop and evolve. Yet participants are often unaware that this is happening alongside of the more overt formal functions that a professional body serves. This illustrates the point made frequently in this book, that informal learning is not well understood. It also suggests that although much about professional know how is tacit, such know how can be shared and enhanced amongst experienced practitioners. Although practice resists complete verbal specification, good practitioners can recognise and acknowledge one another's expertise, and advance it further by mutual support and engagement on matters of common interest. Hence, our claim that continuing education might be carried out much more effectively than has hitherto been the case.

The special capacity that professional bodies have to understand and recognise their own area of expertise is sometimes seen as sinister. Professional bodies can be portrayed as, and sometimes act as, conservative gatekeepers only interested in resisting change and protecting their own interests. No doubt there is some element of truth in this. But professional bodies are also a meeting point for those who are enthusiastic about advancing practice. In the end there is no better arbiter of practice itself than the sincere understandings of the best practitioners. Others can judge the outcomes of practice, but who else can better understand the workings of practice?

2.3.1 Charles' story revisited

Charles' story from chapter five provides a rich example of keeping vocationally relevant in a rapidly changing field – in this case, surveying. It certainly exemplifies the four features of informal learning that we have been discussing. Charles' learning is indeterminate in the various senses mentioned previously. His participation in the development and testing of new technologies and techniques produces personal learning that cannot be pre-specified. It is nested in traditions and practices of the various fields (e.g. engineering, surveying, software writing) that converge in his area of specialisation. As well, his hands-on, trial-and-error approach means that much of the learning is highly contextual, and much of it is tacit. Charles' learning is also very opportunistic. He seeks out and creates suitable learning situations, and he is always on the look out for fresh opportunities. His motivation to stay at the forefront of his rapidly changing field seems to be dominated by a passion for and fascination with the field itself. Thus his learning is significantly concerned with internal goods, though various external goods no doubt accrue to Charles as well. Charles' ongoing learning journey, involving the convergence of what were once disparate fields, is certainly a process of becoming rather than arrival at some pre-determined set of knowledge and skills.

However, Charles' learning journey is highly pre-planned in the sense that he actively seeks out and engages in learning opportunities. But, significant vocational learning and development does not have to be consciously planned. Nor are people always conscious that they are engaged in rich learning, because often it is a by-product of other activities. It is often only with hindsight that the extent and worth of the learning becomes apparent. A common occasion of such rich unconscious learning is the undertaking of new initiatives. The following case study illustrates this point very vividly.

2.3.2 Financial literacy case study
This case study centres on a partnership between a financial institution, a community service organisation and a major educational provider to jointly develop and deliver an educational programme targeted to benefit the community. The financial institution had a history of supporting worthwhile community projects. Social action had always been a core mission of the community service organisation, but it was believed that there must be a better and more sustainable model than the repetitive process of asking corporations for money to implement short-term projects in the community. The educational provider was brought in as the unique project evolved in an educational direction.

In looking for a more substantial and long-term project, questions were asked such as: Which disadvantaged segments of the community should be targeted and where? What types of social action will really make a difference? What initiatives have already addressed these issues? Which community goals have never been tackled? So the project at the start was indeterminate and was to become something bigger than they had ever tackled before. There was no roadmap to follow, no previous practice that could be emulated. The significant learning of those involved was also not foreseen.

The vision of improving financial literacy was identified as having high potential for long-lasting societal and inter-generational impacts, an initiative that could hold a promise to reach a broader population in the long-term, while also teaching practical life skills to those in need. Could children and their parents be taught in parallel to reinforce learning at school and at home? It was decided to aim for this. This was innovation in action. Starting from two people's vision of what might be achieved, a group of individuals across multiple organisations was drawn in to commitment to the same vision. Eventually, an experienced project manager with consulting experience was appointed to be the full-time project coordinator. A steering committee of stakeholders representing major governmental and professional associations was formed and chaired by a senior executive at the financial institution. The elements of professional project management standards were established through commitment to regular meeting schedules and formal documented minutes with action steps and accountabilities.

A major challenge for the group to achieve its vision was to develop a high quality but practical curriculum that could at the same time find a place within the constraints set by existing curriculum. In this the project was fortunate to enlist the support and know how of a senior curriculum specialist. "I had definite ideas about what good curriculum materials should be" he said. "They have to have sound pedagogical objectives and be teacher-friendly. We had to embed the materials into the curriculum outcomes, not as an extra [optional] program on the side". Similarly, suitable adult and community education specialists were found to develop the parent curriculum materials.

> Engagement of disadvantaged parents within a school community is a real challenge. Concepts such as school, education and disclosing personal experiences with money all have negative connotations.

Thus, from the start there was a strong focus on internal goods, not only of community development and enhancement, but also of educational curriculum development and delivery. As the project gathered momentum and was increasingly seen to be successful, there was pressure exerted from within the financial institution to use the initiative as a vehicle to promote its own products. However, the project team were successfully able to insist that the institution's funding of community projects should genuinely be 'not for commercial purposes'. This determined focus on the goods internal to the practice of corporate social responsibility while resisting short-term gain of external goods, seems to be a major part of this project's ongoing success.

By the end of the original funded project timeline, the curriculum specialist was championing a follow-on phase to extend the program into a critical mass of Australian schools across other states. His view was that the project could make a bigger impact on the broader population because "financial literacy is more about making values explicit, about learning responsibility – it's important and needs to be taught". So the next stage was planned. "We were much more articulate in what we wanted to do in the second phase". Due to the clear success of the initial phase, the request for second-phase funding was successful. It was a 50% increase on the funds received for the original phase, making the cumulative grant one of the largest the financial institution had made for a community action initiative.

During the course of a project that is now entering its fourth year of operation, the members of the project team and their respective organisations learned about learning as an emergent, constructed and collective phenomenon and the value of integrity in guiding and shaping individual and group practices. For the three partners, the learning journey has been one discovered, shared and experienced together, through actions in work and practice that shaped and changed individuals and the organisations to which they belonged. The desire to make a difference through personal and socially meaningful work in the hearts of several individuals that comprised this partnership, allowed an intuitive belief and vision to flourish into a practical reality. This learning journey is a continuing process, even though some of the individual personnel have changed, and the project continues to become bigger. The project is now well on the way to making a significant difference to a broadening portion of the national population and hopefully for generations to come. For one of the original project initiators, her credibility and credentials to obtain a new job with another prestigious community organisation are perceived by her to be a direct result of her achievements on the partnership venture. Such was an unforeseen benefit of her informal learning on this initiative.

In reflecting upon what caused this particular project to be so successful and referred to by many participants as the "best that a partnership can be", the participants commented on the shared commitment to the vision and the values exhibited by individuals through many small examples of competent practice. Also singled out by various participants was the value of small actions, ones that engendered trust. The importance of trust for successful cooperative work amongst partners was one clear lesson from this project.

It seems that the practice of corporate social responsibility is moving beyond traditional passive forms of corporate philanthropy to much more proactive forms of collective participation as seen by the roles of the steering committee and various members of this project. The willingness of the funding agency to allow the project to focus on internal goods rather than for commercial benefits was crucial for its success so far.

2.4 Informal Learning and Surviving

We are thinking here of surviving in difficult circumstances of all kinds. This could include surviving in:

- dead end jobs
- oppressive social circumstances, (e.g. unemployment, drug addiction)
- incarceration (e.g. prison)
- internment (e.g. prisoner of war, illegal immigrant)

In all of these kinds of circumstances, many bordering on the horrific, there are accounts available of people surviving and, even, flourishing within them. Such people invariably describe strategies that they were able to adopt, apply and modify through experience; strategies that helped them to adjust to and survive the difficult circumstances. Another common theme in these stories of survival is that the people concerned report that they developed an inner mental life, often based on significant memories but developing over time into fantasies. It seems that this inner mental life provides a welcome arena of freedom and release from the restrictive and, frequently, oppressive physical circumstances that surround and constrain the survivors. Along with this relief from physical hardship gained from a rich inner mental life, survivors typically report an unprecedented sense of their own personal identity. This strong sense of personal identity is closely linked to the development and implementation of strategies to overcome and survive their harsh or oppressive physical circumstances.

We argue that these cases of survival involve informal learning of the kind that we have been investigating throughout this book. In all cases, the four features of informal learning that we have been highlighting are present. Firstly the learning is indeterminate in various senses. It is highly contextual, including being tied to the individual's own life narrative. It is learning that involves trial and error as the learner established what works best for them in these given circumstances. This learning is clearly opportunistic, using whatever is at hand to serve its purpose. This often includes friendship with a like-minded person who is also intent on how to survive. The practice of survival, like any other practice, involves various internal and external goods. However, internal goods such as personal integrity, self-respect, and particular survival goals, both short term and longer term, are prominent in the practice of survival. This informal learning also develops a strong sense of personal identity, of continuously becoming a person who can survive. Of course, there will be arrival at a destination of a kind if freedom or relief from the oppressive circumstances is achieved, but even here a different person from the one who entered the oppressive circumstances has been developed. The next challenge is to become a different person again in the improved situation. There will be no going back to earlier phases.

2.4.1 Anna's story revisited
The features just described can be found in Anna's story (chapter three, section 6.2). Anna as a teenage single mother of two found herself experimenting with strategies that would enable survival in these given circumstances. This included teaming up with others in similar circumstances for cooperative self-help, including learning ways to subvert the social security system. The internal goods of personal integrity and self-respect are prominent in Anna's account of how she progressed through various casual and voluntary work opportunities to achieve her current more substantial and stable position. It is also clear that Anna's informal learning journey is far from over.

3. SHIFTING THE BALANCE

In this book we have challenged ideas about learning in several senses. Firstly, common assumptions about learning have been critiqued and rejected. They have been shown to narrow the scope of our conceptions of learning, thus causing outcomes that are harmful to society and its ongoing development. Secondly, we have argued that learning is something that is much richer than our common conceptual attempts to capture it would suggest. There are dimensions of learning that elude our present formulas and common understandings. Practices of all kinds involve learning, some aspects of which are tacit. But this learning is no less valuable or important for being somewhat tacit. Current policies, with their almost exclusive focus on what can be formalised and codified, are thereby impoverished. Much valuable and worthwhile learning is currently almost invisible to policy. Yet it happens everywhere and it is very significant, as shown by our exemplars and case studies. We want to 'recover' informal learning in the sense that its importance needs to be reflected in policy making and practice. But at the same time, we wish to 're-cover' it in the sense that it needs to be protected against enthusiasts who, in attempting to formalise it, end up changing it into something else, thereby destroying its worth. Thirdly, we have argued the need for a paradigm shift in how we think about learning. Something equivalent to a 'Copernican revolution' seems to be called for. We have suggested a number of concepts that might help to inform this fresh thinking about learning. While from current perspectives what we are calling for might appear to be a revolution, actually it can be viewed as a programme of restoration of the informal to its former standing, both within and without educational institutions. Really, it is a revolution in reverse, a return to a tradition where the valuable role of informal learning is recognised and nurtured.

We think that policy makers and educators should be wary that an ongoing focus on learning as a marketable product will likely lead to a panopticon society. Not only that, but this reduction of learning to specifiable products means that some important kinds of learning are poorly captured or ignored all together. Such a watering down of learning to a lowest common denominator can only undermine the policy objectives that originally powered the learning as product agenda. At least informal learning of all kinds will continue mostly unfettered while ever it continues to be largely ignored by this agenda.

However, there is an accompanying overall trend for policy to seek to more closely formalise learning of all kinds. We have tried to show that formalising informal learning inevitably destroys or, at least, weakens it. So this formalisation trend needs to be reigned in. If policy makers wish to recognise and encourage the informal, a different approach is needed. As we have seen, the contingency and opportunism, that are the hallmarks of the informal, clash with the obsession with pre-specification. In addition, attempts to formalise practice soon reify it into something else. Such a different approach is challenging as it calls for a degree of trust from policy makers. Part of the insistence that courses be revamped to consist of pre-specifiable packaged products, seems to be a lack of trust that teachers and educators will do their jobs professionally. Hence, the move to the panopticon. Such a draconian outlook is bound to fail in relation to informal learning, for the reasons that we have outlined.

But there are also lessons in our arguments for formal learning. Teaching X is generally not practising X. We can recall Dewey's warning (from the Introduction) that there is always a danger of formal teaching becoming remote from the day to day practicalities of everyday life, of it becoming relatively technical and artificial. As we suggested in chapter seven, formal teaching can be far too easily contextualised in terms of external goods, but is not so easily contextualised as a part of the practice of what is actually being taught. Our exemplars and case studies provided clear support for this caveat. If the march of formalisation is not to work against the development of practitioners, links between formal education and practices of many kinds need to be established and enhanced. This would represent an important example of moving to an integrated balance of the formal and informal, a balance which we have been strongly recommending throughout this book. Our fear is that an ongoing emphasis on learning as product, accompanied by endless testing, has already created a narrowing of learning within education systems, a narrowing that is actually inconsistent with stated policy objectives.

In this context, it is clear that we reject the notion of lifelong learning as growing formalisation of learning across the lifespan. Not only is the prospect very unattractive and unpalatable to many, it also threatens to unwittingly destroy what it is intended to achieve. We propose that a fresh understanding of learning, with a better balance of the formal and informal, will lead to much more viable and attractive notions of lifelong learning.

However, at the same time, we wonder whether the term 'learning' has now become so loaded with undesirable connotations, that it may be time to try to find some new term to describe a developing ability to make contextually sensitive judgments. Such a new term would aim to capture the sense of lifelong development and achievement. That is, to avoid such connotations of 'learner' as 'powerless' and 'as yet, incapable'. A new term would aim to get away from the prevalent view of learning as loading up with knowledge in preparation for future application of it, towards a view of learning as becoming.

If, as Dewey claimed, learning is part of living, then how people want to live affects how they want to learn. Thus, learning is politically contextual too. Hence our preferred metaphors and concepts about learning reflect how we want to live. The view that learning is acquisition of products, and its associated metaphors, leads us towards a panopticon society. As liberal humanists, we do not want such a society. Hence we are looking for a fresh account of learning, one within which the learning-living relationship itself is reconceptualised.

REFERENCES

Ackerman, B. (1989) 'Why Dialogue?', *Journal of Philosophy*, 86:1, 5-22.

Adonis, A. & Pollard, S. (1997) *A Class Act: The Myth of Britain's Classless Society*. London: Hamish Hamilton.

Altrichter, H., Posch, P. & Somekh, B. (1993) *Teachers Investigate Their Work*. London & New York: Routledge.

Apple, M.W. (2005) 'Education, Markets and an Audit Culture', *Critical Quarterly*, 47: 1-2, 11-29.

Applebaum, E., Berhhardt, A. & Murnane, R.J. (eds.) (2005) *Low Wage America, How Employers Are Reshaping Opportunity in the Workplace*. New York: Russell Sage Foundation.

Argyris, C. & Schön, D.A. (1974) *Theory in Practice: Increasing Professional Effectiveness*. San Francisco: Jossey Bass.

Argyris, C. & Schön, D.A. (1978) *Organizational Learning: A Theory of Action Perspective*. Reading, MA.: Addison-Wesley.

Ashton, D. & Green, F. (1996) *Education, Training and the Global Economy*. Cheltenham: Edward Elgar.

Bagnall, R.G. (1990) 'Lifelong Education: The Institutionalisation of an Illiberal and Regressive Ideology?', *Educational Philosophy and Theory*, 22: 1, 1-7.

Bagnall, R. (2001) 'Locating Lifelong Learning and Education in Contemporary Currents of Thought and Culture', in D. Aspin, J. Chapman, M. Hatton & Y. Sawano (eds.) *International Handbook of Lifelong Learning*. Dordrecht/Boston/London: Kluwer Academic Publishers, 35-52.

Bailey, C. (1984) *Beyond the Present and the Particular: A Theory of Liberal Education*. London: Routledge & Kegan Paul.

Ball, S.J. (1990) *Politics and Policy Making in Education*. London: Routledge.

Baltes, P.B. & Smith, J. (1990) 'Towards a Psychology of Wisdom and Its Ontogenesis', in R.J. Sternberg (ed.) *Wisdom: Its Nature, Origins, and Development*. New York: Cambridge University Press, 87-120.

Baltes, P.B. & Staudinger, U. (2000) 'Wisdom: A Metaheuristic (Pragmatic) to Orchestrate Mind and Virtue Toward Excellence', *American Psychologist*, 55, 122-135.

Baptiste, I. (1999) 'Beyond Lifelong Learning: A Call to Civically Responsible Change', *International Journal of Lifelong Education*, 18: 2, 94-102.

Bauman, Z. (1998) *Globalisation: The Human Consequences*. Cambridge: Polity Press.

251

Beck, U. (1992) *Risk Society: Towards a New Modernity* (trans. M Ritter). London: Sage.

Beckett, D. (1996) 'Critical Judgement and Professional Practice', *Educational Theory*, 46: 2, 135-149.

Beckett, D. (2001) 'Hot Action at Work: A Different Understanding of "Understanding"', in T. Fenwick (ed.) *Sociocultural Perspectives on Learning Through Work*. New Directions for Adult and Continuing Education No. 92. San Francisco: Jossey Bass.

Beckett, D. (2002) 'Inferential Understanding at Work', in *Philosophy of Education Society of Great Britain Annual Conference 2002, New College, Oxford.*

Beckett, D. & Hager, P. (2000) 'Making Judgments as the Basis for Workplace Learning: Towards An Epistemology of Practice', *International Journal of Lifelong Education*, 19: 4, 300-311.

Beckett, D. & Hager, P. (2002) *Life, Work and Learning: Practice in Postmodernity*. London: Routledge.

Bennett, M. & Hacker, P. (2003) *Philosophical Foundations of Neuroscience*. Malden, MA & Oxford: Blackwell Publishing.

Bereiter, C. (2002) *Education and Mind in the Knowledge Age*. Mahwah, N.J./London: Lawrence Erlbaum Associates.

Berg, I. (1973) *The Great Training Robbery*. Harmondsworth: Penguin.

Bernstein, B. (2001) 'From Pedagogies to Knowledge', in A. Morais, B. Neves, B. Davies, & H. Daniels (eds.) *Towards a Sociology of Pedagogy: The Contribution of Basil Bernstein to Research*. New York: Peter Lang.

Biesta, G. (2005) 'How Is Practice Possible?', in K.R. Howe (ed.) *Philosophy of Education 2005*. Urbana, ILL: Philosophy of Education Society, 344-46.

Billett, S. (2001) *Workplace Learning: Strategies for Effective Practice*. Sydney: Allen & Unwin.

Billett, S. (2002) 'Critiquing Workplace Learning Discourses: Participation and Continuity at Work', *Studies in the Education of Adults*, 34: 1, 56-67.

Billett, S. (2004a) 'Workplace Participatory Practices: Conceptualising Workplaces as Learning Environments', *Journal of Workplace Learning*, 16: 5/6, 312-325.

Billett, S. (2004b) 'Co-participation at Work: Learning Through Work and Throughout Lives', *Studies in the Education of Adults*, 36: 2, 190-205.

Blake, N., Smeyers, P., Smith, R. & Standish, P. (1998) *Thinking Again: Education After Postmodernism*. Westport, Connecticut: Bergin & Garvey.

Bohman, J.F. (1995) 'Public Reason and Cultural Pluralism: Political Liberalism and the Problem of Moral Conflict', *Political Theory*, 23: 2, 253-279.

Boisvert, R.D. (1998) *John Dewey: Rethinking Our Time*. Albany: State University of New York Press.

Boshier, R. (1998) 'Edgar Faure After 25 Years: Down But Not Out', in J. Holford, C. Griffin & P. Jarvis (eds.) *International Perspectives on Lifelong Learning*. London: Kogan Page, 3-20.

Bourdieu, P. (1977) *Outline of a Theory of Practice*. Cambridge: Cambridge University Press.

Bourdieu, P. (1986) 'The Forms of Capital' in J.E.Richardson (ed.) *Handbook of Theory of Research for the Sociology of Education*, (translated by R. Nice). Paris: Greenwood Press.

Bourdieu, P. (1990) *The Logic of Practice*. Cambridge: Polity Press.

Bowden, J. & Marton, F. (1998) *The University of Learning*. London: Kogan Page.

Bowen, J. & Hobson, P. (1974) *Theories of Education: Studies of Significant Innovation in Western Educational Thought*. Sydney: John Wiley & Sons Australasia.

Bown, L. (1990) *Preparing the Future – Women, Literacy and Development. The impact of female literacy on human development and the participation of literate women in change*. London: ActionAid.

Brandom, R. (1994) *Making It Explicit: Reasoning, Representing, and Discursive Commitment*. Cambridge, MA: Harvard University Press.

Brandom, R. (2001) 'Reason, Expression, and the Philosophic Perspective', in C.P. Ragland & S. Heidt (eds.) *What Is Philosophy?* New Haven & London: Yale University Press.

Braverman, H. (1976) *Labor and Monopoly Capital: the Degradation of Work in the Twentieth Century*. New York: Monthly Review.

Brown, A., Rhodes, E. & Carter, R. (2004) 'Supporting Learning in Advanced Supply Systems in the Automotive and Aerospace Industries', in H. Rainbird, A. Fuller & A. Munro (eds.) *Workplace Learning in Context*. London: Routledge, 166-82.

Brown, P. & Hesketh, A. (2004) *The Mismanagement of Talent: Employability, Competition and Careers in the Knowledge Driven Economy*. Oxford: Oxford University Press.

Bruner, J. (1960) *The Process of Education*. Cambridge, MA: Harvard University Press.

Bruner, J. (1996) *The Culture of Education*. Cambridge, MA/London: Harvard University Press.

Buchanan, J., Schofield, K., Briggs, C., Considine, G., Hager, P., Hawke, G., Kitay, J., Meagher, G., McIntyre, J., Mounier, A. & Ryan, S. (2001), *Beyond*

Flexibility: Skills and Work in the Future. Sydney: NSW Board of Vocational Education and Training.

Burke, T. (1994) *Dewey's New Logic: A Reply to Russell.* Chicago/London: The University of Chicago Press.

Carr, D. (1993) 'Guidelines for Teacher Training: The Competency Model', *Scottish Educational Review,* 25:1, 17-25.

Castells, M., Flecha, R., Freire, P., Giroux, H.A., Macedo, D. & Willis, P. (1999) *Critical Education in an Information Age.* Lanham: Bowman & Littlefield.

Castells, M. (1996) *The Rise of the Network Society.* Oxford: Blackwell.

Castells, M. (1997) *The Power of Identity.* Oxford: Blackwell.

Castells, M. (1998) *End of Millennium.* Oxford: Blackwell.

Chisholm, L. (1997) 'Lifelong Learning and Learning Organisations: Twin Pillars of the Learning Society', in F. Coffield (ed.) *A National Strategy for Lifelong Learning.* Newcastle: University of Newcastle upon Tyne, 37-52.

Clark, A.E. & Oswald, A.J. (1996) 'Satisfaction and Comparison Income', *Journal of Public Economics,* 61: 3, 359-381.

Clark J. (2005) 'Explaining Learning: From Analysis to Paralysis to Hippocampus', *Educational Philosophy and Theory,* 37: 5. 667-87.

Coffield, F. (ed.) (1997) *A National Strategy for Lifelong Learning.* Newcastle: University of Newcastle upon Tyne.

Coffield, F. (1998) *Why Is the Beer Always Stronger Up North: Studies of Lifelong Learning in Europe.* Bristol: The Policy Press.

Coffield, F. (1999) *Speaking Truth to Power.* Bristol: The Policy Press.

Coffield, F. (ed.) (2000) *The Necessity of Informal Learning.* Bristol: The Policy Press.

Colley H., Hodkinson P. & Malcolm J. (2003) *Informality and Formality in Learning: a report for the Learning and Skills Research Centre.* London: Learning and Skills Research Centre.

Collins, M. (1998) 'Critical Perspectives and New Beginnings: Reframing the Discourse on Lifelong Learning', in J. Holford, C. Griffin & P. Jarvis (eds.) *International Perspectives on Lifelong Learning.* London: Kogan Page, 44-55.

Collins, R. (1979) *The Credential Society: An Historical Sociology of Education and Stratification.* Orlando: Academic Press.

Commission of the European Communities (1994) *Growth, Competitiveness, Employment: The Challenges and Ways Forward into the 21st Century.* Luxembourg: Office for Official Publications.

Commission of the European Communities (1997) *Study Group on Education and Training Report: Accomplishing Europe Through Education and Training.* Luxembourg: Office for Official Publications.

Conlon, G. (2002) *Determinants of Undertaking Academic and Vocational Qualifications in the UK.* London: Centre for Economics in Education, accessed from http://cee.lse.ac.uk

Coombs, J.R. (1997) 'In Defense of Israel Scheffler's Conception of Moral Education', *Studies in Philosophy and Education*, 16: 2, 175-187.

Cropley, A.J. (1977) *Lifelong Education: a Psychological Analysis.* Oxford: Pergamon.

Cropley, A.J. (Ed.) (1979) *Lifelong Education: A Stocktaking.* Hamburg: UNESCO Institute for Education.

Curtis, S. & Boultwood, M. (1970) *A Short History of Educational Ideas*, (4th edn.). Foxton near Cambridge: University Tutorial Press.

Csikszentmihalyi, M. (1996) *Creativity: Flow and the Psychology of Discovery and Invention.* New York: HarperCollins.

Davis, A. (1998) *The Limits of Educational Assessment.* Oxford: Blackwell.

Davis, A. (2005) 'Learning and the Social Nature of Mental Powers', *Educational Philosophy and Theory*, 37: 5, 635-47.

Dearden, L., McIntosh, S., Myck, M. & Vignoles, A. (2002) *The Returns to Academic, Vocational and Basic Skills in Britain*, in *Bulletin of Economic Research*, London.

Delanty, G. (2003) *Community.* New York: Routledge.

Delors, J. (1996) *Learning: the Treasure Within.* Paris: UNESCO.

Department for Education and Employment (1998) *The Learning Age: a Renaissance for a New Britain.* Green Paper: cm 3790, London: Stationary Office.

Department for Education and Skills (2001) *Participation in Education, Training and Employment by 16-18 Year Olds in England: 1999 and 2000*, accessed from http://www.dfes.gov.uk/statistics/DB/SFR/

Department for Education and Skills (2003) *Executive Summary 14-19* Opportunity and Excellence, accessed from http://www.dfes.gov.uk/14-19.

Derry, J. (2000) 'Foundationalism and Anti-Foundationalism: Seeking Enchantment in the Rough Ground', in V. Oittinen *Evald Ilyenkov's Philosophy Revisited'.* Helsinki: Kikimora. (Typescript supplied by the author)

Dewey, J. (1896) 'The Reflex Arc Concept in Psychology', reprinted in J.A. Boydston (ed.) *The Collected Works of John Dewey: The Early Works 1882-1898*, vol. 5. Carbondale: Southern Illinois University Press, 96-109.

Dewey, J. (1925) *Experience and Nature*, (ed.) J.A. Boydston, vol. 1 of *John Dewey: The Later Works, 1925-1953* (1988 printing). Carbondale & Edwardsville: Southern Illinois University Press.

Dewey, J. (1927) *The Public and its Problems*. Chicago: Swallow Press.

Dewey, J. (1933) *How We Think: a Restatement of the Relation of Reflective Thinking to the Educative Process*. New York: Houghton Mufflin.

Dewey, J. (1938) *Logic: The Theory of Inquiry*, (ed.) J.A. Boydston, vol. 12 of *John Dewey: The Later Works, 1925-1953* (1991 printing). Carbondale & Edwardsville: Southern Illinois University Press.

Dewey, J. (1966) *Democracy and Education*. New York: Free Press, (originally published 1916 New York: Macmillan).

Dewey, J. & Bently, A. (1949) *Knowing and the Known*. Westport, Conn.: Greenwood Press.

Dreyfus, H.L. & Dreyfus, S.E. (1986) *Mind Over Machine: The Power of Human Intuition and Expertise in the Era of the Computer*. Oxford: Blackwell.

Dreyfus, H. (2001) *On the Internet*. London: Routledge.

Duke, C. (2001) 'Lifelong Learning and Tertiary Education: The Learning University Revisited', in D. Aspin, J. Chapman, M. Hatton & Y. Sawano (eds.) *International Handbook of Lifelong Learning*. Dordrecht/Boston/London: Kluwer Academic Publishers, 501-528.

Dunne, J. (1993) *Back to the Rough Ground: 'Phronesis' and 'Techne' in Modern Philosophy and in Aristotle*. Notre Dame: University of Notre Dame Press.

Dunne, J. (2003) 'Arguing for Teaching as a Practice: a Reply to Alasdair MacIntyre', in J. Dunne & P. Hogan (eds.), 353-371.

Dunne, J. & Hogan, P. (eds.) (2003) *Education and Practice: Upholding the Integrity of Teaching and Learning*. Oxford: Blackwell.

Ecclestone, K. & Pryor, J. (2003) 'Learning Careers or Assessment Careers?: The Impact of Assessment Systems on Learning', *British Educational Research Journal*, 29: 4, 471-488.

Edwards, R. (1997) *Changing Places? Flexibility, Lifelong Learning and a Learning Society*. London: Routledge.

Edwards, R., Nicoll, K., Solomon, N. & Usher, R. (2004) *Rhetoric and Educational Discourse: Persuasive Texts?* London: Routledge.

Edwards, R. & Smith, J. (2005) 'Swamping and Spoonfeeding: Literacies for Learning in Further Education, *Journal of Vocational Education and Training*, 57: 1, 47-59.

Elias, N. (1982) *The Civilizing Process: State Formation and Civilization*. Oxford: Blackwell.

Elkjaer, B. (2003) 'Organizational Learning with a Pragmatic Slant', *International Journal of Lifelong Education*, 22: 5, 481-94.

Elstein, A.S., Shulman, L.S. & Sprafka, S.A. (1978) *Medical Problem Solving: An Analysis of Clinical Reasoning*. Chicago: University of Chicago Press.

Emirbayer, M. (1997) 'Manifesto for a Relational Sociology', *The American Journal of Sociology*, 103: 2, 281-317.

Engeström, Y. (1996) 'Developmental Studies of Work as a Testbench of Activity Theory: the Case of Primary Care Medical Practice', in S. Chaiklin & J. Lave *Understanding Practice: Perspectives on Activity and Context*. Cambridge: Cambridge University Press.

Engeström, Y. (1999) 'Activity Theory and Individual and Social Transformation' in Y. Engeström, R. Miettinen & R. Punamaki (eds.) *Perspectives on Activity Theory*. Cambridge: Cambridge University Press,

Engeström, Y. (2001) 'Expansive Learning at Work: Towards an Activity-Theoretical Reconceptualisation', *Journal of Education and Work*, 14: 1, 133-156.

Engeström, Y. (2004) 'The New Generation of Expertise: Seven Theses', in H. Rainbird, A. Fuller & A. Munro (eds.) *Workplace Learning in Context*. London: Routledge, 145-65.

Eraut, M. (1994) *Developing Professional Knowledge and Competence*. London: Falmer.

Eraut, M. (1997) 'Perspectives on Defining "The Learning Society"', *Journal of Education Policy*, 12: 6, 551-558.

Eraut, M., Alderton, J., Cole, G. & Senker, P. (1998) 'Development of Knowledge and Skills in Employment', Research Report 5, University of Sussex Institute of Education.

Eraut, M. (2000) 'Non-Formal Learning, Implicit Learning and Tacit Knowledge', in F. Coffield (ed.) *The Necessity of Informal Learning*. Bristol: The Policy Press.

Eraut, M. (2004a) 'Informal Learning in the Workplace', *Studies in Continuing Education*, 26: 2, 247-276.

Eraut, M. (2004b) 'Transfer of Knowledge Between Education and Workplace Settings', in H. Rainbird, A. Fuller & A. Munro (eds.) *Workplace Learning in Context*. London: Routledge, 201-21.

Evans, K., Hodkinson, P., Unwin, L. (eds.) (2002) *Working to Learn: Transforming Learning in the Workplace*. London: Kogan Page.

Evans, K., Kersh, N. & Sakamoto, A. (2004) 'Learner Biographies: Exploring Tacit Dimensions of Knowledge and Skills', in H. Rainbird, A. Fuller & A. Munro (eds.) *Workplace Learning in Context*. London: Routledge, 222-41.

Falk, C. (1998) 'Sentencing Learners to Life: Retrofitting the Academy for the Information Age', in J. Holford, C. Griffin & P. Jarvis (eds.) *International Perspectives on Lifelong Learning*. London: Kogan Page, 245-55.

Felstead, A. (1993) *Funding Government Training Schemes: Mechanisms and Consequences*. CLMS Working Paper No 2, Accessed from http://www.clms.le.ac.uk

Field, J., (1998), *European Dimensions: Education, Training and the European Union*, Jessica Kingsley, London.

Field, J. & Spence, L. (2000) 'Social Capital and Informal Learning', in F. Coffield (ed.) *The Necessity of Informal Learning*. Bristol: The Policy Press, 32-42.

Field, J. (2005) *Social Capital and Lifelong Learning*. Bristol: The Policy Press.

Foucault, M. (1977) *Discipline and Punish: the Birth of the Prison*. London: Penguin.

Foucault, M. (1980) *Power/Knowledge: Selected Interviews and Other Writings 1972-77*. Brighton: Harvester.

Frazer, E. & Lacey, N. (1993) *The Politics of Community: A Feminist Critique of the Liberal Communitarian Debate*. Brighton: Harvester Wheatsheaf.

Frazer, E. & Lacey, N. (1994) 'MacIntyre, Feminism and the Concept of Practice', in J. Horton & S. Mendus (eds.) *After MacIntyre*. Cambridge: Polity Press.

Freire P. (1972) *Pedagogy of the Oppressed*. Harmondsworth: Penguin.

Fukuyama, F. (1995) *Trust: The Social Virtues and the Creation of Prosperity*. New York: Free Press.

Fukuyama, F. (1999) *The Great Disruption: Human Nature and the Reconstitution of Social Order*. New York: Free Press.

Fuller, A. & Unwin, L. (2003) 'Learning as Apprentices in the Contemporary UK Workplace: Creating and Managing Expansive and Restrictive Participation', *Journal of Education and Work*, 16: 4, 407-26.

Fuller, A. & Unwin, L. (2004) 'Expansive Learning Environments: Integrating Organizational and Personal Development', in H. Rainbird, A. Fuller & A. Munro (eds.) *Workplace Learning in Context*. London: Routledge, 126-44.

Fuller, A., Hodkinson, H., Hodkinson, P. & Unwin, L. (2005) 'Learning As Peripheral Participation in Communities of Practice: A Reassessment of Key Concepts in Workplace Learning', *British Educational Research Journal*, 31: 1, 49-68.

Furedi, F. (2004) *Therapy Culture: Cultivating Vulnerability in an Uncertain Age*. London Routledge.

Gadamer, H.G. (1975) *Truth and Method*. London: Sheed & Ward.

Gallie, W.B. (1956) 'Essentially Contested Concepts', *Proceedings of the Aristotelian Society, LVI.*

Gardner H. (1999) 'Assessment in Context', in Murphy P. (ed.) *Learners, Learning and Assessment.* London: Paul Chapman.

Garrison, J. (1997) *Dewey and Eros: Wisdom and Desire in the Art of Teaching.* New York & London: Teachers College Press.

Garrison, J. (1999) 'John Dewey's Theory of Practical Reasoning', *Educational Philosophy and Theory,* 31: 3, 291-312.

Garrison, J. (2001) 'An Introduction to Dewey's Theory of Functional "Trans-Action": An Alternative Paradigm for Activity Theory', *Mind, Culture, and Activity,* 8: 4, 275-296.

Gelpi, E. (1985) *Lifelong Education and International Relations.* London: Croom Helm.

Giddens, A. (1991) *Modernity and Self-Identity: Self and Society in the Late Modern Age.* Cambridge: Polity Press.

Giddens, A. (1992) *The Consequences of Modernity.* Cambridge: Polity Press.

Giddens, A. (1998) *The Third Way.* Cambridge: Polity Press.

Glock, H.-J. (1996) *A Wittgenstein Dictionary.* Oxford: Blackwell.

Gonczi, A., Hager, P. & Palmer, C. (1994) 'Performance Based Assessment and the NSW Law Society Specialist Accreditation Program', *Journal of Professional Legal Education,* 12: 2, 135-148.

Goodman, N. (1970) 'Seven Strictures on Similarity', in L. Foster & J. Swanson (eds). *Experience and Theory.* London: Duckworth.

Gray, J. (1997) *Endgames: Questions in Late Modern Political Thought.* Cambridge: Polity Press.

Green, F. & Gallie, D. (2002) 'High Skills and High Anxiety: Skills, Hard Work and Mental Well-Being', SKOPE Discussion Paper. Coventry: University of Warwick.

Guile, D. & Young, M (1998) 'Apprenticeship as a Conceptual Basis for a Social Theory of Learning', *Journal of Vocational Education and Training,* 50: 2, 173-192.

Guile, D. & Young, M. (1999) 'Beyond the Institution of Apprenticeship: Towards a Social Theory of Learning as the Production of Knowledge' in P. Ainley & H. Rainbird (eds.) *Apprenticeship: Towards a New Paradigm of Learning.* London: Kogan Page, 111-128.

Guile, D. & Young, M (2003) 'Transfer and Transition in Vocational Education: Some Theoretical Perspectives', in T. Tuomi-Gröhn & Y. Engeström (eds.)

School and Work: New Perspectives on Transfer and Boundary Crossing. Amsterdam: Pergamon, 63-84.

Habermas, J. (1971) *Towards a Rational Society.* London: Heinemann.

Habermas, J. (1972) *Knowledge and Human Interests.* London: Heinemann.

Habermas, J. (1973) *Legitimation Crisis.* Boston: Beacon Press.

Habermas, J. (1984) *The Theory of Communicative Action,* Vol 1. London: Heinemann.

Habermas, J. (1987) *The Theory of Communicative Action,* Vol 2. *Lifeworld and system: A critique of functionalist reason,* (trans. T. McCarthy). Boston: Beacon Press.

Habermas, J. (1989) *The Structural Transformation of the Public Sphere : an inquiry into a category of bourgeois society* (trans. T. Burger with the assistance of F. Lawrence). Cambridge: Polity Press.

Habermas, J. (1992) *The Philosophical Discourse of Modernity.* Cambridge: Polity Press.

Hacker, P.M.S. (1986) *Insight and Illusion: Themes in the Philosophy of Wittgenstein.* Oxford: Clarendon Press.

Hacking, I. (1999) *The Social Construction of What?* Cambridge, MA. & London: Harvard University Press.

Hager, P. (1998) 'Recognition of Informal Learning: Challenges and Issues', *Journal of Vocational Education & Training,* 50: 4, 521-535.

Hager, P. (2000) 'Know-How and Workplace Practical Judgement', *Journal of Philosophy of Education,* 34: 2, 281-296.

Hager, P. (2001) 'Lifelong Learning and the Contribution of Informal Learning', in D. Aspin, J. Chapman, M. Hatton & Y. Sawano (eds.) *International Handbook of Lifelong Learning.* Dordrecht/Boston/London: Kluwer Academic Publishers, 79-92.

Hager, P. (2004a) 'The Conceptualisation and Measurement of Learning at Work', in H. Rainbird, A. Fuller & A. Munro (eds.) *Workplace Learning in Context.* London: Routledge, 242-58.

Hager, P. (2004b) 'The Competence Affair, or Why Vocational Education and Training Urgently Needs a New Understanding of Learning', *Journal of Vocational Education & Training,* 56: 3, 409-433.

Hager, P. (2005a) 'Philosophical Accounts of Learning', *Educational Philosophy and Theory,* 37: 5, 649-66.

Hager, P. (2005b) 'Current Theories of Workplace Learning: A Critical Assessment', in Bascia N., Cumming A., Datnow A., Leithwood K. & Livingstone D. (eds.) *International Handbook of Educational Policy.* Part Two. Dordrecht: Springer, 829-846.

Hager, P. & Beckett, D. (1995) 'Philosophical Underpinnings of the Integrated Conception of Competence', *Educational Philosophy and Theory*, 27: 1, 1-24.

Hager, P. & Smith, E. (2004) 'The Inescapability of Significant Contextual Learning in Work Performance', *London Review of Education*, 2: 1, 33-46.

Halliday, J.S. (1990) *Markets, Managers and Theory in Education*. London: Falmer.

Halliday, J.S. (1996) 'Empiricism in Vocational Education and Training', *Educational Philosophy and Theory*, 28: 1, 40-57.

Halliday, J.S. & Hager, P. (2002) 'Context, Judgement and Learning', *Educational Theory*, 52: 4, 429-445.

Halliday, J.S. (2003) 'Who Wants to Learn Forever? Hyperbole and Difficulty with Lifelong Learning', *Studies in Philosophy and Education*, 22: 3-4, 195-210.

Halliday, J.S. (2004) 'Distributive Justice and Vocational Education', *British Journal of Educational Studies*, 22: 4, 151-165.

Hamlyn, D.W. (1973) 'Human Learning', in R.S. Peters (ed.) *The Philosophy of Education*. London: Oxford University Press.

Hargreaves, D. (1997) 'A Road to the Learning Society', *School Leadership and Management*, 17: 1, 9-21.

Hartley, D. (1998) *Reschooling Society*. London: Falmer.

Harvey, D. (2000) *Spaces of Hope*. Edinburgh: Edinburgh University Press.

Heidegger, M. (1962) *Being and Time*, (trans. J. Macquarrie & E. Robinson) Oxford: Blackwell (originally published 1927 as *Sein und Zeit*).

Hickman, L.A. (1990) *John Dewey's Pragmatic Technology*. Bloomington & Indianapolis: Indiana University Press.

Hickman, L.A. (1998) 'Dewey's Theory of Inquiry', in L.A. Hickman (ed.) *Reading Dewey: Interpretations for a Postmodern Generation*. Bloomington & Indianapolis: Indiana University Press.

Higgins, C. (2003) 'MacIntyre's Moral Theory and the Possibility of an Aretaic Ethics of Teaching', *Journal of Philosophy of Education*, 37: 2, 279-292.

Hillage, J., Uden, T., Aldridge, F. & Eccles, J. (2000) *Adult Learning in England: A Review*, IES Report 369. London: Institute of Employment Studies.

Hirst, P.H. (1974) *Knowledge and the Curriculum*. London: Routledge & Kegan Paul.

Hirst, P.H. (1993) 'Education, Knowledge and Practices', in R. Barrow & P. White (eds.) *Essays in Honour of Paul Hirst*. London: Routledge & Kegan Paul.

Hirst, P. (1994) *Associative Democracy: New Forms of Economic and Social Governance*. Cambridge: Polity Press.

Hirst, P.H. (1998) 'Philosophy of Education: The Evolution of a Discipline', in G. Haydon (ed.) *50 Years of Philosophy of Education: Progress and Prospects*. London: Institute of Education, University of London.

Hirst, P.H. (1999) 'The Nature of Educational Aims', in R. Marples (ed.) *The Aims of Education*. London: Routledge.

Hirst, P.H. & Peters, R. S. (1970) *The Logic of Education*. London: Routledge & Kegan Paul.

Hobsbawn, E. (1994) *The Age of Extremes: A history of the world, 1914-1991*. New York: Vintage Books.

Hodkinson, P. & Hodkinson, H. (2004a) 'The Complexities of Workplace Learning: Problems and Dangers in Trying to Measure Attainment', in H. Rainbird, A. Fuller & A. Munro (eds.) *Workplace Learning in Context*. London: Routledge, 259-75.

Hodkinson, P. & Hodkinson, H. (2004b) 'Rethinking the Concept of Community of Practice in Relation to Schoolteachers' Workplace Learning', *International Journal of Training & Development*, 8: 1, 21-31.

Hodkinson, P. & Hodkinson, H. (2004c) 'A Constructive Critique of Communities of Practice: Moving Beyond Lave and Wenger', OVAL Research Paper 402, University of Technology, Sydney. OVAL Web-site.

Honderich, T. (ed.) (1995) *The Oxford Companion to Philosophy*, Oxford & New York: Oxford University Press.

Horn, J. & Wilburn, D. (2005) 'The Embodiment of Learning', *Educational Philosophy and Theory*, 37: 5, 745-60.

Houle, C. (1980) *Continuing Learning in the Professions*. San Francisco: Jossey Bass.

Hyland, T. (1994) *Competence, Education and NVQs: Dissenting Perspectives*. London: Cassell.

Hyland, T. (1997) 'Reconsidering Competence', *Journal of Philosophy of Education*, 31: 3, 491-505.

Illich, I. & Verne, E. (1976) *Imprisoned in the Global Classroom*. London: Writers & Readers Publishing Cooperative.

Jarvis, P. (1992) *Paradoxes of Learning: On Becoming an Individual in Society*. San Franscisco: Jossey Bass.

Jessup F.W. (1969) 'The Idea of Lifelong Learning', in Jessup F.W. *Lifelong Learning: a Symposium on Continuing Education*. Oxford: Pergamon, 14-31.

Johnson, S. (1998) 'Skills, Socrates and the Sophists: Learning from History', *British Journal of Educational Studies*, 46: 2, 201-213.

Jonathan, R. (1997) *Illusory Freedoms: Liberalism, Education and the Market.* Oxford: Blackwell.

Kallen D. (1979) 'Recurrent Education and Lifelong Learning: Definitions and Distinctions' in T. Schuller & J. Megarry (eds.) *Recurrent Education and Lifelong Learning* (World Yearbook of Education 1979). London: Kogan Page; New York: Nicholls.

Keep, E. & Mayhew, K. (2002) 'Review of the Evidence on the Rate of Returns to Employers of Investment in Training and Employer Training Measures', SKOPE Research paper, Universities of Oxford & Warwick.

Keep, E. (2003) *The State and Power: an elephant and a snake in the telephone box of English VET*, Policy Paper presented at the University of Greenwich 27.11.03., University of Warwick: ESRC Centre on Skills, Knowledge and Organisational Performance.

Kelly, A.V. (1999) *The Curriculum.* (4th edn.). London: Paul Chapman.

Kemmis, S. (2005) 'Knowing Practice: Searching for Saliences', *Pedagogy, Culture & Society*, 13: 3, 391-426.

Kennedy, H. (1997) *Learning Works: widening participation in further education.* Coventry: Further Education Funding Council.

Knapper, C.K. & Cropley, A.J. (1985) 'Lifelong Toil and Trouble: Good Work, Smart Workers, and the Integration of Academic and Vocational Education', *Learning and Higher Education.* New York: Croom Helm.

Knowles, M. (1980) *The Modern Practice of Adult Education: From Pedagogy to Andragogy* (revised edn.). Chicago: Follett.

Kozlowski, S. (1995) 'Organizational Change, Informal Learning, and Adaptation: Emerging Trends in Training and Continuing Education', *The Journal of Continuing Higher Education*, 43: 1, 2-11.

Kuhn, T.S. (1962) *The Structure of Scientific Revolutions*, (2nd enlarged edn. 1970). Chicago: University of Chicago Press.

Lafer, G. (2002) *The Job Training Charade.* New York: Cornell University Press.

Lakatos, I. (1978) *The Methodology of Scientific Research Programmes.* Cambridge: Cambridge University Press.

Lakoff, G. & Johnson, M. (1980) *Metaphors We Live By.* Chicago: University of Chicago Press.

Lakoff, G. & Johnson, M. (1999) *Philosophy in the Flesh: The Embodied Mind and Its Challenge to Western Thought.* New York: Basic Books.

Lave, J. & Wenger, E. (1991) *Situated Learning: Legitimate Peripheral Participation.* Cambridge: Cambridge University Press.

Lave, J. (1996) 'The Practice of Learning', in S. Chaiklin & J. Lave, *Understanding Practice: Perspectives on Activity and Context*. Cambridge: Cambridge University Press.

Lawson, K. (1979) *Philosophical Concepts and Values in Adult Education* (revised edn.). Milton Keynes: The Open University Press.

Lawson, K. (1982) 'Lifelong Education: Concept or Policy?', *International Journal of Lifelong Education*, 1: 2, 97-108.

Little, A. (2002) *The Politics of Community*. Edinburgh: Edinburgh University Press.

Livingstone, D.W. (2001) *Adults' Informal Learning: Definitions, Findings, Gaps and Future Research*. NALL Working Paper No 21. At www.oise.utoronto.ca/depts/sese/csew/nall/res/21adultsinformallearning.htm, March 2002.

Livingstone, D.W. (2005) Review of H. Colley et al. *Informality and Formality in Learning, Studies in the Education of Adults*, 37: 2, 228-9.

Long, H.B., Apps, J.W. & Hiemstra, R. (1985) *Philosophical and Other Views on Lifelong Learning*. Athens, Georgia: Adult Education Department, College of Education, University of Georgia.

Luntley, M. (2003) *Wittgenstein: Meaning and Judgement*. Oxford: Blackwell.

Luntley, M. (2004) 'Growing Awareness', *Journal of Philosophy of Education*, 38: 1, 1-20.

Lyotard, J.F. (1984) *The Postmodern Condition: A Report on Knowledge*. Manchester: Manchester University Press.

MacIntyre, A. (1981) *After Virtue*. London: Duckworth.

MacIntyre, A. (1987) 'The Idea of an Educated Public' in G. Haydon (ed.) *Education and Values*. London: Institute of Education.

MacIntyre, A. (1988) *Whose Justice? Which Rationality?* London: Duckworth.

MacIntyre, A. (1990) *Three Rival Versions of Moral Enquiry*. London: Duckworth.

MacIntyre, A. (1994) 'A Partial Response to my Critics', in J. Horton & S. Mendus (eds.) *After MacIntyre*. Cambridge: Polity Press.

MacIntyre, A. (1999a) *Dependent Rational Animals: Why Human Beings Need the Virtues*. London: Duckworth.

MacIntyre, A. (1999b) 'How to Seem Virtuous Without Actually Being So', in M. Halstead & T. McLaughlin (eds.) *Education in Morality*. London: Routledge.

MacIntyre, A. & Dunne, J. (2002) 'Alasdair MacIntyre on Education: In Dialogue with Joseph Dunne', *Journal of Philosophy of Education*, 36: 1, 1-19.

Mackenzie, J. (2000) 'On Representation', in International Network of Philosophers of Education 7th Biennial Conference 2002, Sydney, August 18-21. (*Proceedings* Vol. 2).

Macrae, S., Maguire, M. & Ball, S. (1997) 'Whose Learning Society? A Tentative Deconstruction', *Journal of Education Policy*, 12: 6, 499-511.

Magee, B. (1998) *Confessions of a Philosopher*. London: Phoenix.

Marginson, S. (1993) *Education and Public Policy in Australia*. Cambridge (UK) & Melbourne: Cambridge University Press.

Marsick, V. & Watkins, K. (1990) *Informal and Incidental Learning in the Workplace*. London: Routledge.

Marshall, J.D. (1996) *Michel Foucault: Personal Autonomy and Education*. Dordrecht: Kluwer.

McLaughlin, T. (2003) 'Teaching as a Practice and a Community of Practice: the limits of commonality and the demands of diversity', in J. Dunne & P. Hogan P. (2003), 339-53.

McPherson, I. (2005) 'Reflexive Learning: Stages Towards Wisdom with Dreyfus', *Educational Philosophy and Theory*, 37: 5, 705-718.

Mulcahy, D. (1996) 'Performing Competencies: Of Training Protocols and Vocational Education Practices', *Australian & New Zealand Journal of Vocational Education Research*, 4: 1, 35-67.

Mulhall, S. (1990) *On Being in the World: Wittgenstein and Heidegger on Seeing Aspects*. London: Routledge.

Mulhall, S. (1998) 'Political Liberalism and Civic Education: The Liberal State and its Future Citizens, *Journal of Philosophy of Education*, 32 (2), 161-176.

Mulhall, S. & Swift, A. (1992) *Liberals and Communitarians*. Oxford: Blackwell.

Murdoch, I. (1997) *Existentialists and Mystics: Writings on Philosophy and Literature* (ed. P. Conradi). London: Chatto & Windus.

Murphy, J.B. (1993) *The Moral Economy of Labour – Aristotelian Themes in Economic Theory*. New Haven & London: Yale University Press.

Nietzsche, F. (1994) *On the Genealogy of Morality and Other Writings* (Cambridge Texts in the History of Political Thought, (ed.) K. Ansell-Pearson). Cambridge: Cambridge University Press (originally published in 1887).

Oakeshott, M. (1933) *Experience and its Modes*. Cambridge: Cambridge University Press.

Ohliger, J. (1974) 'Is Lifelong Education a Guarantee of Permanent Inadequacy?', *Convergence*, 7: 2, 47-59.

Olssen, M. (1999) *Michel Foucault: Materialism and Education*. Westport: Bergin & Garvey.

Ozolins, J. (2003) 'On the Deep Purposes of Teaching and Learning', a paper presented to the Annual Conference of the Philosophy of Education Society of Australasia, University of Auckland, 28-29 November 2003.

Organisation for Economic Cooperation and Development (OECD) (1973) *Recurrent Education: A Strategy for Lifelong Learning*. Paris: OECD.

Organisation for Economic Cooperation and Development (OECD) (1994) *Jobs Study: Facts, Analyses, Strategies*. Paris: OECD.

Organisation for Economic Cooperation and Development (OECD) (1998) *Human Capital Investment: An International Comparison*. Paris: OECD.

Passmore, J. (1980) *The Philosophy of Teaching*. London: Duckworth.

Paterson, R. (1979) *Values, Education and the Adult*. London: Routledge & Kegan Paul.

Peters, R.S. (1965) 'Education as Initiation', in R.D. Archambault (ed.) *Philosophical Analysis and Education*. London: Routledge & Kegan Paul.

Phillips, D.C. & Soltis, J.F. (1998) *Perspectives on Learning*, (3rd. edn.). New York & London: Teachers College Press.

Phillips, D.C. & Soltis, J.F. (2003) *Perspectives on Learning*, (4th edn). New York: Teachers College Press.

Pring, R. (1993) 'Liberal Education and Vocational Preparation', in R. Barrow & P. White (eds.) *Essays in Honour of Paul Hirst*. London: Routledge & Kegan Paul, 49-78.

Pring, R. (1995) *Closing the Gap: Liberal Education and Vocational Preparation*. London: Hodder & Stoughton.

Putnam, R. D. (1993) 'The Prosperous Community: Social Capital and Public Life', *The American Prospect*, 4:13.

Putnam, R.D. (2000) *Bowling Alone: The Collapse and Revival of American Community*. New York: Simon & Schuster.

Rainbird, H., Fuller, A. & Munro, A. (2004a) (eds.) *Workplace Learning in Context*. London: Routledge.

Rainbird, H., Munro, A. & Holly, L. (2004b) 'The Employment Relationship and Workplace Learning', in H. Rainbird, A. Fuller & A. Munro (eds.) *Workplace Learning in Context*. London: Routledge, 38-53.

Rawls, J. (1971) *A Theory of Justice*. Cambridge, MA: Harvard University Press.

Rawls, J. (1993) *Political Liberalism*. New York: Columbia University Press.

Rees, G., Ferve, R., Furlong, J. & Gorard, S. (1997) 'Towards a Social Theory of Lifelong Learning: History, Place and the Learning Society', *Journal of Education Policy*, 12, 485-497.

Rhees, R. (1970) *Discussions of Wittgenstein*. London: Routledge Kegan Paul.

Robinson, D.N. (1990) 'Wisdom Through the Ages', in R.J. Sternberg (ed.) *Wisdom: Its Nature, Origins, and Development*. New York: Cambridge University Press, 13-24.

Robinson, P. (1997a) *Water under the Bridge: Changes in Employment in Britain and the OECD*. London: London School of Economics, Centre for Economic Performance.

Robinson, P. (1997b) *The Myth of Parity of Esteem: Earnings and Qualifications*. London: London School of Economics, Centre for Economic Performance.

Robinson, P. (1997c) *Literacy, Numeracy and Economic Performance*. London: London School of Economics, Centre for Economic Performance.

Rogoff, B. (1995) 'Observing Sociocultural Activity on Three Planes: Participatory Appropriation, Guided Participation, and Apprenticeship', in J.J. Wertsch, P. del Rio & A. Alvarez *Sociocultural Studies of Mind*. Cambridge: Cambridge University Press.

Rooney, D. & Solomon, N. (2004) 'Digesting the Metaphor: Exploring Everyday Learning at Work', paper prepared for the 35th SCUTREA Annual Conference, University of Sheffield, July 2004.

Rorty, R. (1998) *Achieving Our Country*. London: Harvard University Press.

Ryle, G. (1949) *The Concept of Mind*. Harmondworth: Penguin. (1963 printing).

Saint-Onge, H. & Wallace, D. (2003) *Leveraging Communities of Practice for Strategic Advantage*. New York: Butterworth Heinemann.

Saljo, R. (2002) 'My Brain's Running Slow Today – The Preference for "Things Ontologies" in Research and Everyday Discourse on Human Thinking', *Studies in Philosophy and Education*, 21, 389-405.

Scheffler, I. (1960) *The Language of Education*. Springfield, IL: Charles C. Thomas.

Schoenfeld, A.H. (1999) 'Looking Toward the 21st Century: Challenges of Educational Theory and Practice', *Educational Researcher*, 28: 7, 4-14.

Schön, D.A. (1983) *The Reflective Practitioner*. New York: Basic Books.

Schön, D.A. (1987) *Educating the Reflective Practitioner*. San Francisco: Jossey-Bass.

Scottish Office (1998) *Opportunity Scotland: a Paper on Lifelong Learning*, cm 4048. Edinburgh: The Stationery Office.

Scottish Further Education Funding Council (2002) *Demand and Supply of Further Education in Scotland*. Edinburgh: SFEFC.

Scottish Qualifications Authority (1997) *Unit Descriptor: Helping clients manage and maintain domestic standards in a home care setting*. Glasgow: SCOTVEC.

Searle, J. (1995) *The Construction of Social Reality*. London: Penguin.

Sellars, W.F. (1956) 'Empiricism and the Philosophy of Mind', in W.F. Sellars (1963) *Science, Perception and Reality*. London: Routledge & Kegan Paul.

Sfard, A. (1998) 'On Two Metaphors for Learning and the Dangers of Choosing Just One', *Educational Researcher*, 27: 2, 4-13.

Shulman, L.S. (2004) *The Wisdom of Practice: Essays on Teaching, Learning, and Learning to Teach*. (ed.) S.M. Wilson. San Francisco: Jossey-Bass.

Shulman, L.S. & Elstein, A.S. (1976) 'Studies of Problem Solving, Judgment, and Decision Making: Implications for Educational Research' in F.N. Kerlinger (ed.) *Review of Research in Education*, Vol. 3. Itasca, IL: Peacock.

Sianesi, B. (2003) *Returns to Education: A Non-technical Summary of CEE Work and Policy Discussion*. London: Institute for Fiscal Studies and Centre for the Economics of Education.

Smeyers, P. & Burbules, N. (2005) 'Practice: A Central Educational Concept', in K.R. Howe (ed.) *Philosophy of Education 2005*. Urbana, ILL: Philosophy of Education Society, 336-343.

Smith, R. (1997) 'Judgement Day', in R. Smith & P. Standish, *Teaching Right and Wrong: Moral Education in the Balance*. Stoke-on-Trent: Trentham Books.

Smith, R. (2003) 'Thinking with Each Other: the Peculiar Practice of the University', *Journal of Philosophy of Education*, 37: 2, 309-324.

Sommerlad, L. (1999) *Informal Learning and Widening Participation: Literature Review*. London: Tavistock Institute.

Standing, G. (1999) *Global Labour Flexibility: Seeking Distributive Justice*. London/New York: Macmillan/St. Martin's Press.

Staudinger, U.M., Smith, J. & Baltes, P.B. (1992) 'Wisdom-Related Knowledge in Life Review Tasks: Age Differences and the Role of Professional Specialization', *Psychology And Aging*, 7, 271-281.

Stern, E. & Sommerlad, E. (1999) *Workplace Learning, Culture and Performance*. London: Institute of Personnel and Development.

Sternberg, R. (2003) *Wisdom, Intelligence, and Creativity Synthesized*. Cambridge: Cambridge University Press.

Stickney, J. (2005) 'Teaching and Learning in Wittgenstein's Philosophic Method', in K.R. Howe (ed.) *Philosophy of Education 2005*. Urbana, ILL: Philosophy of Education Society, 299-307.

Taylor, C. (1994) 'Justice after Virtue', in J. Horton & S. Mendus (eds.) *After MacIntyre*. Cambridge: Polity Press, 16-44.

Te Wiata, I. (in press) 'Title', in P. Hager & S. Holland (eds.) (2006?) *Graduate Attributes, Learning and Employability*. Dordrecht: Springer. (in press).

Tiles, J.E. (1988) *Dewey*, (The Arguments of the Philosophers Series). London & New York: Routledge.

Toulmin, S. (1999) 'Knowledge as Shared Procedures', in Y. Engeström, R. Miettinen & R. Punamaki (eds.) *Perspectives on Action Theory*. Cambridge: Cambridge University Press.

UNESCO (1972) *Learning to Be* (The Faure Report). Paris: UNESCO.

Usher, R. & Edwards, R. (1994) *Postmodernism and Education*. London: Routledge.

Usher, R., Bryant, I. & Johnston, R. (1997) *Adult Education and the Postmodern Challenge: Learning Beyond the Limits*. London & New York: Routledge.

Vanderstraeten, R. (2002) 'Dewey's Transactional Constructivism', *Journal of Philosophy of Education*, 36: 2, 233-246.

Wain, K., (1984), "Lifelong Education – a Deweyan Challenge", *Journal of Philosophy of Education*, 18 (2) 257-264.

Wain, K. (1987) *Philosophy of Lifelong Education*. London: Croom Helm.

Wain, K. (1993) 'Lifelong Education: Illiberal and Repressive?', *Educational Philosophy and Theory*, 25: 1, 58-70.

Wain, K. (2004) *The Learning Society in a Postmodern World: The Education Crisis*. New York: Peter Long.

Waterhouse, P., Wilson, B. & Ewer, P. (1999) *The Changing Nature and Patterns of Work and Implications for VET*. Adelaide: National Centre for Vocational Education Research.

Wenger, E. (1998) *Communities of Practice: Learning, Meaning and Identity*. Cambridge: Cambridge University Press.

Wenger, E., McDermott, R. & Snyder, W. (2002) *Cultivating Communities of Practice: A Guide to Managing Knowledge*. Boston: Harvard Business School Press.

Wertsch, J.V. (1998) *Mind as Action*. New York: Oxford University Press.

Williams, A. (2003) 'Informal Learning in the Workplace: A Case Study of New Teachers', *Educational Studies*, 29: 2/3, 207-219.

Williams, M. (1994) 'The Significance of Learning in Wittgenstein's Later Philosophy', *Canadian Journal of Philosophy*, 24: 2, 173-203.

Winch, C. (1998) *The Philosophy of Human Learning*. London & New York: Routledge.

Winch, C. (2000) *Education, Work and Social Capital*. London: Routledge.

Winch, C. (2002) 'The Economic Aims of Education', *Journal of Philosophy of Education*, 36: 1, 101-119.

Wittgenstein, L. (1953) *Philosophical Investigations* (cited from the 1967 third edn). Oxford: Blackwell.

Wolf, A. (2002) *Does Education Matter? Myths about Education and Economic Growth*. London: Penguin.

World Bank (1996) *Education Sector Strategy*. Washington: World Bank.

Wrathall, M.A. & Malpas, J. (2000) *Heidegger, Coping, and Cognitive Science*, Essays in Honor of Hubert L. Dreyfus, Vols. 1 & 2. Cambridge, Mass./ London: The MIT Press.

Young, M. (1993) 'A Curriculum for the 21st Century? Towards a New Basis for Overcoming Academic/Vocational Divisions', *British Journal of Educational Studies*, 41: 3, 203-222.

AUTHOR INDEX

SUBJECT INDEX